Book of
QUOTATIONS

LUCEM LIBRIS
DISSEMINAMUS

GEDDES &
GROSSET

Published 2004 by Geddes & Grosset, David Dale House,
New Lanark, ML11 9DJ

This arrangement © 2004 Geddes & Grosset

Edited by Judy Hamilton

ISBN 1 84205 184 9

Printed and bound Poland, OZGraf S.A.

Contents

The Ages of Man

Henry [Brooks] Adams, 1838–1918, American historian
Young men have a passion for regarding their elders as senile.
[*The Education of Henry Adams* 1907]

Aeschylus, 525–456 BC, Greek poet
It is always the season for the old to learn.
[Fragments]

Elizabeth Chase Akers, 1832–1911, American writer
Backward, turn backward, O Time, in your flight,
Make me a child again just for tonight!
[*Rock me to Sleep* 1866]

Zoë Akins, 1886–1958, American playwright
Nothing seems so tragic to one who is old as the death of one who is young, and this alone
proves that life is a good thing.
[*The Portrait of Tiero*]

Henri Frédéric Amiel, 1821–81, Swiss writer
To know how to grow old is the masterwork of wisdom, and one of the most difficult chapters
in the great art of living.
[*Journal In Time* 1883]

Anonymous
An old man hath the almanac in his body.
[Italian proverb]

Aristophanes, c.448–c.388BC, Greek playwright
Old men are children for a second time.
[*Clouds c.*423BC]

Jane Austen, 1775–1817, English novelist
On every formal visit a child ought to be of the party, by way of provision for discourse.
[*Sense and Sensibility* 1811]

**Francis Bacon, Baron Verulam of Verulam and Viscount of St Albans, 1561–1626,
English philosopher**
Young men are fitter to invent than to judge, fitter for execution than for counsel, and fitter
for new projects than for settled business.
[*Essays: Of Youth and Age* 1625]

A man that is young in years, may be old in hours, if he have lost no time. But that happeneth rarely.

[*Ibid*]

James Baldwin, 1924–87, American writer
Children have never been very good at listening to their elders, but they have never failed to imitate them.

[In *Esquire* magazine 1960]

Sir J[ames] M[atthew] Barrie, 1860–1937, Scottish playwright
When the first baby laughed for the first time, the laugh broke into a thousand pieces and they all went skipping about, and that was the beginning of the fairies.

[*Peter Pan* 1911]

When you come to write my epitaph, Charles, let it be in these delicious words, "She had a long twenty-nine."

[*Rosalind* 1912]

Simone de Beauvoir, 1908–86, French writer
One is not born a woman, one becomes one.

[*The Second Sex* 1949]

John Berryman [John Allyn Smith], 1914–72, American poet
I always wanted to be old, I wanted to say
I haven't read that for fifteen years.

[*His Toy, His Dream, His Rest* 1968]

The Bible
And he died in a good old age, full of days, riches, and honour: and Solomon his son reigned in his stead.

[*1 Chronicles* 29:28]

Rejoice, O young man, in thy youth; and let thy heart cheer thee in the days of thy youth.

[*Ecclesiastes* 11:9]

When I was a child, I spake as a child, I understood as a child, I thought as a child: but when I became a man, I put away childish things.

[*1 Corinthians* 13:11]

Ambrose [Gwinett] Bierce, 1842–1914, American writer
The fact that boys are allowed to exist at all is evidence of a remarkable Christian forbearance among men.

[*San Francisco News Letter* 1869]

Age: that period of life in which we compound for the vices that we still cherish by reviling those that we have no longer the enterprise to commit.

[*The Devil's Dictionary* 1906]

[Robert] Laurence Binyon, 1869–1943, English poet
They shall grow not old, as we that are left grow old:
Age shall not weary them, nor the years condemn.
At the going down of the sun and in the morning
We will remember them.

[*Poems: For the Fallen* 1914]

8

THE AGES OF MAN

[Prince] Otto [Edward Leopold] von Bismarck, Duke of Lauenburg, 1815–98, Prussian statesman
To youth I have but three words of counsel – work, work, work.
[Sayings of Bismarck]

George [Henry] Borrow, 1803–81, English writer
Youth is the only season for enjoyment, and the first twenty-five years of one's life are worth all the rest of the longest life of man, even though those five and twenty be spent in penury and contempt, and the rest in the possession of wealth, honours, respectability.
[The Romany Rye 1857]

Edward Ernest Bowen, 1836–1901, English schoolteacher
Forty years on, growing older and older,
Shorter in wind, as in memory long,
Feeble of foot, and rheumatic of shoulder,
What will it help you that once you were strong?
[Forty Years On 1872 (Harrow School song)]

Rupert Chawner Brooke, 1887–1915, English poet
They love the Good; they worship Truth;
They laugh uproariously in youth;
(And when they get to feeling old,
They up and shoot themselves, I'm told.)
[The Old Vicarage, Grantchester 1912]

Robert Browning, 1812–89, English poet
Grow old along with me!
The best is yet to be,
The last of life for which the first was made:
Our times are in His hand
Who saith, "A whole I planned,
Youth shows but half; trust God: see all, nor be afraid!"
[Rabbi Ben Ezra 1864]

Bill [William] Bryson, 1951– , American travel writer
It's amazing, isn't it, how you can give a couple of old people a canvas holdall, an assortment of Tupperware containers and a Thermos flask and they can amuse themselves for hours.
[Notes from a Small Island 1996]

Samuel Butler, 1835–1902, English writer
There's many a good tune played on an old fiddle.
[The Way of All Flesh 1903]

Byron, Lord George Gordon [Noel], 6th Baron Byron of Rochdale, 1788–1824, English poet
There is an order
Of mortals on the earth, who do become
Old in their youth, and die ere middle age.
[Manfred 1817]

9

What is the worst of woes that wait on Age?
What stamps the wrinkle deeper on the brow?
To view each loved one blotted from Life's page,
And be alone on earth, as I am now.

[*Childe Harold's Pilgrimage* 1818]

Years steal
Fire from the mind as vigour from the limb;
And Life's enchanted cup but sparkles near the brim.

[*Ibid*]

Lewis Carroll [Charles Lutwidge Dodgson], 1832–92, English mathematician and writer
"You are old, Father William," the young man said,
"And your hair has become very white;
And yet you incessantly stand on your head –
Do you think, at your age, it is right?"

[*Alice's Adventures in Wonderland* 1865]

"In my youth," Father William replied to his son,
"I feared it might injure the brain;
But now that I'm perfectly sure I have none,
Why, I do it again and again."

[*Ibid*]

Child of the pure unclouded brow
And dreaming eyes of wonder!

[*Through the Looking-Glass and What Alice Found There* 1872]

George Chapman, c.1559–1634, English dramatist
Young men think old men are fools; but old men know young men are fools.

[*All Fools* 5 1605]

Sir Winston [Leonard Spencer] Churchill, 1874–1965, British statesman
Twenty to twenty-five! These are the years! Don't be content with things as they are. "The earth is yours and the fullness thereof." Enter upon your inheritance, accept your responsibilities.

[*My Early Life: Roving Commission* 1930]

Cyril Connolly, 1903–74, English writer
Boys do not grow up gradually. They move forward in spurts like the hands of clocks in railway stations.

[*Enemies of Promise* 1938]

John Dewey, 1859–1952, American philosopher
It is strange that the one thing that every person looks forward to, namely old age, is the one thing for which no preparation is made.

[Attributed]

Benjamin Disraeli, 1st Earl of Beaconsfield, 1804–81, British statesman and novelist
Youth is a blunder; manhood a struggle; old age a regret.

[*Coningsby* 1844]

The Youth of a Nation are the Trustees of Posterity.

[*Sybil* 1845]

10

THE AGES OF MAN

John Dryden, 1631–1700, English dramatist

I am resolved to grow fat, and look young till forty!

[*Secret Love, or The Maiden Queen* 1667]

Men are but children of a larger growth.

[*All for Love* 1678]

Finley Peter Dunne ("Mr Dooley"), 1867–1936, American humorist

If ye live enough befure thirty ye won't care to live at all afther fifty.

[*Mr Dooley's Opinions*: *Casual Observations* 1900]

George Eliot [Mary Ann Evans], 1819–80, English novelist

If youth is the season of hope, it is often so only in the sense that our elders are hopeful about us.

[*Middlemarch* 1871–2]

T[homas] S[tearns] Eliot, 1888–1965, American-born English poet

I grow old . . . I grow old . . .
I shall wear the bottoms of my trousers rolled.

[*The Love Song of Alfred J. Prufrock* 1915]

Henri Estienne, 1531–98, French writer

Si jeunesse savoit; si viellesse pouvoit.
(If only youth had the knowledge; if only age had the strength.)

[*Les Prémices* 1594]

F[rancis] Scott [Key] Fitzgerald, 1896–1940, American novelist

Thirty – the promise of a decade of loneliness, a thinning list of single men to know, a thinning briefcase of enthusiasm, thinning hair.

[*The Great Gatsby* 1925]

It is in the thirties that we want friends. In the forties we know they won't save us any more than love did.

[*Notebooks*]

Benjamin Franklin, 1706–90, American scientist and philosopher

At twenty years of age the will reigns; at thirty the wit; at forty the judgment.

[*Poor Richard's Almanac* 1741]

All would live long; but none would be old.

[*Ibid* 1749]

Old boys have their playthings as well as young ones; the difference is only in price.

[*Ibid* 1752]

Gavarni [Sulplice Guillaume (Paul) Chevalier], 1804–66, French artist

Les enfants terribles.
(The embarassing young.)

[Title of a series of prints]

Johann Wolfgang von Goethe, 1749–1832, German poet and playwright

Once a man's thirty, he's already old,
He is indeed as good as dead.
It's best to kill him right away.

[*Faust* 1808–32]

11

Oliver Goldsmith, 1728–74, Irish-born English writer
I love everything that's old; old friends, old times, old manners, old books, old wine.

[*She Stoops to Conquer* 1773]

Thomas Gray, 1716–71, English poet
In gallant trim the gilded vessel goes,
Youth on the prow, and Pleasure at the helm.

[*The Bard* 1757]

Horace Greeley, 1811–72, American journalist
Go West, young man, and grow up with the country.

[*Hints toward Reform* 1850]

[Henry] Graham Greene, 1904–91, English novelist
There is always one moment in childhood when the door opens and lets the future in.

[*The Power and the Glory* 1940]

Joel Chandler Harris, 1848–1908, American writer
I am in the prime of senility.

[Attributed 1906]

William Hazlitt, 1778–1830, English essayist
As we advance in life, we acquire a keener sense of the value of time. Nothing else, indeed, seems of any consequence, and we become misers in this respect.

[*On the Feeling of Immortality in Youth* 1827]

Robert Henryson, c.1425–c.1506, Scottish poet
O youth, be glad into thy flouris green!
O youth, thy flouris fadis ferly sone.

[*The Reasoning Betwixt Youth and Age*]

A[lfred] E[dward] Housman, 1859–1936, English poet and scholar
Now, of my threescore years and ten,
Twenty will not come again
And take from seventy springs a score,
   It only leaves me fifty more.
And since to look at things in bloom
Fifty springs are little room,
About the woodlands I will go
To see the cherry hung with snow.

[*A Shropshire Lad* 1896]

Washington Irving, 1783–1859, American diplomat and writer
Whenever a man's friends begin to compliment him about looking young, he may be sure that they think he is growing old.

[*Bracebridge Hall* 1822]

Jerome K[lapka] Jerome, 1859–1927, English humorous writer
The world must be getting old, I think; it dresses so very soberly now.

[*Idle Thoughts of an Idle Fellow* 1886]

THE AGES OF MAN

Dr Samuel Johnson, 1709–84, English lexicographer
Towering in the confidence of twenty-one.

[In Boswell's *Life of Samuel Johnson 1791*]

In life's last scene what prodigies surprise,
Fears of the brave, and follies of the wise!

[*The Vanity of Human Wishes* 1749]

Charles Kingsley, 1819–75, English churchman and writer
When all the world is young, lad
And all the trees are green;
   And every goose a swan, lad
    And every lass a queen.

[*The Water Babies* 1863]

Rudyard Kipling, 1865–1936, English writer
And the measure of our torment is the measure of our youth.

[*Gentlemen Rankers*]

Charles Lamb, 1775–1834, English essayist
Boys are capital fellows in their own way, among their mates; but they are unwholesome
companions for grown people.

[*The Old and the New Schoolmaster* 1821]

Philip Arthur Larkin, 1922–85, English poet
One of the sadder things, I think,
Is how our birthdays slowly sink:
Presents and parties disappear,
The cards grow fewer year by year,
Till, when on reaches sixty-five,
How many care we're still alive?

[*Collected poems: Dear Charles, My Muse, Asleep or Dead* 1988]

Alan Jay Lerner, 1918–86, American songwriter
Thank heaven for little girls!
For little girls get bigger every day.

[Song: *Thank Heaven for Little Girls 1957*]

Henry Wadsworth Longfellow, 1807–82, American poet
A boy's will is the wind's will,
And the thoughts of youth are long, long thoughts.

[*My Lost Youth* 1855]

There was a little girl
Who had a little curl
Right in the middle of her forehead;
And when she was good
She was very, very good,
But when she was bad she was horrid.

[*There was a Little Girl*]

Standing with reluctant feet,
Where the brook and river meet,
Womanhood and childhood meet!

[*Maidenhood*]

Youth is lovely, age is lonely,
Youth is fiery, age is frosty.

[The Song of Hiawatha 1855]

Ye are better than all the ballads
That ever were sung or said;
For ye are living poems,
And all the rest are dead.

[Children]

Sir John Lubbock, 1st Baron Avebury, 1834–1913, English politician and historian
It is customary, but I think it is a mistake, to speak of happy childhood. Children are often over-anxious and acutely sensitive. Man ought to be man and master of his fate; but children are at the mercy of those around them.

[The Pleasures of Life 1887]

George Macdonald, 1824–1905, Scottish poet and novelist
Where did you come from, baby dear?
Out of the everywhere into here.

[At the Back of the North Wind 1871]

Where did you get your eyes so blue?
Out of the sky as I came through.

[Ibid]

Frank McCourt 1931– , Irish-American author
Worse than the ordinary miserable childhood is the miserable Irish childhood, and worse yet is the miserable Irish Catholic childhood.

[Angela's Ashes 1996]

John Milton, 1608–74, English poet
The childhood shows the man
As morning shows the day.

[Paradise Regained 1671]

Juan Montalvo, 1832–89, Ecuadorean political writer
Old age is an island surrounded by death.

[On Beauty]

Thomas Moore, 1779–1852, Irish poet
What though youth gave love and roses,
Age still leaves us friends and wine.

[National Airs: Spring and Autumn 1815]

Ogden Nash, 1902–71, American humorous writer
Middle age is when you've met so many people that every new person you meet reminds you of someone else.

[Versus 1949]

Sir William Osler, 1849–1919, Canadian physician
The effective, moving, vitalizing work of the world is done between the ages of twenty-five and forty.

[In Harvey Cushing's *Life of Sir William Osler* 1925]

THE AGES OF MAN

My second fixed idea is the uselessness of men above sixty years of age, and the incalculable benefit it would be in commercial, political, and in professional life, if as a matter of course, men stopped work at this age.

[Ibid]

Samuel Pepys, 1633–1703, English diarist
This day I am, by the blessing of God, thirty-four years old, in very good health and mind's content, and in condition of estate much beyond whatever my friends could expect of a child of theirs, this day thirty-four years. The Lord's name be praised! And may I be thankful for it.

[Diary 23 February 1667]

Stephen Phillips, 1864–1915, English actor and poet
A man not old, but mellow, like good wine.

[Ulysses 1902]

Sir Arthur Wing Pinero, 1855–1934, English playwright
From forty till fifty a man is at heart either a stoic or a satyr.

[The Second Mrs Tanqueray 1893]

William Pitt, 1st Earl of Chatham, 1708–78, British statesman
The atrocious crime of being a young man . . . I shall neither attempt to palliate nor deny.

[Speech in the House of Commons 1741]

Plato, c.428–348BC, Greek philosopher
What is the prime of life? May it not be defined as a period of about twenty years in a woman's life, and thirty in a man's?

[The Republic 360BC]

Alexander Pope, 1688–1744, English poet
When men grow virtuous in their old age, they only make a sacrifice to God of the devil's leavings.

[Thoughts on Various Subjects 1727]

Behold the child, by nature's kindly law,
Pleased with a rattle, tickled with a straw:
Some livelier plaything gives his youth delight,
A little louder, but as empty quite:
Scarfs, garters, gold, amuse his riper stage,
And beads and prayerbooks are the toys of age:
Pleased with this bauble still, as that before;
Till tired he sleeps, and life's poor play is o'er.

[Essay on Man 1732–4]

Learn to live well, or fairly make your will;
You've play'd and lov'd, and ate and drank, your fill.
Walk sober off, before a sprightlier age
Comes tittering on, and shoves you from the stage.

[Epistles: Imitations of Horace 1733]

John Ruskin, 1819–1900, English art critic and writer
Give a little love to a child, and you get a great deal back.

[The Crown of Wild Olive 1866]

Antoine de Saint-Exupéry,1900–1944, French aviator and writer
Grown-ups never understand anything for themselves, and it is tiresome for children to be always and forever explaining things to them.

[*The Little Prince* 1943]

Guillaume de Salluste, Seigneur du Bartas, 1544–90, French poet
Who well lives, long lives: for this age of ours
Should not be numbered by years, days and hours

[*Divine Weeks and Works: Fourth Day* 1605]

George Santayana, 1863–1952, Spanish-American philosopher
The young man who has not wept is a savage, and the old man who will not laugh is a fool.

[*Dialogues in Limbo* 1926]

Sir Walter Scott, 1771–1832, Scottish novelist
Just at the age 'twixt boy and youth,
When thought is speech, and speech is truth.

[*Marmion* 1808]

On his bold visage middle age
Had slightly press'd its signet sage,
Yet had not quench'd the open truth
and Fiery vehemence of youth;
Forward and frolic glee was there,
The will to do, the soul to dare.

[*The Lady of the Lake* 1810]

Seneca, c. 4BC–AD65, Roman philosopher
Old age is an incurable disease.

[*Epistolae ad Lucilium c.* AD63]

William Shakespeare, 1564–1616, English dramatist
Your lordship, though not clean past your youth, hath yet some smack of age in you, some relish of the saltness of time.

[*King Henry IV, Part II* 1 1591]

Have you not a moist eye, a dry hand, a yellow cheek, a white beard, an increasing belly? Is not your voice broken, your hand short, your chin double, your wit single, and every part about you blasted with antiquity, and will you yet call yourself young?

[*Ibid*]

And 'tis not hard, I think,
For men so old as we to keep the peace.

[*Romeo and Juliet* 1 1594–5]

Thou wilt fall backward when thou comest to age
For you and I are past our dancing days.

[*Ibid*]

All the world's a stage,
And all the men and women merely players:
They have their exits and their entrances;
And one man in his time plays many parts,
Its acts being seven ages.

[*As You Like It* 2 1598–1600]

Therefore my age is as a lusty winter
Frosty, but kindly.

[*Ibid*]

What is love? 'tis not hereafter;
Present mirth hath present laughter.
What's to come is still unsure:
In delay there lies no plenty;
Then come kiss me, sweet and twenty,
Youth's a stuff will not endure.

[*Twelfth Night* 2 1598–1600]

Age cannot wither her, nor custom stale
Her infinite variety; other women cloy
The appetites they feed, but she makes hungry
Where most she satisfies.

[*Antony and Cleopatra* 2 1606–7]

My salad days,
When I was green in judgment, cold in blood.

[*Ibid* 1]

I would there were no age between sixteen and three-and-twenty, or that youth would sleep
out the rest; for there is nothing in the between but getting wenches with child, wronging the
ancientry, stealing, fighting.

[*The Winter's Tale* 3 1610–11]

Crabbed age and youth cannot live together:
Youth is full of pleasance, age is full of care.

[*The Passionate Pilgrim* 1599, attributed]

Age, I do abhor thee, youth, I do adore thee.

[*Ibid*]

George Bernard Shaw, 1856–1950, Irish playwright
Every man over forty is a scoundrel.

[*Man and Superman: Maxims for Revolutionists* 1903]

Youth, which is forgiven everything, forgives itself nothing: age, which forgives itself anything,
is forgiven nothing.

[*Ibid*]

It's all that the young can do for the old, to shock them and keep them up to date.

[*Fanny's First Play* 1911]

Sydney Smith, 1771–1845, English churchman
That sign of old age, extolling the past at the expense of the present.

[In Lady Holland's *Memoir* 1855]

Robert Southey, 1774–1843, English poet
Live as long as you may, the first twenty years are the longest half of your life.

[*The Doctor, etc* 1834–7]

In the days of my youth I remembered my God!
And He hath not forgotten my age.

[*The Old Man's Comforts, and how he Gained them* 1838]

Muriel Spark, 1918– , Scottish novelist
Give me a girl at an impressionable age, and she is mine for life.

[*The Prime of Miss Jean Brodie* 1962]

One's prime is elusive. You little girls, when you grow up, must be on the alert to recognize your prime at whatever time of your life it may occur.

[*Ibid*]

Sir Richard Steele, 1672–1729, Anglo-Irish essayist
Age in a virtuous person, of either sex, carries in it an authority which makes it preferable to all the pleasures of youth.

[*The Spectator* 1711]

There are so few who can grow old with a good grace.

[*Ibid*]

Gertrude Stein, 1874–1946, American writer
It was not long after that everybody was twenty-six. During the next two or three years all the men were twenty-six years old. It was the right age apparently for the time and place . . . If they were young men they were twenty-six. Later on, much later on, they were twenty-one and twenty-two.

[*The Autobiography of Alice B. Toklas* 1933]

Robert Louis [Balfour] Stevenson, 1850–94, Scottish novelist and poet
Youth is the time to go flashing from one end of the world to the other both in mind and body; to try the manners of different nations; to hear the chimes at midnight; to see sunrise in town and country; to be converted at a revival; to circumnavigate the metaphysics, write halting verses, run a mile to see a fire, and wait all day long in the theatre to applaud "Hernani."

[*Virginibus Puerisque* 1881]

A child should always say what's true,
And speak when he is spoken to,
And behave mannerly at table:
At least as far as he is able.

[*A Child's Garden of Verses* 1885]

Harriet Elizabeth Beecher Stowe, 1811–96, American writer
"Do you know who made you?"
"Nobody, as I knows on," said the child, with a short laugh . . . "I 'spect I grow'd. Don't think nobody ever made me."

[*Uncle Tom's Cabin* 1851–2]

Jonathan Swift, 1667–1745, Irish-born English writer
I swear she's no chicken; she's on the wrong side of thirty, if she be a day.

[*Polite Conversation c.*1738]

I have been assured by a very knowing American of my acquaintance in London, that a young healthy child well nursed is at a year old a most delicious, nourishing, and wholesome food, whether stewed, roasted, baked, or boiled, and I make no doubt that it will equally serve in a fricassee, or a ragout.

[A Modest Proposal for preventing the Children of Ireland from being a Burden to their *Parents or Country* 1729]

Elizabeth Taylor, 1912–75, English novelist
It is very strange that the years teach us patience; that the shorter our time, the greater our capacity for waiting.

[*A Wreath of Roses* 1950]

18

THE AGES OF MAN

Alfred, Lord Tennyson, 1809–92, English poet
An infant crying in the night:
An infant crying for the light:
And with no language but a cry.

[*In Memoriam* 1850]

William Makepeace Thackeray, 1811–63, English novelist
When you think that the eyes of your childhood dried at the sight of a piece of gingerbread, and that a plum-cake was a compensation for the agony of parting with your mamma and sisters; O my friend and brother, you need not be too confident of your own fine feelings.

[*Vanity Fair* 1847–8]

Dylan Thomas, 1914–53, Welsh poet
Do not go gentle into that good night,
Old age should burn and rave at close of day;
Rage, rage against the dying of the light.

[*Do Not Go Gentle* 1945]

Francis Thompson, 1859–1907, English poet
Know you what it is to be a child? . . . It is to believe in love, to believe in loveliness, to believe in belief; it is to be so little that the elves can reach to whisper in your ear; it is to turn pumpkins into coaches, and mice into horses, lowness into loftiness, and nothing into everything, for each child has its fairy godmother in its own soul.

[*Shelley*]

Henry David Thoreau, 1817–62, American naturalist and writer
Age is no better, hardly so well, qualified for an instructor as youth, for it has not profited so much as it has lost.

[*Walden, or Life in the Woods* 1854]

Pete [Peter Dennis Blandford] Townshend, 1945– , British rock musician
Hope I die before I get old.

[Song: *My Generation* 1965]

Sophie Tucker, 1884–1966, Russian-born American entertainer
Life begins at forty.

[Song title]

From birth to age fifteen, a girl needs good parents. From eighteen to thirty-five, she needs good looks. From thirty-five to fifty-five, she needs a good personality. From fifty-five on, she needs good cash.

[Said *c*.1953]

Sir Peter [Alexander] Ustinov, 1921– , English playwright and actor
The young need old men. They need men who are not ashamed of age, not pathetic imitations of themselves . . . Parents are the bones on which children sharpen their teeth.

[*Dear Me* 1977]

Horace Walpole, 4th Earl of Orford, 1717–97, English writer
Old age is no such uncomfortable thing if one gives oneself up to it with a good grace, and don't drag it about "to midnight dances and the public show."

[Letter 1774]

19

Charles Wesley, 1707–88, English preacher
Gentle Jesus, meek and mild,
Look upon a little child,
Pity my simplicity,
Suffer me to come to Thee.

[*Gentle Jesus, Meek and Mild* 1742]

Walt[er] Whitman, 1819–92, American poet
Women sit or move to and fro, some old, some young.
The young are beautiful – but the old are more beautiful than the young.

[*Beautiful Women* 1855]

Youth, large, lusty, loving – youth full of grace, force, fascination,
Do you know that Old Age may come after you with equal grace, force, fascination?

[*Youth, Day, Old Age and Night* 1855]

Oscar [Fingall O'Flahertie Wills] Wilde, 1854–1900, Irish writer
I have never admitted that I am more than twenty-nine, or thirty at the most. Twenty-nine
when there are pink shades, thirty when there are not.

[*Lady Windermere's Fan* 1891]

The old believe everything: the middle-aged suspect everything: the young know everything.

[*Phrases and Philosophies for the Use of the Young Chameleon* 1894]

Thirty-five is a very attractive age. London Society is full of women of the very highest birth
who have, of their own free choice, remained thirty-five for years.

[*The Importance of Being Earnest* 1895]

I became the spendthrift of my own genius and to waste an eternal youth gave me a curious
joy.

[*De Profundis* 1905]

Thomas Woodrow Wilson, 1856–1924, 28th president of the United States
Generally young men are regarded as radicals. This is a popular misconception. The most
conservative persons I ever met are college undergraduates.

[*Address* 1905]

John Wilmot, 2nd Earl of Rochester, 1647–80, English poet
Ancient person, for whom I
All the flattering youth defy,
Long be it ere thou grow old,
Aching, shaking, crazy, cold;
But still continue as thou art,
Ancient person of my heart.

[*A Song of a Young Lady to Her Ancient Lover*]

William Wordsworth, 1770–1850, English poet
The child is father of the man.

[*My Heart Leaps Up* 1802]

The wiser mind
Mourns less for what age takes away
Than what it leaves behind.

[*The Fountain* 1798]

Bliss was it in that dawn to be alive,
But to be young was very heaven.

[*The Prelude* published 1850]

20

Not in entire forgetfulness,
And not in utter nakedness,
But trailing clouds of glory do we come
From God, who is our home:
Heaven lies about us in our infancy!
Shades of the prison house begin to close
Upon the growing boy.

[*Intimations of Immortality* 1807]

Sweet childish days, that were as long
As twenty days are now.

[*To a Butterfly* 1801]

William Butler Yeats, 1865–1939, Irish poet
The years like great oxen tread the world,
And God the herdsman goads them on behind,
And I am broken by their passing feet.

[*The Countess Cathleen* 1891]

When you are old and grey and full of sleep,
And nodding by the fire, take down this book,
And slowly read, and dream of the soft look
Your eyes had once, and of their shadows deep.

[*When You are Old* 1892]

Bald heads forgetful of their sins,
Old, learned, respectable bald heads
Edit and annotate the lines
That young men, tossing on their beds,
Rhymed out in love's despair
To flatter beauty's ignorant ear.

[*The Scholars* 1915]

Edward Young, 1683–1765, English churchman and poet
At thirty, man suspects himself a fool;
Knows it at forty, and reforms his plan;
At fifty chides his infamous delay,
Pushes his prudent purpose to resolve;
In all the magnanimity of thought
Resolves, and re-resolves; then dies the same.

[*Night Thoughts* 1742–5]

Be wise with speed;
A fool at forty is a fool indeed.

[*Love of Fame* 1725–8]

Art, Music and Drama

Joseph Addison, 1672–1719, English essayist
Music, the greatest good that mortals know,
And all of heaven we have below.

[*Song for St Cecilia's Day*]

Anonymous
Painted pictures are dead speakers.

[Proverb]

Music helps not the tooth-ache.

[Proverb]

Aristotle, 384–322BC, Greek philosopher
Art is a higher type of knowledge than experience.

[*Metaphysics c.*322BC]
In part, art completes what nature cannot elaborate; and in part, it imitates nature.

[*Physics c.*320BC]

Jane Austen, 1775–1817, English novelist
I consider music as a very innocent diversion, and perfectly compatible with the profession of a clergyman.

[*Pride and Prejudice* 1813]

Pierre-Augustin Caron de Beaumarchais, 1739–99, French dramatist
Tout finit par des chansons.
(Everything ends in songs.)

[*The Marriage of Figaro* 1784]

Sir Thomas Beecham, 1879–1961, English conductor
Music first and last should sound well, should allure and enchant the ear. Never mind the inner significance.

[In Atkins' and Newman's *Beecham Stories* 1978]
The function of music is to release us from the tyranny of conscious thought.

[*Ibid*]
A distinguished British historian . . . declares that solo singing is favoured in an aristocratic society and communal or choral in a democratic.

[*A Mingled Chime* 1944]
Jazz! Bah – nothing but the debasement of noble brass instruments by blowing them into mutes, hats, caps, nooks, crannies, holes and corners!

[In Brymer's *From Where I Sit* 1979]

[On Mozart] He emancipated music from the bonds of a formal age, while remaining the true voice of the eighteenth century.

[*Ibid*]

Sir [Henry] Max[imilian] Beerbohm, 1872–1956, English writer
"Ah, say that again," she murmured. "Your voice is music." He repeated his question. "Music" she said dreamily; and such is the force of habit that, "I don't," she added, "know anything about music, really. But I know what I like."

[*Zuleika Dobson* 1912]

Ludwig van Beethoven, 1770–1827, German composer
Only the artist, or the free scholar, carries his happiness within him.

[To Kark von Bursy 1816]

[Joseph] Hilaire [Pierre] Belloc, 1870–1953, English writer
It is the best of all trades, to make songs, and the second best to sing them.

[*On Everything* 1909]

The Bible
O come, let us sing unto the Lord; let us make a joyful noise to the rock of our salvation. Let us come before his presence with thanksgiving, and make a joyful noise unto him with psalms.

[*Psalms* 95:1–2]

O sing unto the Lord a new song: sing unto the Lord, all the earth. Sing unto the Lord, bless his name; show forth his salvation from day to day.

[Ibid. 96:1–2]

Ambrose [Gwinett] Bierce, 1842–1914, American writer
Opera: a play representing life in another world, whose inhabitants have no speech but song, no motions but gestures and no postures but attitudes.

[*The Devil's Dictionary* 1906]

Piano: a parlor utensil for subduing the impenitent visitor. It is operated by depressing the keys of the machine and the spirits of the audience.

[Ibid.]

Dramatist, one who adapts plays from the French.

[Ibid.]

Marlon Brando, 1924– , American actor
An actor's a guy who if you ain't talkin' about him, ain't listening.

[In *The Observer* 1956]

Bertolt Brecht, 1898–1956, German dramatist and poet
A theatre that can't be laughed in is a theatre to be laughed at.

[*The Messingkauf Dialogues* 1965]

Sir Thomas Browne, 1605–82, English physician
Sure there is music even in the beauty, and the silent note which Cupid strikes, far sweeter than the sound of an instrument. For there is a music wherever there is a harmony, order or proportion; and thus far we may maintain the music of the spheres; for those well-ordered motions, and regular paces, though they give no sound to the ear, yet to the understanding they strike a note most full of harmony.

[*Religio Medici* 1643]

For even that vulgar and tavern music, which makes one man merry, another mad, strikes in me a deep fit of devotion, and a profound contemplation of the first Composer, there is something in it of divinity more than the ear discovers.

[*Ibid*]

Robert Browning, 1812–89, English poet
Your business is to paint the souls of men.

[*Fra Lippo Lippi* 1855]

Works done least rapidly, Art most cherishes.

[*Old Pictures in Florence* 1855]

It is the glory and good of Art,
That Art remains the one way possible
Of speaking truths, to mouths like mine at least.

[*Paracelsus* 1835]

That's my last Duchess painted on the wall
Looking as if she were alive.

[*My Last Duchess* 1842]

That's the wise thrush; he sings each song twice over,
Lest you should think he never could recapture
The first fine careless rapture!

[*Home Thoughts from Abroad* 1845]

Sir Edward Coley Burne-Jones, 1833–98, English artist
I mean by a picture a beautiful, romantic dream of something that never was, never will be – in a light better than any lights that ever shone – in a land no one can define or remember, only desire – and the forms divinely beautiful – and then I wake up, with the waking of Brynhild.

[Letter]

Fanny Burney [Frances, Madame d'Arblay], 1752–1840, English writer
"Do you come to the play without knowing what it is?"
"Oh, yes, sir, yes, very frequently. I have not time to read playbills. One merely comes to meet one's friends, and show that one's alive."

[*Evelina* 1778]

John Byrom, 1692–1763, English poet
Some say, that Signor Bononcini,
Compar'd to Handel's a mere ninny;
Others aver, to him, that Handel
Is scarcely fit to hold a candle.
Strange! that such high dispute should be
'Twixt Tweedledum and Tweedledee.

[Epigram on the rivalry between the composers
George Frederick Handel and Giovanni Bononcini]

John Milton Cage, 1912–92, American composer
If this word "music" is sacred and reserved for eighteenth and nineteenth century instruments, we can substitute a more meaningful term: organization of sound.

[*Silence* 1961]

Music is edifying, for from time to time it sets the soul in operation.

[*Ibid*]

Miguel de Cervantes [Saavedra], 1547–1616, Spanish dramatist and poet
Good painters imitate nature, bad ones regurgitate it.

[*El Licenciado Vidriera*]

Charlie Chaplin [Sir Charles Spencer Chaplin], 1889–1977, English-born film actor
There are more valid facts and details in works of art than there are in history books.

[*My Autobiography* 1964]

Charles [Philip Arthur George], Prince of Wales, 1948– , British prince
A kind of vast municipal fire station . . . like a monstrous carbuncle on the face of a much-loved and elegant friend.

[Referring to the new extension to the National Gallery in
London, In the *Observer,* June 1984]

Kenneth [Lord] Clark, 1903–83, English art historian
Opera, next to Gothic architecture, is one of the strangest inventions of Western man. It could not have been foreseen by any logical process.

[*Civilization* 1970]

William Cobbett, 1763–1835, English political reformer
Dancing is at once rational and healthful: it gives animal spirits; it is the natural amusement of young people, and such it has been from the days of Moses.

[*Advice to Young Men* 1829]

Jean Cocteau, 1891–1963, French poet and artist
Art is science in the flesh.

[*Le Rappel a l'Ordre*]

Samuel Taylor Coleridge, 1722–1834, English poet
Swans sing before they die–'twere no bad thing
Should certain persons die before they sing.

[*Epigram on a Volunteer Singer*]

As idle as a painted ship
Upon a painted ocean.

[*The Ancient Mariner* 1798]

We have no adequate conception of the perfection of the ancient tragic dance. The pleasure which the Greeks received from it had for its basis difference; and the more unfit the vehicle, the more lively was the curiosity and intense the delight at seeing the difficulty overcome.

[*Table-Talk* 1824]

William Collins, 1721–59, English poet
Too nicely Jonson knew the critic's part,
Nature in him was almost lost to Art.

[*Verses to Sir Thomas Hanmer*]

William Congreve, 1670–1729, English dramatist
Music alone with sudden charms can bind
The wandering sense, and calm the troubled mind.

[*Hymn to Harmony*]

Music has charms to soothe a savage breast.

[*The Mourning Bride* 1697]

25

Aaron Copland, 1900–90, America composer
Music is in a continual state of becoming.

[*Music and Imagination* 1952]

Victor Cousin, 1792–1867, French philosopher
L'art pour l'art.
(Art for art's sake.)

[*Sorbonne Lectures*]

Sir Noel [Pierce] Coward, 1899–1973, English actor and playwright
Extraordinary how potent cheap music is.

[*Private Lives* 1933]

Oliver Cromwell, 1599–1658, English statesman
Mr Lely, I desire you would use all your skill to paint my picture freely like me, and not flatter me at all; but remark all these roughnesses, pimples, and everything as you see me, otherwise I will never pay a farthing for it.

[Attributed]

Dante [Alighieri], 1265–1321, Italian poet
Art, as far as it can, follows nature, as a pupil imitates his master; thus your art must be, as it were, God's grandchild.

[*Inferno*]

John Davidson, 1857–1900, Scottish poet
He doubted, but God said "Even so;
Nothing is lost that's wrought with tears:
The music that you made below
Is now the music of the spheres."

[*A Ballad of Heaven*]

Destouches [Philippe Néricault], 1680–1754, French dramatist
Criticism is easy, art is difficult.

[*Le Glorieux* 1732]

Charles [John Huffam] Dickens, 1812–70, English novelist
There are only two styles of portrait painting; the serious and the smirk.

[*Nicholas Nickleby* 1838–9]

George Eliot [Mary Ann Evans], 1819–80, English novelist
'Tis God gives skill
But not without men's hands; He could not make
Antonio Stradivari's violins
Without Antonio. Get thee to thy easel.

[*Stradivarius*]

T[homas] S[tearns] Eliot, 1888–1965, American-born English poet
No artist produces great art by a deliberate attempt to express his own personality.
[*Essay: Four Elizabethan Dramatists*]

Henry Havelock Ellis, 1859–1939, English psychologist and writer
Every artist writes his own autobiography.

[*The New Spirit* 1890]

26

Ralph Waldo Emerson, 1803–82, American writer
Every genuine work of art has as much reason for being as the earth and the sun.
[*Society and Solitude: Civilization*]
Art is a jealous mistress, and if a man have a genius for painting, poetry, music, architecture, or philosophy, he makes a bad husband and an ill provider.
[*Conduct of Life: Wealth* 1860]
Artists must be sacrificed to their art. Like bees, they must put their lives into the sting they give.
[*Letters and Social Aims: Inspiration*]

Sir Roger L'Estrange, 1616–1704, English pamphleteer
Though this may be play to you, 'tis death to us.
[*Fables from Several Authors*]

Jules Feiffer, 1929– , American cartoonist and writer
Artists can colour the sky red because they *know* it's blue. The rest of us, who aren't artists, must colour things the way they really are, or people might think we're stupid.

Henry Fielding, 1707–54, English novelist
It hath been thought a vast commendation of a painter to say his figures seem to breathe; but surely it is much greater and nobler applause, that they appear to think.
[*Joseph Andrews* 1742]

E[dward] M[organ] Forster, 1879–1970, English novelist
Works of art, in my opinion, are the only objects in the material universe to possess internal order, and that is why, though I don't believe that only art matters, I do believe in Art for Art's sake.
[*Art for Art's Sake*]

José Ortega y Gasset, 1883–1955, Spanish philosopher
Art is incapable of bearing the burden of our lives. When it tries, it fails, losing its essential grace.
[*The Theme of our Time* 1923]

Paul Gauguin, 1848–1903, French artist
Many excellent cooks are spoiled by going into the arts.
[In Cournos' *Modern Plutarch*]
Art is either a plagiarist or a revolutionist.
[In Huneker's *Pathos of Distance*]

Sir William Schwenck Gilbert, 1836–1911, English librettist
For Art stopped short in the cultivated court of the Empress Josephine.
[*Patience* 1881]

A wand'ring minstrel I –
A thing of shreds and patches,
Of ballads, songs and snatches,
And dreamy lullaby.

[*The Mikado* 1885]

Oliver Goldsmith, 1728–74, Irish-born English writer
Here lies David Garrick, describe me, who can,
An Abridgement of all that was pleasant in man.

[*Retaliation* 1774]

On the stage he was natural, simple, affecting;
'Twas only that when he was off he was acting.

[*Ibid*]

Here Reynolds is laid, and to tell you my mind,
He has not left a better or wiser behind;
His pencil was striking, resistless, and grand;
His manners were gentle, complying, and bland.

[*Ibid*]

When they talk'd of their Raphaels, Correggios, and stuff,
He shifted his trumpet, and only took snuff.

[*Ibid*]

Martha Graham, 1894– , American dancer
No artist is ahead of his time. He *is* his time. It is just that others are behind the time.

Woody [Woodrow Wilson] Guthrie, 1912–67, American singer and songwriter
You can't write a good song about a whorehouse unless you've been in one.

[*Broadside* 1964]

Oscar Hammerstein II, 1895–1960, American lyricist
The hills are alive with the sound of music.
[Song: *The Sound of Music*, music written by Richard Rogers In *The Sound of Music* film 1959]

Moss Hart, 1904–61, American playwright
One begins with two people on a stage and one of them had better say something pretty damn quick!

[In *Contemporary Dramatists* 1977]

Jimi Hendrix, 1942–70, American rock musician
Blues is easy to play, but hard to feel.

[In Charles Shaar Murray's *Crosstown Traffic* 1989]

Katharine [Houghton] Hepburn, 1907–2003, American actress
Life's what's important. Walking, houses, family. Birth and pain and joy. Acting's just waiting for a custard pie. That's all.

Sir Alfred [Joseph] Hitchcock, 1899–1980, English-born film director
The length of a film should be directly related to the endurance of the human bladder.

[In *The Observer* 1960]

If I made *Cinderella*, the audience would be looking out for a body in the coach.

Aldous [Leonard] Huxley, 1894–1963, English writer
In the upper and lower churches of St Francis, Giotto and Cimabue showed that art had once worshipped something other than itself.

[*These Barren Leaves* 1925]

Silence is as full of potential wisdom and wit as the unhewn marble of great sculpture.

[*Point Counter Point* 1928]

After silence, that which comes nearest to expressing the inexpressible is music.

[In *Time* 1957]

Since Mozart's day composers have learned the art of making music throatingly and palpitatingly sexual.

[*Along the Road: Notes and Essays of a Tourist* 1925]

28

Dr Samuel Johnson. 1709–84, English lexicographer
When Learning's triumph o'er her barb'rous foes
First rear'd the Stage, immortal Shakespeare rose;
Each change of many-colour'd life he drew,
Exhausted worlds, and then imagin'd new:
Existence saw him spurn her bounded reign,
And panting Time toil'd after him in vain.
[Prologue for the opening of Drury Lane Theatre, London, 1747]
The drama's laws the drama's patrons give.
For we that live to please, must please to live.

[*Ibid*]

James [Augustine Aloysius] Joyce, 1882–1941, Irish writer and poet
Art is the human disposition of sensible or intelligible matter for an aesthetic end.
[*A Portrait of the Artist as a Young Man* 1916]

Pauline Kael, 1919–2001, American film critic
If there is any test that can be applied to movies, it's that the good ones never make you feel virtuous.
[*New Yorker* 1986]

John Keats, 1795–1821, English poet
The voice I hear this passing night was heard
In ancient days by emperor and clown:
Perhaps the self-same song that formed a path
Through the sad heart of Ruth, when, sick for home,
She stood in tears amid the alien corn.
[*Ode to a Nightingale* 1818]
The excellence of every art is its intensity, capable of making all disagreeables evaporate, from their being in close relationship with beauty and truth.
[Letter to his brothers 1817]
So I do believe . . . that works of genius are the first things in this world.
[*Ibid* 1818]

Rudyard Kipling, 1865–1936, English writer
But the Devil whoops, as he whooped of old:
"It's clever, but is it Art?"
[*The Conundrum of the Workshops*]
And each, in his separate star,
Shall draw the Thing as he sees It for the God of Things as They are!
[*When Earth's Last Picture is Painted*]

Walter Savage Landor, 1775–1864, English writer
There is delight in singing, though none hear
Beside the singer.
[*To Robert Browning* 1846]

John [Winston] Lennon, 1940–80, English pop singer and songwriter
Nothing really affected me until Elvis.
[In Davies' *The Beatles* 1968]

[Agnes] Elizabeth Lutyens, 1906–83, English composer
You're avant-garde for twenty years, then suddenly you're an old-fashioned floozie.
[In *The Guardian* 1966]

[Herbert] Marshall McLuhan, 1911–80, Canadian educator
It is one of the peculiar characteristics of the photograph that it isolates single moments in time.
[In Evans' *Pictures on a Page* 1978]

Herman Melville, 1819–91, American novelist
The Marquesan girls dance all over; not only do their feet dance, but their arms, hands, fingers, ay, their very eyes seem to dance in their heads.
[*Typee* 1846]

H[enry] L[ouis] Mencken, 1880–1956, American critic and writer
The great artists of the world are never Puritans, and seldom even ordinarily respectable.
[*Prejudices* 1919–27]

John Milton, 1608–74, English poet
Sometime let gorgeous Tragedy
In sceptred pall come sweeping by,
Presenting Thebes or Pelops' line,
Or the tale of Troy divine.

[*Il Penseroso* 1645]

Or bid the soul of Orpheus sing
Such notes as, warbled to the string,
Drew iron tears down Pluto's cheek.

[*Ibid*]

George Augustus Moore, 1852–1933, Anglo-Irish novelist
Acting is therefore the lowest of the arts, if it is an art at all.
[*Mummer-Worship*]
Art must be parochial in the beginning to be cosmopolitan in the end.
[*Hail and Farewell* 1911–14]

Anna Mary Robertson ("Grandma") Moses, 1860–1961, American painter
A primitive artist is an amateur whose work sells.

Nero [Claudius Caesar Drusus Germanicus], AD37–68, Roman emperor
Qualis artifex pereo!
(What an artist dies with me!)
[Attributed]

Pablo [Ruiz y] Picasso, 1881–1973, Spanish artist
Painting is a blind man's profession. He paints not what he sees, but what he feels, what he tells himself about what he has seen.
[In *Journals* Jean Cocteau 1929]

Edgar Allan Poe, 1809–49, American writer
Were I called upon to define, very briefly, the term "art," I should call it "the reproduction of what the senses perceive in nature through the veil of the soul."
[*Marginalia* 1844–9]

30

Alexander Pope, 1688–1744, English poet
He best can paint them who shall feel them most.

[*Eloisa to Abelard* 1717]

Whether the charmer sinner it, or saint it,
If folly grow romantic, I must paint it.

[*Moral Essays* 1731–5]

Cole [Albert] Porter, 1891–1964, American composer
My Art belongs to Dada.

[Attributed, in *The Oxford Dictionary of Humorous Quotations*]

André Previn, 1929– , American conductor
The basic difference between classical music and jazz is that in the former the music is always greater than its performance – whereas the way jazz is performed is always more important than what is being played.

[In *The Times* 1967]

Francis Quarles 1592–1644, English poet
My soul, sit thou a patient looker-on;
Judge not the play before the play is done:
Her plot hath many changes; every day
Speaks a new scene; the last act crowns the play.

[*Epigram: Respice Finem*]

Quintilian [Marcus Fabius Quintilianus], c. AD35–c. 96, Roman rhetorician
The height of art is to conceal art.

[*De institutione oratoria c.*90]

Vanessa Redgrave, 1937– , English actress
The stage is actor's country. You have to get your passport stamped every so often or they take away your citizenship.

Gioacchino Antonio Rossini, 1792–1868, Italian composer
Beethoven is the greatest composer – but Mozart is the only one.

[Attributed]

John Ruskin, 1819–1900, English art critic and writer
All great art is the work of the whole living creature, body and soul, and – chiefly of the soul.

[*The Stones of Venice* 1851–3]

To see clearly is poetry, prophecy, and religion – all in one.

[*Modern Painters* 1843–60]

No one can explain how the notes of a Mozart melody, or the folds of a piece of Titian's drapery, produce their essential effects. If you do not feel it, no one can by reasoning make you feel it.

[*Ibid*]

It is far more difficult to be simple than to be complicated, far more difficult to sacrifice skill and cease exertion in the proper place, than to expend both indiscriminately.

[*Ibid*]

Life without industry is guilt, industry without art is brutality.

[*Lectures on Art* 1870]

George Santayana, 1863–1952, Spanish-American philosopher
Nothing is really so poor and melancholy as art that is interested in itself and not in its subject.

[*The Life of Reason* 1906]

Sappho, c.650BC–?, Greek poet
For it is not right that in the house of song there be mourning.
Such things befit not us.

[Farewell poem to her daughter]

[Johann Christoph] Friedrich von Schiller, 1759–1805, German poet
Und siegt Natur, so muss die Kunst entweichen.
When Nature conquers, Art must then give way.

[Remark to Goethe]

John Selden, 1584–1654, English antiquary and politician
Pleasures are all alike, simply considered in themselves. He that takes pleasure to hear sermons enjoys himself as much as he that hears plays.

[*Table Talk: Pleasure* 1689]

William Shakespeare, 1564–1616, English dramatist
As in a theatre the eyes of men
After a well-graced actor leaves the stage,
Are idly bent on him that enters next,
Thinking his prattle to be tedious.

[*King Richard II* 5 1595–6]

How sour sweet music is,
When time is broke and no proportion kept!
So it is with the music of men's lives.

[*Ibid*]

I have a reasonable good ear in music. Let's have the tongs and the bones.
[*A Midsummer Night's Dream* 4 1595–6]

I hold the world but as the world, Gratiano;
A stage where every man must play a part,
And mine a sad one.

[*The Merchant of Venice* 1 1596–7]

How sweet the moonlight sleeps upon this bank!
Here we will sit, and let the sounds of music
Creep in our ears; soft stillness and the night
Become the touches of sweet harmony.

[*Ibid*]

I am never merry when I hear sweet music.

[*Ibid*]

The man that hath no music in himself,
Nor is not moved with concord of sweet sounds,
Is fit for treasons, stratagems and spoils;
The motions of his spirit are dull as night,
And his affections dark as Erebus:
Let no such man be trusted.

[*Ibid* 5]

If it be true that good wine needs no bush, 'tis true that a good play needs no epilogue.
[*As You Like It* Epilogue 1598–1600]

If music be the food of love, play on;
Give me excess of it, that, surfeiting,
The appetite may sicken, and so die.
That strain again–it had a dying fall:
O, it came o'er my ear like the sweet sound
That breathes upon a bank of violets,
Stealing and giving odour.

[*Twelfth Night* 1 1598–1600]

The best actors in the world, either for tragedy, comedy, history, pastoral, pastoral-comical, historical-pastoral, tragical-historical, tragical-comical-historical-pastoral, scene individable, or poem unlimited: Seneca cannot be too heavy, nor Plautus too light.

[*Hamlet* 2 1600–1601]

The play, I remember, pleased not the million; 'twas caviare to the general.

[*Ibid*]

The play's the thing
Wherein I'll catch the conscience of the king.

[*Ibid*]

I have heard of your paintings too, well enough; God has given you one face, and you make yourselves another.

[*Ibid*]

Speak the speech, I pray you, as I pronounced it to you, trippingly on the tongue: but if you mouth it, as many of your players do, I had as lief the town-crier spoke my lines. Nor do not saw the air too much with your hand, thus, but use all gently.

[*Ibid*]

Suit the action to the word, the word to the action; with this special observance, that you o'erstep not the modesty of nature.

[*Ibid*]

The purpose of playing, whose end, both at the first and now, was and is, to hold, as 'twere, the mirror up to nature.

[*Ibid*]

Exit, pursued by a bear.

[*The Winter's Tale* 3 stage direction]

George Bernard Shaw, 1856–1950, Irish playwright
The true artist will let his wife starve, his children go barefoot, his mother drudge for his living at seventy, sooner than work at anything but his art.

[*Man and Superman* 1903]

At every one of those concerts in England you will find rows of weary people who are there, not because they really like classical music, but because they think they ought to like it.

[*Ibid*]

A drama critic is a man who leaves no turn unstoned.

[In the *New York Times* 1950]

Percy Bysshe Shelley, 1792–1822, English poet
With hue like that when some great painter dips
His pencil in the gloom of earthquake and eclipse.

[*The Revolt of Islam* 1818]

Music, when soft voices die,
Vibrates in the memory.

[*To –: Music When Soft Voices*]

In honoured poverty thy voice did weave
Songs consecrate to truth and liberty, –
Deserting these, thou leavest me to grieve,
Thus having been, that thou should'st cease to be.

[*To Wordsworth*]

Richard Brinsley Sheridan, 1751–1816, English dramatist
I open with a clock striking, to beget an awful attention in the audience: it also marks the time, which is four o'clock in the morning, and saves a description of the rising sun, and a great deal about gilding the eastern hemisphere.

[*The Critic* 1779]

O Lord, sir, when a heroine goes mad she always goes into white satin.

[*Ibid*]

Philip Dormer Stanhope, 4th Earl of Chesterfield, 1694–1773, English statesman
If you love music, hear it; go to operas, concerts, and pay fiddlers to play to you; but I insist upon your neither piping nor fiddling yourself. It puts a gentleman in a very frivolous, contemptible light.

[*Letters to His Son* 1749]

Igor [Fedorovich] Stravinsky, 1882–1971, Russian-born composer
To listen is an effort, and just to hear is no merit. A duck hears also.

[In the *New York Review of Books* 1957]

Alfred, Lord Tennyson, 1809–92, English poet
The song that nerves a nation's heart,
Is in itself a deed.

[*The Charge of the Heavy Brigade*]

Count Leo [Nikolaevich] Tolstoy, 1828–1910, Russian writer
Art is not a handicraft, it is a transmission of feeling the artist has experienced.

[*What is Art?* 1898]

Spencer Tracy, 1900–1967, American film actor
Acting is not an *important* job in the scheme of things. Plumbing is.

Ivan Sergeyevich Turgenev, 1818–83, Russian novelist
A picture shows me at a glance what it takes dozen of pages of a book to expound.

[*Fathers and Sons* 1862]

Sir Peter [Alexander] Ustinov, 1921– , British playwright and actor
If Botticelli were alive today he'd be working for Vogue.

[In the *Observer* October 21 1962]

Artemus Ward [Charles Farrar Browne], 1834–67, American humorist
I can't sing. As a singist I am not a success. I am saddest when I sing. So are those who hear me. They are sadder even than I am.

[*Artemus Ward, His Travels* 1865]

Andy Warhol [Andrew Warhola], 1926–87, American artist and filmmaker
Being good in business is the most fascinating kind of art . . . Making money is art and working is art and good business is the best art.

[*From A to B and Back Again* 1975]

Edith Wharton, 1862–1937, American novelist
An unalterable and unquestioned law of the musical world required that the German text of French operas sung by Swedish artists should be translated into Italian for the clearer understanding of English-speaking audiences.

[*The Age of Innocence* 1920]

William Whewell, 1794–1866, English scientist and philosopher
In art, truth is a means to an end; in science, it is the only end.

[*The Philosophy of the Inductive Sciences* 1840]

Oscar [Fingall O'Flahertie Wills] Wilde, 1854–1900, Irish writer
The final revelation is that Lying, the telling of beautiful untrue things, is the proper aim of Art.

[*Intentions: The Decay of Lying* 1891]

For there is no art where there is no style, and no style where there is no unity, and unity is of the individual.

[*Ibid: The Critic as Artist*]

Robbie [Robert Peter] Williams, 1974– , British rock singer and songwriter
Let me entertain you.

[Song title 1998]

Sir P[elham] G[reville] Wodehouse, 1881–1975, English-born writer
Has anyone ever seen a dramatic critic in the daytime. Of course not. They come out after dark, up to no good.

[In the *New York Mirror* 1955

William Wordsworth, 1770–1850, English poet
The music in my heart I bore,
Long after it was heard no more.

[*The Solitary Reaper*]

But who is He, with modest looks,
And clad in homely russet brown?
He murmurs near the running brooks A music sweeter than their own.

[*A Poet's Epitaph*]

Frank Lloyd Wright, 1869–1959, American architect
A doctor can bury his mistakes, but an architect can only advise his client to plant vines.

[In *The Sunday Times* 1957]

Beauty

Anacreon, 563–478BC, Greek poet
Nature gave horns to bulls, hooves to horses, speed to hares, the power of swimming to fishes, that of flying to birds, and understanding to men. She had nothing left to give to women save beauty. Beauty is proof against spears and shields. She who is beautiful is more formidable than fire and iron.

[*Fragment c.*500BC]

Anonymous
Beauty is on the eye of the beholder.

[Proverb]

Beauty may have fair leaves, yet bitter fruit.

[Proverb]

The fairest rose at last is withered.

[Proverb]

Francis Bacon, Baron Verulam of Verulam and Viscount of St Albans, 1561–1626, English philosopher
There is no Excellent Beauty, that hath not some strangeness in the proportion.

[*Essays: Of Beauty* 1597]

John Codrington Bampfylde, 1754–c.1796, English poet
Rugged the breast that beauty cannot tame.

[*Sonnet in Praise of Delia*]

Sir [Henry] Max[imilian] Beerbohm, 1872–1956, English writer
Beauty and the lust for learning have yet to be allied.

[*Zuleika Dobson* 1912]

Aphra Behn, 1640–89, English playwright
Do you not daily see fine clothes . . . are more inviting than Beauty unadorn'd?

[*The Rover* 1681]

The Bible
Favour is deceitful, and beauty is vain: but a woman that feareth the Lord, she shall be praised.

[*Proverbs* 31:30]

Whatsoever things are true, whatsoever things are honest, whatsoever things are just, whatsoever things are pure, whatsoever things are lovely, whatsoever things are of good report, if there be any virtue, and if there be any praise, think on these things.

[*Philippians* 4:8]

BEAUTY

Robert Bridges, 1844–1930, English poet
For beauty being the best of all we know
Sums up the unsearchable and secret aims of nature.

[*The Growth of Love* 1876]

Rupert Chawner Brooke, 1887–1915, English poet
Live hair that is
Shining and free; blue-massing clouds; the keen
Unpassioned beauty of a great machine;
The benison of hot water; furs to touch;
The good smell of old clothes.

[*The Great Lover*]

Robert Browning, 1812–89, English poet
If you get simple beauty, and nought else.
You get about the best thing God invents.

[*Fra Lippo Lippi* 1855]

Robert Williams Buchanan, 1841–1901, Scottish writer
Beauty and Truth, though never found, are worthy to be sought.

[*To David in Heaven*]

Edmund Burke, 1729–97, Irish-born English political writer
I never remember that anything beautiful, whether a man, a beast, a bird, or a plant, was ever shown, though it were to a hundred people, that they did not all immediately agree that it was beautiful.

[*The Sublime and Beautiful* 1756]

Byron, Lord George Gordon [Noel], 6th Baron Byron of Rochdale, 1788-1824, English poet
The fatal gift of beauty.

[*Childe Harold's Pilgrimage* 1818]

She walks in beauty like the night
Of cloudless climes and starry skies;
And all that's best of dark and bright
Meet in her aspect and her eyes:
Thus mellow'd to that tender light
Which heaven to gaudy day denies.

[*She Walks in Beauty* 1820]

Joseph Campbell, 1879–1944, Irish poet
As a white candle
In a holy place,
So is the beauty
Of an aged face.

[*The Old Woman*]

Luis Cernuda, 1902–63, Spanish poet
Everything beautiful has its moment and then passes away.

[*Las Ruinas*]

Marcus Tullius Cicero, 106–43BC, Roman statesman
There are two kinds of beauty – loveliness and dignity. We ought to regard loveliness as the quality of woman, dignity that of man.

[*De Officiis* 78BC]

Hartley Coleridge, 1796–1849, English writer
She is not fair to outward view
As many maidens be;
Her loveliness I never knew
Until she smiled on me.
O then I saw her eye was bright,
A well of love, a spring of light.

[Song: *She is not Fair*]

Confucius [K'ung fu-tzu], 551–479BC, Chinese philosopher
Everything has its beauty but not everyone sees it.

[*Analects* c.500BC]

William Congreve, 1670–1729, English dramatist
Beauty is the lover's gift.

[*The Way of the World* 1700]

There is in true beauty, as in courage, somewhat which narrow souls cannot dare to admire.

[*The Old Bachelor* 1693]

John Donne, c.1571–1631, English poet
No spring nor summer beauty hath such grace
As I have seen in one autumnal face.

[*Elegies*: *The Autumnal*]

Henry Havelock Ellis, 1859–1939, English psychologist and writer
Beauty is the child of love.

[*Impressions and Comments*]

Ralph Waldo Emerson, 1803–82, American writer
Beauty is its own excuse for being.

[*The Rhodora* 1839]

Eugene Field, 1850–95, American journalist and poet
So shut your eyes while mother sings
Of wonderful sights that be,
And you shall see the beautiful things
As you rock on the misty sea
Where the old shoe rocked the fishermen three,
Wynken,
Blynken,
And Nod.

[*Dutch Lullaby* (*Wynken, Blynken and Nod*) 1889]

Anne Frank, 1929–45, German-Jewish diarist
Think of all the beauty still left around you and be happy.

[*The Diary of a Young Girl* 1947]

[Hyppolyte] Jean Giraudoux, 1882–1944, French playwright and writer
Blonde beauty doesn't usually last for ever.

[*Tiger at the Gates* 1935]

Sir James Goldsmith, 1933–97, English businessman
Beauty is a social necessity.

[In the *Times* June 10 1994]

Baltasar Gracian, 1601–58, Spanish philosopher
Beauty and folly are generally companions.

[*The Art of Wordly Wisdom* 1647]

[James] Langston Hughes, 1902–67, American poet, playwright and novelist
Why should I want to be White? I am a Negro – and beautiful!

Victor [Marie] Hugo, 1802–85, French novelist and poet
Le beau est aussi utile que l'utile. Plus peut-etre.
(The beautiful is as useful as the useful. Perhaps more so.)

[*Les Misérables* 1862]

David Hume, 1711–76, Scottish philosopher and writer
Beauty in things exists in the mind which contemplates them.

[*Essays, Moral and Political* 1741]

Aldous [Leonard] Huxley, 1894–1963, English writer
Beauty for some provides escape
Who gain a happiness in eyeing
The gorgeous buttocks of the ape
Or Autumn sunsets exquisitely dying.

[*Leda: Ninth Philosopher's Song* 1920]

Ben[jamin] Jonson, 1572–1637, English poet
Underneath this stone doth lie
As much beauty as could die;
Which in life did harbour give
To more virtue than doth live.

[*Epitaph on Elizabeth*]

Immanuel Kant, 1724–1804, German philosopher
The *beautiful* is that which pleases universally without a concept.

[*Critique of Judgement* 1790]

John Keats, 1795–1821, English poet
A thing of beauty is a joy forever;
Its loveliness increases; it will never
Pass into nothingness; but still will keep
A bower quiet for us, and a sleep
Full of sweet dreams, and health, and quiet breathing.

[*Endymion* 1818]

For 'tis the eternal law
That first in beauty should be first in might.

[*Hyperion* 1820]

"Beauty is truth, truth beauty," – that is all
Ye know on earth, and all ye need to know.

[*Ode on a Grecian Urn c.*1819]

I am certain of nothing but the holiness of the heart's affections and the truth of imagination
– what the imagination seizes as beauty must be truth – whether it existed before or not.

[Letter 1817]

Jean Kerr, 1923– , American journalist

I'm tired of all this nonsense about beauty being only skin-deep. That's deep enough. What
do you want – an adorable pancreas?

D[avid] H[erbert] Lawrence, 1885–1930, English novelist and poet

Beauty is an experience, nothing else. It is not a fixed pattern or an arrangement of features.
It is something felt.

[*Essays*]

George Macdonald, 1824–1905, Scottish poet and novelist

Beauty and sadness always go together.

[*Within and Without* 1855]

Marcus Aurelius [Antoninus] [Marcus Annius Verus] AD121–80, Roman emperor

Does beauty need anything more? Nay, no more than law, or truth, or kindness, or modesty.
Which of them owes its virtue to being praised or loses it by being blamed?

[*Meditations c.*170]

Walter John de la Mare, 1873–1956, English poet

Here lies a most beautiful Lady,
Light of step and heart was she;
I think she was the most beautiful lady
That ever was in the West Country.

[*Epitaph*]

Groucho [Julius Henry] Marx, 1895–1977, American comedian

You're the most beautiful woman I've ever seen, which doesn't say much for you.

[*Animal Crackers* film 1930]

John Edward Masefield, 1878–1967, English poet

Beauty you lifted up my sleeping eye
And filled my heart with longing with a look.

[*Sonnets*]

W[illiam] Somerset Maugham, 1874–1965, English novelist

Beauty is something wonderful and strange that the artist fashions out of the chaos of the
world in the torment of his soul.

[*The Moon and Sixpence* 1919]

John Milton, 1608–74, English poet

Beauty is nature's coin, must not be hoarded,
But must be current, and the good thereof
Consists in mutual and partak'n bliss.

[*Comus* 1634]

40

Beauty stands
In the admiration only of weak minds
Led captive.

[*Paradise Regained* 1671]

Molière [Jean-Baptiste Poquelin], 1622–73, French playwright
Beauty of face is a frail ornament, a passing flower, a momentary brightness belonging only to the skin.

[*Les Femmes savantes* 1672]

Camille Paglia, 1947– , American writer
Beauty is our weapon against nature; by it we make objects, giving them limit, symmetry, proportion. Beauty halts and freezes the melting flux of nature.

[*Sexual Personae* 1990]

Pericles, c.493–429BC, Greek statesman
For we are lovers of the beautiful without extravagance, and cultivate our minds without effeminacy.

[*Thucydides*]

Ambrose Philips, c.1675–1749, English politician and poet
The flowers, anew, returning seasons bring!
But beauty faded has not second spring.

[*The First Pastoral*]

Plato, c.428–348BC, Greek philosopher
The good is the beautiful.

[*Lysis*]

When a man loves the beautiful, what does he desire? That the beautiful may be his.

[*Symposium c.*360BC]

Plotinus, c.205–c.270, Greek philosopher
Beauty is rather a light that plays over the symmetry of things than that symmetry itself.

[*Enneads c.*250]

Edgar Allan Poe, 1809–49, American writer
Helen, thy beauty is to me
Like those Nicaean barks of yore,
That gently, o'er a perfumed sea,
The weary, wayworn wanderer bore.
To his own native shore.

[*To Helen* 1831]

Alexander Pope, 1688–1744, English poet
Fair tresses man's imperial race insure,
And beauty draws us with a single hair.

[*The Rape of the Lock* 1714]

Beauties in vain their pretty eyes may roll;
Charms strike the sight, but merit wins the soul.

[*Ibid*]

So peaceful rests, without a stone, a name,
What once had beauty, titles, wealth, and fame,
How loved, how honour'd once, avails thee not,
To whom related, or by whom begot;
A heap of dust alone remains of thee,
'Tis all thou art, and all the proud shall be!

[*Elegy to the Memory of an Unfortunate Lady* 1717]

Jean Paul Richter, 1763–1825, German novelist

Whenever, at a party, I have been in the mood to study fools, I have always looked for a great beauty: they always gather round her like flies around a fruit-stall.

[*Hesperus* 1795]

John Ruskin, 1819–1900, English art critic and writer

Remember that the most beautiful things in the world are the most useless; peacocks and lilies for instance.

[*The Stones of Venice* 1851–3]

Saki [Hector Hugh Munro], 1870–1916, Scottish-born writer

I always say beauty is only sin deep.

[*Reginald's Choir Treat* 1904]

Sappho, c. 650BC–?, Greek poet

What is beautiful is good, and who is good will soon be beautiful.

[*Fragment c.*610BC]

William Shakespeare, 1564–1616, English dramatist

Could I come near your beauty with my nails,
I'd set my ten commandments in your face.

[*King Henry II, Part II* 1 1591]

Beauty itself doth of itself persuade
The eyes of men without an orator.

[*The Rape of Lucrece* 1594]

Is she kind as she is fair?
For beauty lives with kindness.

[*The Two Gentlemen of Verona* 4 1594–5]

For where is any author in the world
Teaches such beauty as a woman's eye?
Learning is but an adjunct to ourself.

[*Love's Labour's Lost* 4 1594–5]

O, she doth teach the torches to burn bright!
It seems she hangs upon the cheek of night
Like a rich jewel in an Ethiope's ear;
Beauty too rich for use, for earth too dear!

[*Romeo and Juliet* 1 1594–5]

Beauty's ensign yet
Is crimson in thy lips and in thy cheeks,
And death's pale flag is not advanced there.

[*Ibid 5*]

BEAUTY

Thus ornament is but the guiled shore
To a most dangerous sea; the beauteous scarf
Veiling an Indian beauty; in a word,
The seeming truth which cunning times put on
To entrap the wisest.

[The Merchant of Venice 3 1596–7]

Beauty provoketh thieves sooner than gold.

[As You Like It 1 1598–1600]

He hath a daily beauty in his life
That makes me ugly.

[Othello 5 1604–5]

From fairest creatures we desire increase,
That thereby beauty's rose might never die.

[Sonnets 1]

Shall I compare thee to a summer's day?
Thou art more lovely and more temperate:
Rough winds do shake the darling buds of May,
And summer's lease hath all too short a date.

[Ibid 18]

To me, fair friend, you never can be old,
For as you were when first your eye I eyed,
Such seems your beauty still. Three winters cold
Have from the forests shook three summers' pride,
Three beauteous springs to yellow autumn turn'd.

[Ibid 104]

Ah! yet doth beauty, like a dial-hand,
Steal from his figure and no pace perceived.

[Ibid]

Beauty is but a vain and doubtful good;
A shining gloss that fadeth suddenly;
A flower that dies when first it 'gins to bud;
A brittle glass that's broken presently.

[The Passionate Pilgrim 1599]

George Bernard Shaw, 1856–1950, Irish playwright
I believe in Michael Angelo, Velasquez, and Rembrandt; in the might of design, the mystery of colour, the redemption of all things by Beauty everlasting, and the message of Art that has made these hands blessed.

[The Doctor's Dilemma 1906]

Percy Bysshe Shelley, 1792–1822, English poet
And the rose like a nymph to the bath addressed,
Which unveiled the depth of her glowing breast,
Till, fold after fold, to the fainting air
The soul of her beauty and love lay bare.

[The Sensitive Plant 1820]

For she was beautiful – her beauty made
The bright world dim, and everything beside
Seemed like the fleeting image of a shade.

[The Witch of Atlas 1820]

My last delight tell them that they are dull,
And bid them own that thou art beautiful.

[*Epipsychidion* 1821]

An isle under Ionian skies,
Beautiful as a wreck of Paradise.

[*Ibid*]

Wallace Stevens 1879–1955, American poet
Beauty is momentary in the mind –
The fitful tracing of a portal;
But in the flesh it is immortal.
The body dies; the body's beauty lives.

[*Peter Quince at the Clavier* 1923]

James Thomson, 1700–48, Scottish poet
Loveliness
Needs not the foreign aid of ornament,
But is when unadorned adorned the most.

[*The Seasons: Autumn* 1726–30]

James Thomson, 1834–82, Scottish poet
Perfect beauty is its own sole end.

[*Weddah* 1871]

Thus beauty is that pearl a poor man found;
Which could not be surrendered, changed, or sold,
Which he might never bury in the ground,
Or hide away within his girdle-fold.

[*Ibid*]

Count Leo [Nikolaevich] Tolstoy, 1828–1910, Russian writer
It is amazing how complete is the delusion that beauty is goodness.
[*The Kreutzer Sonata* 1890]

Lew[is] Wallace, 1827–1905, American novelist
Beauty is altogether in the eye of the beholder.

[*The Prince of India*]

Edmund Waller, 1606–87, English poet
Small is the worth
Of beauty from the light retir'd;
Bid her come forth,
Suffer herself to be desir'd,
And not blush so to be admir'd.

[*Go, Lovely Rose!* 1664]

Sir William Watson, 1858–1935, English poet
O be less beautiful, or be less brief.

[*Autumn*]

Simone Weil, 1909–43, French essayist and philosopher
Beauty always promises, but never gives anything.
[*Selected Essays: Human Personality* 1962]

Oscar [Fingall O'Flahertie Wills] Wilde, 1854–1900, Irish writer

Beauty is the only thing that time cannot harm. Philosophies fall away like sand, and creeds follow one another like the withered leaves of autumn; but what is beautiful is a joy for all seasons and a possession for all eternity.

[*The English Renaissance of Art 1882*]

It is better to be beautiful than to be good. But . . . it is better to be good than to be ugly.

[*The Picture of Dorian Gray* 1891]

At least
I have not made my heart a heart of stone,
Nor starved my boyhood of its goodly feast,
Nor walked where Beauty is a thing unknown.

[*Apologia*]

Naomi Wolf, 1962– , American author

"Beauty" is a currency system like the gold standard. Like any economy, it is determined by politics, and in the modern age in the West it is the last, best belief system that keeps male dominance intact.

[*The Beauty Myth* 1990]

[Adeline] Virginia Woolf, 1882–1941, English novelist and critic

She bore about with her, she could not help knowing it, the torch of her beauty; she carried it erect into any room that she entered; and after all, veil it as she might, and shrink from the monotony of bearing that it imposed on her, her beauty was apparent.

[*To the Lighthouse* 1927]

William Wordsworth, 1770–1850, English poet

Fair seed-time had my soul, and I grew up
Fostered alike by beauty and by fear.

[*The Prelude*]

Sweet Highland Girl, a very shower
Of beauty is thy earthly dower.

[*To a Highland Girl* 1803]

It is a beauteous evening, calm and free.

[*Sonnet* 1807]

Some happy tone
Of meditation, slipping in between
The beauty coming and the beauty gone.

[*Most sweet it is* 1835]

Sir Henry Wotton,1568–1639, English diplomat and poet

You meaner beauties of the night,
That poorly satisfy our eyes
More by your number than your light
You common people of the skies;
What are you, when the moon shall rise.

[*On his Mistress, the Queen of Bohemia* 1624]

William Butler Yeats, 1865–1939, Irish poet

Land of Heart's Desire,
Where beauty has no ebb, decay no food,
But joy is wisdom, Time an endless song.

[*The Land of Heart's Desire* 1894]

45

A woman of so shining loveliness
That men threshed corn at midnight by a tress,
A little stolen tress.

[*The Secret Rose* 1896]

MacDonagh and MacBride
And Connolly and Pearse
Now and in time to be,
Wherever green is worn,
Are changed, changed utterly:
A terrible beauty is born.

[*Easter 1916* 1917]

I know what wages beauty gives,
How hard a life her servant lives,
Yet praise the winters gone:
There is not a fool can call me friend,
And I may dine at journey's end
With Landor and with Donne.

[*To a Young Beauty* 1918]

In courtesy I'd have her chiefly learned;
Hearts are not had as a gift but hearts are earned
By those that are not entirely beautiful.

[*A Prayer for My Daughter* 1919]

The innocent and the beautiful
Have no enemy but time.

[*In Memory of Eva Gore-Booth and Con Markiewicz* 1929]

Only God, my dear,
Could love you for yourself alone
And not your yellow hair.

[*For Anne Gregory* 1932]

Liberty

John Quincy Adams, 1767–1848, 6th president of the United States
Individual liberty is individual power, and as the power of a community is a mass compounded of individual powers, the nation which enjoys the most freedom must necessarily be in proportion to its numbers the most powerful nation.

[Letter 1822]

Joseph Addison, 1672–1719, English essayist
A day, an hour of virtuous liberty
Is worth a whole eternity in bondage.

[*Cato* 1713]

Anonymous
Lean liberty is better than fat slavery.

[Proverb]

'Tis liberty that every one loves.

[Proverb]

Susan B[rownell] Anthony, 1820–1906, American reformer
The true Republic: men, their rights and nothing more; women, their rights and nothing less.

[1872]

Francis Bacon, Baron Verulam of Verulam and Viscount of St Albans, 1561–1626, English philosopher
But the most ordinary cause of a single life, is Liberty; especially in certain self-pleasing and humorous minds, which are so sensible of every restraint as they will go near to think their girdles and garters to be bonds and shackles.

[*Essays: Of Marriage and Single Life* 1623]

Men in great places are thrice servants: servants of the Sovereign or State; servants of Fame; and servants of Business ... It is a strange desire to seek Power and to lose Liberty.

[*Ibid: Of Great Place*]

Menachem Begin, 1913–92, Israeli statesman
Who will condemn the hatred of evil that springs from the love of what is good and just?

[*The Revolt* 1951]

The Bible
And ye shall know the truth, and the truth shall make you free.

[*John* 8:32]

With a great sum obtained I this freedom. And Paul said, But I was free born.

[*Acts* 22:28]

47

Edmund Burke, 1729–97, Irish-born English political writer

Freedom and not servitude is the cure of anarchy; as religion and not atheism, is the true remedy for superstition.

[*On Conciliation with America: The Thirteen Resolutions* 1775]

Abstract liberty, like other mere abstractions, is not to be found.

[*Ibid*]

Robert Burns, 1759–96, Scottish poet

Man's inhumanity to man,
Makes countless thousands mourn!

[*Man Was Made to Mourn* 1786]

Freedom and whisky gang thegither,
Tak aff your dram!

[*The Author's Earnest Cry and Prayer*]

Now's the day, and now's the hour;
See the front o' battle lour;
See approach proud Edward's power –
Chains and slavery!

[*Bruce before Bannockburn*]

Liberty's in every blow! –
Let us do or die!.

[*Ibid*]

A fig for those by law protected!
Liberty's a glorious feast!
Courts for cowards were erected,
Churches built to please the priest!

[*Love and Liberty* (or *The Jolly Beggars*)]

Byron, Lord George Gordon [Noel], 6th Baron Byron of Rochdale, 1788–1824, English poet

Yet, Freedom! yet thy banner, torn, but flying,
Streams like the thunderstorm *against* the wind.

[*Childe Harold's Pilgrimage* 1818]

Hereditary Bondsmen! know ye not
Who would be free themselves must strike the blow?

[*Ibid*]

Lydia Maria Child, 1802–80, American abolitionist

[On slaves] They have stabbed themselves for freedom – jumped into the waves for freedom – fought like very tigers for freedom! But they have been hung, and burned, and shot – and their tyrants have been their historians.

[*An Appeal on Behalf of That Class of Americans called Africans* 1833]

Samuel Taylor Coleridge, 1772–1834, English poet

For what is freedom, but the unfettered use
Of all the powers which God for use had given?

[*The Destiny of Nations*]

William Cowper, 1731–1800, English poet

Freedom has a thousand charms to show,
That slaves, howe'er contented, never know.

[*Table-Talk* 1782]

Slaves cannot breathe in England; if their lungs
Receive our air, that moment they are free;
They touch our country, and their shackles fall.

[*The Task: The Timepiece* 1785]

John Philpot Curran, 1750–1817, Irish lawyer and patriot
The condition upon which God hath given liberty to men is eternal vigilance; which condition
if he break, servitude is at once the consequence of his crime, and the punishment of his guilt.

[Speech 1790]

Charles [John Huffam] Dickens, 1812–70, English novelist
I only ask to be free. The butterflies are free. Mankind will surely not deny to Harold
Skinpole what it concedes to the butterflies!

[*Bleak House* 1853]

Thomas Drummond, 1797–1840, Scottish engineer and statesman
Property has its duties as well as its rights.

[Letter to the Earl of Donoughmore 1838]

John Dryden, 1631–1700, English dramatist
I am as free as Nature first made man,
Ere the base laws of servitude began,
When wild in woods the noble savage ran.

[*The Conquest of Granada* 1670]

Paul Laurence Dunbar, 1872–1906, American poet
It is not a carol of joy or glee,
But a prayer that he sends from his heart's deep core . . .
I know why the caged bird sings!

[*Sympathy* 1899]

Benjamin Franklin, 1706–90, American scientist and philosopher
They that can give up essential liberty to obtain a little temporary safety deserve neither
liberty nor safely.

[*Historical Review of Pennsylvania* 1759]

William Lloyd Garrison, 1805–79, American abolitionist
Wherever there is a human being, I see God-given rights inherent in that being, whatever may
be the sex or complexion.

[In W.P. and F.J.T. Garrison *William Lloyd Garrison* 1885–9]

Edward Gibbon, 1737–94, English historian
Corruption, the most infallible symptom of constitutional liberty.

[*Decline and Fall of the Roman Empire* 1776–88]

Oliver Goldsmith, 1728–74, Irish-born English writer
This is Liberty-hall, gentlemen.

[*She Stoops to Conquer* 1773]

Samuel Gompers 1850–1924, English-born American labour leader
Show me the country that has no strikes and I'll show the country in which there is no liberty.

[Speech]

49

Gracchus [François Noël Babeuf], 1760–97, French revolutionary
Let the revolting distinction of rich and poor disappear once and for all, the distinction of great and small, of masters and valets, of governors and governed. Let there be no other difference between human beings than those of age and sex. Since all have the same needs and the same faculties, let there be one education for all, one food for all.

[*Manifesto of the Equals c.*1795]

Patrick Henry, 1736–99, American statesman
Is life so dear, or peace so sweet, as to be purchased at the price of chains and slavery? Forbid it, almighty God! I know not what course others may take, but as for me, give me liberty or give me death!

[Speech 1775]

Eric Hoffer, 1902–83, American philosopher and dockworker
When people are free to do as they please, they usually imitate each other.

[*The Passionate State of Mind* 1955]

Oliver Wendell Holmes, 1809–94, American physician and writer
The freeman casting with unpurchased hand
The vote that shakes the turrets of the land.

[*Poetry: a Metrical Essay*]

Aldous [Leonard] Huxley, 1894–1963, English writer
That all men are equal is a proposition to which, at ordinary times, no sane individual has ever given his assent.

[*Proper Studies*]

Henrik Ibsen, 1828–1906, Norwegian dramatist
The most dangerous enemy to truth and freedom in our midst is the compact majority. Yes, the damned, compact, liberal majority.

[*An Enemy of the People* 1882]
You should never put on your best trousers when you go out to fight for freedom and truth.

[*Ibid*]

James I, 1394–1437, king of Scotland
The bird, the beast, the fish eke in the sea,
They live in freedom everich in his kind;
And I a man, and lackith liberty.

[*The Kingis Quair*]

Thomas Jefferson, 1743–1826, 3rd president of the United States
The God who gave us life gave us liberty at the same time.

[*Summary View of the Rights of British America*]
We hold these truths to be self-evident – that all men are created equal; that they are endowed by their Creator with certain inalienable rights; that among these are life, liberty, and the pursuit of happiness.

[*The Declaration of Independence*]
The tree of liberty must be refreshed from time to time with the blood of patriots and tyrants. It is its natural manure.

[Letter 1787]

Dr Samuel Johnson, 1709–84, English lexicographer

Sir, we *know* our will is free, and *there's* an end on't.

[1769. In Boswell's *Life of Samuel Johnson 1791*]

"Junius," fl. 1769–72 [?Sir Philip Francis, 1740–1818, British civil servant]

The liberty of the press is the *Palladium* of all the civil, political, and religious rights of an Englishman.

[*Letters* dedication]

Brian Keenan, 1950– , Irish teacher and writer

Yes, I want something. I want my freedom, I want to live like a man, I am not an animal.

[*An Evil Cradling* 1992]

Martin Luther King Jr, 1929–68, American churchman and civil rights activist

Injustice anywhere is a threat to justice everywhere.

[Letter 1963]

I have a dream that one day on the red hills of Georgia the sons of former slaves and the sons of former slave-owners will be able to sit down together at the table of brotherhood.

[Speech 1963]

Nonviolent action, the Negro saw, was the way to supplement, no replace, the process of change. It was the way to divest himself of passivity without arraying himself in vindictive force.

[*Why We Can't Wait* 1964]

Free at last, free at last
Thank God Almighty
I'm free at last.

[Words from a speech, chosen as his epitaph]

Emma Lazarus, 1849–87, American poet

Give me your tired, your poor,
Your huddled masses yearning to breathe free,
The wretched refuse of your teeming shore,
Send these, the homeless, tempest-tossed, to me:
I lift my lamp beside the golden door.

[*The New Colossus* 1883 (inscribed on the pedestal of the Statue of Liberty, New York)]

Nikolai Lenin [Vladimir Ilyich Ulyanov], 1870–1924, Russian revolutionary leader

It is true that liberty is precious – so precious that it must be rationed.

[Attributed]

Abraham Lincoln, 1809–65, 16th president of the United States

In giving freedom to the slave, we assure freedom to the free – honourable alike in what we give and what we preserve.

[Message to Congress 1862]

That this nation, under God, shall have a new birth of freedom, and that government of the people, by the people, and for the people, shall not perish from the earth.

[*The Gettysburg Address* 1863]

I have always thought that all men should be free; but if any should be slaves, it should be first those who desire it for themselves, and secondly those who desire it for others. Whenever I hear anyone arguing for slavery, I feel a strong impulse to see it tried on him personally.

[Address to an Indiana regiment 1865]

Richard Lovelace, 1618–57/8, English poet

Stone walls do not a prison make,
Nor iron bars a cage;
Minds innocent and quiet take
That for an hermitage:
If I have freedom in my love
And in my soul am free,
Angels alone, that soar above,
Enjoy such liberty.

[*To Althea from Prison* 1649]

Magna Carta, 1215

It shall be lawful in future for anyone to leave our kingdom and return safely and securely, by land and water, save, in the public interest, for a short period in time of war.

[Article 42]

Nelson Mandela, 1918– , South African statesman

Our march to freedom is irreversible. . . . I have fought against white domination and I have fought against black domination. I have cherished the ideal of a democratic and free society in which all persons live together in harmony and with equal opportunity. It is an ideal which I hope to live for and to achieve. But if need be, it is an ideal for which I am prepared to die.

[Speech on release from prison, Cape Town, 1990]

José [Julian] Martí, 1853–95, Cuban patriot and poet

Men have no special right because they belong to one race or another: the word man defines all rights.

[*My Race* 1893]

Golda Meir, 1898–1978, Israeli stateswoman

We only want that which is given naturally to all peoples of the world, to be masters of our own fate, only of our fate, not of others, and in cooperation and friendship with others.

[Address to an Anglo-American committee of inquiry 1946]

John Stuart Mill, 1806–73, English philosopher

The only freedom which deserves the name is that of pursuing our own good in our own way, so long as we do not attempt to deprive others of theirs, or impede their efforts to obtain it.

[*On Liberty* 1859]

The liberty of the individual must be thus far limited; he must not make himself a nuisance to other people.

[*Ibid*]

John Milton, 1608–74, English poet

Give me the liberty to know, to utter, and to argue freely according to conscience, above all liberties.

[*Areopagitica* 1644]

No man who knows aught, can be so stupid to deny that all men naturally were born free.

[*Tenure of Kings and Magistrates* 1649]

[The blood of the Indians] has been so unjustly, so cruelly, and so often shed by the hands of the Spaniards: since God has made of one blood all nations of men for to dwell on all the face of the earth . . . All great and extraordinary wrongs done to particular persons ought to be considered as in a manner done to all the rest of the human race.

[Manifesto to the Lord Protector in favour of war against Spain 1655]

Preferring
Hard liberty before the easy yoke
Of servile Pomp.

[*Paradise Lost* 1668]

Eyeless in Gaza at the mill with slaves.

[*Samson Agonistes* 1671]

I did but prompt the age to quit their clogs
By the known rules of ancient liberty,
When straight a barbarous noise environs me
Of owls and cuckoos, asses, apes, and dogs.

[*Sonnet: On the Same*]

Licence they mean when they cry liberty.
For who loves that, must first be wise and good.

[*Ibid*]

Molière [Jean-Baptiste Poquelin], 1622–73, French playwright
Il se faut réserver une arrière boutique . . . en laquelle nous établissions notre vraie liberté.
(We must keep a little back shop . . . where we may establish our own true liberty.)

[*Essais*]

Joshua [Mqabuko Nyongolo] Nkomo, 1917–99, Zimbabwean nationalist and politician
The price of freedom can never be too high.

[*The Story of My Life* 1984]

George Orwell [Eric Arthur Blair], 1903–50, English novelist and critic
All animals are equal, but some animals are more equal than others.

[*Animal Farm* 1945]

Thomas Paine, 1737–1809, English political writer
Those who expect to reap the blessings of freedom must, like men, undergo the fatigue of supporting it.

[*The American Crisis* 1777]

Laurence Johnston Peter, 1919–90, Canadian-born American educator
Most hierarchies were established by men, who now monopolize the upper levels, thus depriving women of their rightful share of opportunities to achieve incompetence.

[*The Peter Principle* 1969]

William Pitt, 1759–1806, British statesman
Necessity is the plea for every infringement of human freedom. It is the argument of tyrants; it is the creed of slaves.

[Speech in the House of Commons 1783]

Marie Jeanne Philipon Roland de la Platière, 1754–93, French revolutionary
O Liberté! que de crimes on commet en ton nom!
(O Liberty! what crimes are committed in your name!)

[On seeing a statue of Liberty from the scaffold]

Sir Karl Raimund Popper, 1902–94, Austrian-born English philosopher
We must plan for freedom, and not only for security, if for no other reason than that only freedom can make security secure.

[*The Open Society and its Enemies* 1945]

Red Cloud, 1822–1909, American Oglala Sioux Indian chief

[On American federal troops] We were told that they wished merely to pass through our country . . . to seek for gold in the far west . . . yet before the ashes of the council fire are cold, the Great Father is building his forts among us. You have heard the sound of the white soldier's axe upon the Little Piney. His presence here is . . . an insult to the spirits of our ancestors. Are we then to give up our sacred graves to be ploughed for corn? Dakotas, I am for war

[Speech in Fort Laramie, Wyoming 1866]

Jean Jacques Rousseau, 1712–78, Swiss-born French philosopher

L'homme est né libre, et partout il est dans les fers.
(Man is born free, and everywhere he is in chains.)

[*The Social Contract* 1762]

[Ahmed] Salman Rushdie, 1947– , British novelist

"Free speech is a non-starter," says one of my Islamic extremist opponents. No sir, it is not. Free speech is the whole thing, the whole ball game. Free speech is life itself.

[Speech delivered in New York, 1999, under sentence of *fatwa* following publication of *The Satanic Verses* 1988.]

Jean-Paul Sartre, 1905–80, French philosopher and writer

Man is condemned to be free.

[*Existentialism and Humanism* 1948]

William Shakespeare 1564–1616, English dramatist

I must have liberty
Withal, as large a charter as the wind,
To blow on whom I please.

[*As You Like It* 2 1598–1600]

George Bernard Shaw, 1856–1950, Irish playwright

Equality is fundamental in every department of social organization.

[*Man and Superman: Maxims for Revolutionists* 1903]

Liberty means responsibility. That is why most men dread it.

[*Ibid*]

Percy Bysshe Shelley, 1792–1822, English poet

I hated thee, fallen tyrant! I did groan
To think that a most unambitious slave,
Like thou shouldst dance and revel on the grave
Of Liberty.

[*Feelings of a Republican on the Fall of Bonaparte*]

Let there be light! said Liberty,
And like sunrise from the sea,
Athens arose!

[*Hellas* 1821]

Isaac Bashevis Singer, 1904–91 , American Yiddish novelist

When you betray somebody else, you also betray yourself.

[In the *New York Times Magazine* 1978]

Adam Smith, 1723–90, Scottish philosopher
No society can surely be flourishing and happy, of which the far greater part of the members are poor and miserable.

[*The Wealth of Nations* 1776]

Samuel Francis Smith, 1808–95, American writer
My country, 'tis of thee,
Sweet land of liberty,
Of thee I sing.

[*America* 1831]

Alexander Solzhenitsyn, 1918– , Russian novelist
You took my freedom away a long time ago and you can't give it back because you haven't got it yourself.

[*The First Circle* 1968]

Herbert Spencer, 1820–1903, English philosopher
No one can be perfectly free till all are free; no one can be perfectly moral till all are moral; no one can be perfectly happy till all are happy.

[*Social Statics* 1851]

Edmund Spenser, c.1552–99, English poet
What more felicity can fall to creature,
Than to enjoy delight with liberty.

[*Complaints* 1591]

John Addington Symonds, 1840–93, English writer
These things shall be! A loftier race
Than e'er the world hath known, shall rise,
With flame of freedom in their souls
And light of knowledge in their eyes.

[*New and Old: A Vista* 1880]

Tecumseh, c.1768–1813, American Shawnee Indian chief
Once they were a happy race. Now they are made miserable by the white people, who are never contented but are always encroaching.

[Speech to Governor Harrison 1810]

Sell a country! Why not sell the air, the clouds and the great sea, as well as the earth? Did not the Great Spirit make them all for the use of his children.

[*Ibid*]

[Sithu] U Thant, 1909–74, Burmese secretary-general of the United Nations
The world will not live in harmony so long as two-thirds of its inhabitants find difficulty in living at all.

[In *The Observer* 1969]

Margaret Hilda Thatcher, Baroness Thatcher of Kesteven, 1925– , British politician
Let me give you my vision: a man's right to work as he will, to spend what he earns, to own property, to have the State as servant and not as master – these are the British inheritance. They are the essence of a free country and on that freedom all our other freedoms depend.

[Speech, Blackpool 1975. In *The Path to Power*]

James Thomson, 1700–1748, Scottish poet, and David Mallet or Malloch, c.1705–1765, Scottish writer
When Britain first, at Heaven's command,
Arose from out the azure main,
This was the charter of the land,
And guardian angels sung this strain –
"Rule, Britannia, rule the waves;
Britons never will be slaves."

[Alfred: A Masque 1740]

James Thomson, 1834–82, Scottish poet
Those pale and languid rich ones
Who are always and never free.

[Sunday at Hampstead]

Bertrand Barère de Vieuzac, 1755–1841, French revolutionary
L'arbre de la liberté ne croît qu'arrosé par le sang des tyrans.
(The tree of liberty grows only when watered by the blood of tyrants.)

[Speech 1792]

Voltaire [François Marie Arouet], 1694–1778, French philosopher and writer
La Liberté est née en Angleterre des querelles des tyrans.
(Liberty was born in England from the quarrels of tyrants.)

[Lettres Philosophiques]

Ils ne se servent de la pensée que pour autoriser leurs injustices, et n'emploient les paroles que pour déguiser leurs pensés.
(They use thought only to warrant their injustices, and employ words only to conceal their thoughts.)

[Le Chapon et la poularde (The Capon and the Pullet)]

George Washington, 1732–99, 1st president of the United States
Liberty, when it begins to take root, is a plant of rapid growth.

[Letter 1788]

Daniel Webster, 1782–1852, American statesman
Liberty and Union, now and for ever, one and inseparable.

[Speech in the Senate 1830]

Simone Weil, 1909–43, French essayist and philosopher
Liberty, taking the word in its concrete sense, consists in the ability to choose.

William Carlos Williams, 1883–1963, American novelist and poet
Freedom is an indivisible word. If we want to enjoy it, and fight for it, we must be prepared to extend it to everyone, whether they are rich or poor, whether they agree with us or not, no matter what their race or the colour of their skin.

[One World]

Thomas Woodrow Wilson, 1856–1924, 28th president of the United States
The history of liberty is a history of resistance.

[Speech 1812]

LIBERTY

William Wordsworth, 1770–1850, English poet
We must be free or die, who speak the tongue
That Shakespeare spake; the faith and morals hold
Which Milton held.

[Sonnet: It is not to be thought of]

Two voices are there; one is of the sea,
One of the mountains; each a mighty voice:
In both from age to age thou didst rejoice,
They were thy chosen music, Liberty!

[Sonnet: Thought of a Briton on the Subjugation of Switzerland]

In sundry moods, 'twas pastime to be bound
Within the Sonnet's scanty plot of ground;
Pleased if some souls (for such there needs must be)
Who have felt the weight of too much liberty,
Should find some solace there, as I have found.

[Nuns fret not 1807]

Books, Literature and Reading

[Amos] Bronson Alcott, 1799–1888, American philosopher
One must be a wise reader to quote wisely and well.

[*Table Talk: Quotation* 1877]

William Allingham, 1824–1889, Irish poet and diarist
A man who keeps a diary pays,
Due toll to many tedious days;
But life becomes eventful – then,
His busy hand forgets his pen.
Most books, indeed, are records less
Of fullness than of emptiness.

[*A Diary: March 24–28, 1864* 1907]

Anonymous
If you drop gold and books, pick up the books first, then the gold.

[Proverb]

Antiphanes of Macedonia, *fl* 360BC
Idly inquisitive tribe of grammarians, who dig up the poetry of others by the roots . . . Get away, bugs, that bite secretly at the eloquent.

[*Greek Anthology*]

Matthew Arnold, 1822–88, English poet and critic
Poetry is simply the most beautiful, impressive and widely effective mode of saying things, and hence its importance.

[*Essays in Criticism: Heinrich Heine*]

Jane Austen, 1775–1817, English novelist
We all talk Shakespeare, use his similes, and describe with his descriptions.

[*Mansfield Park* 1814]

I think I may boast myself to be, with all possible vanity, the most unlearned and uninformed female who ever dared to be an authoress.

[Letter 1815]

The little bit (two inches wide) of ivory on which I work with so fine a brush as produces little effect after much labour.

[*Ibid* 1816]

"And what are you reading, Miss ——?" "Oh! it is only a novel!" replies the young lady; while she lays down her book with affected indifference, or momentary shame. It is only *Cecilia*, or *Camilla*, or *Belinda*; or, in short, only some work in which the greatest powers of the mind are

58

displayed, in which the most thorough knowledge of human nature, the happiest delineations of its varieties, the liveliest effusions of wit and humour, are conveyed to the world in the best chosen language

[*Northanger Abbey* 1818]

Francis Bacon, Baron Verulam of Verulam and Viscount of St Albans, 1561–1626, English philosopher

Some books are to be tasted, others to be swallowed, and some few to be chewed and digested; that is, some books are to be read only in parts; others to be read but not curiously; and some few to be read wholly, and with diligence and attention. Some books also may be read by deputy, and extracts made of them by others.

[*Essays: Of Studies* 1597]

Reading maketh a full man, conference a ready man, and writing an exact man.

[*Ibid*]

Histories make men wise; poets, witty; the mathematics, subtile; natural philosophy, deep; moral, grave; logic and rhetoric, able to contend.

[*Ibid*]

Thomas Beer, 1889–1940, American writer

I agree with one of your reputable critics that a taste for drawing-rooms has spoiled more poets than ever did a taste for gutters.

[*The Mauve Decade*]

[Joseph] Hilaire [Pierre] Belloc, 1870–1953, English writer

Child, do not throw this book about;
Refrain from the unholy pleasure
Of cutting all the pictures out.
Preserve it as your chiefest treasure.

[*A Bad Child's Book of Beasts* 1896]

When I am dead, I hope it may be said
"His sins were scarlet, but his books were read.

[*On His Books*]

Jeremy Bentham, 1748–1832, English philosopher

Prose is when all the lines except the last go on to the end. Poetry is when some of them fall short of it

[In Packe's *Life of John Stuart Mill*]

Richard Bentley, 1662–1742, English classical scholar

[Of Pope's translation of the *Iliad*] A very pretty poem, Mr Pope, but it's not Homer.

[Attributed]

The Bible

My heart is inditing a good matter: I speak of the things which I have made touching the king: my tongue is the pen of a ready writer.

[*Psalms* 45:1]

Of making many books there is no end; and much study is a weariness of the flesh.

[*Ecclesiastes* 12:12]

Pilate answered, What I have written I have written.

[*John* 19:22]

Ambrose [Gwinett] Bierce, 1842–1914, American writer

Novel: a short story padded.

[*The Devil's Dictionary* 1906]

The first three essentials of the literary art are imagination, imagination and imagination.

[*Ibid*]

"Old books? The devil take them!" Goby said.
"Fresh every day must be my books and bread."
Nature herself approves the Goby rule
And gives us every moment a fresh fool.

[*Ibid*]

Augustine Birrell, 1850–1933, British politician and writer

Libraries are not made; they grow.

[*Obiter Dicta: Book-Buying* 1884]

Charlotte Brontë, 1816–55, English novelist

Novelists should never allow themselves to weary of the study of real life.

[*The Professor* 1846]

John Buchan, 1st Baron Tweedsmuir, 1875–1940, Scottish writer and statesman

Scott was a master but not a schoolmaster of language, and sometimes grammar and syntax go by the board.

[Sir Walter Scott]

[Frank] Gelett Burgess, 1866–1951, American humorist

I never saw a Purple Cow
I never hope to see one;
But I can tell you, anyhow,
I'd rather see than be one.

[*The Purple Cow* 1895]

Ah, yes, I wrote "The Purple Cow" –
I'm sorry, now, I wrote it! But I can tell you, anyhow,
I'll kill you if you quote it!

[*Cinq Ans Après* 1914]

Robert Burns, 1759–96, Scottish poet

A chiel's amang you takin' notes,
And, faith, he'll prent it!

[*On the late Captain Grose's Peregrinations through Scotland*]

Hail, Poesie! thou nymph reserv'd!
In chase o' thee, what crowds hae swerv'd
Frae Common Sense, or sunk ennerv'd
'Mang heaps o' clavers.

[*Sketch*]

[On an unidentified critic] Thou eunuch of language: thou butcher, imbruing thy hands in the bowels of orthography: thou arch-heretic in pronunciation: thou pitch-pipe of affected emphasis: thou carpenter, mortising the awkward joints of jarring sentences: thou squeaking dissonance of cadence: thou pimp of gender: thou scape-gallows from the land of syntax: thou scavenger of mood and tense: thou murderous accoucheur of infant learning: thou *ignis fatuus*, misleading the steps of benighted ignorance: thou pickle-herring in the puppet-show of nonsense.

[*c*.1791]

Robert Burton, 1577–1640, English churchman and writer
Hence it is clear how much more cruel the pen is than the sword.

[*Anatomy of Melancholy* 1621]

They lard their lean books with the fat of others' works.

[*Ibid*]

Samuel Butler, 1612-80, English poet
For rhyme the rudder is of verses,
With which, like ships, they steer their courses.

[*Hudibras* 1663]

But those that write in rhyme still make
The one verse for the other's sake.

[*Ibid*]

Byron, Lord George Gordon [Noel], 6th Baron Byron of Rochdale, 1788–1824, English poet
'Tis pleasant, sure, to see one's name in print;
A book's a book, although there's nothing in't.

[*English Bards and Scotch Reviewers* 1809]

With just enough of learning to misquote.

[*Ibid*]

Who, both by precept and example, shows
That prose is verse, and verse is merely prose.

[*Ibid*]

Think you, if Laura had been Petrarch's wife,
He would have written sonnets all his life?

[*Don Juan* 1819–24]

'Tis strange – but true; for truth is always strange;
Stranger than fiction.

[*Ibid*]

If I could always read, I should never feel the want of society.

[*Journal* 1814]

Thomas Carlyle, 1795–1881, Scottish historian and writer
My books are friends that never fail me.

[Letter 1817]

A well-written Life is almost as rare as a well-spent one.

[*Critical and Miscellaneous Essays* 1827]

How does the poet speak to men, with power, but by being still more a man than they?

[*Essays: Burns*]

All that mankind has done, thought, gained or been: it is lying as in magic preservation in the pages of books.

[*Heroes and Hero Worship* 1840]

Lewis Carroll [Charles Lutwidge Dodgson], 1832–1898, English mathematician and writer
"What is the use of a book," thought Alice, "without pictures or conversations?"

[*Alice's Adventures in Wonderland* 1865]

George Chapman, c.1559–1634, English dramatist
And let a scholar all Earth's volumes carry,
He will be but a walking dictionary.

[*Tears of Peace*]

His naked Ulysses, clad in eternal fiction.

[*The Odysseys of Homer* 1616]

Geoffrey Chaucer, 1340?–1400, English poet
For out of olde feldes, as men seith,
Cometh al this newe corn from yere to yere;
And out of olde bokes, in good feith,
Cometh al this newe science that men lere.

[*The Parliament of Fowls*]

G[ilbert] K[eith] Chesterton, 1874–1936, English writer
There is a great deal of difference between the eager man who wants to read a book, and the
tired man who wants a book to read.

[*Charles Dickens*]

Samuel Taylor Coleridge, 1772–1834, English poet
No man was ever yet a great poet, without being at the same time a profound philosopher.

[*Biographia Literaria* 1817]

That willing suspension of disbelief for the moment, which constitutes poetic faith.

[*Ibid*]

Not the poem which we have *read*, but that to which we *return*, with the greatest pleasure,
possesses the genuine power, and claims the name of *essential poetry*.

[*Lectures on Shakespeare and Milton*]

I wish our clever young poets would remember my homely definitions of prose and poetry;
that is, prose = words in their best order; poetry = the *best* words in the best order.

[*Table Talk* 1827]

William Cowper, 1731–1800, English poet
Thousands . . .
Kiss the book's outside who ne'er look within.

[*Expostulation*]

There is a pleasure in poetic pains
Which only poets know.

[*The Task II: The Timepiece* 1785]

Quentin Crisp, 1908–99, English eccentric and writer
An autobiography is an obituary in serial form with the last instalment missing.

[*The Naked Civil Servant* 1968]

Dante (Alighieri), 1265–1321, Italian poet
Onorate l'altissimo poeta.
(Honour the greatest poet.)

[*The Divine Comedy*]

René Descartes, 1596–1650, French philosopher
The reading of all good books is like a conversation with the finest men of past centuries.

[*Le Discourse de la Méthode* 1637]

Charles [John Huffam] Dickens, 1812–70, English novelist
Mr Dickens writes too often and too fast . . . If he persists much longer in this course, it requires not gift of prophecy to foretell his fate – he has risen like a rocket, and he will come down like a stick.

[Anonymous review of *Pickwick Papers* 1838]

Wentworth Dillon, 4th Earl of Roscommon, c.1633–1685, Irish writer
And choose an author as you choose a friend.

[*Essay on Translated Verse*]

Benjamin Disraeli, 1st Earl of Beaconsfield, 1804–81, British statesman and novelist
An author who speaks about his own books is almost as bad as a mother who talks about her own children.

[At a banquet 1873]

When I want to read a novel I write one.

[In Moneypenny and Buckle's *Life of Disraeli*]

Isaac D'Israeli, 1766–1848, English antiquary and writer
There is an art of reading, as well as an art of thinking, and an art of writing.

[*The Literary Character* 1795]

John Donne, c. 1571–1631, English poet
I am two fooles, I know,
For loving, and for saying so
In whining Poetry.

[*The Triple Foole*]

T[homas] S[tearns] Eliot, 1888–1965, American-born English poet
Many are engaged in writing books and printing them
Many desire to see their names in print,
Many read nothing but the race reports.

[*The Rock* 1934]

Ralph Waldo Emerson, 1803–82, American writer
Language is fossil poetry.

[*Essays: The Poet* 1844]

Never read any book that is not a year old.

[*Society and Solitude: Books* 1870]

Edward FitzGerald, 1809–83, English writer and translator
Here with a Loaf of Bread beneath the Bough,
A Flask of Wine, a Book of Verse – and Thou
Beside me singing in the Wilderness –
And Wilderness is Paradise enow.

[*The Rubaiyat of Omar Khayyam* 1859]

F[rancis] Scott [Key] Fitzgerald, 1896–1940, American novelist
All good writing is *swimming under water* and holding your breath.

[Letter to his daughter Francis. In Wilson's *The Crack-Up: with Other Uncollected Pieces, Note-Books and Unpublished Letters* 1945]

Anne Frank, 1929–45, German-Jewish diarist
If I read a book that impresses me, I have to take myself firmly in hand before I mix with other people; otherwise they would think my mind rather queer.
[*The Diary of a Young Girl* 1947]

José Ortega y Gasset, 1883–1955, Spanish philosopher
Poetry has become the higher algebra of metaphors.
[*The Dehumanization of Art* 1925]

Edward Gibbon, 1737–94, English historian
My early and invincible love of reading . . . I would not exchange for the treasures of India.
[*Memoirs* 1796]

Oliver Goldsmith, 1728–74, Irish-born English poet
As writers become more numerous, it is natural for readers to become more indolent.
[*The Bee* 1759]
I . . . showed her that books were sweet, unreproaching companions to the miserable, and that if they could not bring us to enjoy life, they could at least teach us to endure it.
[*The Vicar of Wakefield* 1766]

Thomas Hardy, 1840–1928, English novelist and poet
Of course poets have morals and manners of their own, and custom is no argument with them.
[*The Hand of Ethelberta*]

William Hazlitt, 1778–1830, English essayist
It is better to be able neither to read nor write than to be able to do nothing else.
[*Table Talk: On the Ignorance of the Learned* 1821–2]
When I take up a work that I have read before (the oftener the better) I know what I have to expect. The satisfaction is not lessened by being anticipated.
[*The Plain Speaker: On Reading Old Books* 1826]

[Christian Johann] Heinrich Heine, 1797–1856, German poet
Wherever they burn books they will also, in the end, burn human beings.
[*Almansor: A Tragedy* 1823]

Joseph Heller, 1923–99, American novelist
He knew everything about literature except how to enjoy it.
[*Catch-22* 1961]

Ernest [Miller] Hemingway, 1899–1961, American novelist
All modern American literature comes from one book by Mark Twain called *Huckleberry Finn.*
[*Green Hills of Africa* 1935]

William Henry, Duke of Gloucester, 1743–1805, British prince
Another damned, thick, square book! Always scribble, scribble, scribble. Eh! Mr Gibbon?
[Attributed]

[Sir] Anthony Hope [Hawkins], 1863–1933, English novelist
I wish you would read a little poetry sometimes. Your ignorance cramps my conversation.
[*The Dolly Dialogues* 1894]

Horace [Quintus Horatius Flaccus], 65–8BC, Roman poet
Genus irritabile vatum.
(The touchy race of poets.)

[*Epistles*]

A[lfred] E[dward] Housman, 1859–1936, English poet and scholar
Even when poetry has a meaning, as it usually has, it may be inadvisable to draw it out . . .
Perfect understanding will sometimes almost extinguish pleasure.

[*The Name and Nature of Poetry* 1933]

David Hume, 1711–76, Scottish philosopher and writer
Never literary attempt was more unfortunate than my Treatise of Human Nature. It fell dead-born from the press.

[*My Own Life* 1777]

Aldous [Leonard] Huxley, 1894–1963, English writer
The proper study of mankind is books.

[*Chrome Yellow* 1921]

It is far easier to write ten passably effective sonnets, good enough to take in the not too inquiring critic, than one effective advertisement that will take in a few thousand of the uncritical buying public.

[*On the Margin*]

A bad book is as much of a labour to write as a good one; it comes as sincerely from the author's soul.

[*Point Counter Point* 1928]

William Ralph Inge, 1860–1954, English churchman
Literature flourishes best when it is half a trade and half an art.

[*The Victorian Age*]

Henry James, 1843–1916, American-born English writer
It takes a great deal of history to produce a little literature.

[*Life of Nathaniel Hawthorne* 1879]

The only obligation to which in advance we may hold a novel, without incurring the accusation of being arbitrary, is that it be interesting.

[*The Art of Fiction: Partial Portraits*]

What is character but the determination of incident? What is incident but the illustration of character?

[*Ibid*]

The historian, essentially, wants more documents than he can really use; the dramatist only wants more liberties than he can really take.

[*The Aspern Papers* 1888]

Dr Samuel Johnson, 1709–84, English lexicographer
What is written without effort is in general read without pleasure.

[*Johnsonian Miscellanies*]

[On literary criticism] You may abuse a tragedy, though you cannot write one. You may scold a carpenter who has made you a bad table, though you cannot make a table. It is not your trade to make tables.

[In Boswell's *Life of Samuel Johnson* 1791]

A man ought to read just as inclination leads him; for what he reads as a task will do him little good.

[*Ibid*]

[When asked if he had read a new book through] No, Sir, do *you* read books *through*?

[*Ibid*]

A man will turn over half a library to make one book.

[*Ibid*]

The stream of time, which is continually washing the dissoluble fabricks of other poets, passes without injury by the adamant of Shakespeare.

[*Edition of Shakespeare* preface]

John Keats, 1795–1821, English poet
Poetry should surprise by a fine excess, and not by singularity; it should strike the reader as a wording of his own highest thoughts, and appear almost a remembrance.

[Letter 1818]

I have met with women whom I really think would like to be married to a poem, and to be given away by a novel.

[Letter 1819]

A drainless shower
Of light is poesy; 'tis the supreme of power;
'Tis might half slumb'ring on its own right arm.

[*Ibid*]

And they shall be accounted poet kings
Who simply tell the most heart-easing things.

[*Ibid*]

The poet and the dreamer are distinct,
Diverse, sheer opposite, antipodes.
The one pours out a balm upon the world,
The other vexes it.

[*The Fall of Hyperion* 1820]

Helen [Adams] Keller, 1880–1968, deaf-blind American writer
Literature is my Utopia. Here I am not disfranchised. No barrier of the senses shuts me out from the sweet, gracious discourse of my book friends. They talk to me without embarrassment or awkwardness.

[*The Story of My Life* 1902]

John Fitzgerald Kennedy, 1917–63, 35th president of the United States
When power leads man toward arrogance, poetry reminds him of his limitations. When power narrows the areas of man's concern, poetry reminds him of the richness and diversity of his existence. When power corrupts, poetry cleanses, for art establishes the basic human truths which must serve as the touchstone of our judgment.

[Speech 1963]

[Alfred] Joyce Kilmer, 1886–1918, American poet
I think that I shall never see
A poem lovely as a tree.

[*Trees* 1913]

Poems are made by fools like me,
But only God can make a tree.

[*Ibid*]

Rudyard Kipling, 1865–1936, English writer
The cure for this ill is not to sit still,
Or frowst with a book by the fire;
But to take a large hoe and shovel also,
And dig till you gently perspire.

[Just So Verses]

Charles Lamb, 1775–1834, English essayist
I love to lose myself in other men's minds. When I am not walking, I am reading; I cannot sit and think. Books think for me.

[Last Essays of Elia 1833]

Walter Savage Landor, 1775–1864, English writer
Prose on certain occasions can bear a great deal of poetry: on the other hand, poetry sinks and swoons under a moderate weight of prose.

[Imaginary Conversations 1824]

Andrew Lang, 1844–1912, Scottish writer
A house full of books, and a garden full of flowers.

[Ballade of True Wisdom]

Stephen Butler Leacock, 1869–1944, Canadian economist and humorist
The classics are only primitive literature. They belong to the same class as primitive machinery and primitive music and primitive medicine.

[Behind the Beyond 1913]

Edward Lear, 1812–88, English writer and artist
How pleasant to know Mr Lear!
Who has written such volumes of stuff!
Some think him ill-tempered and queer,
But a few think him pleasant enough.

[Nonsense Songs preface 1871]

Georg Christoph Lichtenberg, 1742–99, German scientist and writer
There can hardly be a stranger commodity in the world than books. Printed by people who don't understand them; sold by people who don't understand them; bound, criticized and read by people who don't understand them, and now even written by people who don't understand them.

[A Doctrine of Scattered Occasions]

Samuel Lover, 1797–1868, Irish novelist and artist
When once the itch of literature comes over a man, nothing can cure it but the scratching of a pen.

[Handy Andy 1842]

Martin Luther, 1483–1546, German religious reformer
The multitude of books is a great evil. There is no limit to this fever for writing; everyone must be an author; some out of vanity, to acquire celebrity and raise up a name; others for the sake of mere gain.

[Table-Talk 1569]

Thomas Babington Macaulay, 1st Baron Macaulay, 1800–1859, English historian
Perhaps no person can be a poet, or even can enjoy poetry, without a certain unsoundness of mind.

[*Essays: On Milton*]

With the dead there is no rivalry. In the dead there is no change. Plato is never sullen. Cervantes is never petulant. Demosthenes never comes unseasonably. Dante never stays too long. No difference of political opinion can alienate Cicero. No heresy can excite the horror of Bossuet.

[*Essays: Lord Bacon*]

A person who professes to be a critic in the delicacies of the English language ought to have the Bible at his fingers' ends.

[Letter to his sister 1831]

John Milton, 1608–74, English poet
Books are not absolutely dead things, but do contain a potency of life in them to be as active as that soul was whose progeny they are; nay they do preserve as in a vial the purest efficacy and extraction of that living intellect that bred them.

[*Areopagitica* 1644]

As good almost kill a man as kill a good book; who kills a man kills a reasonable creature, God's image; but he who destroys a good book kills reason itself, kills the image of God, as it were in the eye.

[*Ibid*]

Rhyme being no necessary adjunct or true ornament of poem or good verse, in longer works especially, but the invention of a barbarous age, to set off wretched matter and lame metre.

[*The Verse.* Preface to *Paradise Lost* 1668]

Who reads
Incessantly, and to his reading brings not
A spirit and judgment equal or superior
(And what he brings, what needs he elsewhere seek?)
Uncertain and unsettled still remains,
Deep vers'd in books and shallow in himself.

[*Paradise Regained* 1671]

Nancy Freeman Mitford, 1904–73, English writer
I have only read one book in my life, and that is *White Fang*. It's so dreadfully good I've never bothered to read another.

[*In Pursuit of Love*]

Michel [Eyquem] de Montaigne, 1533–92, French essayist
All the world knows me in my book, and my book in me.

[*Essays* 1580]

Hannah More, 1745–1833, English writer
He liked those literary cooks
Who skim the cream of others' books;
And ruin half an author's graces
By plucking *bon-mots* from their places.

[*Florio*]

John Morley, 1st Viscount Morley of Blackburn, 1838–1923, English politician
Literature, the most seductive, the most deceiving, the most dangerous of professions.

[*Burke* 1879]

Vladimir Nabokov, 1899–1977, Russian-born American writer and critic
A novelist is, like all mortals, more fully at home on the surface of the present than in the ooze of the past.

[*Strong Opinions* 1973]

John Boyle O'Reilly, 1844–90, Irish writer
You may grind their souls in the self-same mill,
You may bind them, heart and brow;
But the poet will follow the rainbow still,
And his brother will follow the plough.

[*The Rainbow's Treasure*]

Dorothy [Rothschild] Parker, 1893–1967, American writer
This is not a novel to be tossed aside lightly. It should be thrown with great force.

Plato, c. 428–348BC, Greek philosopher
Poets utter great and wise things which they do not themselves understand.

[*The Republic c.*370BC]

Alexander Pope, 1688–1744, English poet
Let such teach others who themselves excel,
And censure freely who have written well.

[*Essay on Criticism* 1711]

Some have at first for Wits then Poets past,
Turn'd Critics next, and prov'd plain fools at last.

[*Ibid*]

True ease in writing comes from art, not chance,
As those move easiest who have learn'd to dance.
The bookful blockhead, ignorantly read,
With loads of learned lumber in his head.

[*Ibid*]

Poetic justice, with her lifted scale,
Where, in nice balance, truth with gold she weighs,
And solid pudding against empty praise.

[*The Dunciad* 1728]

While pensive Poets painful vigils keep,
Sleepless themselves, to give their readers sleep.

[*Ibid*]

And he, whose fustian's so sublimely bad
It is not poetry, but prose run mad.

[*Ibid*]

Satire or sense, alas! can Sporus feel,
Who breaks a butterfly upon a wheel?

[*Ibid*]

Vain was the chief's, the sage's pride!
They had no poet, and they died.

[*Imitations of Horace* 1733]

Ezra [Loomis] Pound, 1885–1972, American poet

Free us for we perish
In this ever-flowing monotony
Of ugly print marks, black
Upon white parchment.

[*The Eyes*]

Will[iam Penn Adair] Rogers, 1879–1935, American humorist

When you put down the good things you ought to have done, and leave out the bad ones you did do – that's memoirs.

[*The Autobiography of Will Rogers* 1949]

Martin Joseph Routh, 1755–1854, English academic

Always verify your references, sir!

[Attributed]

John Ruskin, 1819–1900, English art critic and writer

Life being very short, and the quiet hours of it few, we ought to waste none of them in reading valueless books.

[*Seasame and Lilies* 1865]

All books are divisible into two classes: the books of the hour, and the books of all time.

[*Ibid*]

If a book is worth reading, it is worth buying.

[*Ibid*]

Bertrand [Arthur William] Russell, 3rd Earl Russell, 1872–1970, English philosopher

There are two motives for reading a book: one, that you enjoy it, the other that you can boast about it.

[*The Conquest of Happiness* 1930]

Carl Sandburg, 1878–1967, American poet

Slang is a language that rolls up its sleeves, spits on its hands and goes to work.

[In the *New York Times* 1959]

Jean-Paul Sartre, 1905–80, French philosopher and writer

The writer, a free man addressing free men, has only one subject – freedom.

[*What is Literature?*]

William Shakespeare, 1564–1616, English dramatist

Come, and take choice of all my library,
And so beguile thy sorrow.

[*Titus Andronicus* 4 1593–4]

Study is like the heaven's glorious sun,
That will not be deep-search'd with saucy looks;
Small have continual plodders ever won,
Save base authority from others' books.

[*Love's Labour's Lost* 1 1594–5]

Devise, wit; write, pen; for I am for whole volumes in folio.

[*Ibid*]

He hath never fed of the dainties that are bred in a book; he hath not eat paper, as it were; he hath not drunk ink.

[*Ibid*]

From women's eyes this doctrine I derive:
They sparkle still the right Promethean fire;
They are the books, the arts, the academes,
That show, contain, and nourish all the world.

[*Ibid* 4]

That book in many's eyes doth share the glory,
That in gold clasps locks in the golden story.

[*Romeo and Juliet* 1 1594–5]

The lunatic, the lover and the poet
Are of imagination all compact.

[*A Midsummer Night's Dream* 5 1595–6]

The lover, all as frantic,
Sees Helen's beauty in a brow of Egypt:
The poet's eye, in a fine frenzy rolling,
Doth glance from heaven to earth, from earth to heaven;
And as imagination bodies forth
The forms of things unknown, the poet's pen
Turns them to shapes and gives to airy nothing
A local habitation and a name.

[*Ibid*]

Tear him for his bad verses, tear him for his bad verses.

[*Julius Caesar* 3 1598–1600]

To be a well-favoured man is the gift of fortune; but to write and read comes by nature.

[*Much Ado About Nothing* 3 1598–1600]

This is the very false gallop of the verses.

[*As You Like it* 3 1598–1600]

Truly, I would the gods had made thee poetical.

[*Ibid*]

O Sir, we quarrel in print, by the book; as you have books for good manners: I will name you the degrees. The first, the Retort Courteous; the second, the Quip Modest; the third, the Reply Churlish; the fourth, the Reproof Valiant; the fifth, the Countercheck Quarrelsome; the sixth, the Lie with Circumstance; the seventh, the Lie Direct.

[*Ibid* 5]

Speaks three or four languages word for word without book.

[*Twelfth Night* 1 1598-1600]

If this were played upon a stage now, I could condemn it as an improbable fiction.

[*Ibid*]

Your face, my thane, is as a book where men
May read strange matters.

[*Macbeth* 1 1605–6]

In nature's infinite book of secrecy
A little can I read.

[*Antony and Cleopatra* 1 1606–7]

Knowing I loved my books, he furnish'd me
From mine own library with volumes that
I prize above my dukedom.

[*The Tempest* 1 1611–12]

O! let my books be then the eloquence
And dumb presagers of my speaking breast.

[*Sonnets* 23]

John Sheffield, 1st Duke of Buckingham and Normandy, 1648–1721, English politician and poet

Of all those arts in which the wise excel,
Nature's chief masterpiece is writing well.

[Essay on Poetry 1682]

Read Homer once, and you can read no more,
For all books else appear so mean, so poor,
Verse will seem prose; but still persist to read,
And Homer will be all the books you need.

[Ibid]

Percy Bysshe Shelley, 1792–1822, English poet

Most wretched men
Are cradled into poetry by wrong,
They learn in suffering what they teach in song.

[Julian and Maddalo 1818]

Poetry is the record of the best and happiest moments of the happiest and best minds.

[A Defence of Poetry 1821]

Poets are the unacknowledged legislators of the world.

[Ibid]

Richard Brinsley Sheridan, 1751–1816, English dramatist

You shall see them on a beautiful quarto page, where a neat rivulet of text shall meander through a meadow of margin.

[The School for Scandal 1777]

Sir Philip Sidney,1554–86, English soldier, statesman and poet

"Fool" said my Muse to me, "look in thy heart and write."

[Astrophel and Stella c.1582]

B[urrhus] F[rederic] Skinner, 1904– , American psychologist

We shouldn't teach great books; we should teach a love of reading.

[In R. Evans' *B.F. Skinner: The Man and His Ideas* 1968]

[Lloyd] Logan Pearsall Smith, 1865–1946, American-born English writer

A bestseller is the gilded tomb of a mediocre talent.

[Afterthoughts: Art and Letters 1931]

People say that life is the thing, but I prefer reading.

[Ibid: Myself]

Sydney Smith, 1771–1845, English churchman

The motto I proposed for the *[Edinburgh] Review* was: *Tenui musam meditamur avena* – "We cultivate literature upon a little oatmeal."

[Works]

No furniture so charming as books.

[In Lady Holland's *Memoirs* 1855]

Live always in the best company when you read.

[Ibid]

I never read a book before reviewing it; it prejudices a man so.

[In H. Pearson's *The Smith of Smiths* 1934]

Alexander Solzhenitsyn, 1918– , Russian novelist
A great writer is, so to speak, a second government in his country. And for that reason no regime has ever loved great writers, only minor ones.
[*The First Circle* 1964]

World literature is . . . a kind of collective body and a common spirit, a living unity of the heart which reflects the growing spiritual unity of mankind.
[Nobel lecture 1972]

Robert Southey, 1774–1843, English poet
Your true lover of literature is never fastidious.
[*The Doctor, etc* 1834–7]

Sir Richard Steele, 1672–1729, Anglo-Irish essayist
Reading is to the mind what exercise is to the body.
[*The Tatler* 1709–11]

Robert Louis [Balfour] Stevenson, 1850–94, Scottish novelist and poet
Books are good enough in their own way, but they are a mighty bloodless substitute for life.
[*Virginibus Puerisque: An Apology for Idlers* 1881]

Jonathan Swift, 1667–1745, Irish-born English writer
Books, like men their authors, have no more than one way of coming into the world, but there are ten thousand to go out of it, and return no more.
[*A Tale of a Tub* 1704]

Good God! what a genius I had when I wrote that book [*The Tale of a Tub*].
[In Sir Walter Scott's *Life of Swift* 1824]

William Makepeace Thackeray, 1811–63, English novelist
There are a thousand thoughts lying within a man that he does not know till he takes up the pen to write.
[*The History of Henry Esmond* 1852]

Dylan Thomas, 1914–53, Welsh poet
These poems, with all their crudities, doubts, and confusions, are written for the love of Man and in praise of God, and I'd be a damn' fool if they weren't.
[Note in *Collected Poems* 1952]

Thomas à Kempis, c.1380–1471, Augustinian monk and writer
Verily, when the day of judgment comes, we shall not be asked what we have read, but what we have done.
[*De Imitatione Christi*]

James Thomson, 1700–48, Scottish poet
A bard here dwelt, more fat than bard beseems.
[*The Castle of Indolence*]

Henry David Thoreau, 1817–62, American naturalist and writer
How many a man has dated a new era in his life from the reading of a book.
[*Walden, or Life in the Woods* 1854]

Martin Farquhar Tupper, 1810–89, English writer
A good book is the best of friends, the same today and for ever.
[*Proverbial Philosophy: Of Reading* 1838]

Mark Twain [Samuel Langhorne Clemens], 1835–1910, American writer
A classic is something that everybody wants to have read and nobody wants to read.

[Speeches: The Disappearance of Literature]

William Walker, 1623–84, English poet
Learn to read slow: all other graces
Will follow in their proper places.

[The Art of Reading]

John Wesley 1703–91, English preacher
Beware you be not swallowed up in books! An ounce of love is worth a pound of knowledge.

[In Southey's *Life of Wesley* 1820]

E[lwyn] B[rooks] White, 1899–1985, American humorist
A writer is like a bean plant – he has his little day, and then gets stringy.

[Letter to Harold Ross 1938]

Walt[er] Whitman, 1819–92, American poet
The proof of a poet is that his country absorbs him as affectionately as he has absorbed it.

[Leaves of Grass 1855 preface]

Camerado, this is no book,
Who touches this touches a man,
(Is it night? Are we here together alone?)
It is I you hold and who holds you.
I spring from the pages into your arms – decease calls me forth.

[So Long!]

Oscar [Fingall O'Flahertie Wills] Wilde, 1854–1900, Irish writer
Movement, that problem of the visible arts, can be truly realized by Literature alone. It is Literature that shows us the body in its swiftness and the soul in its unrest.

[Intentions: The Critic as Artist 1891]
There is no such thing as a moral or an immoral book. Books are well written or badly written. That is all.

[The Picture of Dorian Gray 1891]
You should study the Peerage, Gerald. It is the one book a young man about town should know thoroughly, and it is the best thing in fiction the English have done.

[A Woman of No Importance 1893]
I never travel without my diary. One should always have something sensational to read in the train.

[The Importance of Being Earnest 1895]
The good ended happily, and the bad unhappily. That is what Fiction means.

[Ibid]

William Carlos Williams, 1883–1963, American novelist and poet
A cool of books
will sometimes lead the mind to libraries
of a hot afternoon, if books can be found
cool to the sense to lead the mind away.

[The Selected Poems of William Carlos Williams: The Library 1976]

John Wilson, d.1889, English bookseller

O for a Booke and a shadie nooke,
Eyther in-a-doore or out;
With the grene leaves whisp'ring overhede,
Or the Streete cryes all about.
Where I maie Reade all at my ease,
Both of the Newe and Olde;
For a jollie goode Booke whereon to looke
Is better to me than Golde.

[From a catalogue of second-hand books]

William Wordsworth, 1770–1850, English poet

We must be free or die, who speak the tongue
That Shakespeare spake; the faith and morals hold
Which Milton held.

[*Sonnets Dedicated to Liberty*]

Scorn not the Sonnet. Critic, you have frowned,
Mindless of its just honours; with this key
Shakespeare unlocked his heart.

[*Sonnet: Scorn not the Sonnet*]

We poets in our youth begin in gladness;
But thereof comes in the end despondency and madness.
[*The Leech-Gatherer; or Resolution and Independence*]

The light that never was, on sea or land;
The consecration, and the poet's dream.
[*Elegiac Stanzas suggested by a Picture of Peele Castle in a Storm*]

Every great and original writer, in proportion as he is great and original, must himself create the taste by which he is to be relished.

[Letter]

Poetry is the spontaneous overflow of powerful feelings: it takes its origin from emotion recollected in tranquility: the emotion is contemplated till, by a species of reaction, the tranquility gradually disappears, and an emotion, kindred to that which was before the subject of contemplation, is gradually produced, and does itself actually exist in the mind.

[*Lyrical Ballads* preface 1800]

William Butler Yeats, 1865–1939, Irish poet

I think it better that in times like these
A poet's mouth be silent, for in truth
We have no gift to set a statesman right.

[*On being asked for a War Poem* 1916]

A good writer should be so simple that he has no faults, only sins.

[*The Death of Synge*]

We have no longer in any country a literature as great as the literature of the old world, and that is because the newspapers, all kinds of second-rate books, the preoccupation of men with all kinds of practical changes, have driven the living imagination out of this world.

[*Samhain* 1904]

Work and Business

Dean Acheson, 1893–1971, American statesman
A memorandum is written not to inform the reader but to protect the writer.

[In *Wall Street Journal* September 8 1977]

Anonymous
Plain dealing is more often praised than practised.

[Proverb]

Do business, but be not a slave to it.

[Proverb]

All work and no play makes Jack a dull boy.

[Proverb]

Susan B[rownell] Anthony, 1820–1906, American reformer
Join the union, girls, and together say Equal Pay for Equal Work.

[*The Revolution* 1868]

[Justin] Brooks Atkinson, 1894–1984, American essayist
There is a good deal of solemn cant about the common interests of capital and labor. As matters stand, their only common interest is that of cutting each other's throat.

[*Once Around the Sun* 1951]

Jane Austen, 1775–1817, English novelist
"I am afraid," replied Elinor, "that the pleasure of an employment does not always evince its propriety."

[*Sense and Sensibility* 1811]

Sir J[ames] M[atthew] Barrie, 1860–1937, Scottish playwright
A young Scotsman of your ability let loose upon the world with £300, what could he not do? It's almost appalling to think of; especially if he went among the English.

[*What Every Woman Knows* 1908]

[Joseph] Hilaire [Pierre] Belloc, 1870–1953, English writer
Lord Finchley tried to mend the Electric Light
Himself. It struck him dead: and serve him right!
It is the business of the wealthy man
To give employment to the artisan.

[*Epigrams*]

WORK AND BUSINESS

The Bible
Be ye strong therefore, and let not your hands be weak: for your work shall be rewarded.
[*2 Chronicles* 15:7]
They that go down to the sea in ships, that do business in great waters; These see the works of the Lord, and his wonders in the deep.
[*Psalms* 107:23–4]
No man can serve two masters: for either he will hate the one, and love the other; or else he will hold to the one, and despise the other. Ye cannot serve God and mammon.
[*Matthew* 6:24]

Ambrose [Gwinett] Bierce, 1842–1914, American writer
Corporation: an ingenious device for obtaining individual profit without individual responsibility.
[*The Devil's Dictionary* 1906]
Economy: purchasing the barrel of whiskey that you do not need for the price of the cow that you cannot afford.
[*Ibid*]
Insurance: an ingenious modern game of chance in which the player is permitted to enjoy the comfortable conviction that he is beating the man who keeps the table.
[*Ibid*]
Merchant: one engaged in a commercial pursuit. A commercial pursuit is one in which the thing pursued is a dollar.
[*Ibid*]
Abasement: a decent and customary mental attitude in the presence of wealth or power. Peculiarly appropriate in an employee when addressing an employer.
[*Ibid*]

William Blake, 1757–1827, English poet and artist
The busy bee has no time for sorrow.
[*The Marriage of Heaven and Hell: Proverbs of Hell* 1791]

W[illiam] E[dward] B[urghardt] Du Bois, 1868–1963, American civil rights leader
The return from your work must be the satisfaction which that work brings you and the world's need of that work. With this, life is heaven, or as near heaven as you can get. Without this – with work which you despise, which bores you, and which the world doest not need – this life is hell.
[*To His Newborn Great-Grandson* 1958]

Elizabeth Barrett Browning, 1806–61, English poet
Let no one till his death
Be called unhappy. Measure not the work
Until the day's out and the labour done.
[*Aurora Leigh* 1857]

Robert Browning, 1812–89, English poet
Oh, if we draw a circle premature
Heedless of far gain,
Greedy for quick returns of profit, sure,
Bad is our bargain.
[*A Grammarian's Funeral*]

77

Edmund Burke, 1729–97, Irish-born English political writer

Young man, there is America – which at this day serves for little more than to amuse you with stories of savage men, and uncouth manners; yet shall, before you taste of death, show itself equal to the whole of that commerce which now attracts the envy of the world.

[Speech 1775]

Robert Burns, 1759–96, Scottish poet

We labour soon, we labour late,
To feed the titled knave, man,
And a' the comfort we're to get,
Is that ayont the grave, man.

[*The Tree of Liberty*]

The best laid schemes o' mice an' men
Gang aft a-gley.

[*To a Mouse*]

Byron, Lord George Gordon [Noel], 6th Baron Byron of Rochdale, 1788–1824, English poet

Such hath it been – shall be – beneath the sun
The many still must labour for the one.

[*The Corsair* 1814]

Thomas Carlyle, 1795–1881, Scottish historian and writer

A man willing to work, and unable to find work, is perhaps the saddest sight that fortune's inequality exhibits under the sun.

[*Chartism* 1834]

A fair day's wages for a fair day's work: it is as just a demand as governed men ever made of governing.

[*Past and Present* 1843]

Blessed is he who has found his work; let him ask no other blessedness.

[*Ibid*]

Captains of industry.

[*Ibid*]

Work is the grand cure of all the maladies and miseries that ever beset mankind.

[Rectorial address, Edinburgh, 1866]

Geoffrey Chaucer, c.1340–1400, English poet

Nowher so bisy a man as he ther nas,
And yet he seemed bisier than he was.

[*The Canterbury Tales: The Sergeant of the Lawe c.*1387]

G[ilbert] K[eith] Chesterton, 1874–1936, English writer

And I dream of the days when work was scrappy,
And rare in our pockets the mark of the mint,
When we were angry and poor and happy,
And proud of seeing our names in print.

[*A Song of Defeat*]

Sir Winston [Leonard Spencer] Churchill, 1874–1965, British statesman

Give us the tools, and we will finish the job.

[Radio broadcast 1941]

Henry Clay, 1777–1852, American statesman
The call for free trade is as unavailing as the cry of a spoiled child for the moon. It never has existed; it never will exist.

[Speech in the Senate 1832]

R[obin] G[eorge] Collingwood, 1889–1943, philosopher and archaeologist
Perfect freedom is reserved for the man who lives by his own work and in that work does what he wants to do.

[*Speculum Mentis*]

Charles Caleb Colton, c.1780–1832, English writer
Of the professions it may be said that soldiers are becoming too popular, parsons too lazy, physicians too mercenary, and lawyers too powerful.

[*Lacon* 1820]

Calvin Coolidge, 1872–1933, 30th president of the United States
The business of America is business.

[Speech 1925]

Sir Noel [Pierce] Coward, 1899–1973, English actor and playwright
Work is much more fun than fun.

[In *The Observer* 1963]

William Cowper, 1731–1800, English poet
A business with an income at its heels
Furnishes always oil for its own wheels.

[*Retirement* 1782]

Absence of occupation is not rest,
A mind quite vacant is a mind distress'd.

[*Ibid*]

Quentin Crisp, 1908–99, English eccentric and writer
There was no need to do any housework at all. After the first four years the dirt doesn't get any worse.

[*The Naked Civil Servant* 1968]

Clarence Seward Darrow, 1857–1938, American lawyer
With all their faults, trade unions have done more for humanity than any other organization of men that ever existed. They have done more for decency, for honesty, for education, for the betterment of the race, for the developing of character in man, than any other association of men.

[*The Railroad Trainman* 1909]

Thomas Dekker, c.1570–1632, English dramatist
Work apace, apace, apace, apace;
Honest labour bears a lovely face.

[*Patient Grissill* 1603]

Charles [John Huffam] Dickens, 1812–70, English novelist
Here's the rule, for bargains: "Do other men, for they would do you." That's the true business precept.

[*Martin Chuzzlewit* 1843–4]

Oh, let us love our occupations,
Bless the squire and his relations,
Live upon our daily rations,
And always know our proper stations.

[*The Chimes* 1845]

Maria Edgeworth, 1768–1849, Irish novelist

Well! some people talk of morality, and some of religion, but give me a little snug property.

[*The Absentee* 1812]

Business was his aversion; pleasure was his business.

[*The Contrast*]

Benjamin Franklin, 1706–90, American scientist and philosopher

No nation was ever ruined by trade.

[*Thoughts on Commercial Subjects*]

Necessity never made a good bargain.

[*Poor Richard's Almanack* 1735]

John Kenneth Galbraith, 1908– , Canadian-born American economist

Meetings are indispensable when you don't want to do anything.

[*Ambassador's Journal* 1969]

The salary of the chief executive of the large corporation is not a market award for achievement. It is frequently in the nature of a warm personal gesture by the individual to himself.

[*Annals of an Abiding Liberal* 1980]

Oliver Goldsmith, 1728–74, Irish-born English writer

Trade's unfeeling train
Usurp the land and dispossess the swain.

[*The Deserted Village* 1770]

And honour sinks where commerce long prevails.

[*The Traveller* 1764]

Samuel Goldwyn, 1882–1974, Polish-born American film producer

I don't want any yes-men around me. I want everybody to tell me the truth even if it costs them their jobs.

[Attributed]

Maxim Gorky [Aleksei Maksimovich Peshkov], 1868–1936

When work is a pleasure, life is a joy. When work is a duty, life is slavery.

[*The Lower Depths* 1903]

Richard Long Harkness, 1907–77, American journalist

What is a committee? A group of the unwilling, picked from the unfit, to do the unnecessary.

[*New York Herald Tribune* 1960]

Sir John Henry Harvey-Jones, 1924– , English industrial executive

Industry is a bit like the human body. The cells are continuously dying and unless new cells are created, sooner or later the whole thing will collapse and disappear.

[*Making it Happen: Reflections on Leadership* 1987]

Robert Heller, 1919– , American business writer
The first myth of management is that it exists. The second myth of management is that success equals skill.

[The Great Executive Dream]

George Henry, 1839–97, English economist
The man who gives me employment, which I must have or suffer, that man is my master, let me call him what I will.

[Social Problems]

Sir A[lan] P[atrick] Herbert, 1890–1971, English humorous writer
This high official, all allow,
Is grossly overpaid.
There wasn't any Board; and now
There isn't any trade.

[On the President of the Board of Trade]

Herbert [Clark] Hoover, 1874–1964, 31st president of the United States
Please find me a one-armed economist so we will not always hear: "On the other hand . . ."

[Attributed]

E[dgar] W[atson] Howe, 1853–1937, American writer
Doing business without advertising is like winking at a girl in the dark: you know what you are doing, but nobody else does.

Elbert Hubbard, 1856–1915, American writer and editor
If you want work well done, select a busy man: the other kind has no time.

[The Note Book 1927]

Victor [Marie] Hugo, 1802–85, French novelist and poet
Nothing is more dangerous than discontinued labour; it is habit lost. A habit easy to abandon, difficult to resume.

[Les Misérables 1862]

David Hume, 1711–76, Scottish philosopher and writer
Avarice, the spur of industry.

[Essays: Of Civil Liberty 1741–2]

Jerome K[lapka] Jerome, 1859–1927, English humorous writer
I like work; it fascinates me. I can sit and look at it for hours. I love to keep it by me: the idea of getting rid of it nearly breaks my heart.

[Three Men in a Boat 1889]

It is impossible to enjoy idling thoroughly unless one has plenty of work to do.

[The Idle Thoughts of an Idle Fellow 1889]

Dr Samuel Johnson, 1709–84, English lexicographer
Trade could not be managed by those who manage it if it had much difficulty.

[Letter to Mrs Hester Thrale 1779]

Benjamin Franklin King, 1857–94, American humorist
Nothing to do but work,
Nothing to eat but food,
Nothing to wear but clothes
To keep one from going nude.

[*The Pessimist*]

Charles Kingsley, 1819–75, English churchman and writer
Do the work that's nearest,
Though it's dull at whiles,
Helping, when you meet them,
Lame dogs over stiles.

[*The Invitation*]

Philip Arthur Larkin, 1922–85, English poet
Why should I let the toad *work*
Squat on my life?
Can't I use my wit as a pitchfork
And drive the brute off?

[*Toads*]

Karl Liebknecht, 1871–1919, German political leader
The basic law of capitalism is you or I, not both you and I.

[Speech 1907]

Abraham Lincoln, 1809–65, 16th president of the United States
With malice towards none; with charity for all; with firmness in the right, as God gives us to
see the right, let us strive on to finish the work we are in.

[Second Inaugural address 1865]
My father taught me to work; he did not teach me to love it.

Eric [Robert Russell] Linklater, 1899–1974, Scottish novelist
While swordless Scotland, sadder than its psalms,
Fosters its sober youth on national alms
To breed a dull provincial discipline,
Commerce its god and golf its anodyne.

[*Preamble to a Satire*]

Jack London [John Griffith Chaney], 1876–1916, American writer
In an English ship, they say, it is poor grub, poor pay, and easy work; in an American ship,
good grub, good pay, and hard work. And this is applicable to the working populations of
both countries.|

[*The People of the Abyss*]

John Lyly, c.1554–1606, English playwright
A comely old man as busie as a bee.

[*Euphues and his England* 1580]

Don[ald Robert Perry] Marquis, 1878–1937, American novelist, playwright and poet
Alas! The hours we waste in work
And similar inconsequence,
Friends, I beg you not to shirk
Your daily task of indolence.

[*The Almost Perfect State* 1927]

Karl Marx, 1818–83, and Friedrich Engels, 1820–95, German philosophers
The workers have nothing to lose but their chains. They have a world to gain. Workers of the world, unite!

[*The Communist Manifesto* 1848]

Augustus De Morgan, 1806–71, English mathematician
Great fleas have little fleas upon their backs to bite 'em,
And little fleas have lesser fleas, and so *ad infinitum*,
And the great fleas themselves, in turn, have greater fleas to go on,
While those again have greater still, and greater still, and so on.

[*A Budget of Paradoxes*]

Ogden Nash, 1902–71, American humorous writer
I sit in an office at 244 Madison Avenue,
And say to myself You have a responsible job, havenue?

[*Spring comes to Murray Hill*]

Cyril Northcote Parkinson, 1909–93, English political scientist
Work expands so as to fill the time available for its completion.

[*Parkinson's Law, The Pursuit of Progress* 1958]

Laurence Johnston Peter, 1919–90, Canadian-born American educator
An economist is an expert who will know tomorrow why the things he predicted yesterday didn't happen today.

[*Peter's Quotations* 1977]

Sir Joshua Reynolds, 1723–92, English painter
If you have great talents, industry will improve them: if you have but moderate abilities, industry will supply their deficiency.

[*Discourses*]

David Ricardo, 1772–1823, English economist
When wages are low profits must be high.

[*Collected Works* 1846]

Franklin Delano Roosevelt, 1882–1945, 32nd president of the United States
No business which depends for existing on paying less than living wages to its workers has any right to continue in this country. By business I mean the whole of commerce as well as the whole of industry; by workers I mean all workers – the white-collar class as well as the man in overalls; and by living wages I mean more than a bare subsistence level – I mean the wages of decent living.

[Address 1933]

Theodore Roosevelt, 1858–1919, 26th president of the United States

No man needs sympathy because he has to work . . . Far and away the best prize that life offers is the chance to work hard at work worth doing.

[Address 1903]

Bertrand [Arthur William] Russell, 3rd Earl Russell, 1872–1970, English philosopher

Unless a man has been taught what to do with success after getting it, the achievement of it must inevitably leave him a prey to boredom.

[*The Conquest of Happiness*]

Anthony Sampson, 1926– , English writer

We are an indispensable team; *you* are overmanned; *they* are redundant.

[In *The Observer* 1981]

William Scott, Baron Stowell, 1745–1836, English lawyer

A dinner lubricates business.

William Shakespeare 1564–1616, English dramatist

'Tis a very excellent piece of work, madam lady: would 'twere done!

[*The Taming of the Shrew* 1 1593–4]

If all the year were playing holidays,
To sport would be as tedious as to work.

[*King Henry IV, Part I* 1 1597–8]

I am not yet of Percy's mind, the Hotspur of the north; he that kills me some six or seven dozen of Scots at a breakfast, washes his hands, and says to his wife, "Fie upon this quiet life! I want work."

[*Ibid* 2]

For so work the honey-bees,
Creatures that by a rule in nature teach
The act of order to a peopled kingdom.
They have a king and officers of sorts;
Where some, like magistrates, correct at home,
Others, like merchants, venture trade abroad,
Others, like soldiers, armed in their stings,
Make boot upon the summer's velvet buds,
Which pillage they with merry march bring home
To the tent-royal of their emperor;
Who, busied in his majesty, surveys
The singing masons building roofs of gold,
The civil citizens kneading up the honey,
The poor mechanic porters crowding in
Their heavy burdens at the narrow gate,
The sad-eyed justice, with his surly hum,
Delivering o'er to executors pale
The lazy dawning drone.

[*King Henry V* 1 1598–1600]

O that we now had here
But one ten thousand of those men in England
That do no work today!

[*Ibid*]

Has this fellow no feeling of his business?

[*Hamlet* 5 1600–1601]

The hand of little employment hath the daintier sense.

[Ibid]

To business that we love we rise betime,
And go to 't with delight.

[Antony and Cleopatra 4 1606–7]

Let me have no lying: it becomes none but tradesmen.

[The Winter's Tale 4 1610–11]

George Bernard Shaw, 1856–1950, Irish playwright
A day's work is a day's work, neither more nor less, and the man who does it needs a day's sustenance, a night's repose, and due leisure, whether he be painter or ploughman.

[An Unsocial Socialist]

Adam Smith, 1723–90, Scottish philosopher
The real price of every thing, what every thing really costs to the man who wants to acquire it, is the toil and trouble of acquiring it.

[The Wealth of Nations 1776]

A monopoly granted either to an individual or to a trading company has the same effect as a secret in trade or manufactures. The monopolists, by keeping the market constantly understocked, by never fully supplying the effectual demand, sell their commodities much above the natural price, and raise their emolument, whether they consist in wages or profit, greatly above their natural rate.

[Ibid]

People of the same trade seldom meet together, even for merriment and diversion, but the conversation ends in a conspiracy against the public, or in some contrivance to raise prices. It is impossible indeed to prevent such meetings by any law which either could be executed, or would be consistent with liberty and justice.

[Ibid]

Philip Dormer Stanhope, 4th Earl of Chesterfield, 1694–1773, English statesman
Without some dissimulation no business can be carried on at all.

[Letters to His Son 1749]

Idleness is only the refuge of weak minds.

[Ibid]

Robert Louis [Balfour] Stevenson, 1850–94, Scottish novelist and poet
Extreme *busyness*, whether at school or college, kirk or market, is a symptom of deficient vitality.

[Virginibus Puerisque: An Apology for Idlers 1881]

Everyone lives by selling something.

[Across the Plains 1892]

Surely we should find it both touching and inspiriting, that in a field from which success is banished, our race should not cease to labour.

[Ibid]

Studs [Louis] Terkel, 1912– , American writer
Perhaps it is this spectre that most haunts working men and women: the planned obsolescence of people that is of a piece with the planned obsolescence of the things they make. Or sell.

[Working 1972]

William Makepeace Thackeray, 1811–63, English novelist
Business first; pleasure afterwards.

[The Rose and the Ring 1855]

"No business before breakfast, Glum!" says the King. "Breakfast first, business next."

[*Ibid*]

Jill Tweedie, 1936–93, English journalist
How to be an effective secretary is to develop the kind of lonely self-abnegating sacrificial instincts usually possessed only by the early saints on their way to martyrdom.

[*It's Only Me* 1980]

Umberto I, 1844–1900, king of Italy
È un incidente del mestiere.
(It is an incident of the profession.)

[On escaping assassination]

Virgil *or* Vergil [Publius Vergilius Maro], 70–19BC, Roman poet
Labor omnia vincit.
(Work conquers all.)

[*Georgics*]

Voltaire [François Marie Arouet], 1694–1778, French philosopher and writer
[On England] *Dans ce pays-ci il est bon de tuer de temps en temps un amiral pour encourager les autres.*
(In this country it is considered good from time to time to kill an admiral to encourage the others.)

[*Candide* 1759]

Work keeps us from three great evils, boredom, vice, and need.

[*Ibid*]

We must look after our garden. When man was put in the Garden of Eden, he was put there to work; that proves that man was not born for rest. Let us work without question, that is the only way to make life tolerable.

[*Ibid*]

Isaac Watts, 1674–1748, English poet and hymn-writer
How doth the little busy bee
Improve each shining hour,
And gather honey all the day
From every opening flower!

[*Divine Songs for the use of Children: Against Idleness and Mischief* 1715]

Simone Weil, 1909–43, French essayist and philosopher
What a country calls its vital economic interests are not the things that enable its citizens to live, but the things that enable it to make war. Petrol is more likely than wheat to be a cause of international conflict.

[*The Need for Roots* 1949]

Arthur Wellesley, 1st Duke of Wellington, 1769–1852, English soldier and statesman
My rule always was to do the business of the day in the day.

[In Stanhope's *Notes of Conversations with the Duke of Wellington*]

E[lwyn] B[rooks] White, 1899–1985, American humorist
The trouble with the profit system has always been that it was highly unprofitable to most people.

[*One Man's Meat* 1944]

WORK AND BUSINESS

Katherine Whitehorn, 1926– , English journalist
I yield to no one in my admiration for the office as a social centre, but it's no place to get any work done.

[Sunday Best]

Oscar [Fingall O'Flahertie Wills] Wilde, 1854–1900, Irish writer
Work is the refuge of people who have nothing better to do.

[The Soul of Man under Socialism]

Andrew Jackson Young, 1932– , American politician
Nothing is illegal if a hundred businessmen decide to do it.

[1976]

Crime, Justice and the Law

Woody Allen [Allen Stewart Konigsberg], 1935– , American writer, actor and film director

I think crime pays. The hours are good, you travel a lot.

[*Take the Money and Run*]

Anonymous

Lizzie Borden took an axe,
And gave her mother forty whacks.
When she saw what she had done,
She gave her father forty-one.

[*The Crimes of Lizzie Borden*]

Lawyers' houses are built on the heads of fools.

[Proverb]

Law cannot persuade where it cannot punish.

[Proverb]

St Thomas Aquinas, 1225–74, Italian theologian

Human law is law only by virtue of its accordance with right reason, and by this means it is clear that it flows from Eternal law. In so far as it deviates from right reason it is called an Unjust law; and in such a case, it is no law at all, but rather an assertion of violence.

[*Summa Theologiae c.*1260]

Hannah Arendt, 1906–75, German-born American philosopher

No punishment has ever possessed enough power of deterrence to prevent the commission of crimes. On the contrary, whatever the punishment, once a specific crime has appeared for the first time, its reappearance is more likely than its initial emergence could ever have been.

[*Eichmann in Jerusalem* 1963]

Francis Bacon, Baron Verulam of Verulam and Viscount of St Albans, 1561–1626, English philosopher

One of the Seven was wont to say: "That laws were like cobwebs; where the small flies were caught, and the great brake through."

[*Apothegms*]

Revenge is a kind of wild justice.

[*Essays: Of Revenge*]

Opportunity makes a thief.

[Letter 1598]

Henry Ward Beecher, 1813–87, American preacher
Riches without law are more dangerous than is poverty without law.
[*Proverbs from Plymouth Pulpit* 1870]

[Enoch] Arnold Bennett, 1867–1931, English novelist
The price of justice is eternal publicity.
[*Things That Have Interested Me*]

Jeremy Bentham, 1748–1832, English philosopher
All punishment is mischief; all punishment in itself is evil.
[*Principles of Morals and Legislation* 1789]
It is with government as with medicine, its only business is the choice of evils. Every law is an evil, for every law is an infraction of liberty.
[*Ibid*]

The Bible
And Cain said unto the Lord, My punishment is greater than I can bear.
[*Genesis* 4:13]
Who made thee a prince and a judge over us?
[*Exodus* 2:14]
But the path of the just is as the shining light, that shineth more and more unto the perfect day. The way of the wicked is as darkness; they know not at what they stumble.
[*Proverbs* 4:18–19]
Stolen waters are sweet.
[*Ibid* 9:17]
He maketh his sun to rise on the evil and on the good, and sendeth rain on the just and the unjust.
[*Matthew* 5:45]
Lay not up for yourselves treasures upon earth, where moth and rust doth corrupt, and where thieves break through and steal.
[*Ibid* 6:19]
Judge not, that ye be not judged. For with what judgement ye judge, ye shall be judged: and with what measure ye mete, it shall be measured to you again
[*Ibid* 7:1–2]
I say unto you, that likewise joy shall be in heaven over one sinner that repenteth, more than over ninety and nine just persons, which need no repentance.
[*Luke* 15:7]
For as many as have sinned without law shall also perish without law: and as many as have sinned in the law shall be judged by the law.
[*Romans* 2:12]
These, not having the law, are a law unto themselves.
[*Ibid* 2:14]

Ambrose [Gwinett] Bierce, 1842–1914, American writer
Justice: a commodity which in a more or less adulterated condition the State sells to the citizen as a reward for his allegiance, taxes and personal service.
[*The Devil's Dictionary* 1906]
Lawyer: one skilled in circumvention of the law.
[*Ibid*]
Litigation: a machine which you go into as a pig and come out of as a sausage.
[*Ibid*]

Mercy: an attribute beloved of detected offenders.

[Ibid]

William Blake, 1757–1827, English poet and artist
As, long agone,
When men were first a nation grown,
Lawless they lived, till wantonness
And liberty began to increase,
And one man lay in another's way;
The laws were made to keep fair play.

[Blind Man's Buff]

Prisons are built with stones of Law, brothels with bricks of Religion.
[The Marriage of Heaven and Hell: Proverbs of Hell c.1790–93]

Charles Synge Christopher Bowen, Baron Bowen of Colwood, 1835–94, English judge
The rain it raineth on the just
And also on the unjust fella:
But chiefly on the just, because
The unjust steals the just's umbrella.

[In Sichel's Sands of Time]

Bertolt Brecht, 1898–1956, German dramatist and poet
What is robbing a bank compared with founding a bank?

[The Threepenny Opera 1928]

Emily Jane Brontë, 1818–48, English novelist
O dreadful is the check – intense the agony –
When the ear begins to hear and the eye begins to see;
When the pulse begins to throb, the brain to think again;
The soul to feel the flesh and the flesh to feel the chain!

[The Prisoner]

Byron, Lord George Gordon [Noel], 6th Baron Byron of Rochdale, 1788–1824, English poet
Know ye the land where the cypress and myrtle
Are emblems of deeds that are done in their clime?
Where the rage of the vulture, the love of the turtle,
Now melt into sorrow, now madden to crime.

[The Bride of Abydos 1813]

William Camden, 1551–1623, English historian
Agree, for the law is costly.

[Remains Concerning Britain 1614]

Albert Camus, 1913–60, Algerian-born French philosopher and novelist
Absolute freedom mocks at justice. Absolute justice denies freedom.

[The Rebel 1951]

Lewis Carroll [Charles Lutwidge Dodgson], 1832–92, English mathematician and writer
"I'll be judge, I'll be jury," said cunning old Fury;
"I'll try the whole cause, and condemn you to death."

[Alice's Adventures in Wonderland 1865]

Raymond Chandler, 1888–1959, American novelist

Organised crime is just the dirty side of the sharp dollar.

[*The Long Good-bye* 1953]

Harold Chapin, 1885–1915, American actor and playwright

In the eyes of a British jury, for a woman to offer a reason for doing anything only makes her offence the blacker.

[*The New Morality* 1920]

Marcus Tullius Cicero, 106–43BC Roman statesman

The fundamentals of justice are that no one shall suffer wrong, and that the public good be served.

[*De Officiis* 78BC]

Guilt is present in the hesitation, even though the deed be not committed.

[*Ibid*]

The greatest incitement to crime is the hope of escaping punishment.

[*Pro Milone c.* 50BC]

For laws are dumb in the midst of arms.

[*Ibid*]

The good of the people is the highest law.

[*Ibid*]

Sir Edward Coke, 1552–1634, English judge

The gladsome light of jurisprudence.

[*Institutes: First Institute* 1628]

Sir Arthur Conan Doyle, 1859–1930, English novelist

"Wonderful!" I ejaculated. "Commonplace," said Holmes.

[*A Study in Scarlet* 1887]

You know my methods. Apply them.

[*The Sign of Four* 1890]

Singularity is almost invariably a clue. The more featureless and commonplace a crime is, the more dificult it is to bring it home.

[*The Adventures of Sherlock Holmes* 1892]

"Excellent!" I cried. "Elementary," said he.

[*The Memoirs of Sherlock Holmes* 1894]

William Congreve, 1670–1729, English dramatist

See how love and murder will out.

[*The Double Dealer* 1693]

Richard Joseph Daley, 1902–76, American politician

Get the thing straight once and for all: the policeman isn't there to create disorder. The policeman is there to preserve disorder.

[Said while mayor of Chicago, 1968]

Eugene Victor Debs, 1855–1926, American politician

While there is a lower class, I am in it. While there is a criminal class I am of it. While there is a soul in prison, I am not free.

[*Labor and Freedom*]

Daniel Defoe, 1660–1731, English novelist
When kings the sword of justice first lay down,
They art no kings, though they possess the crown.
Titles are shadows, crowns are empty things,
The good of subjects is the end of kings.

[*The True-Born Englishman* 1701]

Charles [John Huffam] Dickens, 1812–70, English novelist
"If the law supposes that," said Mr Bumble . . . "the law is a ass – a idiot."

[*Oliver Twist* 1837–8]

John Dryden, 1631–1700, English dramatist
Forgiveness to the injured does belong;
For they ne'er pardon who have done the wrong.

[*The Conquest of Granada* 1670]

So easy still it proves in factious times
With public zeal to cancel private crimes.

[*Absalom and Achitophel* 1681]

George Eliot [Mary Ann Evans], 1819–80, English novelist
The law's made to take care o' raskills.

[*The Mill on the Floss* 1860]

T[homas] S[tearns] Eliot, 1888–1965, American-born English poet
And when you reach the scene of crime – *Macavity's not there!*

[*Macavity: the Mystery Cat* 1939]

Ralph Waldo Emerson, 1803–82, American writer
No law can be sacred to me but that of my nature. Good and bad are but names very readily transferable to that or this; the only right is what is after my own constitution; the only wrong what is against it.

[*Essays*: *Self-Reliance* 1841]

George Farquhar, 1678–1707, Irish playwright
Crimes, like virtues, are their own rewards.

[*The Inconstant* 4 1703]

Henry Fielding, 1707–54, English novelist
I am as sober as a judge.

[*Don Quixote in England* 1734]

Thwackum was for doing justice, and leaving mercy to heaven.

[*Tom Jones* 1749]

Joseph Fouché, 1759–1820, French minister of police
C'est plus qu'un crime; c'est une faute.
It is worse than a crime: it is a blunder.

[On the execution of the Duc d'Enghien, an abducted royalist emigré, 1804]

Anatole France [Jacques Anatole Thibault], 1844–1924, French novelist and critic
The law, in its majestic equality, forbids the rich as well as the poor to sleep under bridges, to beg in the streets, and to steal bread.

[In Cournos' *Modern Plutarch*]

Christopher [Harris] Fry, 1907– , English poet and playwright
I know I am not
A practical person; legal matters and so forth
Are Greek to me, except, of course,
That I understand Greek.

[The Lady's not for Burning 1949]

Elizabeth Fry [*née* Gurney], 1780–1845, English Quaker prison reformer
Does capital punishment tend to the security of the people? By no means. It hardens the
hearts of men, and makes the loss of life appear light to them; and it renders life insecure,
inasmuch as the law holds out that property is of greater value than life.

[In Sarah Hale's *Women's Record: Sketches of All Distinguished Women* 1853]

Mohandas Karamchand ("Mahatma") Gandhi, 1869–1948, Indian political leader
That action alone is just which does not harm either party to a dispute.

John Gay, 1685–1732, English poet and playwright
The charge is prepar'd; the lawyers are met;
The judges all rang'd (a terrible show!).

[The Beggar's Opera 1728]

Sir William Schwenck Gilbert, 1836–1911, English librettist
And many a burglar I've restored
To his friends and his relations.

[Trial by Jury 1875]

When constabulary duty's to be done,
A policeman's lot is not a happy one.

[The Pirates of Penzance 1879]

As some day it may happen that a victim must be found,
I've got a little list – I've got a little list
Of society offenders who might well be underground,
And who never would be missed – who never would be missed.

[The Mikado 1885]

My object all sublime
I shall achieve in time –
To let the punishment fit the crime.

[Ibid]

Oliver Goldsmith, 1728–74, Irish-born English writer
Laws grind the poor, and rich men rule the law.

[The Traveller 1764]

Kenneth Grahame, 1859–1932, English writer
The burglars vanished silently into the laurels, with horrid implications!

[The Golden Age: The Burglars 1895]

Ulysses S[impson] Grant, 1822–85, 18th president of the United States
I know of no method to secure the repeal of bad or obnoxious laws so effective as their
stringent execution.

[Inaugural address 1869]

St Gregory VII, c. 1020–1085, Italian pope
I have loved justice and hated iniquity: therefore I die in exile.

[Last words]

[Billings] Learned Hand, 1872–1961, American judge
I should like to have every court begin, "I beseech ye in the bowels of Christ, think that we may be mistaken."

[*Morals in Public Life* (quoting Cromwell) 1951]

Justice, I think, is the tolerable accommodation of the conflicting interests of society, and I don't believe there is any royal road to attain such accommodations concretely.

[In Hamburger's *The Great Judge* 1946]

Thomas Hardy, 1840–1928, English novelist and poet
"Justice" was done, and the President of the Immortals (in Aeschylean phrase) had ended his sport with Tess.

[*Tess of the D'Urbervilles* 1891]

Lord Gordon Hewart, 1870–1943, English jurist
It is not merely of some importance but is of fundamental importance that justice should not only be done, but should manifestly and undoubtedly be seen to be done.

[In court, 1923. In Jackson's *The Chief*]

Oliver Wendell Holmes, 1841–1935, American judge
The life of the law has not been logic: it has been experience.

[*The Common Law* 1881]

Thomas Jefferson, 1743–1826, 3rd president of the United States
It is not only vain, but wicked, in a legislator to frame laws in opposition to the laws of nature, and to arm them with the terrors of death. This is truly creating crimes in order to punish them.

[*Notes on the Crimes Bill* 1779]

Every man is under the natural duty of contributing to the necessities of society; and this is all the laws should enforce on him.

[Letter 1816]

Dr Samuel Johnson, 1709–84, English lexicographer
Depend upon it, sir, when a man knows he is to be hanged in a fortnight, it concentrates his mind wonderfully.

[September 1777. In Boswell's *Life of Samuel Johnson* 1791]

Rudyard Kipling, 1865–1936, English writer
The Saxon is not like us Normans. His manners are not so polite.
But he never means anything serious till he talks about justice and right,
When he stands like an ox in the furrow with his sullen set eyes on your own,
And grumbles, "This isn't fair dealing," my son, leave the Saxon alone.

[*Norman and Saxon*]

Abraham Lincoln, 1809–65, 16th president of the United States
Why should there not be a patient confidence in the ultimate justice of the people? Is there any better or equal hope in the world.

[Inaugural address 1861]

He reminds me of the man who murdered both his parents, and then, when sentence was about to be pronounced, pleaded for mercy on the grounds that he was an orphan.

[In Gross's *Lincoln's Own Stories*]

Charles Macklin, c.1697–1797, Irish actor and dramatist
The law is a sort of hocus-pocus science, that smiles in yer face while it picks yer pocket: and the glorious uncertainty of it is of mair use to the professors than the justice of it.

[*Love à la Mode* 1759]

Magna Carta, 1215
To no one will we sell, to no one will we refuse or delay right or justice.

[Article 40]

Lord Mansfield, 1705–93, English jurist
Consider what you think justice requires, and decide accordingly. But never give your reasons; for your judgement will probably be right, but your reasons will certainly be wrong.

[In Campbell's *Lives of the Chief Justices*]

Marcus Aurelius [Antoninus] [Marcus Annius Verus] AD121–80, Roman emperor
A wrongdoer is often a man who has left something undone, not always one who has done something.

[*Meditations c.*170]

Andrew Marvell, 1621–78, English poet and politician
Had we but world enough, and time,
This coyness, Lady, were no crime.

[*To his Coy Mistress* 1650]

John Milton, 1608–74, English poet
Yet I shall temper so
Justice with mercy, as may illustrate most
Them fully satisfied, and thee appease.

[*Paradise Lost* 1667]

Reinhold Niebuhr, 1892–1971, American religious thinker
Man's capacity for justice makes democracy possible, but man's inclination to injustice makes democracy necessary.

[*The Children of Light and the Children of Darkness* 1944]

Christopher North [John Wilson], 1785–1854, Scottish journalist
Laws were made to be broken.

[*Noctes Ambrosianae* 1830]

Oliver North 1943– , American soldier
[On the Iran-Contra affair] When I heard the words criminal investigation my mindset changed considerably.

[In *New York Times*, July 10 1987]

Thomas Otway, 1652–85, English dramatist
Honest men are the soft easy cushions on which knaves repose.

[*Venice Preserv'd* 1682]

95

Blaise Pascal, 1623–62, French mathematician and writer
Justice without strength is helpless, strength without justice is tyrannical. . . Unable to make what is just strong, we have made what is strong just.

[*Pensées* 1670]

William Pitt, 1st Earl of Chatham, 1708–78, British statesman
Where law ends, tyranny begins.

[Speech in the House of Lords, 1770]

Alexander Pope, 1688–1744, English poet
The hungry judges soon the sentence sign,
And wretches hang that jurymen may dine.

[*The Rape of the Lock* 1712]

Poetic Justice, with her lifted scale;
Where, in nice balance, truth with gold she weighs,
And solid pudding against empty praise.

[*The Dunciad* 1728]

Order is heaven's first law.

[*Essay on Man* 1732–4]

Pierre Joseph Proudhon, 1809–65, French social philosopher and writer
If I were asked to answer the following question: "What is slavery?" and I should answer in one word, "Murder!" my meaning would be understood at once. No further argument would be required to show that the power to take from a man his thought, his will, his personality, is a power of life and death, and that to enslave a man is to kill him. Why, then, to this other question: "What is property?" may I not likewise answer "Theft"?

[*What is Property?* 1840]

Thomas De Quincey, 1785–1859, English writer
If once a man indulge himself in murder, very soon he comes to think little of robbing; and from robbing he next comes to drinking and Sabbath-breaking, and from that to incivility and procrastination.

[*Murder Considered as One of the Fine Arts* 1827]

Robert Rice, 1916– , American criminologist
Crime is a logical extension of the sort of behaviour that is often considered perfectly respectable in legitimate business.

[*The Business of Crime*]

Jean Jacques Rousseau, 1712–78, Swiss-born French philosopher
Good laws lead to the making of better ones; bad ones bring about worse.

[*The Social Contract* 1762]

Charles Louis de Secondat, Baron de Montesquieu, 1689–1755, French philosopher
Useless laws weaken the necessary laws.

[*The Spirit of the Laws* 1748]

John Selden, 1584–1654, English antiquary and politician
Ignorance of the law excuses no man; not that all men know the law, but because 'tis an excuse every man will plead, and no man can tell how to refute him.

[*Table Talk: Judgments* 1689]

Seneca, c. 4BC–AD65, Roman philosopher
There is no crime without a precedent.

[*Hippolytus c.* 60]

William Shakespeare, 1564–1616, English dramatist
Who steals my purse, steals trash; 'tis something, nothing;
'Twas mine, 'tis his, and has been slave to thousands;
But he that filches from me my good name
Robs me of that which not enriches him
And makes me poor indeed.

[*Othello* 3 1604–5]

The first thing we do, let's kill all the lawyers.

[*King Henry VI, Part II* 4 1591]

The quality of mercy is not strain'd,
It droppeth as the gentle rain from heaven
Upon the place beneath: it is twice blest;
It blesseth him that gives and him that takes:
'Tis mightiest in the mightiest: it becomes
The throned monarch better than his crown.

[*The Merchant of Venice* 3 1596–7]

Wrest once the law to your authority:
To do a great right, do a little wrong.

[*Ibid* 4]

For, as thou urgest justice, be assured
Thou shalt have justice, more than thou desirest.

[*Ibid*]

But mercy is above this sceptred sway;
It is enthroned in the hearts of kings,
It is an attribute to God himself;
And earthly power doth then show likest God's
When mercy seasons justice.

[*Ibid* 4]

Old father antic the law.

[*King Henry IV, Part I* 1 1597–8]

For the watch to babble and talk is most tolerable and not to be endured.

[*Much Ado About Nothing* 3 1598–1600]

The most peaceable way for you, if you do take a thief, is to let him show himself what he is
and steal out of your company.

[*Ibid*]

Flat burglary as ever was committed.

[*Ibid* 4]

Still you keep o' the windy side of the law.

[*Twelfth Night* 3 1598–1600]

But that I am forbid
To tell the secrets of my prison-house,
I could a tale unfold whose lightest word
Would harrow up thy soul, freeze thy young blood,
Make thy two eyes, like stars, start from their spheres,
Thy knotted and combined locks to part,
And each particular hair to stand an end,
Like quills upon the fretful porpentine.

[*Hamlet* 1 1600–1601]

Murder most foul, as in the best it is;
But this most foul, strange and unnatural.

[*Ibid*]

I will speak daggers to her, but use none.

[*Ibid* 3]

O, my offence is rank, it smells to heaven;
It hath the primal eldest curse upon't,
A brother's murder.

[*Ibid*]

May one be pardon'd and retain the offence?

[*Ibid*]

The jury, passing on the prisoner's life,
May in the sworn twelve have a thief or two
Guiltier than him they try.

[*Measure for Measure* 2 1604–5]

Every true man's apparel fits your thief.

[*Ibid* 4]

They say, best men are moulded out of faults;
And, for the most, become much more the better
For being a little bad.

[*Ibid* 5]

The robb'd that smile steals something from the thief.

[*Othello* 1 1604–5]

See how yond justice rails upon yond simple thief.
Hark, in thine ear: change places; and handy-dandy, which is the justice, which is the thief?

[*King Lear* 4 1604–5]

Come, let's away to prison:
We two alone will sing like birds i' the cage.

[*Ibid* 5]

But in these cases
We shall have judgment here; that we but teach
Bloody instructions, which, being taught, return,
To plague the inventor; this even-handed justice
Commends the ingredients of our poison'd chalice
To our own lips.

[*Macbeth* 1 1605–6]

The time has been,
That, when the brains were out, the man would die,
And there an end; but now they rise again,
With twenty mortal murders on their crowns,
And push us from our stools.

[*Ibid* 3]

I'll example you with thievery:
The sun's a thief, and with his great attraction
Robs the vast sea: the moon's an arrant thief,
And her pale fire she snatches from the sun:
The sea's a thief, whose liquid surge resolves
The moon into salt tears: the earth's a thief,
That feeds and breeds by a composture stolen
From general excrement: each thing's a thief.

[*Timon of Athens* 4 1607–8]

Percy Bysshe Shelley, 1792–1822, English poet
I met Murder on the way –
He had a mask like Castlereagh.

[The Mask of Anarchy 1819]

O[renthal] J[ames] Simpson, 1947– , American football player
[On facing charges of murder] I'm absolutely, one hundred per cent, not guilty.

[In the New York Times July 23 1994]

Sir Sydney Alfred Smith, 1883–1969, New Zealand-born medico-legal expert
No child is born a criminal: no child is born an angel: he's just born.

Tobais [George] Smollett, 1721–71, Scottish novelist and surgeon
Hark ye, Clinker, you are a most notorious offender. You stand convicted of sickness, hunger, wretchedness, and want.

[Humphrey Clinker 1771]

[Edmund] John Millington Synge, 1871–1909, Irish playwright
Drink a health to the wonders of the western world, the pirates, preachers, poteen-makers, with the jobbing jockies; parching peelers, and the juries fill their stomachs selling judgments of the English law.

[The Playboy of the Western World 1907]

Thomas Stephen Szasz, 1920– , American psychiatrist
Men are rewarded and punished not for what they do, but rather for how their acts are defined. This is why men are more interested in better justifying themselves than better behaving themselves.

[The Second Sin 1973]

Miguel de Unamuno [y Jugo], 1864–1936, Spanish philosopher
Every peasant has a lawyer inside of him, just as every lawyer, no matter how urbane he may be, carries a peasant within himself.

[Civilization is Civilism]

Voltaire [François Marie Arouet], 1694–1778, French philosopher and writer
He who is merely just is severe.

[Letter to Frederick the Great 1740]

Divided by interests, and united by crime.

[Mérope 1743]

Fear follows crime, and is its punishment.

[Semiramis]

It is better to risk saving a guilty person than to condemn an innocent one.

[Zadig 1747]

William Watson, c.1559–1603, English writer
Fiat justitia et ruant coeli.
Let justice be done though the heavens fall.

[Questions Concerning Religion and State 1602]

Evelyn [Arthur St John] Waugh, 1903–66, English writer
I came to the conclusion may years ago that almost all crime is due to the repressed desire for aesthetic expression.

[Decline and Fall 1928]

Oscar [Fingall O'Flahertie Wills] Wilde, 1854–1900, Irish writer

For Man's grim Justice goes its way,
And will not swerve aside:
It slays the weak, it slays the strong,
It has a deadly stride.

[*The Ballad of Reading Goal* 1898]

There is no chapel on the day
On which they hang a man.

[*Ibid*]

The vilest deeds like poison-weeds
Bloom well in prison-air:
It is only what is good in Man
That wastes and withers there:
Pale Anguish keeps the heavy gate
And the Warder is Despair.

[*Ibid*]

I know not whether Laws be right,
Or whether Laws be wrong;
All that we know who lie in gaol
Is that the wall is strong;
And that each day is like a year,
A year whose days are long.

[*Ibid*]

Mary Wollstonecraft, 1759–97, English writer

It is justice, not charity, that is wanting in the world.

[*A Vindication of the Rights of Women* 1792]

Executions, far from being useful examples to the survivors, have, I am persuaded, a quite contrary effect, by hardening the heart they ought to terrify. Besides, the fear of an ignominious death, I believe, never deterred anyone from the commission of a crime, because in committing it the mind is roused to activity about present circumstances.

[*Letters written in Sweden, Norway and Denmark* 1796]

Richard Nathaniel Wright, 1908–60, American writer

How can law contradict the lives of millions of people and hope to be administered successfully?

[*Native Son* 1940]

Death, Parting and Sorrow

Joseph Addison, 1672–1719, English essayist
See in what peace a Christian can die.

[Spoken on his deathbed]

Woody Allen [Allen Stewart Konigsberg], 1935– , American writer, actor and film director
On the plus side, death is one of the few things that can be done as easily as lying down.

[*Getting Even* 1972]

Sir Kingsley Amis, 1922–95, English novelist and poet
Death has got something to be said for it:
There's no need to get out of bed for it;
Wherever you be,
They bring it to you, free.

[*Collected Poems: Delivery Guaranteed* 1979]

Anaxandrides, *fl.* 376BC, Greek writer
It is good to die before one has done anything deserving death.

[*Fragment c.*376BC]

Anonymous
You can shed tears that she is gone
or you can smile because she has lived.

[*She Is Gone*, chosen as preface for the order of service for the funeral of Elizabeth the Queen Mother, April 9 2002]

Old men go to death; but death comes to young men.

[Proverb]

Six feet of earth make all men equal.

[Proverb]

W[ystan] H[ugh] Auden, 1907–73, English-born poet
To save your world you asked this man to die:
Would this man, could he see you now, ask why?

[*Epitaph for an Unknown Soldier*]

Berthold Auerbach, 1812–82, German novelist
We hear the rain fall, but not the snow. Bitter grief is loud, calm grief is silent.

[*Auf der Hohe* 1865]

Francis Bacon, Baron Verulam of Verulam and Viscount of St Albans, 1561–1626, English philosopher

Men fear Death as children fear to go in the dark; and as that natural fear in children is increased with tales, so is the other.

[Essays: Of Death]

Revenge triumphs over Death; Love slights it; Honour aspireth to it; Grief flieth to it.

[Ibid]

It is as natural to die as to be born; and to a little infant perhaps the one is as painful as the other.

[Ibid]

Honoré de Balzac, 1799–1850, French novelist

What does farewell mean, if not death? But will death itself be a farewell?

[Louis Lambert]

Sir J[ames] M[atthew] Barrie, 1860–1937, Scottish playwright

Every time a child says "I don't believe in fairies," there is a little fairy somewhere that falls down dead.

[Peter Pan 1911]

To die will be an awfully big adventure.

[Ibid]

Henry Ward Beecher, 1813–87, American preacher

Now comes the mystery.

[Last words 1887]

[Joseph] Hilaire [Pierre] Belloc, 1870–1953, English writer

Loss and Possession, death and life are one,
There falls no shadow where there shines no sun.

[For a Sundial]

The Bible

For dust thou art, and unto dust shalt thou return.

[Genesis 3:19]

Where thou diest, will I die, and there will I be buried: the Lord do so to me, and more also, if ought but death part thee and me.

[Ruth 1:17]

Saul and Jonathan were lovely and pleasant in their lives, and in their death they were not divided.

[2 Samuel 1:23]

And the king was much moved, and went up to the chamber over the gate, and wept: and as he went, thus he said, O my son Absalom, my son, my son Absalom! would God I had died for thee, O Absalom, my son, my son!

[Ibid 18:33]

Yea, though I walk through the valley of the shadow of death, I will fear no evil: for thou art with me; thy rod and thy staff they comfort me.

[Psalms 23:4]

A good name is better than precious ointment; and the day of death than the day of one's birth.

[Ecclesiastes 7:1]

He will swallow up death in victory; and the Lord God will wipe away tears from off all faces.

[Isaiah 15:8]

And behold joy and gladness, slaying oxen, and killing sheep, eating flesh, and drinking wine: let us eat and drink; for tomorrow we shall die.

[*Ibid* 22:13]

For the king of Babylon stood at the parting of the way, at the head of the two ways.

[*Ezekiel* 21:21]

For the wages of sin is death; but the gift of God is eternal life through Jesus Christ our Lord.

[*Romans* 6:23]

The last enemy that shall be destroyed is death.

[*1 Corinthians* 15:26]

Death is swallowed up in victory. O death, where is thy sting? O grave, where is thy victory.

[*Ibid* 15:51–55]

For to me to live is Christ, and to die is gain.

[*Philippians* 1:21]

For we brought nothing into this world, and it is certain we can carry nothing out.

[*1 Timothy* 6:7]

And I looked, and behold a pale horse: and his name that sat on him was Death.

[*Revelation* 6:8]

And God shall wipe away all tears from their eyes; and there shall be no more death, neither sorrow, nor crying, neither shall there be any more pain: for the former things are passed away.

[*Ibid* 21:4]

Judge none blessed before his death.

[*Ecclesiasticus* 11:28]

But the souls of the righteous are in the hand of God, and there shall no torment touch them. In the sight of the unwise they seemed to die: and their departure is taken for misery, And their going from us to be utter destruction: but they are in peace.

[*Wisdom of Solomon* 3:1]

In the midst of life we are in death.

[*The Book of Common Prayer: The Burial of the Dead*]

We therefore commit his body to the ground; earth to earth, ashes to ashes, dust to dust; in sure and certain hope of the Resurrection to eternal life.

[*Ibid*]

William Blake, 1757–1827, English poet and artist
Drive your cart and your plough over the bones of the dead.

[*The Marriage of Heaven and Hell: Proverbs of Hell c.*1790–93]

Catherine Bramwell Booth, 1884–1987, Salvation Army Leader
It's a strange experience to live so near to death. You find yourself planning something, then you pull yourself up and think, "I may not be here" . . . I'm in love with living.

[On the eve of her 100th birthday]

George [Henry] Borrow, 1803–81, English writer
There's night and day, brother, both sweet things; sun, moon, and stars, brother, all sweet things; there's likewise a wind on the heath. Life is very sweet, brother; who would wish to die?

[*Lavengro* 1851]

John Bright, 1811–89, English politician
The Angel of Death has been abroad throughout the land; you may almost hear the beating of his wings.

[Speech in the House of Commons 1855]

103

Emily Jane Brontë, 1818–48, English novelist and poet
I lingered round them, under that benign sky: watched the moths fluttering among the heath and harebells; listened to the soft wind breathing through the grass; and wondered how anyone could ever imagine unquiet slumbers for the sleepers in that quiet earth.

[*Wuthering Heights* 1847]

Rupert Chawner Brooke, 1887–1915, English poet
And the worst friend and enemy is but Death.

[*Peace*]

If I should die, think only this of me:
That there's some corner of a foreign field
That is for ever England. There shall be
In that rich earth a richer dust concealed.

[*The Soldier* 1915]

Thomas Brown, 1663–1704, English writer
A leap into the dark.

[*Letters from the Dead*]

Sir Thomas Browne, 1605–82, English physician
We all labour against our own cure, for death is the cure of all diseases.

[*Religio Medici* 1643]

I am not so much afraid of death, as ashamed thereof; 'tis the very disgrace and ignominy of our natures.

[*Ibid*]

Elizabeth Barrett Browning, 1806–61, English poet
It is a place where poets crowned may feel the heart's decaying;
It is a place where happy saints may weep amid their praying.
Yet let the grief and humbleness, as low as silence, languish:
Earth surely now may give her calm to whom she gave her anguish.

[*Cowper's Grave*]

Robert Browning, 1812–89, English poet
What is he buzzing in my ears?
"Now that I come to die,
Do I view the world as a vale of tears?"
Ah, reverend sir, not I!

[*Confessions*]

Who knows but the world may end tonight?

[*The Last Ride Together*]

Robert Burns, 1759–96, Scottish poet
O Death! the poor man's dearest friend,
The kindest and the best!
Welcome the hour my aged limbs
Are laid with thee at rest!
The great, the wealthy fear thy blow,
From pomp and pleasure torn;
But, oh! a blest relief to those
That weary-laden mourn.

[*Man was Made to Mourn* 1786]

The friend of man, the friend of truth,
The friend of age, and guide of youth
If there's another world, he lives in bliss;
If there is none, he made the best of this.

[*On Wm Muir in Tarbolton Mill*]

Samuel Butler, 1835–1902, English writer

It costs a lot of money to die comfortably.

[*Note Books c.*1890]

To himself every one is an immortal; he may know that he is going to die, but he can never know that he is dead.

[*Ibid*]

Byron, Lord George Gordon [Noel], 6th Baron Byron of Rochdale, 1788–1824, English poet

Fare thee well! and if for ever,
Still for ever, fare thee well.

[*Fare Thee Well*]

'Tis vain to struggle – let me perish young –
Live as I lived, and love as I have loved;
To dust if I return, from dust I sprung.

[*Stanzas to the Po*]

Saint Peter sat by the celestial gate:
His keys were rusty, and the lock was dull,
So little trouble had been given of late.

[*The Vision of Judgement*]

Old man! 'tis not so difficult to die.

[*Manfred* 1817]

Death in the front, Destruction in the rear!

[*Childe Harold's Pilgrimage* 1818]

There, swan-like, let me sing and die.

[*Ibid*]

'Tis strange the mind, that very fiery particle,
Should let itself be snuff'd out by an article.

[*Ibid*]

Et tu, Brute! You too, Brutus!

[Dying words]

William Camden, 1551–1623, English historian

Betwixt the stirrup and the ground
Mercy I asked, mercy I found.

[*Epitaph for a Man Killed by Falling from his Horse*]

Charles II, 1630–85, king of England, Scotland and Ireland

He had been, he said, an unconscionable time dying; but he hoped that they would excuse him.

[Said on his deathbed: in Macaulay's *History of England* 1848]

Marcus Tullius Cicero, 106–43BC, Roman statesman

No man can be ignorant that he must die, nor be sure that he may not this very day.

[*De Senectute c.*78BC]

John Clare, 1793–1864, English poet
He could not die when the trees were green,
For he loved the time too well.

[*The Dying Child* 1820]

John [Marwood] Cleese, 1939– , English comic actor and writer
I'm getting very curious about what I'm going to do after I'm dead. . . People think I'm weird, of course. I think it's weird to believe that mental health consists in pretending you're immortal. Anyway, what's so bad about death? Most of the best people are dead, you know.
[In Jonathan Margolis' *Cleese Encounters*]

Stephen Grover Cleveland, 1837–1908, 22nd and 24th president of the United States
I have tried so hard to do the right.

[Last words]

Arthur Hugh Clough, 1819–61, English poet
Thou shalt not kill; but need'st not strive
Officiously to keep alive.

[*The Latest Decalogue* 1862]

[Sidonie Gabrielle Claudine] Colette, 1873–1954, French novelist
It takes time for the absent to assume their true shape in our thoughts. After death they take on a firmer outline and then cease to change.

[*Earthly Paradise*]

Confucius [K'ung fu-tzu], 551–479BC, Chinese philosopher
If we treat the dead as if they were wholly dead it shows want of affection; if we treat them as wholly alive it shows want of sense. Neither should be done.

[*The Book of Rites* c.500BC]

David ("Davy") Crockett, 1786–1836, American frontiersman
I leave this rule for others when I'm dead,
Be always sure you're right – then go ahead.

[*Autobiography* 1834]

Oliver Cromwell, 1599–1658, English statesman
It is not my design to drink or to sleep, but my design is to make what haste I can to be gone.

[Dying words]

Dante (Alighieri), 1265–1321, Italian poet
All hope abandon, ye who enter!

[*The Divine Comedy: Inferno*]

These have not hope of death.

[*Ibid*]

Charles [John Huffam] Dickens, 1812–70, English novelist
Grief never mended no broken bones, and as good people's wery scarce, what I says is, make the most on 'em.

[*Sketches by Boz: Gin Shops* 1836–7]

"People can't die, along the coast," said Mr Peggotty, "except when the tide's pretty nigh out. They can't be born, unless it's pretty nigh in – not properly born, till flood. He's a going out with the tide.

[*David Copperfield* 1849–50]

It is a far, far better thing that I do, than I have ever done; it is a far, far better rest that I go to, than I have ever known.

[*A Tale of Two Cities* 1859]

Emily Dickinson, 1830–1886, American poet

My life closed twice before its close;
It yet remains to see
If Immortality unveil
A third event to me,
So huge, so hopeless to conceive
As these that twice befell.
Parting is all we know of heaven
And all we need of hell.

[*My life closed twice before its close*]

Benjamin Disraeli, 1st Earl of Beaconsfield, 1804–81, British statesman and novelist

Grief is the agony of an instant; the indulgence of grief the blunder of a life.

[*Vivian Grey* 1827]

Those who have known grief seldom seem sad.

[*Endymion* 1880]

John Donne, c.1571–1631, English poet

No man is an island, entire of itself; every man is a piece of the continent, a part of the main; if a clod be washed away by the sea, Europe is the less, as well as if a promontory were, as well as if a manor of thy friends or of thine own were; any man's death diminishes me, because I am involved in mankind; and therefore never send to know for whom the bell tolls; it tolls for thee.

[*Devotions upon Emergent Occasions* 1624]

One short sleep past, we wake eternally,
And death shall be nor more; Death, thou shalt die.

[*Holy Sonnets*]

Michael Drayton, 1563–1631, English poet

Since there's not help, come let us kiss and part.

[*Sonnets* 61]

Now at the last gasp of Love's latest breath,
When, his pulse failing, Passion speechless lies,
When Faith is kneeling by his bed of death,
And Innocence is closing up his eyes,
Now if thou wouldst, when all have given him over,
From death to life thou mightst him yet recover.

[*Ibid*]

George Eliot [Mary Ann Evans], 1819–80, English novelist

In every parting there is an image of death.

[*Scenes of Clerical Life* 1857]

Ralph Waldo Emerson, 1803–82, American writer

Goodbye, proud world! I'm going home;
Thou art not my friend, and I'm not thine.

[*Poems: Goodbye* 1847]

Robert Emmet, 1778–1803, Irish patriot

Let there be no inscription upon my tomb. Let no man write my epitaph. No man can write my epitaph. I am here ready to die. I am not allowed to vindicate my character; and when I am prevented from vindicating myself, let no man dare calumniate me. Let my character and motives repose in obscurity and peace, till other times and other men can do them justice.

[At his trial, 1803]

Kathleen Ferrier, 1912–53, English opera singer

Now I'll have *eine kleine* pause.

[Last words]

Henry Fielding, 1707–54, English novelist

It hath been often said, that it is not death, but dying which is terrible.

[*Amelia* 1751]

Edward FitzGerald, 1809–83, English writer and translator

One thing is certain the rest is lies;
The flower that once has blown forever dies.

[*The Rubaiyat of Omar Khayyam* 1857]

John Fletcher, 1579–1625, and Philip Massinger, 1583–1640, English dramatists

Death hath a thousand doors to let out life.
I shall find one.

[*A Very Woman c.*1625]

Jean de La Fontaine, 1621–95, French poet

La mort ne surprend point le sage, Il est toujours prêt à partir.
(Death does not surprise the wise man, he is always ready to leave.)

[*Fables: La Mort et le Mourant* 1671]

Benjamin Franklin, 1706–90, American scientist and philosopher

The body of Benjamin Franklin, Printer, (like the cover of an old book, its contents torn out and stripped of its lettering and gilding), lies here, food for worms; but the work shall not be lost, for it will (as he believed) appear once more in a new and more elegant edition, revised and corrected by the Author.

[Epitaph on himself, 1728]

Frederick the Great [Frederick II], 1712–86, king of Prussia

Perhaps nature wants us, at the end of our days, to be disgusted with life, so that we may leave this world with less regret.

[Letter 1783]

Gaius [Julius Caesar], c.100–44BC, Roman statesman

Nothing is easier than to blame the dead.

[*The Gallic War c.*51BC]

Thomas Gray, 1716–71, English poet

Some village Hampden, that with dauntless breast
The little tyrant of his fields withstood;
Some mute inglorious Milton here may rest,
Some Cromwell guiltless of his country's blood.

[*Elegy Written in a Country Churchyard* 1851]

Far from the madding crowd's ignoble strife
Their sober wishes never learn'd to stray;
Along the cool sequester'd vale of life
They kept the noiseless tenor of their way.

[*Ibid*]

Thomas Hardy, 1840–1928, English novelist and poet
All her shining keys will be took from her, and her cupboards opened, and little things 'a
didn't wish seen, anybody will see, and her wishes and ways will all be as nothing.

[*The Mayor of Casterbridge* 1886]

William Hazlitt, 1778–1830, English essayist
No young man believes he shall ever die.

[*On the Feeling of Immortality in Youth*]

Seamus Heaney, 1939– , Irish poet
Wearing a poppy bruise on his left temple,
He lay in the four foot box as in his cot.
No gaudy scars, the bumper knocked him clear.
A four foot box, a foot for every year.

[*Mid-Term Break*]

[Christian Johann] Heinrich Heine, 1797–1856, German poet
[On God] Of course he will forgive me; that's his business.

[Last words]

O. Henry [William Sydney Porter], 1862–1910, American writer
Turn up the lights – I don't want to go home in the dark.
[Last words, quoting a popular song by Harry H. Williams (1879–1922)]

John Heywood, c.1497–c.1580, English epigrammatist
Let the world slide, let the world go:
A fig for care, and a fig for woe!
If I can't pay, why I can owe,
And death makes equal the high and low.

[*Be Merry Friends*]

Thomas Hobbes, 1588–1679, English political philosopher
No arts; no letters; no society; and which is worst of all, continual fear and danger of violent
death; and the life of man solitary, poor, nasty, brutish, and short.

[*Leviathan* 1651]

Thomas Hood, 1799–1845, English poet
Our very hopes belied our fears,
Our fears our hopes belied –
We thought her dying when she slept,
And sleeping when she died!

[*The Deathbed*]

They went and told the sexton and
The sexton toll'd the bell.

[*Faithless Sally Brown*]

Horace [Quintus Horatius Flaccus], 65–8BC, Roman poet

Pale Death, with impartial foot, strikes at poor men's hovels and the towers of kings.

[*Odes*]

A[lfred] E[dward] Housman, 1859–1936, English poet and scholar

And silence sounds no worse than cheers
After death has stopped the ears.

[*A Shropshire Lad: To an Athlete Dying Young* 1896]

The man that runs away
Lives to die another day.

[*Ibid: The Day of Battle*]

Dolores Ibarruri ("La Pasionaria"), 1895–1989, Spanish revolutionary

It is better to die on your feet than to live on your knees.

[Speech 1936]

Helen [Maria Fiske] Hunt Jackson, 1830–85, American writer

Oh write of me, not "Died in bitter pains,"
But "Emigrated to another star!"

[*Emigravit*]

Thomas Jonathan ("Stonewall") Jackson, 1824–63, American Confederate general

Let us cross over the river, and rest under the trees.

[Last words]

Thomas Jefferson, 1743–1826, 3rd president of the United States

There is a fullness of time when men should go, and not occupy too long the ground to which others have a right to advance.

[Letter 1811]

I enjoy good health: I am happy in what is around me, yet I assure you I am ripe for leaving all this year, this day, this hour.

[*Ibid* 1816]

Sir Elton John [Reginald Kenneth Dwight], 1947– , British rock musician

And it seems to me you lived your life
Like a candle in the wind,
Never knowing who to cling to when the rain set in.

[Song: Candle In The Wind 1973]

Your candle burned out long before
Your legend ever did.

[*Ibid*]

Dr Samuel Johnson, 1709–84, English lexicographer

Prepare for death if here at night you roam,
And sign your will before you sup from home.

[*London*]

It matters not how a man dies, but how he lives.

[1769. In Boswell's *Life of Samuel Johnson* 1791]

All grief for what cannot in the course of nature be helped soon wears away.

[1777. In *Ibid*]

John Keats, 1795–1821, English poet
Darkling I listen; and for many a time
I have been half in love with easeful Death.

[*Ode to a Nightingale* 1818]

Thou was not born for death, immortal Bird!
No hungry generations tread thee down.

[*Ibid*]

John Keble, 1792–1866, English churchman and poet
Abide with me from morn till eve,
For without Thee I cannot live;
Abide with me when night is nigh,
For without Thee I dare not die.

[*The Christian Year: Evening* 1827]

Alphonse Marie Louis de Lamartine, 1790–1869, French statesman
What is our life but a succession of preludes to that unknown song whose first solemn note is
sounded by death?

[*Méditations Poétiques* 1820]

Timothy Leary, 1920–96, American psychologist
How you die is the most important thing you ever do. It's the exit, the final scene of the glorious epic of your life. It's the third act and, you know, everything builds up to the third act.

[In *The Guardian* December 2 1995.]

George Henry Lewes, 1817–78, English writer
The only cure for grief is action.

[*The Spanish Drama* 1846]

Georg Christoph Lichtenberg, 1742–99, German scientist and writer
I am always grieved when a man of real talent dies. The world needs such men more than
Heaven does.

[*Aphorismen* 1902–8]

Abraham Lincoln, 1809–65, 16th president of the United States
The world will little note nor long remember what we say here, but it can never forget what
they did here . . . It is rather for us to be here dedicated to the great task remaining before us
– that from these honoured dead we take increased devotion to that cause for which they gave
the last full measure of devotion; that we here highly resolve that these dead shall not have
died in vain.

[*The Gettysburg Address* 1863]

Henry Wadsworth Longfellow, 1807–82, American poet
There is no grief like the grief which does not speak.

[*Hyperion* 1839]

Louis VI (Louis the Fat), 1078–1137, king of France
Better a thousand times to die with glory than live without honour.

[Attributed]

Lucretius, c.99–c.55BC, Roman poet
Why shed tears that thou must die? For if thy past life has been one of enjoyment, and if all
thy pleasures have not passed through thy mind, as through a sieve, and vanished, leaving not

a rack behind, why then dost thou not, like a thankful guest, rise cheerfully from life's feast, and with a quiet mind go take thy rest?

[*De Natura Rerum* 57BC]

Thomas Babington Macaulay, 1st Baron Macaulay, 1800–59, English historian
There are not ten people in the world whose deaths would spoil my dinner, but there are one or two whose deaths would break my heart.

[Letter to Hannah Macaulay 1833]

Then out spake brave Horatius,
The captain of the gate:
"To every man upon this earth
Death cometh soon or late;
And how can man die better
Than facing fearful odds
For the ashes of his fathers
And the temples of his gods?"

[*Lays of Ancient Rome: Horatius* 1842]

Horace Mann, 1796–1859, American lawyer and educator
Be ashamed to die until you have won some victory for humanity.

[Address to students 1859]

Marcus Aurelius [Antoninus] [Marcus Annius Verus] AD121–80, Roman emperor
The act of dying is also one of the acts of life.

[*Meditations c.*170]

Mary, Queen of Scots, 1542–87, queen of Scotland
In my end is my beginning.

[Her motto after capture by the English 1568]

Mary Tudor, 1516–58, queen of England and Ireland
When I am dead and opened, you shall find "Calais" lying in my heart.

[In Holinshed's *Chronicles* 1577]

Cotton Mather, 1663–1728, American churchman
Is this dying? Is this all? Is this what I feared when I prayed against a hard death? Oh, I can bear this! I can bear it!

[Spoken on his deathbed]

Menander, c.343–291BC, Greek poet
Whom the gods love dies young.

[*Moyostikhoi c.*300BC]

H[enry] L[ouis] Mencken, 1880–1956, American critic and writer
Of all escape mechanisms, death is the most efficient.

[*A Book of Burlesques* 1928]

John Milton, 1608–74, English poet
Of Man's first disobedience, and the fruit
Of that forbidden tree, whose mortal taste
Brought death into the world, and all our woe.

[*Paradise Lost* 1667]

O'er many a frozen, many a fiery Alp,
Rocks, caves, lakes, fens, bogs, dens, and shades of death.

[*Ibid*]

I fled, and cry'd out Death;
Hell trembl'd at the hideous Name, and sigh'd.

[*Ibid*]

And over them triumphant Death his dart
Shook, but delay'd to strike, though oft invok'd
With vows, as their chief good, and final hope.

[*Ibid*]

Lady Mary Wortley Montagu, 1689–1762, English writer
He left a world he was weary of with the cool indifference you quit a dirty inn, to continue
your journey to a place where you hope for better accommodation.

[Letter 1759]

Thomas Moore, 1779–1852, Irish poet
Oh! ever thus, from childhood's hour,
I've seen my fondest hopes decay;
I never lov'd a tree or flow'r,
But 'twas the first to fade away.
I never nurs'd a dear gazelle,
To glad me with its soft black eye,
But when it came to know me well,
And love me, it was sure to die!

[*Lalla Rookh: The Fire Worshippers* 1817]

Sir Thomas More, 1478–1535, English statesman
I pray you, I pray you, Mr Lieutenant, see me safe up, and for my coming down let me shift
for myself.

[To the Governor of the Tower of London before his execution]

William Morris, 1834–96, English artist and poet
Wilt thou do the deed and repent it? thou hadst better never been born:
Wilt thou do the deed and exalt it? then thy fame shall be outworn:
Thou shalt do the deed and abide it, and sit on thy throne on high,
And look on today and tomorrow as those that never die.

[*Sigurd the Volsung* 1876]

John Muir, 1838–1914, Scottish-born American naturalist
On no subject are our ideas more warped and pitiable than on death . . . Let children walk
with nature, let them see the beautiful blendings and communions of death and life, their
joyous inseparable united, as taught in woods and meadows, plains and mountains and
streams of our blessed star, and they will learn that death is stingless indeed, and as beautiful
as life, and that the grave has no victory, for it never fights. All is divine harmony.

[*A Thousand-Mile Walk to the Gulf* 1916]

Dame Iris Murdoch, 1919–99, English novelist and philosopher
Bereavement is a darkness impenetrable to the imagination of the unbereaved.

[The Sacred and Profane Love Machine 1974]

Sir Henry John Newbolt, 1862–1938, English poet
The river of death has brimmed his banks,
And England's far, and Honour a name,
But the voice of a schoolboy rallies the ranks:
"Play up! play up! and play the game!"

[*Vitai Lampada*]

Dorothy [Rothschild] Parker, 1893–1967, American writer
[When told that Calvin Coolidge had died] How could they tell?

[Attributed 1933]

Razors pain you
Rivers are damp;
Acids stain you;
And drugs cause cramp.
Guns aren't lawful,
Nooses give;
Gas smells awful;
You might as well live.

[*Enough Rope: Résumé* 1926]

Anna Pavlova, 1885–1931, Russian-born ballerina
Get my Swan costume ready.

[Last words]

Octavio Paz, 1914–98, Mexican poet
We are condemned
to kill time:
Thus we die
bit by bit.

[*Cuento de los Jardines* 1968]

Samuel Pepys, 1633–1703, English diarist
I went out to Charing Cross, to see Major-General Harrison hanged, drawn and quartered;
which was done there, he looking as cheerful as any man could do in that condition.

[*Diary* 13 October 1660]

Sylvia Plath, 1932–63, American-born poet
Dying
Is an art, like everything else.
I do it exceptionally well.

[*Lady Lazarus* 1966]

Plato, c.428–348BC, Greek philosopher
The hour of departure has arrived, and we go our ways – I to die, and you to live. Which is
better God only knows.

[*Dialogues Phaedo*]

Man is a prisoner who has no right to open the door of his prison and run away . . . A man
should wait, and not take his own life until God summons him.

[*Ibid*]

114

Edward Pollock, 1823–58, English poet

The one who goes is happier
Than those he leaves behind.

[The Parting Hour]

Alexander Pope, 1688–1744, English poet

Thus let me live, unseen, unknown,
Thus unlamented let me die,
Steal from the world, and not a stone
Tell where I lie.

[Ode on Solitude]

By foreign hands thy dying eyes were closed,
By foreign hands thy decent limbs composed,
By foreign hands thy humble grave adorned,
By strangers honoured and by strangers mourned.

[Elegy to the Memory of an Unfortunate Lady 1717]

Such were the notes thy once-loved poet sung,
Till death untimely stopp'd his tuneful tongue.

[Epistle to Robert, Earl of Oxford]

But thousands die, without or this or that,
Die, and endow a college or a cat.

[Moral Essays 1731–5]

Posidippus, *fl.* c.275BC, Greek writer

Of all the boons that man asks of the gods, he prays most fervently for an easy death.

*[Fragment c.*75BC]

Marcel Proust, 1871–1922, French novelist

Happiness is beneficial for the body, but it is grief that develops the powers of the mind.

[Remembrance of Things Past 1913–26]

Sir Walter Raleigh, c.1552–1618, English explorer and poet

O eloquent, just, and mighty Death! whom none could advise, thou hast persuaded; what none hath dared, thou hast done; and whom all the world hath flattered, thou only hast cast out of the world and despised: thou hast drawn together all the far-stretched greatness, all the pride, cruelty, and ambition of men, and covered it all over with these two narrow words, *Hic jacet!*

[History of the World 1614]

Cecil John Rhodes, 1853–1902, South African politician

So much to do; so little done.

[Said on his deathbed]

Theodore Roosevelt, 1858–1919, 26th president of the United States

Put out the light.

[Last words]

Christina Georgina Rossetti, 1830–94, English poet

When I am dead, my dearest,
Sing no sad songs for me.

[When I am Dead]

115

Better by far you should forget and smile
Than that you should remember and be sad.

[Ibid]

Dante Gabriel Rossetti, 1828–82, English poet

A sonnet is a moment's monument, –
Memorial from the Soul's eternity
To one dead deathless hour.

[The House of Life Introduction 1870]

When vain desire at last and vain regret
Go hand in hand to death.

[Ibid: The One Hope]

Nicholas Rowe, 1674–1718, English playwright

Death is the privilege of human nature,
And life without it were not worth our taking.

[The Fair Penitent 1703]

Arundhati Roy, 1961– , Indian novelist

The Loss of Sophie Mol stepped softly around the Ayemenem House like a quiet thing in socks. It hid in books and food. In Mammachi's violin case. In the scabs of the sores on Chacko's shins that he constantly worried. In his slack, womanish legs.
It is curious how sometimes the memory of death lives on for so much longer than the life it purloined. Over the years, as the memory of Sophie Mol (. . .) slowly faded, the Loss of Sophie Mol grew robust and alive.

[The God of Small Things 1997]

Saki [Hector Hugh Munro], 1870–1916, Scottish-born writer

Waldo is one of those people who would be enormously improved by death.

[Beasts and Super-Beasts: The Feast of Nemesis 1914]

J[erome] D[avid] Salinger, 1919– , American novelist

I hope to hell when I do die somebody has sense enough to just dump me in the river or something. Anything except sticking me in a goddam cemetery.

[The Catcher in the Rye 1951]

Arthur Schopenhauer, 1788–1860, German philosopher

Each day is a little life; every walking and rising a little birth, every fresh morning a little youth, every going to rest and sleep a little death.

[Our Relation to Ourselves 1851]

After your death you will be what you were before your birth.

[Parerga and Paralipomena 1851]

Sir Walter Scott, 1771–1832, Scottish novelist

And come he slow, or come he fast,
It is but Death who comes at last.

[Marmion 1808]

Alan Seeger, 1888–1916, English poet

I have a rendezvous with Death
At some disputed barricade,
At midnight in some flaming town.

[I Have a Rendezvous with Death]

DEATH, PARTING AND SORROW

Peter ("Pete") Seeger, 1919– , American folksinger

Where have all the flowers gone?
The girls have picked them every one.
Oh, when will they ever learn.

[*Where Have All the Flowers Gone?* 1961]

Samuel Sewall, 1652–1730, American judge

About midnight my dear wife expired to our great astonishment, especially mine.

[*Diary* 26 May 1720]

William Shakespeare 1564–1616, English dramatist

Fear no more the heat o' the sun,
Nor the furious winter's rages;
Thou thy worldly task hast done,
Home art gone, and ta'en thy wages.

[*Cymbeline* 4 1609–10]

Lord, Lord! methought, what pain it was to drown!
What dreadful noise of waters in mine ears!
What ugly sights of death within mine eyes!
Methought I saw a thousand fearful wrecks;
Ten thousand men that fishes gnaw'd upon.

[*King Richard III* 1 1592–3]

Good night, good night! parting is such sweet sorrow,
That I shall say good night till it be morrow.

[*Romeo and Juliet* 2 1594–5]

Eyes, look your last!
Arms, take your last embrace.

[*Ibid* 5]

Doomsday is near; die all, die merrily.

[*King Henry IV, Part I* 3 1597–8]

A man can die but once.

[*King Henry IV, Part II* 3 1597–8]

If we are mark'd to die, we are enow
To do our country loss; and if to live
The fewer men, the greater share of honour.

[*King Henry V* 4 1598–1600]

This day is call'd the feast of Crispian,
He that outlives this day, and comes safe home,
Will stand a tip-toe when this day is named,
And rouse him at the name of Crispian.

[*Ibid*]

Patch grief with proverbs.

[*Much Ado About Nothing* 5 1598–1600]

Done to death by slanderous tongues.

[*Ibid*]

Men have died from time to time and worms have eaten them, but not for love.

[*As You Like It* 4 1598–1600]

Come away, come away, death,
And in sad cypress let me be laid;
Fly away, fly away, breath;
I am slain by a fair cruel maid.
My shroud of white, stock all with yew,
O, prepare it!
My part of death, no one so true
Did share it.

[*Twelfth Night* 2 1598–1600]

Set honour in one eye and death i' the other,
And I will look on both indifferently.

[*Julius Caesar* 1 1598–1600]

When beggars die, there are no comets seen;
The heavens themselves blaze forth the death of princes.

[*Ibid* 2]

Cowards die many times before their deaths;
The valiant never taste of death but once.

[*Ibid*]

Why, he that cuts off twenty years of life
Cuts off so many years of fearing death.

[*Ibid* 3]

As Caesar loved me, I weep for him; as he was fortunate, I rejoice at it; as he was valiant, I honour him; but as he was ambitious, I slew him. There is tears for his love; joy for his fortune; honour for his valour; and death for his ambition.

[*Ibid*]

If we do not meet again, why, we shall smile!
If not, why then, this parting was well made.

[*Ibid* 5]

Thou know'st 'tis common; all that lives must die,
Passing through nature to eternity.

[*Hamlet* 1 1600–1601]

To be or not to be: that is the question:
Whether 'tis nobler in the mind to suffer
The slings and arrows of outrageous fortune,
Or to take arms against a sea of troubles,
And by opposing end them? To die: to sleep;
No more; and by a sleep to say we end
The heartache and the thousand natural shocks
That flesh is heir to, 'tis a consummation
Devoutly to be wished. To die, to sleep:
To sleep: perchance to dream: ay, there's the rub;
For in that sleep of death what dreams may come
When we have shuffled off this mortal coil,
Must give us pause.

[*Ibid* 3]

Sweets to the sweet: farewell.

[*Ibid* 5]

Be absolute for death; either death or life
Shall thereby be the sweeter. Reason thus with life:
If I do lose thee, I do lose a thing
That none but fools would keep: a breath thou art,
Servile to all the skyey influences.

[*Measure for Measure* 3 1604–5]

The sense of death is most in apprehension;
And the poor beetle, that we tread upon,
In corporal sufferance finds a pang as great
As when a giant dies.

[*Ibid*]

If I must die
I will encounter darkness as a bride,
And hug it in mine arms.

[*Ibid*]

The weariest and most loathed wordly life
That age, ache, penury and imprisonment
Can lay on nature is a paradise
To what we fear of death.

[*Ibid*]

Nothing in his life
Became him like the leaving it; he died
As one that had been studied in his death
To throw away the dearest thing he ow'd,
As 'twere a careless trifle.

[*Macbeth* 1 1605–6]

Methought I heard a voice cry "Sleep no more!
Macbeth does murder sleep," the innocent sleep,
Sleep that knits up the ravell'd sleave of care,
The death of each day's life, sore labour's bath,
Balm of hurt minds, great nature's second course,
Chief nourisher in life's feast.

[*Ibid* 2]

Shake off this downy sleep, death's counterfeit,
And look on death itself!

[*Ibid*]

Hear it not, Duncan; for it is a knell
That summons thee to heaven or to hell.

[*Ibid*]

Tomorrow, and tomorrow, and tomorrow,
Creeps in this petty pace from day to day,
To the last syllable of recorded time;
And all our yesterdays have lighted fools
The way to dusty death. Out, out, brief candle!
Life's but a walking shadow, a poor player
That struts and frets his hour upon the stage,
And then is heard no more; it is a tale
Told by an idiot, full of sound and fury
Signifying nothing.

[*Ibid* 5]

Blow wind! come, wrack!
At least we'll die with harness on our back.

[*Ibid* 5]

I am dying, Egypt, dying; only
I here importune death while, until
Of many thousand kisses the poor last
I lay upon thy lips.

[*Antony and Cleopatra* 4 1606–7]

What's brave, what's noble,
Let's do it after the high Roman fashion,
And make death proud to take us.

[*Ibid*]

Finish, good lady; the bright day is done,
And we are for the dark.

[*Ibid* 5]

Give me my robe, put on my crown; I have
Immortal longings in me.

[*Ibid*]

If thou and nature can so gently part,
The stroke of death is as a lover's pinch
Which hurts, and is desired.

[*Ibid*]

But if the while I think on thee, dear friend,
All losses are restored and sorrows end.

[*Sonnets* 30 1609]

Like as the waves make towards the pebbled shore,
So do our minutes hasten to their end.

[*Ibid* 60]

Tired with all these, for restful death I cry.

[*Ibid* 56]

In me thou see'st the twilight of such day
As after sunset fadeth in the west,
Which by and by black night doth take away,
Death's second self, that seals up all in rest.

[*Ibid* 73]

He that dies pays all debts.

[*The Tempest* 3 1611–12]

George Bernard Shaw, 1856–1950, Irish playwright
In heaven an angel is nobody in particular.

[*Man and Superman: Maxims for Revolutionists* 1903]

Life levels all men: death reveals the eminent.

[*Ibid*]

Wilfred [John Joseph] Sheed, 1930– , English-born American novelist
Suicide . . . is about life, being in fact the sincerest form of criticism life gets.

[*The Good Word* 1978]

Percy Bysshe Shelley, 1792–1822, English poet
How wonderful is Death,
Death and his brother Sleep.

[*Queen Mab* 1813]

120

First our pleasures die – and then
Our hopes, and then our fears – and when
These are dead, the debt is due.

[*Prometheus Unbound* 1818–19]

Peace is in the grave.
The grave hides all things beautiful and good:
I am a God and cannot find it there.

[*Ibid*]

Death is the veil which those who live call life:
They sleep, and it is lifted.

[*Ibid*]

Dust claims dust – and we die too.

[*Death* 1820]

It might make one in love with death, to think that one should be buried in so sweet a place.

[*Adonais* preface, 1821]

He has outsoared the shadow of our night;
Envy and calumny and hate and pain,
And that unrest which men miscall delight
Can touch him not and torture not again.

[*Ibid*]

To that high Capital, where kingly Death
Keeps his pale court in beauty and decay.

[*Ibid*]

Oh, cease! must hate and death return?
Cease! must men kill and die?
Cease! drain not to its dregs the urn
Of bitter prophecy.
The world is weary of the past,
Oh, might it die or rest at last!

[*Hellas* 1821]

Some say that gleams of a remoter world
Visit the soul in sleep, – that death is slumber.

[*Mont Blanc*]

The flower that smiles today
Tomorrow dies.

[*Mutability*]

Simonides of Ceos, c.556–c.468BC, Greek poet
Go tell the Spartans, thou that passeth by,
That here, obedient to the laws, we lie.

[Epitaph for the Spartans who fell at Thermopylae 480BC]

Florence Margaret ("Stevie") Smith, 1902–71, English poet
I was much too far out all my life
And not waving but drowning.

[*Not Waving but Drowning* 1957]

Tobias [George] Smollett, 1721–71, Scottish novelist and surgeon
Death's like the best bower anchor, as the saying is, it will bring us all up.

[*Roderick Random* 1748]

121

Sophocles, c.496–c.406BC, Greek poet
Death is not the greatest of ills; it is worse to want to die, and not be able to.

[*Electra c.*450BC]

Edmund Spenser, c.1552–99, English poet
Sleep after toil, port after stormy seas,
Ease after war, death after life, does greatly please.

[*The Faerie Queene* 1590–96]

Stanislaus {Leszczynski}, 1677–1766, king of Poland
He who fears death dies every time he thinks of it.

[*Oeuvres du philosophe bienfaisant* 1763]

Laurence Sterne, 1713–68, English churchman and writer
"He shall not die, by G – – ," cried my uncle Toby. – The Accusing Spirit, which flew up to heaven's chancery with the oath, blushed as he gave it in; and the Recording Angel, as he wrote it down, dropped a tear upon the word, and blotted it out for ever.

[*Tristram Shandy* 1760]

Robert Louis [Balfour] Stevenson, 1850–94, Scottish novelist and poet
Under the wide and starry sky,
Dig the grave and let me lie.

[*Underwoods: Requiem* 1887]

This be the verse you grave for me:
"Here he lies where he longed to be;
Home is the sailor, home from sea,
And the hunter home from the hill."

[*Ibid*]

Here lies one who meant well, tried a little, failed much: – surely that may be his epitaph of which he need not be ashamed.
[*Across the Plains* 1892]

Suetonius [Gaius Suetonius Tranquillus], ADc.70–c.140, Roman biographer
Ave, Imperator, morituri te salutant.
(Hail, Caesar, those about to die salute thee.)

[*Life of Claudius*]

Jonathan Swift,1667–1745, Irish-born English writer
I shall be like that tree, I shall die at the top.

[In Walter Scott's *Memoirs of Jonathan Swift* 1814]

[Edmund] John Millington Synge, 1871–1909, Irish playwright
I have put away sorrow like a shoe that is worn out and muddy, for it is I have had a life that will be envied by great companies.

[*Deirdre of the Sorrows* 1910]

Henry John Temple, 3rd Viscount Palmerston, 1784–1865, British statesman
Die, my dear Doctor, that's the last thing I shall do!

[Attributed last words]

DEATH, PARTING AND SORROW

Alfred, Lord Tennyson, 1809–92, English poet
Their meetings made December June,
Their every parting was to die.

[*In Memoriam* 1850]

Half a league, half a league,
Half a league onward,
All in the valley of Death
Rode the six hundred.

[*The Charge of the Light Brigade* 1854]

Their's not to make reply,
Their's not to reason why,
Their's but to do and die:
Into the valley of Death
Rode the six hundred.

[*Ibid*]

Twilight and evening bell,
And after that the dark!
And may there be no sadness of farewell,
When I embark.

[*Crossing the Bar* 1889]

For men may come and men may go,
But I go on for ever.

[*The Brook*]

Tertullian, c.160–c.230, Roman Christian theologian
It is a poor thing for anyone to fear that which is inevitable.

[*The Testimony of the Christian Soul c.*210]

Lewis Thomas, 1913– 93, American scientist
We are, perhaps uniquely among the earth's creatures, the worrying animal. We worry away our lives, fearing the future, discontent with the present, unable to take in the idea of dying, unable to sit still.

[*The Medusa and the Snail* 1979]

Francis Thompson, 1859–1907, English poet
She went her unremembering way,
She went and left in me
The pang of all the partings gone,
And partings yet to be.
[*Daisy*]

James Thomson, 1834–82, Scottish poet
The City is of Night; perchance of Death,
But certainly of Night; for never there
Can come the lucid morning's fragrant breath
After the dewy dawning's cold grey air.

[*The City of Dreadful Night* 1874]

Ivan Sergeyevich Turgenev, 1818–83, Russian novelist
Go and try to disprove death. Death will disprove you, and that's all.

[*Fathers and Sons* 1862]

Mark Twain [Samuel Langhorne Clemens], 1835–1910, American writer
All say, "How hard it is that we have to die" – a strange complaint to come from the mouths of people who have had to live.
[*Pudd'nhead Wilson* 1894]
Death, the only immortal who treats us all alike, whose pity and whose peace and whose refuge are for all – the soiled and the pure, the rich and the poor, the loved and the unloved.
[*Notebooks* 1935 (written on his deathbed)]
The reports of my death are greatly exaggerated.
[Cable to Associated Press from Europe]

George Washington, 1732–99, 1st president of the United States
Doctor, I die hard, but I am not afraid to go.
[Last words]

Ethel Waters, 1896–1977, American actress and singer
I'm not afraid to die, honey. In fact, I'm kind of looking forward to it. I know that the Lord has his arms wrapped around this big, fat sparrow.

John Webster, c.1578–c.1632, English dramatist
I saw him now going the way of all flesh.
[*Westward Hoe* 1607]

Death hath ten thousand several doors
For men to take their exit.
[*The Duchess of Malfi* c.1614]

Oscar [Fingall O'Flahertie Wills] Wilde, 1854–1900, Irish writer
For he who lives more lives than one
More deaths than one must die.
[*The Ballad of Reading Gaol* 1898]
[On being faced with a large bill for an operation] I suppose that I shall have to die beyond my means.
[In R.H. Sherard's *Life of Oscar Wilde*]
A thing is not necessarily true because a man dies for it.
[*Sebastian Melmoth*]

William Wordsworth, 1770–1850, English poet
There is
One great society alone on earth;
The noble Living and the noble Dead.
[*The Prelude* 1799–1805]

Sir Henry Wotton, 1568–1639, English diplomat and poet
He first deceased; she for a little tried
To live without him, liked it not, and died.
[*The Death of Sir Albertus Morton's Wife*]

William Butler Yeats, 1865–1939, Irish poet
I know that I shall meet my fate
Somewhere among the clouds above;
Those that I fight I do not hate,
Those that I guard I do not love.
[*An Irish Airman Foresees his Death* 1919]

124

O but we talked at large before
The sixteen men were shot,
But who can talk of give and take,
What should be and what not
While those dead men are loitering there
To stir the boiling pot?

[*Sixteen Dead Men* 1920]

A man awaits his end
Dreading and hoping all;
Many times he died,
Many times rose again.

[*Death* 1929]

What can they know that we know that know the time to die?

[*The Curse of Cromwell* 1937]

A drunkard is a dead man
And all dead men are drunk.

[*A Drunken Man's Praise of Sobriety* 1938]

Edward Young, 1683–1765, English churchman and poet
Death but entombs the body; life the soul.

[*Night III; Night Thoughts*]

Education and Knowledge

Henry [Brooks] Adams, 1838–1918, American historian
A teacher affects eternity; he can never tell where his influence stops.

[*The Education of Henry Adams* 1907]

Those who seek education in the paths of duty are always deceived by the illusion that power in the hands of friends is an advantage to them.

[*Ibid*]

John Quincy Adams, 1767–1848, 6th president of the United States
To furnish the means of acquiring knowledge is . . . the greatest benefit that can be conferred upon mankind. It prolongs life itself and enlarges the sphere of existence.

[*Report on the establishment of the Smithsonian Institution c.*1846]

Joseph Addison, 1672–1719, English essayist
Education is a companion which no misfortune can depress, no crime can destroy, no enemy can alienate, no despotism can enslave. At home a friend, abroad an introduction, in solitude a solace, and in society an ornament. It chastens vice, it guides virtue, it gives, at once, grace and government to genius. Without it, what is man? A splendid slave, a reasoning savage.

[*The Spectator* 1711]

[Amos] Bronson Alcott, 1799–1888, American philosopher
To be ignorant of one's ignorance is the malady of the ignorant.

[*Table Talk: Discourse* 1877]

Anonymous
A little knowledge is a dangerous thing.

[Proverb]

Knowledge in youth is wisdom in age.

[Proverb]

Knowledge is silver among the poor, gold among the nobles, and a jewel among princes.

[Italian proverb]

Francis Bacon, Baron Verulam of Verulam and Viscount of St Albans, 1561–1626, English philosopher
If a man will begin with certainties, he shall end in doubts; but if he will be content to begin with doubts, he shall end in certainties.

[*The Advancement of Learning* 1605]

I have taken all knowledge to be my province.

[Letter 1592]

126

Sir J[ames] M[atthew] Barrie, 1860–1937, Scottish playwright
Facts were never pleasing to him. He acquired them with reluctance and got rid of them with relief. He was never on terms with them until he had stood them on their heads.

[*Love Me Never or For Ever*]

Jacques [Martin] Barzun, 1907– , French-born American scholar.
The young man who is not a radical about something is a pretty poor risk for education.

[*Teacher in America*]

The Bible
Wisdom is the principal thing; therefore get wisdom: and with all thy getting get understanding.

[*Proverbs* 4:7]

He that hath knowledge spareth his words: and a man of understanding is of an excellent spirit.

[*Ibid* 17:27]

For in much wisdom is much grief: and he that increaseth knowledge increaseth sorrow.

[*Ecclesiastes* 1:18]

Paul, thou art beside thyself; much learning doth make thee mad.

[*Acts* 26:24]

Ambrose [Gwinett] Bierce, 1842–1914, American writer
Education: that which discloses to the wise and disguises from the foolish their lack of understanding.

[*The Devil's Dictionary* 1906]

Erudition: dust shaken out of a book into an empty skull.

[*Ibid*]

Learning: the kind of ignorance distinguishing the studious.

[*Ibid*]

Charles Synge Christopher Bowen, Baron Bowen of Colwood, 1835–94, English judge
[On a metaphysician] A blind man in a dark room – looking for a black hat – which isn't there.

[Attributed]

Bertolt Brecht, 1898–1956, German dramatist and poet
The world of knowledge takes a crazy turn
When teachers themselves are taught to learn.

[*The Life of Galileo* 1939]

Jacob Bronowski, 1908–74, Polish-born British scientist
That is the essence of science: ask an impertinent question, and you are on the way to a pertinent answer.

[*The Ascent of Man* 1973]

It is important that students bring a certain ragamuffin barefoot irreverence to their studies; they are not here to worship what is known, but to question it.

[*The Ascent of Man* 1975]

Charlotte Brontë, 1816–55, English novelist
Prejudices, it is well known, are most difficult to eradicate from the heart whose soil has never been loosened or fertilized by education; they grow there, firm as weeds among stones.

[*Jane Eyre* 1847]

127

Henry Peter Brougham, 1st Baron Brougham and Vaux, 1778–1868, British law reformer
The schoolmaster is abroad, and I trust to him, armed with his primer, against the soldier in full military array.

[Speech in the House of Commons 1828]

Education makes a people easy to lead, but difficult to drive; easy to govern, but impossible to enslave.

[Attributed]

Sir William Browne, 1692–1774, English physician
The King to Oxford sent a troop of horse,
For Tories own no argument but force:
With equal care to Cambridge books he sent,
For Whigs allow no force but argument.

[Reply to Trapp (see Trapp below)]

[John] Anthony Burgess [Wilson], 1917–93, English-born novelist and critic
None of the teachers knew very much about what they taught and it was pathetic, sometimes, the way they tried to make our schooldays happy.

[*One Hand Clapping*]

Edmund Burke, 1729–97, Irish-born English political writer
Learning will be cast into the mire and trodden down under the hoofs of a swinish multitude.

[*Reflections on the Revolution in France* 1790]

Robert Burns, 1759–96, Scottish poet
His locked, letter'd, braw brass collar,
Show'd him the gentleman and scholar.

[*The Twa Dogs*]

Nicholas Murray Butler, 1862–1947, American philosopher
An expert is one who knows more and more about less and less.

[Address, Columbia University, New York]

Thomas Carlyle, 1795–1881, Scottish historian and writer
The true university of these days is a collection of books.

[*Heroes and Hero Worship: The Hero as Divinity* 1840]

[On political economy] The Dismal Science.

[*Latter-day Pamphlets: The Present Time* 1850]

Carlos Castaneda, 1925?–1998, American anthropologist and writer.
When a man begins to learn, he is never clear about his objectives. His purpose is faulty; his intent is vague. He hopes for rewards that will never materialize, for he knows nothing of the hardships of learning.

[*The Teachings of Don Juan*, 1968]

Geoffrey Chaucer, c.1340–1400, English poet
And French she spake ful fayre and fetisly,
After the scole of Stratford-atte-Bowe.

[*The Canterbury Tales: Prologue* c.1387]

And gladly wolde he lerne and gladly teche.

[*Ibid*]

Sir Winston [Leonard Spencer] Churchill, 1874–1965, British statesman
It is a good thing for an uneducated man to read books of quotations . . . The quotations when engraved upon the memory give you good thoughts. They also make you anxious to read the authors and look for more.

[*My Early Life*: *Roving Commission* 1930]

Arthur Hugh Clough, 1819–61, English poet
Grace is given of God, but knowledge is bought in the market.

[*The Bothie of Tober-na-Vuolich* 1848]

Samuel Taylor Coleridge, 1772–1834, English poet
To most men, experience is like the stern lights of a ship, which illumine only the track it has passed.

[To Thomas Allsop *c*.1820]

Confucius [K'ung fu-tzu], 551–479BC, Chinese philosopher
Learning without thought is labour lost; thought without learning is perilous.

[*Analects c.*500BC]

William Cowper, 1731–1800, English poet
Knowledge is proud that he has learn'd so much;
Wisdom is humble that he knows no more.

[*The Task: The Winter Walk at Noon* 1785]

René Descartes, 1596–1650, French philosopher
One cannot conceive anything so strange and so implausible that it has not already been said by one philosopher or another.

[*Le Discours de la Méthode* 1637]

Charles [John Huffam] Dickens, 1812–70, English novelist
A smattering of everything and a knowledge of nothing.

[*Sketches by Boz* 1836–7]

Mr Weller's knowledge of London was extensive and peculiar.

[*Pickwick Papers* 1837–7]

"Now what I want is, Facts. Teach these boys and girls nothing but Facts. Facts alone are wanted in life. Plant nothing else, and root out everything else . . . Stick to Facts, sir!"

[*Hard Times* 1854]

Diogenes [Laertius], *fl.* 2nd century BC, Greek historian
On one occasion Aristotle was asked how much educated men were superior to those uneducated; "As much," said he, "as the living are to the dead."

[*Lives of the Philosophers c.*150BC]

Benjamin Disraeli, 1st Earl of Beaconsfield, 1804–81, British statesman and novelist
A university should be a place of light, of liberty, and of learning.

[Speech in the House of Commons 1873]

Fyodor Mikhailovich Dostoevsky, 1821–81, Russian novelist
You are told a lot about your education, but some beautiful, sacred memory, preserved since childhood, is perhaps the best education of all. If a man carries many such memories into life with him, he is saved for the rest of his days. And even if only one good memory is left in our hearts, it may also be the instrument of our salvation one day.

[*The Brothers Karamazov* 1880]

129

John Dryden, 1631–1700, English dramatist
By education most have been misled;
So they believe, because they so were bred,
The priest continues what the nurse began,
And thus the child imposes on the man.

[*The Hind and the
Panther* 1687]

Umberto Eco, 1932– , Italian novelist and semiotician
Learning does not consist only of knowing what we must or we can do, but also of knowing what we could do and perhaps should not do.

[*The Name of the Rose*, 1980]

Albert Einstein, 1879–1955, German-born mathematical physicist
It is the supreme art of the teacher to awaken joy in creative expression and knowledge.

[*Out of My Later Years* 1950]

Henry Fielding, 1707–54, English novelist
Public schools are the nurseries of all vice and immorality.

[*Joseph Andrews* 1742]

Anatole France [Jacques Anatole Thibault], 1844–1924, French novelist and critic
The whole art of teaching is only the art of awakening the natural curiosity of young minds for the purpose of satisfying it afterwards.

[*The Crime of Sylvestre
Bonnard* 1881]

Thomas Fuller, 1608–61, English churchman and writer
Learning hath gained most by those books by which the printers have lost.

[*The Holy State and the
Profane State: Of Books* 1642]

James Abram Garfield, 1831–81, 20th president of the United States
Next in importance to freedom and justice is popular education, without which neither freedom nor justice can be permanently maintained.

[Letter of
acceptance 1880]

Sir William Schwenck Gilbert, 1836–1911, English librettist
You must lie upon the daisies and discourse in novel phrases of your complicated state of mind,
The meaning doesn't matter if it's only idle chatter of a transcendental kind.

[*Patience* 1881]

"If this young man expresses himself in terms too deep for *me*,
Why, what a very singularly deep young man this deep young man must be!"

[*Ibid*]

Oliver Goldsmith, 1728–74, Irish-born English writer
A man severe he was, and stern to view;
I knew him well, and every truant knew;
Well had the boding tremblers learn'd to trace
The day's disasters in his morning face;
Full well they laugh'd, with counterfeited glee,
At all his jokes, for many a joke had he;
Full well the busy whisper, circling round,
Convey'd the dismal tidings when he frown'd;
Yet he was kind; or if severe in aught,
The love he bore to learning was in fault.

[*The Deserted Village* 1770]

In arguing too, the parson own'd his skill,
For e'en though vanquish'd, he could argue still;
While words of learned length and thund'ring sound
Amazed the gazing rustics rang'd around,
And still they gaz'd, and still the wonder grew,
That one small head could carry all he knew.

[*Ibid*]

Kenneth Grahame, 1859–1932, English writer
The clever men at Oxford
Know all that there is to be knowed.
But they none of them know half as much
As intelligent Mr Toad.

[*The Wind in the Willows* 1908]

William Harvey, 1578–1657, English physician
All we know is still infinitely less than all that still remains unknown.

[*De Motu Cordis et Sanguinis* 1628]

William Hazlitt, 1778–1830, English essayist
Boys who shine at school do not make the greatest figures when they grow up and come out into the world.

[*Table Talk: On the Ignorance of the Learned* 1821–2]

Joseph Heller, 1923–99, American novelist
To know that you do not know is to know a great deal.
[*Picture This* 1988]

Oliver Wendell Holmes, 1809–94, American physician and writer
The world's great men have not commonly been great scholars, nor its great scholars great men.

[*The Autocrat of the Breakfast Table* 1858]

Science is a first-rate piece of furniture for a man's upper chamber, if he has common sense on the ground floor.

[*The Poet at the Breakfast Table* 1872]

Thomas Hughes, 1822–96, English writer
Life isn't all beer and skittles; but beer and skittles, or something better of the same sort, must form a good part of every Englishman's education.

[*Tom Brown's Schooldays* 1857]

Thomas Henry Huxley, 1825–95, English biologist
If a little knowledge is dangerous, where is the man who has so much as to be out of danger?
[*On Elemental Instruction in Physiology* 1877]
Perhaps the most valuable result of all education is the ability to make yourself do the thing you have to do, when it ought to be done, whether you like it or not; it is the first lesson that ought to be learned; and however early a man's training begins, it is probably the last lesson that he learns thoroughly.
[*Technical Education* 1877]

Eugene Ionesco, 1912–94, Romanian-born French playwright
Arithmetic leads to Philology, and Philology leads to Crime.
[*The Lesson*]

Dr Samuel Johnson, 1709–84, English lexicographer
Integrity without knowledge is weak and useless, and knowledge without integrity is dangerous and dreadful.
[*Rasselas* 1759]
Knowledge is of two kinds. We know a subject ourselves, or we know where we can find information upon it.
[1775. In Boswell's *Life of Samuel Johnson* 1791]
Dictionaries are like watches; the worse is better than none, and the best cannot be expected to go quite true.
[In Mrs Piozzi's *Anecdotes* 1786]

John Fitzgerald Kennedy, 1917–63, 35th president of the United States
Liberty without learning is always in peril and learning without liberty is always in vain.
[On the 90th anniversary of Vanderbilt University 1963]

William Lamb, 2nd Viscount Melbourne, 1779–1848, English statesman
I don't know, Ma'am, why they make all this fuss about education; none of the Pagets can read or write, and they get on well enough.
[Remark to Queen Victoria]

Thomas Babington Macaulay, Baron Macaulay, 1800–1859, English historian
Every schoolboy knows who imprisoned Montezuma, and who strangled Atahualpa.
[*Essays: Lord Clive*]
[On Richard Steele] He was a rake among scholars, and a scholar among rakes.
[*Essays: Aikin's Life of Addison*]

Christopher Marlowe, 1564–93, English dramatist
Nature that fram'd us of four elements,
Warring within our breasts for regiment,
Doth teach us all to have aspiring minds:
Our souls, whose faculties can comprehend
The wondrous architecture of the world:
And measure every wand'ring planet's course,
Still climbing after knowledge infinite,
And always moving as the restless Spheres,
Will us to wear ourselves and never rest,
Until we reach the ripest fruit of all,
That perfect bliss and sole felicity,
The sweet fruition of an earthly crown.
[*Tamburlaine the Great* 1590]

John Milton, 1608–74, English poet
Where there is much desire to learn, there of necessity will be much arguing, much writing, many opinions; for opinion in good men is but knowledge in the making.

[*Areopagitica* 1644]

Maria Montessori, 1870–1952, Italian educationist and physician
If education is always to be conceived along the same antiquated lines of a mere transmission of knowledge, there is little to be hoped from it in the bettering of man's future. For what is the use of transmitting knowledge if the individual's total development lags behind?

[*The Absorbent Mind* 1949]

Johann Heinrich Pestalozzi,1746–1827, Swiss educationist
Not art, not·books, but life itself is the true basis of teaching and education
[In Heinz and Ruth Norden's *The Education of Man: Aphorisms* 1951]

Alexander Pope, 1688–1744, English poet
A little learning is a dangerous thing;
Drink deep, or taste not the Pierian spring:
There shallow draughts intoxicate the brain,
And drinking largely sobers us again.

[*Essay on Criticism* 1711]

Know then thyself, presume not God to scan,
The proper study of mankind is man.

[*Moral Essays* 1734]

'Tis education forms the common mind:
Just as the twig is bent, the tree's inclined.

[*Ibid*]

Ezra [Loomis] Pound, 1885–1967, American poet
Real education must ultimately be limited to men who insist on knowing; the rest is mere sheep-herding.

[*ABC of Reading*]

Sir Walter Alexander Raleigh, 1861–1922, English academic
In an examination those who do not wish to know ask questions of those who cannot tell.
[*Laughter from a Cloud: Some Thoughts on Examinations*]

Cecil John Rhodes, 1853–1902, South African politician
Educational relations make the strongest tie.
[In his will, establishing the Rhodes Scholarship scheme]

Sir Walter Scott, 1771–1832, Scottish novelist
All men who have turned out worth anything have had the chief hand in their own education.
[Letter 1830]

Peter ("Pete") Seeger, 1919– , American folksinger
Do you know the difference between education and experience? Education is when you read the fine print; experience is what you get when you don't.
[In Linda Botts' *Loose Talk* 1980]

William Shakespeare, 1564–1616, English dramatist
Thou hast most traitorously corrupted the youth of the realm in erecting a grammar school; and whereas, before, our forefathers had no other books but the score and tally, thou hast

caused printing to be used, and, contrary to the king, his crown and dignity, thou hast built a paper-mill.

[*King Henry VI, Part II* 4 1591]

Away with him, away with him! he speaks Latin.

[*Ibid*]

An unlesson'd girl, unschool'd, unpractised;
Happy in this, she is not yet so old
But she may learn.

[*The Merchant of Venice* 3 1596–7]

And then the whining schoolboy, with his satchel
And shining morning face, creeping like snail
Unwillingly to school.

[*As You Like It* 2 1598–1600]

Be innocent of the knowledge, dearest chuck,
Till thou applaud the deed.

[*Macbeth* 3 1605–6]

John Sheffield, 1st Duke of Buckingham and Normandy, 1648–1721, English politician and poet
Learn to write well, or not to write at all.

[*Essay on Satire* 1680]

Richard Brinsley Sheridan, 1751–1816, English dramatist
A progeny of learning.

[*The Rivals* 1775]

Isaac Bashevis Singer, 1904–91, American Yiddish novelist
Out knowledge is a little island in a great ocean of non-knowledge.

[In the *New York Times Magazine* 1978]

Socrates, c.469–399BC, Greek philosopher
There is only one good, knowledge, and one evil, ignorance.

[In Diogenes Laertius' *Lives of Eminent Philosophers* c.150BC]

Solon, c.640–c.558BC, Greek legislator
But I grow old always learning many things.

[In Plutarch's *Solon*]

Herbert Spencer, 1820–1903, English philosopher
Education has for its object the formation of character.

[*Social Statics* 1850]

Science is organized knowledge.

[*Essays on Education* 1861]

Sir Richard Steele, 1672–1729, Anglo-Irish essayist
Though her mien carries much more invitation than command, to behold her is an immediate check to loose behaviour; to love her is a liberal education.

[*The Tatler*]

John Addington Symonds, 1840–93, English writer
These things shall be! A loftier race
Than e'er the world hath known, shall rise,
With flame of freedom in their souls
And light of knowledge in their eyes.

[*New and Old: A Vista* 1880]

Charles Maurice de Talleyrand-Perigord, 1754–1838, French statesman
Ils n'ont rien appris, ni rien oublié.
(They have learned nothing and forgotten nothing.)

[Attributed]

Alfred, Lord Tennyson, 1809–92, English poet
To follow knowledge like a sinking star,
Beyond the utmost bound of human thought.

[*Ulysses* 1833]

Knowledge comes, but wisdom lingers.

[*Locksley Hall* 1842]

Joseph Trapp, 1679–1747, English academic
The King, observing with judicious eyes,
The state of both his universities,
To Oxford sent a troop of horse, and why?
That learned body wanted loyalty;
To Cambridge books, as very well discerning
How much that loyal body wanted learning.

[On George I's donation of a library to Cambridge (see Brown above)]

George Macaulay Trevelyan, 1876–1962, English historian
Education . . . has produced a vast population able to read but unable to distinguish what is
worth reading.

[*English Social History* 1942]

John Tyndall, 1820–93, Irish-born physicist
Charles Darwin, the Abraham of scientific men – a searcher as obedient to the command of
truth as was the patriarch to the command of God.

[*Fragments of Science: Science and Man*]

Sir Peter [Alexander] Ustinov, 1921– , English playwright and actor
I am convinced that it is of primordial importance to learn more every year than the year
before. After all, what is education but a process by which a person begins to learn how to
learn.

[*Dear Me* 1977]

Peter De Vries, 1910–93, American novelist and journalist
I was thinking that we all learn by experience, but some of us have to go to summer school.

[*Tunnel of Love* 1954]

Evelyn [Arthur St John] Waugh, 1903–66, English writer
Assistant masters came and went . . . Some liked little boys too little and some too much.

[*A Little Learning*]

Anyone who has been to an English public school will always feel comparatively at home in prison.

[Decline and Fall 1928]

I took Art as my second subject one semester. I'd have taken it as my first subject only Dad lost his money in religion so I had to learn a trade.

[The Loved One 1948]

Simone Weil, 1909–43, French essayist and philosopher

Culture is an instrument wielded by professors to manufacture professors, who when their turn comes, will manufacture professors.

[The Need for Roots 1949]

James Abbott McNeill Whistler, 1834–1903, American-born painter

[In reply to the question in court, "For two days' labour, you ask two hundred guineas?"] No, I ask it for the knowledge of a lifetime.

[The Gentle Art of Making Enemies]

Oscar [Fingall O'Flahertie Wills] Wilde, 1854–1900, Irish writer

Education is an admirable thing, but it is well to remember from time to time that nothing that is worth knowing can be taught.

[Intentions: The Critic as Artist 1891]

Edward Young, 1683–1765, English poet

Some for renown, on scraps of learning dote,
And think they grow immortal as they quote.

[Love of Fame 1725–8]

Eternity, Time and the Seasons

Jane Ace, 1905–74, American actress
Time wounds all heels.

[In Goodman Ace's *The Fine Art of Hypochondria; or How Are You?* 1966]

John Quincy Adams, 1767–1848, 6th president of the United States
My stern chase after time is, to borrow a simile from Tom Paine, like the race of a man with a wooden leg after a horse.

[*Diary* 25 March 1844]

Joseph Addison, 1672–1719, English essayist
'Tis the divinity that stirs within us,
'Tis Heaven itself that points out an hereafter,
And intimates Eternity to man.
Eternity! – thou pleasing-dreadful thought!

[*Cato* 1713]

Woody Allen [Allen Stewart Konigsberg], 1935– , American writer, actor and film director
I don't want to achieve immortality through my work. I want to achieve it through not dying.

[In E. Lax's *Woody Allen and His Comedy*]

Anonymous
If all things were eternal,
And nothing their end bringing,
If this should be, then how should we
Here make an end of singing?

[*If All The World Were Paper*]

Eternity has no grey hairs.

[Proverb]

Time and words can never be recalled.

[Proverb]

February makes a bridge, and March breaks it.

[Proverb]

Aristotle 384–322BC, Greek philosopher
One swallow does not make a summer.

[*The Nicomachean Ethics c.*340BC]

137

Francis Bacon, Baron Verulam of Verulam and Viscount of St Albans, 1561–1626, English philosopher

And he that will not apply New Remedies, must expect New Evils; for Time is the greatest Innovator.

[Essays: Of Innovations]

[Joseph] Hilaire [Pierre] Belloc, 1873–1953, English writer

I am a sundial, and I make a botch
Of what is done much better by a watch.

[On a Sundial, 1938]

The Bible

While the earth remaineth, seedtime and harvest, and cold and heat, and summer and winter, and day and night shall not cease.

[Genesis 8:22]

My times are in thine hand: deliver me from the hand of mine enemies, and from them that persecute me.

[Psalms 31:15]

For a thousand years in thy sight are but as yesterday when it is past, and as a watch in the night.

[Ibid 90:4]

The thing that hath been, it is that which shall be; and that which is done is that which shall be done: and there is no new thing under the sun.

[Ecclesiastes 1:9]

To everything there is a season, and a time to every purpose under the heaven: A time to be born, and a time to die; a time to plant, and a time to pluck up that which is planted; A time to kill, and a time to heal; a time to break down, and a time to build up; A time to weep, and a time to laugh; a time to mourn, and a time to dance; A time to cast away stones, and a time to gather stones together; a time to embrace, and a time to refrain from embracing; A time to get, and a time to lose; a time to keep, and a time to cast away; A time to rend, and a time to sew; a time to keep silence, and a time to speak; A time to love, and a time to hate; A time of war, and a time of peace.

[Ibid 3:1–8]

I returned, and saw under the sun, that the race is not to the swift, nor the battle to the strong, neither yet bread to the wise, nor yet riches to men of understanding, nor yet favour to men of skill; but time and chance happeneth to them all.

[Ibid 9:11–12]

For, lo, the winter is past, the rain is over and gone; the flowers appear on the earth; the time of the singing of birds is come, and the voice of the turtle is heard in our land.

[Song of Solomon 2:11–12]

And let us not be weary in well-doing: for in due season we shall reap, if we faint not.

[Galatians 6:9]

Ambrose [Gwinett] Bierce, 1842–1914, American writer

Dawn: the time when men of reason go to bed.

[The Devil's Dictionary 1906]

William Blake, 1757–1827, English poet and artist

To see a world in a grain of sand,
And heaven in a wild flower,
Hold infinity in the palm of your hand,
And eternity in an hour.
[*Auguries of Innocence* 1805]
He who bends to himself a joy
Doth the winged life destroy;
But he who kisses the joy as it flies
Lives in eternity's sunrise.

[*Gnomic Verses*]

Jorge Luis Borges, 1899–1986, Argentinian writer

Time is the substance from which I am made. Time is a river which carries me along, but I am the river; it is a tiger that devours me, but I am the tiger; it is a fire that consumes me, but I am the fire.

[*Labyrinths: A New Rufutation of Time* 1962]

Robert Bridges, 1844–1930, English poet

Spring goeth all in white,
Crowned with milk-white may:
In fleecy flocks of light
O'er heaven the white clouds stray.

[*Spring goeth all in White*]

Robert Browning, 1812–89, English poet

Never the time and the place
And the loved one all together!

[*Never the Time and the Place*]

The year's at the spring
And day's at the morn;
Morning's at seven;
The hillside's dew-pearled;
The lark's on the wing;
The snail's on the thorn:
God's in his heaven –
All's right with the world!

[*Pippa Passes* 1841]

In the morning of the world,
When earth was nigher heaven than now.

[*Ibid*]

He said, "What's time? Leave Now for dogs and apes!
Man has Forever."

[*A Grammarian's Funeral*]

Jean de La Bruyère, 1645–96, French moralist

Those who make the worse use of their time are the first to complain of its brevity.

[*Caractères* 1688]

John Baldwin Buckstone, 1802–79, English actor and playwright
On such an occasion as this,
All time and nonsense scorning,
Nothing shall come amiss,
And we won't go home till morning.

[Billy Taylor]

John William Burgon, 1813–88, English churchman and poet
Match me such marvel save in Eastern clime,
A rose-red city half as old as Time.

[Petra 1845]

Byron, Lord George Gordon [Noel], 6th Baron Byron of Rochdale, 1788–1824, English poet
Time writes no wrinkle on thine azure brow:
Such as creation's dawn beheld, thou rollest now.
[Childe Harold's Pilgrimage 1818]

The English winter – ending in July,
To recommence in August.

[Don Juan 13 1819–24]

Henry Carey, c.1690–1743, English poet and musician
Of all the days that's in the week
I dearly love but one day –
And that's the day that comes betwixt
A Saturday and Monday.

[Sally in our Alley 1713]

Thomas Carlyle, 1795–1881, Scottish historian and writer
The illimitable, silent, never-resting thing called Time, rolling, rushing on, swift, silent, like an all embracing ocean-tide, on which we and all the Universe swim like exhalations.
[Heroes and Hero Worship 1 1840]

Julia Fletcher Carney, 1823–1908, American teacher
Little drops of water, little grains of sand,
Make the mighty ocean and the pleasant land.
So the little minutes, humble though they be,
Make the mighty ages of eternity.

[Little Things]

Lewis Carroll [Charles Lutwidge Dodgson], 1832–92, English mathematician and writer
"The time has come," the Walrus said,
"To talk of many things:
Of shoes – and ships – and sealing wax –
Of cabbages – and kings –
And why the sea is boiling hot
And whether pigs have wings.

[Through the Looking-Glass and What Alice Found There 1872]

Geoffrey Chaucer, c.1340–1400, English poet
The tyme, that may not sojourne,
But goth, and may never retourne,
As watir that doun renneth ay,
But never drope retourne may.

[Romaunt of the Rose]

Samuel Taylor Coleridge, 1772–1834, English poet
And the spring comes slowly up this way.

[Christabel 1816]

Summer has set in with its usual severity.

[Quoted in a letter by Charles Lamb 1826]

Sir Noel [Pierce] Coward, 1899–1973, English actor and playwright
Time is the reef upon which all our frail mystic ships are wrecked.

[Blithe Spirit 1941]

I don't give a hoot about posterity. Why should I worry about what people think of me when I'm dead as a doornail anyway.

[Present Laughter]

William Cowper, 1731–1800, English poet
O Winter, ruler of th' inverted year.

[The Task: The Winter Evening 1785]

William Henry Davies, 1871–1940, Welsh poet
What is this life if, full of care,
We have no time to stand and stare?

[Leisure]

Charles [John Huffam] Dickens, 1812–70, English novelist
It was the best of times, it was the worst of times, it was the age of wisdom, it was the age of foolishness, it was the epoch of belief, it was the epoch of incredulity, it was the season of Light, it was the season of Darkness, it was the spring of hope, it was the winter of despair, we had everything before us, we had nothing before us, we were all going direct to Heaven, we were all going direct the other way.

[A Tale of Two Cities 1859]

Benjamin Disraeli, 1st Earl of Beaconsfield, 1804–81, British statesman and novelist
Time is the great physician.

[Endymion 1880]

Henry Austin Dobson, 1840–1921, English writer
Time goes, you say? Ah no!
Alas, Time stays, *we* go.

[The Paradox of Time]

Sir Francis Drake, c.1540–96, English admiral
There's plenty of time to win this game, and to thrash the Spaniards too.

[As the Armada was sighted while he played bowls, 1588]

John Dryden, 1631–1700, English dramatist
A very merry, dancing, drinking,
Laughing, quaffing, and unthinking time.

[*Secular Masque*]

Jonathan Edwards, 1703–58, American theologian
We can have but little sense of what an eternal duration is; it swallows up all thought and imagination: if we set ourselves to think upon it, we are presently lost.

[*Sinners in Zion Tenderly Warned* 1740]

T[homas] S[tearns] Eliot, 1888–1965, American-born English poet
Wearily, as one would turn to nod goodbye to Rochefoucauld,
If the street were time and he at the end of the street.

[*The Boston Evening Transcript*]

April is the cruellest month, breeding
Lilacs out of the dead land, mixing
Memory and desire, stirring
Dull roots with spring rain.

[*The Burial of the Dead* 1922]

Elizabeth I, 1533–1603, queen of England and Ireland
All my possessions for a moment of time.

[Last words]

Ralph Waldo Emerson, 1803–82, American writer
A day is a miniature eternity.

[*Journals* 1839]

Write it on your heart that every day is the best day in the year. No man has learned anything rightly until he knows that every day is Doomsday.

[*Society and Solitude: Works and Days* 1870]

Euripides, c.480–406BC, Greek dramatist
Time will reveal everything. It is a babbler, and speaks even when not asked.

[*Fragment c.*425BC]

Edward FitzGerald, 1809–83, English writer and translator
Come, fill the Cup, and in the Fire of Spring
The Winter Garment of Repentance fling:
The Bird of Time has but a little way
To fly – and Lo! the Bird is on the Wing.

[*The Rubaiyat of Omar Khayyam* 1857]

Benjamin Franklin, 1706–90, American scientist and philosopher
Early to bed and early to rise, makes a man healthy, wealthy and wise.

[*Poor Richard's Almanack* 1735]

Lost time is never found again.

[*Ibid* 1748]

Remember that time is money.

[*Advice to a Young Tradesman* 1748]

Dost thou love life? Then do not squander time, for that's the stuff life is made of.

[*Poor Richard's Almanack* 1746]

Thomas Fuller, 1608–61, English churchman and writer
It is always darkest just before the day dawneth.
[*A Pisgah-Sight of Palestine* 1650]

Johann Wolfgang von Goethe, 1749–1832, German poet and playwright
One has has time enough, if only one applies it well.
[*Dichtung und Wahrheit* 1831]
How great is my inheritance, how wide and spacious,
Time is my inheritance, my estate is time.
[*Wilhelm Meisters Wanderjahre*]

Baltasar Gracian, 1601–58, Spanish philosopher
All that really belongs to us is time; even he who has nothing else has that.
[*The Art of Worldly Wisdom* 1647]

Rosa Guy [Rosa Cuthbert], 1928– , Trinidadian-born American writer
Even forever comes to an end.
[*A Measure of Time* 1983]

Walter Hagen, 1892–1969, American golfer
Don't hurry, don't worry. You're only here for a short visit. So be sure to stop and smell the flowers.
[In the *New York Times* 1977]

Thomas Hardy, 1840–1928, English novelist and poet
Time and circumstance, which enlarge the views of most men, narrow the views of women almost invariably.
[*Jude the Obscure* 1895]

William Harrison, 1535–93, English topographer
Tempora mutantur, et nos mutamur in illis.
(The times are changing, and we are changing in them.)
[*Description of Britain* in Holinshed's *Chronicle* 1577]

Nathaniel Hawthorne, 1804–64, American novelist
The Past lies upon the Present like a giant's body.
[*The House of Seven Gables* 1851]

Robert Herrick, 1591–1674, English poet and churchman
Gather ye rosebuds while ye may,
Old Time is still a-flying:
And this same flower that smiles today,
Tomorrow will be dying.
[*Hesperides: To the Virgins, to Make Much of Time* 1648]

Thomas Hood, 1799–1845, English poet
Spring it is cheery,
Winter is dreary,
Green leaves hang, but the brown must fly;
When he's forsaken,
Wither'd and shaken,
What can an old man do but die.
[*Ballad*]

Horace [Quintus Horatius Flaccus], 65BC–8BC, Roman poet

Time will bring to light whatever is hidden, and it will conceal and cover up what is now shining with the greatest splendour.

[*Epistles c.*19BC]

Mark Antony de Wolfe Howe, 1864–1960,

Now, thieving Time, take what you must –
Quickness to hear, to move, to see;
When dust is drawing near to dust
Such diminutions needs must be.
Yet leave, O leave exempt from plunder
My curiosity, my wonder!

[*Thieving Time* 1951]

Aldous [Leonard] Huxley, 1894–1963, English writer

Past time is only evil at a distance.

[*After Many a Summer*]

Jerome K[lapka] Jerome, 1859–1927, English humorous writer

Time is but the shadow of the world upon the background of Eternity.

[*Three Men in a Boat* 1889]

Ben[jamin] Jonson, 1572–1637, English poet

He was not of an age, but for all time.

[*To the Memory of Shakespeare*]

Franz Kafka, 1883–1924, Austrian writer

Only our concept of time makes it possible for us to speak of the Day of Judgment by that name; in reality it is a summary court in perpetual session.

[Letters, in Max Brod's
Franz Kafka]

John Keats, 1795–1821, English poet

Thou still unravish'd bride of quietness,
Thou foster-child of silence and slow time.

[*Ode on a Grecian Urn c.*1819]

Season of mists and mellow fruitfulness,
Close bosom-friend of the maturing sun.

[*To Autumn*]

C[live] S[taples] Lewis, 1898–1963, English writer

The Future is something which everyone reaches at the rate of sixty minutes an hour, whatever he does, whoever he is.

[*The Screwtape Letters* 1941]

Abraham Lincoln, 1809–65, 16th president of the United States
Time! what an empty vapour 'tis!
And days, how swift they are:
Swift as an Indian arrow –
Fly on like a shooting star;
The present moment just is here,
Then slides away in haste,
That we can never say they're ours,
But only say they're past.

[Untitled poem *c.*1828]

Henry Wadsworth Longfellow, 1807–82, American poet
Art is long, and Time is fleeting,
And our hearts, though stout and brave,
Still, like muffled drums, are beating
Funeral marches to the grave.

[*Voices of the Night: A Psalm of Life* 1839]

Lucretius, c.99–c.55BC, Roman poet
Summarum summa est aeternum.
(The sum of all sums is eternity.)

[*De Natura Rerum* 57BC]

Do you not see even stones yield to the power of time, lofty towers fall to decay, and rocks moulder away? Temples and statues of the gods go to ruin, nor can the gods themselves prolong their date or get reprieve from fate.

[*Ibid*]

Marcus Aurelius [Antoninus] [Marcus Annius Verus] AD121–80, Roman emperor
Time is like a river. As soon as a thing is seen it is carried away and another takes its place, and then that other is carried away also.

[*Meditations c.*170]

Christopher Marlowe, 1564–93, English dramatist
Stand still, you ever-moving spheres of Heaven
That time may cease, and midnight never come.

[*Dr Faustus* 1588]

O lente, lente currite, noctis equi:
The stars move still, time runs, the clock will strike,
The devil will come, and Faustus must be damn'd.

[*Ibid*]

Andrew Marvell, 1621–78, English poet and politician
But at my back I always hear
Time's wingèd chariot drawing near;
And yonder all before us lie
Deserts of vast eternity.

[*To his Coy Mistress* 1650]

W[illiam] Somerset Maugham, 1874–1965, English novelist
It is bad enough to know the past; it would be intolerable to know the future.
[In Richard Hughes' *Foreign Devil* 1972]

Norman Alexander McCaig, 1910–96, Scottish poet
On shaven grass a summer's litter lies
Of paper bags and people. One o'clock
Booms on the leaves with which the trees are quilted
And wades away through air, making it rock
On flower-beds that have blazed and dazed and wilted.

[*A Common Grace: Nude in a Fountain* 1960]

Maurice Merleau-Ponty, 1908–61, French philosopher
Time presupposes a view of time. It is, therefore, not like a river, not a flowing substance.

[*Phenomenology of Perception* 1945]

John Milton, 1608–74, English poet
Time will run back, and fetch the age of gold,
And speckl'd vanity
Will sicken soon and die.

[*On the Morning of Christ's Nativity: The Hymn*]

Thus with the year
Seasons return, but not to me returns
Day, or the sweet approach of ev'n or morn.

[*Paradise Lost* 1667]

With thee conversing I forget all time,
All seasons and their change, all please alike.

[*Ibid*]

O dark, dark, dark, amid the blaze of noon,
Irrecoverably dark, total Eclipse
Without all hope of day!

[*Samson Agonistes* 1671]

Now the bright morning Star, Day's harbinger,
Comes dancing from the East, and leads with her
The Flow'ry May.

[*Song on May Morning*]

Time, the subtle thief of youth.

[*Sonnets* 7]

Wilson Mizner, 1876–1933, American gambler
Life's a tough proposition, and the first hundred years are the hardest.

[Saying]

Thomas Moore, 1779–1852, Irish poet
'Tis the last rose of summer
Left blooming alone;
All her lovely companions
Are faded and gone.

[*Irish Melodies* 1801–34: *The Last Rose of Summer*]

Christopher [Darlington] Morley, 1890–1957, American writer
April prepares her green traffic light and the world thinks Go.

[*John Mistletoe* 1931]

Napoleon I [Napoleon Bonaparte], 1769–1821, emperor of France
You may ask me for anything you like except time.

[To one of his officers, 1803]

Friedrich Wilhelm Nietzsche, 1844–1900, German philosopher and poet

All things return eternally, and ourselves with them: we have already existed times without number, and all things with us.

[*Thus Spake Zarathustra* 1885]

Ovid [Publius Ovidius Naso], 43BC–AD18, Roman poet

Tempora labuntur or *Tempus fugit.*
(Time flies.)

[*Fasti c.* AD5]

Tempus edax rerum.
(Time the devourer of all things.)

[*Metamorphoses* 15]

Thomas Paine, 1737–1809, English political writer

These are the times that try men's souls.

[*The American Crisis* 1777]

Blaise Pascal, 1623–62, French mathematician and writer

I have only made this letter longer because I lack the time to make it shorter.

[*Lettres Provinciales* 1656–7]

Time cures sorrows and squabbles because we all change, and are no longer the same persons. Neither offender nor the offended is the same.

[*Pensées* 1670]

Thomas Love Peacock, 1785–1866, English essayist and poet

How troublesome is day!
It calls us from our sleep away;
It bids us from our pleasant dreams awake,
And sends us forth to keep or break
Our promises to pay.
How troublesome is day!

[*Fly-by-Night* 1837]

Alfred Edward Perlman, 1902–96, American business executive

After you've done a thing the same way for two years, look it over carefully. After five years look at it with suspicion, and after ten years throw it away and start all over again.

[In the *New York Times* 1958]

Sylvia Plath, 1932–63, American-born poet

It is only time that weighs upon our hands.
It is only time, and that is not material.

[*Winter Trees : Three Women* 1971]

Plato, c.428–348BC, Greek philosopher

Time brings everything.

[*Greek Anthology* 9]

Pliny the Younger, AD62–c.114, Roman statesman

The happier the time, the faster it goes.

[*Letters c.* 110]

Alexander Pope, 1688–1744, English poet
Time conquers all, and we must Time obey.

[*Pastorals: Winter*]

Ezra [Loomis] Pound, 1885–1972, American poet
Winter is icummen in,
Lhude sing Goddamn,
Raineth drop and staineth slop
And how the wind doth ramm!
Sing: Goddamn.

[*Ancient Music*]

E. Annie [Edna Ann] Proulx, 1935– , American journalist, novelist and short story writer
It was spring. Sodden ground, smell of earth. The wind beat through twigs, gave off a greenish odour like struck flints. Coltsfoot in the ditches; furious dabs of tulips stuttering in gardens. Slanting rain. Clock hands leapt to pellucid evenings. The sky riffled like cards in a chalk–white hand.

[*The Shipping News* 1993]

Marcel Proust, 1871–1922, French novelist
The time which we have at our disposal every day is elastic; the passions that we feel expand it, those that we inspire contract it; and habit fills up what remains.

[*Remembrance of Things Past* 1913–26]

Publilius Syrus, *fl.* 1st century BC, Roman writer
Every day learns from that which preceded it.

[*Sententiae c.*50BC]

Sir Walter Raleigh, c.1552–1618, English explorer and poet
Even such is Time, that takes in trust
Our youth, our joys, our all we have,
And pays us but with earth and dust.

[Written the night before his death]

Will[iam Penn Adair] Rogers, 1879–1935, American humorist
Half our life is spent trying to find something to do with the time we have rushed through life trying to save.

[*The Autobiography of Will Rogers* 1949]

Vita [Victoria Mary] Sackville-West, 1892–1962, English writer, poet and gardener
Forget not the bees in winter, though they sleep,
For winter's big with summer in her womb.

[*The Land: Spring* 1927]

George Santayana, 1863–1952, Spanish-American philosopher
To be interested in the changing seasons is, in this middle zone, a happier state of mind than to be hopelessly in love with spring.

[*Little Essays*]

Jean-Paul Sartre, 1905–80, French philosopher and writer
Three o'clock is always too late or too early for anything you want to do.

[*La Nausée* 1949]

[Johann Christoph] Friedrich von Schiller, 1759–1805, German poet
Time consecrates;
And what is grey with age becomes religion.

[*Die Piccolomini* 4]

Sir Walter Scott, 1771–1832, Scottish novelist
There's a gude time coming.

[*Rob Roy* 1817]

Seneca, c.4BC–AD65, Roman philosopher
Veritatem dies aperit.
Time discovers the truth.

[*De Ira c.*43]

Time heals what reason cannot.

[*Agamemnon c.*60]

William Shakespeare 1564–1616, English dramatist
Now is the winter of our discontent
Made glorious summer by this sun of York.

[*King Richard III* 1 1592–3]

When well apparell'd April on the heel
Of limping winter treads.

[*Romeo and Juliet* 1 1594–5]

Night's candles are burnt out, and jocund day
Stands tiptoe on the misty mountain tops.

[*Ibid* 3]

O, call back yesterday, bid time return.

[*King Richard II* 3 1595–6]

How many things by season season'd are
To their right praise and true perfection!

[*The Merchant of Venice* 5 1596–7]

Fleet the time carelessly, as they did in the golden world.

[*As You Like It* 1 1598–1600]

Blow, blow, thou winter wind,
Thou art not so unkind
As man's ingratitude.

[*Ibid*]

Time travels in divers paces with divers persons. I'll tell you who Time ambles withal, who
Time trots withal, who Time gallops withal and who he stands still withal.

[*Ibid* 3]

Thus the whirligig of time brings in his revenges.

[*Twelfth Night* 5 1598–1600]

Thou know'st 'tis common; all that lives must die,
Passing through nature to eternity.

[*Hamlet* 1 1600–01]

The time is out of joint: O cursed spite,
That ever I was born to set it right.

[*Ibid*]

[On the players] They are the abstract and brief chronicles of the time.

[*Ibid* 2]

149

For who would bear the whips and scorns of time,
The oppressor's wrong, the proud man's contumely,
The pangs of despised love, the law's delay,
The insolence of office and the spurns
That patient merit of the unworthy takes,
When he himself might his quietus make
With a bare bodkin?

[*Ibid* 3]

The end crowns all;
And that old common arbitrator, Time,
Will one day end it.

[*Troilus and Cressida* 4 1601–3]

A forted residence 'gainst the tooth of time
And razure of oblivion.

[*Measure for Measure* 5 1604–5]

If you can look into the seeds of time,
And say which grain will grow and which will not.

[*Macbeth* 1 1605–6]

Come what come may,
Time and the hour runs through the roughest day.

[*Ibid*]

Tomorrow, and tomorrow, and tomorrow,
Creeps in this petty pace from day to day
To the last syllable of recorded time,
And all our yesterdays have lighted fools
The way to dusty death. Out, out, brief candle!

[*Ibid* 5]

Shall I compare thee to a summer's day?
Thou art more lovely and more temperate.
Rough winds do shake the darling buds of May
And summer's lease hath all too short a date.

[*Sonnets* 18 1609]

But thy eternal summer shall not fade.

[*Ibid*]

When to the sessions of sweet silent thought
I summon up remembrance of things past,
I sigh the lack of many a thing I sought,
And with old woes new wail my dear time's waste.

[*Ibid* 30]

Being your slave, what should I do but tend
Upon the hours and times of your desire?
I have no precious time at all to spend,
Nor services to do, till you require.
Nor dare I chide the world-without-end hour
Whilst I, my sovereign, watch the clock for you,
Nor think the bitterness of absenced sour
When you have bid your servant once adieu.

[*Ibid* 57]

To me, fair friend, you never can be old,
For as you were when first your eye I eyed,
Such seems your beauty still. Three winters cold
Have from the forests shook three summers' pride,
Three beauteous springs to yellow autumn turn'd.

[*Ibid* 114]

When in the chronicle of wasted time
I see descriptions of the fairest wights,
And beauty making beautiful old rhyme
In praise of ladies dead and lovely knights.

[*Ibid* 116]

A sad tale's best for winter.

[*The Winter's Tale* 2 1610–11]

In the dark backward and abysm of time.

[*The Tempest* 1 1611–12]

Percy Bysshe Shelley, 1792–1822, English poet
Day after day a weary waste of hours.

[*Alastor* 1816]

O wild West Wind, thou breath of Autumn's being,
Thou, from whose unseen present the leaves dead
Are driven, like ghosts from an enchanter fleeing.

[*Ode to the West Wind* 1820]

O, Wind,
If Winter comes, can Spring be far behind?

[*Ibid*]

The One remains, the many change and pass;
Heaven's light forever shines, Earth's shadows fly;
Life, like a dome of many-coloured glass,
Stains the white radiance of eternity,
Until Death tramples it to fragments.

[*Adonais* 1821]

Samuel Smiles, 1812–1904, Scottish writer
Those who have most to do, and are willing to work, will find the most time.

[*Self-Help* 1859]

Robert Southwell, 1561–95, English poet
Time and wind stay no man's pleasure.

[*St Peter's Complaint* 1595]

Herbert Spencer, 1820–1903, English philosopher
Time: that which man is always trying to kill, but which ends in killing him.

[*Definitions*]

Philip Dormer Stanhope, 4th Earl of Chesterfield, 1694–1773, English statesman
I recommend you to take care of the minutes, for hours will take care of themselves.

[*Letters to His Son* 4 October 1749]

Know the true value of time; snatch, seize and enjoy every moment of it. No idleness, no
laziness, no procrastination.

[*Ibid* 26 December 1749]

Henry David Thoreau, 1817–62, American naturalist and writer
As if you could kill time without injuring eternity.

[*Walden, or Life in the Woods* 1854]

Time is but the stream I go fishing in.

[*Ibid*]

James Grover Thurber, 1894–1961, American humorist
Early to rise and early to bed makes a male healthy and wealthy and dead.

[*Fables for Our Times* 1941]

Henry Vaughan, 1621–95, English poet and physician
I saw Eternity the other night,
Like a great ring of pure and endless light,
All calm, as it was bright;
And round beneath it, Time in hours, days, years,
Driv'n by the spheres
Like a vast shadow mov'd; in which the world
And all her train were hurl'd

[*Silex Scintillans: The World* 1650]

Virgil *or* Vergil [Publius Vergilius Maro], 70–19BC, Roman poet
Sed fugit interea, fugit inrreparabile tempus.
(Time meanwhile flies, flies never to return.)

[*Georgics*]

Sir William Watson, 1858–1935, English poet
April, April,
Laugh thy girlish laughter,
Then, the moment after,
Weep thy golden tears!

[*Song* 1896]

Isaac Watts, 1674–1748, English poet and hymn-writer
A thousand ages in thy sight
Are like an evening gone,
Short as the watch that ends the night
Before the rising sun.

[*Psalm 90*]

Time, like an ever-rolling stream,
Bears all its sons away.

[*Ibid*]

Oscar [Fingall O'Flahertie Wills] Wilde, 1854–1900, Irish writer
And down the long and silent street
The dawn, with silver-sandalled feet,
Crept like a frightened girl.

[*The Harlot's House* 1885]

Tennessee Williams [Thomas Lanier Williams], 1911–83, American playwright
Time is the longest distance between two places.

[*The Glass Menagerie* 1 1944]

Family Life, Home and Marriage

Joseph Addison, 1672–1719, English essayist
Themistocles, the great Athenian general, being asked whether he would choose to marry his daughter to an indigent man of merit, or to a worthless man of an estate, replied that he would prefer a man without an estate, to an estate with a man.

[*The Fortune Hunter*]

A woman seldom asks advice before she has bought her wedding clothes.

[*The Spectator* 475]

[Amos] Bronson Alcott, 1799–1888, American philosopher
As the homes, so the state.

[*Tablets* 1868]

Anonymous
He who marrieth does well, but he who marrieth not, better.

[Proverb]

Marry in haste and repent at leisure; 'tis good to marry late or never.

[Proverb]

Susan B[rownell] Anthony, 1820–1906, American reformer
Marriage, to women as to men, must be a luxury, not a necessity; an incident of life, not all of it. And the only possible way to accomplish this great change is to accord to women equal power in the making, shaping and controlling of the circumstances of life.

[Speech 1875]

Aristophanes, c.448–c.388BC, Greek playwright
A man, though he be grey-haired, can always get a wife. But a woman's time is short.

[*Lysistrata c.*411BC]

Jane Austen, 1775–1817, English novelist
It is a truth universally acknowledged, that a single man in possession of a good fortune must be in want of a wife.

[*Pride and Prejudice* 1813]

A lady's imagination is very rapid; it jumps from admiration to love to matrimony in a moment

[*Ibid*]

Happiness in marriage is entirely a matter of chance.

[*Ibid*]

What is the difference in matrimonial affairs between the mercenary and the prudent motive?

[*Ibid*]

Lord, how ashamed I should be of not being married before three and twenty!

[*Ibid*]

A family of ten children will always be called a fine family, where there are heads, and arms, and legs enough for that number.

[*Northanger Abbey* 1818]

Francis Bacon, Baron Verulam of Verulam and Viscount of St Albans, 1561–1626, English philosopher

He that hath wife and children, hath given hostages to fortune; for they are impediments to great enterprises, either of virtue or mischief.

[*Essays: Of Marriage and Single Life* 1625]

Certainly, wife and children are a kind of discipline of humanity,

[*Ibid*]

Wives are young men's mistresses; companions for middle age; and old men's nurses.

[*Ibid*]

The joys of parents are secret, and so are their griefs and fears.

[*Ibid: Of Parents and Children*]

Children sweeten labours, but they make misfortunes more bitter.

[*Ibid*]

Honoré de Balzac, 1799–1850, French novelist

No man should marry until he has studied anatomy and dissected at least one woman.

[*The Physiology of Marriage* 1830]

The majority of husbands remind me of an orangutang trying to play the violin.

[*Ibid*]

Being a husband is a whole-time job. That is why so many husbands fail. They cannot give their entire attention to it.

[*The Title*]

Sir [Henry] Max[imilian] Beerbohm, 1872–1956, English writer

They were a tense and peculiar family, the Oedipuses, weren't they?

[In D. Cecil's *Max: a Biography* 1965]

Bhartrihari, *fl.* 7th century, Hindu poet

What is the perfect way to happiness? To stay at home.

[*The Niti Sataka c.*625]

The Bible

Honour thy father and thy mother: that thy days may be long upon the land which the Lord thy God giveth thee.

[*Exodus 20*:12]

A wise son maketh a glad father: but a foolish son is the heaviness of his mother.

[*Proverbs 10*:1]

He that spareth his rod hateth his son: but he that loveth him chasteneth.

[*Ibid 13*:24]

Whoso findeth a wife findeth a good thing, and obtaineth favour of the Lord.

[*Ibid 18*:22]

Train up a child in the way he should go: and when he is old, he will not depart from it.

[*Ibid 22*:6]

The fathers have eaten sour grapes, and the children's teeth are set on edge.

[*Ezekiel 18*:2]

But from the beginning of the creation God made them male and female. For this cause shall a man leave his father and mother, and cleave to his wife. And they twain shall be one flesh: so then they are no more twain but one flesh. What therefore God hath joined together, let not man put asunder.

[*Mark* 10:6–9]

Whosoever shall put away his wife, and marry another, committeth adultery against her. And if a woman shall put away her husband and be married to another, she committeth adultery.

[*Ibid* 10:11–12]

Let every man have his own wife, and let every woman have her own husband. Let the husband render unto the wife due benevolence: and likewise also the wife unto the husband.

[*1 Corinthians* 7: 2–3]

I say therefore to the unmarried and widows, It is good for them if they abide even as I. But if they cannot contain, let them marry: for it is better to marry than to burn.

[*Ibid* 7:8–9]

Likewise, ye husbands, dwell with them according to knowledge, giving honour unto the wife, as unto the weaker vessel, and as being heirs together of the grace of life.

[*1 Peter* 3:7]

Ambrose [Gwinett] Bierce, 1842–1914, American writer

Marriage: the state or condition of a community consisting of a master, a mistress and two slaves, making in all, two.

[*The Devil's Dictionary* 1906]

Wedding: a ceremony at which two persons undertake to become one, one undertakes to become nothing, and nothing undertakes to become supportable.

[*Ibid*]

A bad marriage is like an electrical thrilling machine: it makes you dance, but you can't let go.

[*Collected Works* 1911]

Josh Billings [Henry Wheeler Shaw], 1818–85, American humorist

There's no cure for laziness, but I've known a second wife to hurry it some.

[Lecture in San Francisco 1885]

Charlotte Brontë, 1816–55, English novelist

If there is one notion I hate more than another, it is that of marriage – I mean marriage in the vulgar, weak sense, as a mere matter of sentiment.

[*Shirley* 1849]

Alfred and I intended to be married in this way almost from the first; we never meant to be spliced in the humdrum way of other people.

[*Villette* 1853]

Robert Burns. 1759–96, Scottish poet

To make a happy fireside clime
To weans and wife,
That's the true pathos and sublime
Of human life.

[*Epistle to Dr Blacklock*]

Ah, gentle dames' it gars me greet
To think how mony counsels sweet,
How mony lengthen'd, sage advices
The husband frae the wife despises!

[*Tam O'Shanter* 1791]

155

Robert Burton, 1577–1640, English churchman and writer
One was never married, and that's his hell; another is, and that's his plague.

[*The Anatomy of Melancholy* 1621]

Wilhelm Busch, 1832–1908, German artist and poet
Becoming a father is easy enough,
But being one can be rough.

[*Julchen* 1877]

William Camden, 1551–1623, English historian
Age and wedlock lames man and beast.

[*Remains Concerning Britain* 1605]

Will Carleton, 1845–1912, American writer
Draw up the papers, lawyer, and make 'em good and stout,
For things are running crossways, and Betsey and I are out.

[*Betsey and I Are Out* 1873]

Miguel de Cervantes [Saavedra], 1547–1616, Spanish dramatist and poet
There are but two families in the world as my grandmother used to say, the Haves and the Have-nots.

[*Don Quixote* 1615]

You are a king by your own fireside, as much as any monarch in his throne.

[*Ibid*]

Geoffrey Chaucer, c.1340–1400, English poet
She was a worthy womman al hir lyve:
Housbondes at chirche dore she hadde fyve,
Withouten oother coompaignye in youthe –
But therof nedeth nat to speke as nowthe.

[*The Canterbury Tales: The Wife of Bath* c.1387]

Wommen desiren have sovereynetee
As wel over hir housbond as hir love,
And for to been in maistrie hym above.

[*Ibid*]

G[ilbert] K[eith] Chesterton, 1874–1936, English writer
"My country, right or wrong," is a thing that no patriot would think of saying except in a desperate case. It is like saying, "My mother, drunk or sober."

[*The Defendant*]

Dame Agatha Christie, 1891–1976, English detective-story writer
An archaeologist is the best husband a woman can have; the older she gets, the more interested he is in her.

Sir Winston [Leonard Spencer] Churchill, 1874–1965, British statesman
There is no finer investment for any community than putting milk into babies.

[Radio broadcast 1943]

Lady Astor: If I were your wife, I should flavour your coffee with poison!
Sir Winston: And If I were your husband, madam, I should drink it.

[Attributed]

Family Life, Home and Marriage

Marcus Tullius Cicero, 106–43BC, Roman statesman
The first bond of society is marriage; the next, children; then the family.

[*De Officiis* 78BC]

Charles Caleb Colton, c.1780–1832, English writer
Marriage is a feast where the grace is sometimes better than the dinner.

[*Lacon* 1820]

Confucius [K'ung fu-tzu], 551–479BC, Chinese philosopher
Marriage lies at the bottom of all government.

[*The Book of Rites c.*500BC]

William Congreve, 1670–1729, English dramatist
Courtship to marriage, as a very witty prologue to a very dull play.

[*The Old Bachelor* 1693]

Married in haste, we may repent at leisure.

[*Ibid*]

Let us be very strange and well bred: Let us be as strange as if we had been married a great while, and as well bred as if we were not married at all.

[*The Way of the World* 1700]

Randle Cotgrave, d.c.1634, English lexicographer
Every bird likes its own nest best.

[*French-English Dictionary* 1611]

Sir Noel [Pierce] Coward, 1899–1973, English actor and playwright
We must all be very kind to Auntie Jessie,
For she's never been a Mother or a Wife,
You mustn't throw your toys at her,
Or make a vulgar noise at her,
She hasn't led a very happy life.

[*We Must All Be Very Kind To Auntie Jessie*]

Honeymooning is a very overrated amusement.

[*Private Lives* 1 1930]

William Cowper, 1731–1800, English poet
But strive to be a man before your mother.

[*Motto to Connoisseur*]

Said John – It is my wedding day,
And all the world would stare,
If wife should dine at Edmonton,
And I should dine at Ware.

[*John Gilpin* 1782]

Domestic happiness, Thou only bliss
Of Paradise that has surviv'd the fall!

[*The Task: The Garden* 1785]

George Crabbe, 1754–1832, English poet and churchman
Taught by care, the patient man and wife
Agree to share the bittersweet of life.

[*The Parish Register* 1807]

Mrs Dinah Maria Craik, 1826–87, English melodramatist
Oh, my son's my son till he gets him a wife,
But my daughter's my daughter all her life.

[Young and Old]

Richard Crashaw, c.1612–1649, English poet
I would be married, but 'd have no wife,
I would be married to a single life.

[On Marriage]

Sir John Davies, 1569–1626, English poet
Every groom is a king at home.

[The Scourge of Folly 1611]

Charles [John Huffam] Dickens, 1812–70, English novelist
Wen you're a married man, Samivel, you'll understand a good many things as you don't
understand now; but vether it's worth while goin' through so much to learn so little, as the
charity boy said ven he got to the end of the alphabet, is a matter o' taste.

[Pickwick Papers 1836–7]

Accidents will occur in the best-regulated families; and in families not regulated by that
pervading influence which sanctifies while it enhances the – a – I would say, in short, by the
influence of Woman, in the lofty character of Wife, they may be expected with confidence,
and must be born with philosophy.

[David Copperfield 1849–50]

Benjamin Disraeli, 1st Earl of Beaconsfield, 1804–81, British statesman and novelist
I have always thought that every woman should marry, and no man.

[Lothair 1870]

Marriage is the greatest earthly happiness when founded on complete sympathy.

[Letter to Gladstone]

John Dryden 1631–1700 English dramatist
And all to leave what with his toil he won
To that unfeather'd two-legged thing, a son.

[Absalom and Achitophel 1681]

Here lies my wife: here let her lie,
Now she's at rest, and so am I.

[Epitaph Intended for Dryden's Wife]

Isadora Duncan [Angela Duncan], 1877–1927, American dancer and choreographer
Any intelligent woman who reads the marriage contract and then goes into it, deserves all the
consequences.

[My Life 1927]

George Eliot [Mary Ann Evans], 1819–80, English novelist
I should like to know what is the proper function of women, if it is not to make reasons for
husbands to stay at home, and still stronger reasons for bachelors to go out

[The Mill on the Floss 1860]

Euripides, c.480–406BC, Greek dramatist
Divorce is not honourable to women.

[Medea 431BC]

James H[erman] Elroy Flecker, 1884–1915, English poet

Half to forget the wandering and the pain,
Half to remember days that have gone by,
And dream and dream that I am home again!

[*Brumana*]

Phineas Fletcher, 1582–1650, English poet

A saint abroad, at home a fiend.

[*The Purple Island* 1633]

Jean de La Fontaine, 1621–95, French poet

It is impossible to please all the world and also one's father.

[*Fables* 1671]

Lena Guilbert Ford, d.1918, American poet

Keep the home fires burning, while your hearts are yearning,
Though your lads are far away they dream of home;
There's a silver lining through the dark clouds shining,
Turn the dark cloud inside out, till the boys come home.

[*Keep the Home Fires Burning*]

Stephen Collins Foster, 1826–64, American songwriter

All up and down de whole creation,
Sadly I roam,
Still longing for de old plantation,
And for de old folks at home.

[*My Old Kentucky Home*]

Benjamin Franklin, 1706–90, American scientist and philosopher

Where there's marriage without love, there will be love without marriage.

[*Poor Richard's Almanack* 1734]

Keep your eyes wide open before marriage and half shut afterwards.

[*Ibid* 1758]

Robert [Lee] Frost, 1875–1963, American poet

Home is the place where, when you have to go there,
They have to take you in.

[*The Death of the Hired Man* 1914]

The greatest thing in family life is to take a hint when a hint is intended – and not to take a hint when a hint isn't intended.

[*Comment*]

Thomas Fuller, 1608–61, English churchman and writer

They that marry ancient people, merely in expectation to bury them, hang themselves in hope that one will come and cut the halter.

[*The Holy and Profane State: Of Marriage* 1642]

Mrs Elizabeth Cleghorn Gaskell, 1810–65, English novelist

A man is so in the way in the house.

[*Cranford* 1853]

159

John Gay, 1685–1732, English poet and playwright

Do you think your mother and I should have liv'd comfortably so long together, if ever we had been married?

[*The Beggar's Opera* 1728]

One wife is too much for most husbands to hear
But two at a time there's no mortal can bear.

[*Ibid*]

Johann Wolfgang von Goethe, 1749–1832, German poet and playwright

The sum which two married people owe to one another defies calculation. It is an infinite debt, which can only be discharged through all eternity.
[*Elective Affinities* 18091]

Robert von Ranke Graves, 1895–1985, English poet

Why have such scores of lovely, gifted girls
Married impossible men?
Simple self-sacrifice may be ruled out,
And missionary endeavour, nine times out of ten.

[*Collected Poems: A Slice of Wedding Cake* 1975]

Germaine Greer, 1939– , Australian feminist writer

Mothers carefully, diligently, constantly build up the confidence of their sons. Fathers give only fitful testimony to the lovability of their daughters.

[*Daddy, We hardly Knew You* 1990]

Felicia Dorothea Hemans, 1793–1835, English poet

The stately homes of England,
How beautiful they stand!
Amidst their tall ancestral trees,
O'er all the pleasant land.

[*The Homes of England*]

O. Henry [William Sydney Porter], 1862–1910, American writer

If men knew how women pass the time when they are alone, they'd never marry.

[*Memoirs of a Yellow Dog*]

Sir A[lan] P[atrick] Herbert, 1890–1971, English humorous writer

The critical period in matrimony is breakfast time.

[*Uncommon Law* 1935]

Robert Herrick, 1591–1674, English poet

He loves his bonds who, when the first are broke,
Submits his neck unto a second yoke.

[*Hesperides* 1648]

Hesiod, *fl.* 8th century BC, Greek poet

Marry in the springtime of thy life, neither much above or below the age of thirty. Thy wife should be a virgin in her nineteenth year.

[*Works and Days c.*700BC]

Thomas Jefferson, 1743–1826, 3rd president of the United States
A lively and lasting sense of filial duty is more effectually impressed on the mind of a son or daughter by reading *King Lear*, than by all the dry volumes of ethics and divinity that ever were written.

[Letter 1771]

The happiest moments of my life have been the few which I have passed at home in the bosom of my family.

[*Ibid* 1790]

The happiness of the domestic fireside is the first boon of Heaven; and it is well it is so, since it is that which is the lot of the mass of mankind.
[*Ibid* 1813]

Dr Samuel Johnson, 1709–84, English lexicographer
I am sometimes disposed to think with the severer casuists of most nations that marriage is rather permitted than approved, and that none, but by the instigation of a passion too much indulged, entangle themselves with indissoluble compacts.

[*Rasselas* 1759]

Marriage has many pains, but celibacy has no pleasures.

[*Ibid*]

A man is in general better pleased when he has a good dinner upon his table than when his wife talks Greek.

[*Johnsonian Miscellanies*]

With secret course, which no loud storms annoy,
Glides the smooth current of domestic joy.

[Added to Goldsmith's *Traveller*]

Erica Jong, 1942– , American writer and poet
Bigamy is having one husband too many. Monogamy is the same.

[*Fear of Flying* 1973]

Carl Gustav Jung, 1875–1961, Swiss psychiatrist
Seldom, or perhaps never, does a marriage develop into an individual relationship smoothly and without crises; there is no coming to consciousness without pain.

[*Contributions to Analytical Psychology* 1928]

John Keats, 1795–1821, English poet
The roaring of the wind is my wife and the stars through the window pane are my children. The mighty abstract idea I have of beauty in all things stifles the more divided and minute domestic happiness ... The opinion I have of the generality of women – who appear to me as children to whom I would rather give a sugar plum than my time, forms a barrier against matrimony which I rejoice in.

[Letter to his brother and sister 1818]

John Keble, 1792–1866. English churchman and poet
Sweet is the smile of home; the mutual look,
When hearts are of each other sure.

[*The Christian Year* 1827]

The voice that breathed o'er Eden,
That earliest wedding day.

[*Holy Matrimony*]

Rudyard Kipling, 1865–1936, English writer
The bachelor may risk 'is 'ide
To 'elp you when you're downed;
But the married man will wait beside
Till the ambulance comes round.

[*The Married Man*]

Philip Arthur Larkin, 1922–85, English poet
They fuck you up, your mum and dad.
They do not mean to, but they do.
They fill you with the faults they had
And add some extra, just for you.

[*This Be The Verse*]

Stephen Butler Leacock, 1869–1944, Canadian economist and humorist
The parent who could see his boy as he really is, would shake his head and say: "Willie is no good: I'll sell him."

[*The Lot of the Schoolmaster*]

Robert E[dward] Lee, 1807–70, American Confederate general
Never marry unless you can do so into a family that will enable your children to feel proud of both sides of the house.

[To John Hood, Texas, 1856]

Abraham Lincoln, 1809–65, 16th president of the United States
Whatever woman may cast her lot with mine, should any ever do so, it is my intention to do all in my power to make her happy and contented; and there is nothing I can imagine that would make me more unhappy than to fail in that effort.

[Letter 1837]

Marriage is neither heaven nor hell. It is simply purgatory.

[Attributed 1864]

John Locke, 1632–1704, English philosopher
He that will have his son have a respect for him and his orders, must himself have a greater reverence for his son.

[*Some Thoughts Concerning Education* 1693]

Henry Wadsworth Longfellow, 1807–82, American poet
The men that women marry,
And why they marry them, will always be
A marvel and a mystery to the world.

[*Michael Angelo*]

Sir [Edward Montague] Compton Mackenzie, 1883–1972, English novelist
Prostitution. Selling one's body to keep one's soul: this is the meaning of the sins that were forgiven to the woman because she loved much: one might say of most marriages that they were selling one's soul to keep one's body.

[*The Adventures of Sylvia Scarlett*]

Gabriel Garcia Márquez, 1928– , Colombian novelist
The problem with marriage is that it ends every night after making love and it must be rebuilt every morning before breakfast.

[*Love in the Time of Cholera* 1985]

Menander, c.343–291BC, Greek poet
A daughter is an embarrassing and ticklish possession.

[Perinthis c.300BC]

Marriage, to tell the truth, is an evil, but it is a necessary evil.

[Fragment c.300BC]

Spike [Terence Alan] Milligan, 1918–2002, Irish comedian and writer
She was growing up, and that was the direction I wanted her to take. Who wants a daughter that grows sideways?

[Indefinite Articles]

A[lan] A[lexander] Milne, 1882–1956, English writer
James James
Morrison Morrison
Weatherby George Dupree
Took great
Care of his Mother,
Though he was only three.

[When We Were Very Young: Disobedience 1924]

John Milton, 1608–74, English poet
Nothing lovelier can be found
In woman, than to study household good,
And good works in her husband to promote.

[Paradise Lost 1667]

Molière [Jean-Baptiste Poquelin], 1622–73, French playwright
Le mariage, Agnès, n'est pas un badinage.
Marriage, Agnes, is not a joke.

[L'Ecole des femmes 1662]

William Cosmo Monkhouse, 1840–1901, English art critic and poet
There was an old party of Lyme,
Who married three wives at one time.
When asked, "Why the third?" He replied,
"One's absurd,
And bigamy, sir, is a crime.

[Limerick]

Thomas Moore, 1779–1852, Irish poet
"Come, come," said Tom's father, "at your time of life,
There's no longer excuse for thus playing the rake –
It is time you should think, boy, of taking a wife – "
"Why, so it is, father – whose wife shall I take?"

[A Joke Versified]

Christopher [Darlington] Morley, 1890–1957. American writer
There is no prince or prelate
I envy – no, not one.
No evil can befall me –
By God, I have a son'

[Secret Laughter]

Ralph Nader, 1934– , American writer and reformer

Young wives are the leading asset of corporate power. They want the suburbs, a house, a settled life. And respectability. They want society to see they have exchanged themselves for something of value.

Napoleon I [Napoleon Bonaparte], 1769–1821, emperor of France

It is horrible to see oneself die without children.

[To Gaspard Gourgaud, St Helena 1817]

Ogden Nash, 1902–71, American humorous writer

I hope my tongue in prune juice smothers
If I belittle dogs and mothers.

[*Versus: I Do, I Will, I Have* 1949]

Cardinal John Henry Newman, 1801–90, English churchman and poet

Lead, kindly Light, amid the encircling gloom,
Lead Thou me on;
The night is dark, and I am far from home.

[*Lead Kindly Light*]

George Orwell [Eric Arthur Blair], 1903–50, English novelist and critic

[On England] It resembles a family, a rather stuffy Victorian family, with not many black sheep in it but with all its cupboards bursting with skeletons. It has rich relations who have to be kow-towed to and poor relations who are horribly sat upon, and there is a deep conspiracy about the source of the family income. It is a family in which the young are generally thwarted and most of the power is in the hands of irresponsible uncles and bedridden aunts. Still, it is a family.

[*England, Your England*]

John Howard Payne, 1791–1852, American playwright

'Mid pleasures and palaces though we may roam,
Be it ever so humble, there's no place like home.

[*Clari, the Maid of Milan* 1823]

Samuel Pepys, 1633–1703, English diarist

My wife, who, poor wretch, is troubled with her lonely life.

[*Diary* 19 December 1662]

Saw a wedding in the church; and strange to see what delight we married people have to see these poor fools decoyed into our condition.

[*Ibid* 25 December 1665]

Home, and, being washing day, dined upon cold meat.

[*Ibid* 4 April 1666]

Alexander Pope, 1688–1744, English poet

Go, like the Indian, in another life
Expect thy dog, thy bottle, and thy wife.

[*Essay on Man* 1732–4]

Chaste to her husband, frank to all beside,
A teeming mistress, but a barren bride.

[*Moral Essays* 1731–5]

She who ne'er answers till a husband cools,
Or, if she rules him, never shows she rules;
Charms by accepting, by submitting sways,
Yet has her humour most when she obeys.

[Ibid]

Not louder shrieks to pitying heaven are cast,
When husbands or when lapdogs breathe their last.

[The Rape of the Lock 1714]

Ezra [Loomis] Pound, 1885–1972, American poet
O how hideous it is
To see three generations of one house gathered together!
It is like an old tree with shoots,
And with some branches rotted and falling.

[Commission]

Come, let us pity those who are better off than we are.
Come, my friend, and remember
That the rich have butlers and no friends,
And we have friends and no butlers.
Come, let us pity the married and unmarried.

[The Garret]

Publilius Syrus, *fl.* 1st century BC, Roman writer
It is mind, not body, that makes marriage last.

[Sententiae c.50BC]

Bertrand [Arthur William] Russell, 3rd Earl Russell, 1872–1970, English philosopher
The more civilized people become the less capable they seem of lifelong happiness with one partner.

[Marriage and Morals 1929]

Ihara Saikaku [Hirayama Togo], 1642–93, Japanese novelist
Marrying off your daughter is a piece of business you may expect to do only once in a lifetime, and, bearing in mind that none of the losses are recoverable later, you should approach the matter with extreme caution.

[Nippon Eitai-gura]

And why do people wilfully exhaust their strength in promiscuous living, when their wives are on hand from bridal night till old age – to be taken when required, like fish from a private pond.

[Ibid]

Saki [Hector Hugh Munro], 1870–1916, Scottish-born writer
The Western custom of one wife and hardly any mistresses.

[Reginald in Russia 1910]

Charles Monroe Schulz, 1922–2000, American cartoonist
Big sisters are the crab grass in the lawn of life.

[Peanuts 1952]

William Shakespeare, 1564–1616, English dramatist
She's beautiful and therefore to be woo'd
She is a woman, therefore to be won.

[King HenryVI, Part I 5 1591]

165

This is the way to kill a wife with kindness.

[*The Taming of the Shrew* 4 1593–4]

Such duty as the subject owes the prince
Even such a woman oweth to her husband.

[*Ibid* 5]

Home-keeping youth have ever homely wits.

[*The Two Gentlemen of Verona* 1 1594–5]

The cuckoo then, on every tree,
Mocks married men; for thus sings he,
Cuckoo;
Cuckoo, cuckoo: O world of fear,
Unpleasing to a married ear.

[*Love's Labour's Lost* 5 1594–5]

It is a wise father that knows his own child.

[*The Merchant of Venice* 2 1596–7]

As 'tis ever common
That men are merriest when they are from home.

[*King Henry V* 1 1598–1600]

Benedick the married man.

[*Much Ado About Nothing* 1 1598–1600]

I have a good eye, uncle; I can see a church by daylight.

[*Ibid* 2]

Men are April when they woo, December when they wed: maids are May when they are
maids, but the sky changes when they are wives.

[*As You Like It* 4 1598–1600]

And in these degrees have they made a pair of stairs to marriage which they will climb
incontinent, or else be incontinent before marriage.

[*Ibid* 5]

Many a good hanging prevents a bad marriage.

[*Twelfth Night* 1 1598–1600]

I am all the daughters of my father's house,
And all the brothers too.

[*Ibid* 2]

You are my true and honourable wife,
As dear to me as are the ruddy drops
That visit my sad heart.

[*Julius Caesar* 2 1598–1600]

A young man married is a man that's marr'd.

[*All's Well That Ends Well* 2 1601–1603

O curse of marriage,
That we can call these delicate creatures ours,
And not their appetites! I had rather be a toad,
And live upon the vapour of a dungeon,
Than keep a corner in the thing I love
For others' uses.

[*Othello* 3 1604–1605]

I have given suck and know
How tender 'tis to love the babe that milks me:
I would, while it was smiling in my face,
Have pluck'd my nipple from his boneless gums,
And dash'd the brains out, had I so sworn as you
Have done to this.

[*Macbeth* 1 1605–6]

Dost thou not see my baby at my breast,
That sucks the nurse asleep.

[*Antony and Cleopatra* 5 1606–7]

Let me not to the marriage of true minds
Admit impediments. Love is not love
Which alters when it alteration finds.

[*Sonnets* 116 1609]

George Bernard Shaw, 1856–1950, Irish playwright
Those who talk most about the blessings of marriage and the constancy of its vows are the very people who declare that if the chain were broken and the prisoners left free to choose, the whole social fabric would fly asunder. You cannot have the argument both ways. If the prisoner is happy, why lock him in? If he is not, why pretend that he is?

[*Man and Superman* 1903]

Marriage is popular because it combines the maximum of temptation with the maximum of opportunity.

[*Ibid*: *Maxims for Revolutionists* 1903]

Home is the girl's prison and the woman's workhouse.

[*Ibid*]

Home life as we understand it is no more natural to us than a cage is natural to a cockatoo.

[*Getting Married* 1908]

Percy Bysshe Shelley, 1792–1822, English poet
A system could not well have been devised more studiously hostile to human happiness than marriage.

[*Queen Mab* notes 1813]

Richard Brinsley Sheridan, 1751–1816, English dramatist
'Tis safest in matrimony to begin with a little aversion.

[*The Rivals* 1775]

Tobias [George] Smollett, 1721–71, Scottish novelist and surgeon
A seafaring man may have a sweetheart in every port; but he should steer clear of a wife as he would avoid a quicksand.

[*Sir Launcelot Greaves* 1762]

Stanislaus [Leszczynski], 1677–1766 king of Poland
Men and women, in marrying, make a vow to love one another. Would it not be better for their happiness if they made a vow to please one another?

[*Oeuvres du philosophe bienfaisant* 1763]

Laurence Sterne, 1713–68, English churchman and writer
I wish either my father or my mother, or indeed both of them, as they were in duty both equally bound to it, had minded what they were about when they begot me.

[*Tristram Shandy* 1760]

Robert Louis [Balfour] Stevenson, 1850–94, Scottish novelist and poet

Even if we take matrimony at its lowest, even if we regard it as no more than a sort of friendship recognized by the police.

[*Virginibus Puerisque* 1881]

Lastly (and this is, perhaps, the golden rule), no woman should marry a teetotaller, or a man who does not smoke.

[*Ibid*]

Marriage is like life in this – that it is a field of battle, and not a bed of roses.

[*Ibid*]

Marriage is a step so grave and decisive that it attracts light-headed, variable men by its very awfulness.

[*Ibid*]

In marriage, a man becomes slack and selfish, and undergoes a fatty degeneration of his moral being.

[*Ibid*]

Times are changed with him who marries; there are no more bypath meadows, where you may innocently linger, but the road lies long and straight and dusty to the grave.

[*Ibid*]

To marry is to domesticate the Recording Angel. Once you are married, there is nothing left for you, not even suicide, but to be good.

[*Ibid*]

Jonathan Swift, 1667–1745, Irish-born English writer

The reason why so few marriages are happy, is, because young ladies spend their time in making nets, not in making cages.

[*Thoughts on Various Subjects* 1706]

Jeremy Taylor, 1613–67, English churchman

He that loves not his wife and children, feeds a lioness at home and broods a nest of sorrows.

[*Sermons: Married Love*]

Alfred, Lord Tennyson, 1809–92, English poet

A happy bridesmaid makes a happy bride.

[*The Bridesmaid*]

Don't thou marry for munny, but go wheer munny is!

[*Northern Farmer: New Style*]

William Makepeace Thackeray, 1811–63, English novelist

This I set down as a positive truth. A woman with fair opportunities and without an absolute hump, may marry whom she likes.

[*Vanity Fair* 1847–8]

Remember, it's as easy to marry a rich woman as a poor woman.

[*Pendennis* 1848–50]

Margaret Hilda Thatcher, Baroness Thatcher of Kesteven, 1925– , British politician

I could combine being a good mother with being an effective professional woman, as long as I organized everything intelligently down to the last detail.

[*The Path to Power*]

We have become a grandmother.

[In the *Times* March 1989]

James Thomson, 1834–82, Scottish poet
Give a man a pipe he can smoke,
Give a man a book he can read:
And his home is bright with a calm delight,
Though the room be poor indeed.

[*Gifts*]

Count Leo [Nikolaevich] Tolstoy, 1828–1910, Russian writer
All happy families resemble one another; every unhappy family is unhappy in its own way.
[*Anna Karenina* 1876]

Mark Twain [Samuel Langhorne Clemens], 1835–1910, American writer
In Boston they ask, How much does he know? In New York, How much is he worth? In Philadelphia, Who were his parents?
[*What Paul Bourget Thinks of Us*]

Peter De Vries, 1910–93, American novelist and journalist
There are times when parenthood seems nothing but feeding the mouth that bites you.
[*Tunnel of Love* 1954]

Artemus Ward [Charles Farrar Browne], 1834–67, American humorist
[On Brigham Young, Mormon leader] He is dreadfully married. He's the most married man I ever saw in my life.
[*Artemus Ward's Lectures* 1869]

Mae West, 1892–1980, American entertainer
Marriage is a great institution, but I'm not ready for an institution yet.
[Attributed]

Oscar [Fingall O'Flahertie Wills] Wilde, 1854–1900, Irish writer
Twenty years of romance make a woman look like a ruin; but twenty years of marriage make her something like a public building.
[*A Woman of No Importance* 1893]
Children begin by loving their parents. After a time they judge them. Rarely, if ever, do they forgive them.
[*Ibid*]
Women have become so highly educated that nothing should surprise them except happy marriages.
[*Ibid*]
All women become like their mothers. That is their tragedy. No man does. That is his.
[*Ibid*]
You don't seem to realize, that in married life three is company and two is none.
[*The Importance of Being Earnest* 1895]

Thornton [Niven] Wilder, 1897–1975, American playwright
The best part of married life is the fights. The rest is merely so-so.
[*The Matchmaker* 1954]

Sir P[elham] G[reville] Wodehouse, 1881–1975, English-born writer
It is no use telling me that there are bad aunts and good aunts. At the core they are all alike. Sooner or later, out pops the cloven hoof.
[*The Code of the Woosters*]

169

Chumps always make the best husbands. When you marry, Sally, grab a chump. Tap his forehead first, and if it rings solid, don't hesitate. All the unhappy marriages come from the husbands having brains.

[*The Adventures of Sally*]

Mary Wollstonecraft, 1759–97, English writer
The absurd duty, too often inculcated, of obeying a parent only on account of his being a parent, shackles the mind, and prepares it for a slavish submission to any power but reason.

[*A Vindication of the Rights of Women* 1792]

[Adeline] Virginia Woolf, 1882–1941, English novelist and critic
Those comfortably padded lunatic asylums which are known, euphemistically, as the stately homes of England.

[*The Common Reader* 1925]

Henry Clay Work, 1832–84, American songwriter
Father, dear father, come home with me now,
The clock in the steeple strikes one.

[*Come Home, Father*]

Eating and Drinking

Henry Aldrich, 1647–1710, English churchman
If all be true that I do think,
There are five reasons we should drink:
Good wine – a friend – or being dry –
Or lest we should be by and by –
Or any other reason why.

[*Five Reasons for Drinking*]

Anonymous
I always eat peas with honey,
I've done it all my life,
They do taste kind of funny,
But it keeps them on the knife.

[*Peas*]

Hunger makes good kitchen.

[Proverb]

Eat at pleasure, drink by measure.

[Proverb]

Wine is a turn-coat; first a friend, then an enemy.

[Proverb]

James Beard, 1903–85, American cookery writer
A gourmet who thinks of calories is like a tart who looks at her watch.

[Caption to his photograph in a New York bar]

Pierre-Augustin Caron de Beaumarchais, 1732–99, French dramatist
Drinking when we are not thirsty and making love all year round, madam; that is all there is
to distinguish us from other animals.

[*The Marriage of Figaro* 1784]

Thomas Becon, 1512–67, English cleric
For when the wine is in, the wit is out.

[*Catechism*]

Sir John Betjeman, 1906–84, English poet
Phone for the fish-knives, Norman,
As Cook is a little unnerved;
You kiddies have crumpled the serviettes
And I must have things daintily served.

[A Few Late Chrysanthemums: How to Get On in Society 1954]

171

The Bible

And the ravens brought him bread and flesh in the morning, and bread and flesh in the evening; and he drank of the brook.

[*I Kings* 17:6]

Stolen waters are sweet, and bread eaten in secret is pleasant.

[*Proverbs* 9:17]

Wine is a mocker, strong drink is raging: and whosoever is deceived thereby is not wise.

[*Ibid* 20:1]

Thou preparest a table before me in the presence of mine enemies: thou anointest my head with oil; my cup runneth over.

[*Psalms* 23:6]

And behold joy and gladness, slaying oxen, and killing sheep, eating flesh, and drinking wine: let us eat and drink; for tomorrow we shall die.

[*Ibid* 22:13]

They reel to and fro, and stagger like a drunken man, and are at their wit's end.

[*Ibid* 107:27]

And when he had taken the five loaves and the two fishes, he looked up to heaven, and blessed, and brake the loaves, and gave them to his disciples to set before them; and the two fishes divided he among them all. And they did all eat, and were filled. And they took up twelve baskets full of the fragments, and of the fishes. And they that did eat of the loaves were about five thousand men.

[*Mark* 6: 41–44]

Drink no longer water, but use a little wine for thy stomach's sake and thine often infirmities.

[*I Timothy* 5:23]

Wine is as good as life to a man, if it be drunk moderately: what life is then to a man that is without wine? for it was made to make men glad.

[*Ecclesiasticus* 31:27]

Ambrose [Gwinett] Bierce, 1842–1914, American writer

Abdomen: the temple of the god Stomach, in whose worship, with sacrificial rights, all true men engage.

[*The Devil's Dictionary* 1906]

"I was in the drawing-room, enjoying my dinner," said Brillat-Savarin, beginning an anecdote. "What!" interrupted Rochebriant, "eating dinner in a drawing-room?" "I must beg you to observe, monsieur," explained the great gastronome, "that I did not say I was eating my dinner, but enjoying it. I had dined an hour before."

[*Ibid*]

Edible: good to eat, and wholesome to digest, as a worm to a toad, a toad to a snake, a snake to a pig, a pig to a man, and a man to a worm.

[*Ibid*]

Hospitality: the virtue which induces us to feed and lodge certain persons who are not in need of food and lodging.

[*Ibid*]

Rarebit: a Welsh rabbit, in the speech of the humorless, who point out that it is not a rabbit. To whom it may be solemnly explained that the comestible known as toad-in-the-hole is really not a toad, and that *riz-de-veau à la financière* is not the smile of a calf prepared after the recipe of a she banker.

[*Ibid*]

Sauce: the one infallible sign of civilization and enlightenment. A people with no sauces has one thousand vices; a people with one sauce has only nine hundred and ninety-nine. For every sauce invented and accepted a vice is renounced and forgiven.

[*Ibid*]

Wine: fermented grape-juice known to the Women's Christian Union as "liquor," sometimes as "rum." Wine, madame, is God's next best gift to man.

[*Ibid*]

Anthelme Brillat-Savarin, 1755–1826, French gourmet and writer
A meal without wine is like a day without sunshine.

[*The Physiology of Taste* 1825]

Rupert Chawner Brooke, 1887–1915, English poet
Stands the Church clock at ten to three?
And is there honey still for tea?

[*The Old Vicarage, Grantchester* 1912]

Robert Browning, 1812–89, English poet
So munch on, crunch on, take your muncheon
Breakfast, supper, dinner, luncheon!

[*The Pied Piper of Hamelin* 1879]

Edmund Burke, 1729–97, Irish-born English political writer
And having looked to government for bread, on the very first scarcity they will turn and bite the hand that fed them.

[*Thoughts and Details on Scarcity*]

Robert Burns, 1759–96, Scottish poet
I was na fou, but just had plenty.

[*Death and Dr Hornbook* 1785]

There's some are fou o' love divine,
There's some are fou o' brandy;
An monie jobs that day begin,
May end in houghmagandie
Some ither day.

[*The Holy Fair* 1785]

The halesome parritch, chief of Scotia's food.

[*The Cottar's Saturday Night* 1785]

Freedom and whisky gang the gither!

[*The Author's Earnest Cry and Prayer*]

Great chieftain o' the pudding-race.

[*Address to a Haggis*]

Go, fetch to me a pint o' wine,
And fill it in a silver tassie;
That I may drink before I go.
A service to my bonnie lassie.

[*My Bonnie Mary* 1786]

Some hae meat and canna eat,
And some wad eat that want it;
But we hae meat, and we can eat,
And sae the Lord be thankit.

[*The Selkirk Grace* 1793, attributed]

Byron, Lord George Gordon [Noel], 6th Baron Byron of Rochdale, 1788–1824, English poet

There's nought, no doubt, so much the spirit calms
As rum and true religion.

[*Don Juan* 1819–24]

Let us have wine and women, mirth and laughter,
Sermons and soda water the day after.

[*Ibid*]

All human history attests
That happiness for man – the hungry sinner! –
Since Eve ate apples, much depends on dinner.

[*Ibid*]

Lewis Carroll [Charles Lutwidge Dodgson], 1832–92, English mathematician and writer

Jam tomorrow and jam yesterday – but never jam today.

[*Through the Looking-Glass and What Alice found there* 1872]

"A loaf of bread," the Walrus said,
"Is what we chiefly need:
Pepper and vinegar besides
Are very good indeed –
Now if you're ready, Oysters dear,
We can begin to feed."

[*Through the Looking-Glass and What Alice Found There* 1872]

Miguel de Cervantes [Saavedra], 1547–1616, Spanish dramatist and poet

I drink when I have occasion for it, and sometimes when I have not.

[*Don Quixote* 1615]

G[ilbert] K[eith] Chesterton, 1874–1936, English writer

And Noah he often said to his wife when he sat down to dine,
"I don't care where the water goes if it doesn't get into the wine."

[*Wine and Water*]

Irvin [Shrewsbury] Cobb, 1876–1944, American humorist

[On "corn licker"] It smells like gangrene starting in a mildewed silo, it tastes like the wrath to come, and when you absorb a deep swig of it you have all the sensations of having swallowed a lighted kerosene lamp.

[To the Distillers' Code Authority, National Recovery Administration]

Samuel Taylor Coleridge, 1772–1834, English poet

Water, water, everywhere,
And all the boards did shrink;
Water, water, everywhere.
Nor any drop to drink.

[*The Ancient Mariner* 1798]

Cyril [Vernon] Connolly, 1903–74, English writer

Imprisoned in every fat man a thin one is wildly signalling to be let out.

[*The Unquiet Grave* 1944]

174

Quentin Crisp, 1908–99, English eccentric and writer
My favourite food is Guinness. It's the only food that doesn't have to be cooked or kept in the refrigerator.
[In the *Daily Express* April 27 1989]

Michael [Kirk] Douglas, 1944– , American film actor
Lunch is for wimps.
[*Wall Street* film screenplay by Stanley Weiser and Oliver Stone, directed by Oliver Stone 1987]

T[homas] S[tearns] Eliot, 1888–1965, American-born English poet
I have measured out my life with coffee spoons.
[*The Love Song of J. Alfred Prufrock* 1915]

Should I, after tea and cakes and ices,
Have the strength to force the moment to its crisis?
[*Ibid*]

They are rattling breakfast plates in the basement kitchens,
And along the trampled edges of the street
I am aware of the damp souls of housemaids
Sprouting despondently at area gates.
[*Morning at the Window*]

Epictetus, c. AD50–c.120, Greek philosopher
He is a drunkard who takes more than three glasses, though he be not drunk.
[*Encheiridion c.*110]

Epicurus, c. 341–270BC, Greek philosopher
We should look for someone to eat and drink with before looking for something to eat and drink, for dining alone is leading the life of a lion or wolf.
[*Aphorisms c.*300BC]

François de Salignac de la Mothe Fénélon, 1651–1715, French churchman
Some of the most dreadful mischiefs that afflict mankind proceed from wine; it is the cause of disease, quarrels, sedition, idleness, aversion to labour, and every species of domestic disorder.
[*Télémaque* 1699]

Ludwig Andreas Feuerbach, 1804–72, German philosopher
Der Mensch is was er isst.
Man is what he eats.
[Preface to Moleschott's *Lehre der Nahrungsmittel* 1850]

John Ford, 1586–c.1640, English dramatist
We can drink till all look blue.
[*The Lady's Trial* 1638]

Benjamin Franklin, 1706–90, American scientist and philosopher
To lengthen thy life, lessen thy meals.
[*Poor Richard's Almanac* 1733]

Mohandas Karamchand ("Mahatma") Gandhi, 1869–1948, Indian political leader
Man becomes what he eats. The grosser the food the grosser the body.
[*Harijan* 1933]

Sir William Schwenck Gilbert, 1836–1911, English librettist
A taste for drink, combined with gout,
Had doubled him up for ever.

[*The Gondoliers* 1889]

Robert von Ranke Graves, 1895–1985, English poet
He grips the tankard of brown ale
That spills a generous foam:
Oft-times he drinks, they say, and winks
At drunk men lurching home.

[*The General Elliott*]

Ernest [Miller] Hemingway, 1899–1961, American novelist
This wine is too good for toast-drinking, my dear. You don't want to mix emotions up with a wine like that. You lose the taste.

[*The Sun Also Rises* 1926]

Henry IV, 1553–1610, king of France
Les grand mangeurs et les grands dormeurs sont incapables de rien faire de grand.
(Great eaters and great sleepers are incapable of doing anything that is great.)

[Attributed]

George Herbert, 1593–1633, English poet
Drink not the third glasse, – which thou can'st not tame
When once it is within thee.

[*The Temple: The Church Porch* 1633]

Thomas Hood, 1799–1845, English poet
Oh! God! that bread should be so dear, And flesh and blood so cheap.

[*The Song of the Shirt* 1843]

A[lfred] E[dward] Housman, 1859–1936, English poet and scholar
And malt does more than Milton can
To justify God's ways to man.
Ale, man, ale's the stuff to drink
For fellows whom it hurts to think.

[*A Shropshire Lad* 1896]

Eugene Ionesco, 1912–94, Romanian-born French playwright
Yoghurt is very good for the stomach, the lumbar regions, appendicitis and apotheosis.

[*The Bald Prima Donna* 1956]

Washington Irving, 1783–1859, American diplomat and writer
They who drink beer will think beer.

[*The Sketch-book: Stratford* 1819–20]

Thomas Jefferson, 1743–1826, 3rd president of the United States
[On beer] I wish to see this beverage become common instead of the whiskey which kills one third of our citizens, and ruins their families.

[Letter 1815]

EATING AND DRINKING

Dr Samuel Johnson, 1709–84, English lexicographer
For a man seldom thinks with more earnestness of anything than he does of his dinner.
[In Mrs Piozzi's *Anecdotes of Samuel Johnson* 1786]

Ben[jamin] Jonson, 1572–1637, English poet
Drink to me only with thine eyes,
And I will pledge with mine;
Or leave a kiss but in the cup,
And I'll not look for wine.

[*The Forest: To Celia* 1616]

Juvenal [Decimus Junius Juvenalis], c.AD60–c.136, Roman satirist
Panem et circenses.
(Bread and circuses.)

[*Satires*]

James Kirkup, 1918– , English poet
Lumps of sparkling sugar
Sling themselves out of their crystal bowl
With a disordered fountain's
Ornamental stops and starts.
The milk describes a permanent parabola
Girdled with satellites of spinning tarts.

[*Tea in a Space-Ship*]

Walter Savage Landor, 1775–1864, English writer
I shall dine late; but the dining room will be well lighted, the guests few and select.
[*Imaginary Conversations* 1824]

George Martin Lane, 1823–1912, American academic
The waiter roars it through the hall:
"We don't give bread with one fish-ball."

[*One Fish-ball*]

Fran Lebowitz, 1951– , American journalist and writer
A great many people in Los Angeles are on strict diets that restrict their intake of synthetic foods. The reason for this appears to be a widely-held belief that organically grown fruit and vegetables make the cocaine work faster.

[*Social Studies* 1983]

Henry Sambrooke Leigh, 1837–83, English writer
If you wish to grow thinner, diminish your dinner,
And take to light claret instead of pale ale;
Look down with an utter contempt upon butter,
And never touch bread till it's toasted – or stale.

[*Carols of Cockayne* 1869]

Marie Antoinette, 1755–93, queen of France
Qu'ils mangent de la brioche.
(Let them eat cake.)

[Attributed]

W[illiam] Somerset Maugham, 1874–1965, English novelist

At a dinner party one should eat wisely but not too well, and talk well but not too wisely.

[A Writer's Notebook 1949]

H[enry] L[ouis] Mencken, 1880–1956, American critic and writer

I've made it a rule never to drink by daylight and never to refuse a drink after dark.

[In the *New York Post* 1945]

Dixon Lanier Merritt, 1879–1954, American journalist

A rare old bird is the pelican,
His beak holds more than his belican.
He can take in his beak
Enough food for a week.
I'm darned if I know how the helican!

[The Pelican 1910]

A[lan] A[lexander] Milne, 1882–1956, English writer

I do like a little bit of butter to my bread.

[When We Were Very Young 1924]

What is the matter with Mary Jane?
She's crying with all her might and main,
And she won't eat her dinner – rice pudding again –
What *is* the matter with Mary Jane?

[When We Were Very Young 1924]

It was just as if somebody inside him were saying, "Now then, Pooh, time for a little something."

[Winnie the Pooh 1926]

Molière [Jean-Baptiste Poquelin], 1622–73, French playwright

He makes his cook his merit, and the world visits his dinners and not him.

[Le Misanthrope 1666]

Il faut manger pour vivre et non pas vivre pour manger.
(One should eat to live, not live to eat.)

[L'Avare 1668]

Je vis de vonne soupe et non de beau langage.
(It's good food and not fine words that keeps me alive.)

[Les Femmes Savantes 1672]

Thomas Moore, 1779–1852, Irish poet

Yet, who can help loving the land that has taught us
Six hundred and eighty-five ways to dress eggs.

[The Fudge Family in Paris]

J[ohn Cameron Andrieu] B[ingham Michael] Morton, ("Beachcomber"), 1893–1979, English author and journalist

Vegetarians have wicked, shifty eyes, and laugh in a cold and calculating manner. They pinch little children, steal stamps, drink water, favour beards . . . wheeze, squeak, drawl and maunder.

[By The Way]

John Motley Morehead, 1796–1866, American politician

It's a long time between drinks.

[Said while Governor of North Carolina]

178

Napoleon I [Napoleon Bonaparte], 1769–1821, emperor of France
An army marches on its stomach.

[Attributed]

Ogden Nash, 1902–71, American humorous writer
You two can be what you like, but since I am the big fromage in this family, I prefer to think of myself as the Gorgon Zola.

[*Medusa and the Mot Juste*]

Samuel Pepys, 1633–1703, English diarist
Strange to see how a good dinner and feasting reconciles everybody.

[*Diary* 9 November 1665]

William Pitt, 1759–1806, British statesman
I think I could eat one of Bellamy's veal pies.

[Last words]

François Rabelais, c.1494–c.1553, French physician and writer
L'appetit vient en mangeant.
(The appetite comes with eating.)

[*Gargantua* 1534]

Michael Wayne Rosen, 1946– , English writer and poet
I love chocolate cake.
And when I was a little boy
I loved it even more.

[*Chocolate Cake*]

Saki [Hector Hugh Munro], 1870–1916, Scottish-born writer
I loathe rice pudding, it's so wholesome.

[*The Watched Pot*]

The cook was a good cook, as cooks go; and as cooks go, she went.

[*Reginald on Besetting Sins* 1904]

Siegfried Sassoon, 1886–1967, English poet
A sallow waiter brings me beans and pork. . .
Outside there's fury in the firmament.
Ice-cream, of course, will follow; and I'm content.
O Babylon! O Carthage! O New York!

[*Storm on Fifth Avenue*]

Charles Monroe Schulz, 1922–2000, American cartoonist
No matter how hard you try, you can't bend a cracker.

[*For the Love of Peanuts* 1963]

John Selden, 1584–1654, English antiquary and politician
'Tis not the drinking that is to be blamed, but the excess.

[*Table Talk: Humility* 1689]

Seneca, c.4BC–AD65, Roman philosopher
Drunkenness is simply voluntary insanity.

[*Epistolae ad Lucilium* c.AD63]

William Shakespeare, 1564–1616, English dramatist

There shall be in England seven halfpenny loaves sold for a penny: the three hooped pot shall have ten hoops; and I will make it a felony to drink small beer.

[*King Henry VI, Part II* 4 1591]

O, who can hold a fire in his hand
By thinking on the frosty Caucasus?
Or cloy the hungry edge of appetite
By bare imagination of a feast?

[*King Richard II* 1 1595–6]

Falstaff sweats to death,
And lards the lean earth as he walks along.

[*King Henry IV Part I* 2 1597–8]

He hath eaten me out of house and home.

[*Ibid*]

Who with a body fill'd and vacant mind,
Gets him to rest, cramm'd with distressful bread.

[*King Henry V* 4 1598–1600]

I am a great eater of beef and I believe that does harm to my wit.

[*Twelfth Night* 1 1598–1600]

Now in the name of all the gods at once,
Upon what meat doth this our Caesar feed,
That he is grown so great?

[*Julius Caesar* 1 1598–1600]

He was a man
Of an unbounded stomach.

[*King Henry VIII* 4 1613]

I have very poor and unhappy brains for drinking: I could wish courtesy would invent some other custom of entertainment.

[*Othello* 2 1604–5]

Come, come, good wine is a good familiar creature, if it be well used.

[*Ibid* 2:3:313]

But mice and rats and such small deer,
Have been Tom's food for seven long year.

[*King Lear* 3 1605–6]

I have yet
Room for six scotches more.

[*Antony and Cleopatra* 4 1606–7]

George Bernard Shaw, 1856–1950, Irish playwright

I'm only a beer teetotaller, not a champagne teetotaller.

[*Candida* 1898]

There is no love sincerer than the love of food.

[*Man and Superman* 1903]

Percy Bysshe Shelley, 1792–1822, English poet

We'll have tea and toast,
Custards for supper, and an endless host
Of syllabubs and jellies and mince-pies,
And other such lady-like luxuries.

[Letter to Maria Gisborne]

Eating and Drinking

Goldwin Smith, 1823–1910, English historian
King Nebuchadnezzar was turned out to grass
With oxen, horses and the savage ass.
The king surveyed the unaccustomed fare
With an inquiring but disdainful air
And murmured as he cropped the unwonted food,
"It may be wholesome but it is not good."

[*Lines parodying Newdigate Prize poems*]

Sydney Smith, 1771–1845, English churchman
Oh, green and glorious! Oh, herbaceous treat!
'Twould tempt the dying anchorite to eat:
Back to the world he'd turn his fleeting soul,
And plunge his fingers in the salad-bowl!
Serenely full, the epicure would say,
Fate cannot harm me, I have dined to-day!

[In Lady Holland's *Memoir of the Reverend Sydney Smith: Recipe for Salad* 1855]

Socrates, c.469–399BC, Greek philosopher
Bad men live that they may eat and drink, whereas good men eat and drink that they may live.

[In Plutarch's *How Young Men Ought to hear Poems*]

Sir J[ohn] C[ollings] Squire, 1884–1958, English poet
But I am not so think as you drunk I am.

[*Ballade of Soporific Absorption*]

Robert Louis [Balfour] Stevenson, 1850–94, Scottish novelist and poet
Fifteen men on the Dead Man's Chest –
Yo-ho-ho, and a bottle of rum!
Drink and the devil had done for the rest –
Yo-ho-ho, and a bottle of rum!

[*Treasure Island* 1881–2]

Go, little book, and wish to all,
Flowers in the garden, meat in the hall,
A bin of wine, a spice of wit,
A house with lawns enclosing it,
A living river by the door,
A nightingale in the sycamore.

[*Underwoods: Envoy* 1887]

William Stevenson, c.1530–1575, English academic
I cannot eat but little meat,
My stomach is not good;
But sure I think that I can drink
With him that wears a hood.

[*Gammer Gurton's Needle* (disputed)]

Jonathan Swift, 1667–1745, Irish-born English writer
Fingers were made before forks, and hands before knives.

[*Polite Conversation* c.1738]

It was a bold man that first ate an oyster.

[*Ibid*]

James Grover Thurber, 1894–1961, American humorist
Seeing isn't believing, it's eating that's believing.

[Caption to his photograph in a New York bar]

Mark Twain [Samuel Langhorne Clemens], 1835–1910, American writer
I might glorify my bill of fare until I was tired; but after all, the Scotchman would shake his head and say, "Where's your haggis?" and the Fijian would sigh and say, "Where's your missionary?"

[*A Tramp Abroad* 1879]

Peter De Vries, 1910–93, American novelist and journalist
"Do you like codfish balls?"
"I don't know, I've never attended any."

[*The Mackerel Plaza* 1958]

Horace Walpole, 4th Earl of Orford, 1717–97, English writer
I have a partiality for drunkenness, though I never practised it: it is a reality; but what is sobriety, only the absence of drunkenness?

[Letter 1789]

Izaak Walton, 1593–1683, English writer on fishing
This dish of meat is too good for any but anglers, or very honest men.

[*The Compleat Angler* 1653]

William Carlos Williams, 1883–1963, American novelist and poet
I have eaten
the plums
that were in
the icebox
and which
you were probably
saving
for breakfast.

[*Poems: This is Just to Say* 1934]

[Adeline] Virginia Woolf, 1882–1941, English novelist and critic
One cannot think well, love well, sleep well, if one has not dined well.

[*A Room of One's Own* 1929]

William Wordsworth, 1770–1850, English poet
And homeless near a thousand homes I stood,
And near a thousand tables pined and wanted food.

[*Guilt and Sorrow* 1791–4]

Drink, pretty creature, drink.

[*The Pet Lamb* 1800]

William Butler Yeats, 1865–1939, Irish poet
Come swish around, my pretty punk,
And keep me dancing still
That I may stay a sober man
Although I drink my fill.

[*A Drunken Man's Praise of Sobriety* 1938]

Fools and Foolishness

Sir William Alexander, Earl of Stirling, c.1567–1640, Scottish poet
Yet with great toil all that I can attain
By long experience, and in learned schools,
Is for to know my knowledge is but vain,
And those that think them wise are greatest fools.

[*The Tragedy of Croesus* 1604]

Anonymous
Fools and madmen ought not to be left in their own company.

[Proverb]

There's no fool like an old fool.

[Proverb]

When a fool helps, the more he helps, the worse things get.

[Chinese Proverb]

Phineas Taylor Barnum, 1810–91, American showman
You can fool some of the people all the time, and all of the people some of the time, but you can't fool all of the people all the time.

[Attributed]

The Bible
Even a fool, when he holdeth his peace, is counted wise: and he that shutteth his lips is esteemed a man of understanding.

[*Proverbs* 17:28]

It is an honour for a man to cease from strife: but every fool will be meddling.

[*Ibid* 20:3]

Answer not a fool according to his folly, lest thou also be like unto him. Answer a fool according to his folly, lest he be wise in his own conceit. He that sendeth a message by the hand of a fool cutteth off the feet and drinketh damage.

[*Ibid* 26:4–6]

The heart of the wise is in the house of mourning: but the heart of fools is in the house of mirth. It is better to hear the rebuke of the wise, than for a man to hear the song of fools.

[*Ecclesiastes* 7:4–61]

Be not hasty in thy spirit to be angry: for anger resteth in the bosom of fools.

[*Ibid* 7:9]

For ye suffer fools gladly, seeing ye yourselves are wise.

[*2 Corinthians* 11:19]

Ambrose [Gwinett] Bierce, 1842–1914, American writer

Folly: that "gift and faculty divine" whose creative and controlling energy inspires Man's mind, guides his actions and adorns his life.

[*The Devil's Dictionary* 1906]

Fool: a person who pervades the domain of intellectual speculation and diffuses himself through the channels of moral activity. He it was who invented letters, printing, the railroad, the steamboat, the telegraph, the platitude, and the circle of the sciences. He created patriotism and taught the nations war – founded theology, philosophy, law, medicine and Chicago. He established monarchical and republican government. His grandmotherly hand has warmly tucked in the set sun of civilization, and in the twilight he prepares man's evening meal of milk-and-mortality and turns down the covers of the universal grave. And after the rest of us shall have retired for the night of eternal oblivion he will sit up to write a history of human civilization.

[*Ibid*]

William Blake, 1757–1827, English poet and artist

A fool sees not the same tree that a wise man sees.

[*Marriage of Heaven and Hell: Proverbs of Hell* c.1790–93]

Nicolas Boileau-Despréaux, 1636–1711, French poet

A fool always finds a greater fool to admire him.

[*L'Art poétique* 1674]

Jane Brereton, 1685–1740, English poet

The picture, plac'd the busts between,
Adds to the thought much strength;
Wisdom and Wit are little seen,
But Folly's at full length.

[*On Mr Nash's Picture at Full Length between the Busts of Sir Isaac Newton and Mr Pope*
(alsoattributed to Lord Chesterfield)]

Byron, Lord George Gordon [Noel], 6th Baron Byron of Rochdale, 1788–1824, English poet

I'll publish right or wrong:
Fools are my theme, let satire be my song.

[*English Bards and Scotch Reviewers* 1809]

We are the fools of time and terror: Days
Steal on us, and steal from us; yet we live,
Loathing our life, and dreading still to die.

[*Manfred* 1817]

Thomas Carlyle, 1795–1881, Scottish historian and writer

A Parliament speaking through reporters to Buncombe and the twenty-seven million, mostly fools.

[*Latter-day Pamphlets: Parliaments* 1850]

Miguel de Cervantes [Saavedra], 1547–1616, Spanish dramatist and poet

He's a muddled fool, full of lucid intervals.

[*Don Quixote* 1615]

Colly Cibber, 1671–1757, English playwright

If I can please myself with my own follies, have I not a plentiful provision for life?

[*Apology for His Life* 1740]

Charles Caleb Colton, c.1780–1832, English writer

The follies of the fool are known to the world, but are hidden from himself; the follies of the wise are known to himself, but hidden from the world.

[*Lacon* 1820]

Confucius [K'ung fu-tzu], 551–479BC, Chinese philosopher

For one word a man is often deemed to be wise, and for one word he is often deemed to be foolish. We should be careful indeed what we say.

[*Analects c.*500BC]

William Cowper, 1731–1800, English poet

How much a dunce that has been sent to roam
Excels a dunce that has been kept at home.

[*The Progress of Error* 1782]

'Tis hard if all is false that I advance –
A fool must now and then be right, by chance.

[*Conversation* 1782]

The Dhammapada, c.AD100

Though a fool spend all his life with wise men, he will know the truth no more than a spoon knows the taste of soup.

Fyodor Mikhailovich Dostoevsky, 1821–1881, Russian novelist

The cleverest of all, in my opinion, is the man who calls himself a fool at least once a month.

[*A Writer's Diary* 1873]

Michael [Kirk] Douglas, 1944– , American film actor

A fool and his money are lucky enough to get together in the first place.

[*Wall Street* film 1987. Screenplay by Stanley Weiser and Oliver Stone, directed by Oliver Stone]

Albert Einstein, 1879–1955, German-born mathematical physicist

Before God we are all equally wise – equally foolish.

[Address at the Sorbonne, Paris]

George Eliot [Mary Ann Evans, 1819–80, English novelist

I'm not denyin' the women are foolish: God Almighty made 'em to match the men.

[*Adam Bede* 1859]

T[homas] S[tearns] Eliot, 1888–1965, American-born English poet

When lovely woman stoops to folly and
Paces about her room again, alone,
She smoothes her hair with automatic hand,
And puts a record on the gramophone.

[*The Waste Land: The Fire Sermon* 1922]

Euripides, c.480–406BC, Greek dramatist

The fool speaks only folly.

[*Bacchae c.*410BC]

W.C. Fields [William Claude Dunkinfield], 1879–1946, American actor

Never give a sucker an even break.

[Attributed]

Jean de La Fontaine, 1621–95, French poet

Alas! we see that at all times the
Small have suffered from the follies of the Great.

[*Fables* 1671]

Bernard le Bovier de Fontenelle, 1657–1757, French writer

The follies of the fathers are no warning to the children.

[*Dialogues des morts* 1683]

Benjamin Franklin, 1706–90, American scientist and philosopher

Experience keeps a dear school, but fools will learn in no other.

[*Poor Richard's Almanack* 1743]

To be intimate with a foolish friend is like going to bed with a razor.

[*Ibid* 1754]

It is ill manners to silence a fool, and cruelty to let him go on.

[*Ibid*]

The first degree of folly is to conceit one's self wise; the second to profess it; the third to despise counsel.

[*Ibid*]

Oliver Goldsmith, 1728–74, Irish-born English writer

When lovely woman stoops to folly,
And finds too late that men betray,
What charm can soothe her melancholy?
What art can wash her guilt away?
The only art her guilt to cover,
To hide her shame from every eye,
To give repentance to her lover
And wring his bosom is – to die.

[*The Vicar of Wakefield* 1766]

Thomas Gray, 1716–71, English poet

Thought would destroy their paradise.
No more; – where ignorance is bliss,
'Tis folly to be wise.

[*Ode on a Distant Prospect of Eton College* 1747]

Oscar Hammerstein II, 1895–1960, American lyricist

Fools give you reasons, wise men never try.

[Song: *Some Enchanted Evening*. In *South Pacific* 1949]

Tom [Thomas J] Hanks, 1956– , American actor

Stupid is as stupid does.

[*Forrest Gump* film 1994. Screenplay by Eric Roth, directed by Robert Zemeckis, based on Winston Groom's novel]

Henry IV, 1553–1610, king of France

[On James VI of Scotland and I of England] The wisest fool in Christendom.

[Attributed]

The Hitopadesa, c.500

Of the child unborn, the dead, and the fool, the two first, and not the last, are the least to be lamented; for the two first cause but a transient sorrow, whilst the last is an eternal plague.

Thomas Hobbes, 1588–1679, English political philosopher

For words are wise men's counters, they do but reckon by them; but they are the money of fools.

[*Leviathan* 1651]

[Sir] Anthony Hope [Hawkins], 1863–1933, English novelist

His foe was folly and his weapon wit.

[Memorial to W.S. Gilbert]

Aldous [Leonard] Huxley, 1894–1963, English writer

The solemn foolery of scholarship for scholarship's sake.

[*The Perennial Philosophy* 1945]

Henrik Ibsen, 1828–1906, Norwegian dramatist

Fools are in a terrible, overwhelming majority, all the wide world over.

[*An Enemy of the People* 1882]

Eugene Ionesco, 1912–94, Romanian-born French playwright

Characters in a play don't always have to be bigger fools than in everyday life.

[*Foursome*]

Benjamin Jonson, 1572–1637, English poet

To be a fool born is a disease incurable.

[*Volpone* 1605]

Rudyard Kipling, 1865–1936, English writer

Then ye returned to your trinkets; then ye contented your souls
With the flannelled fools at the wicket or the muddied oafs at the goals.

[*The Islanders*]

And the end of the fight is a tombstone white with the name of the late deceased,
And the epitaph drear: "A fool lies here who tried to hustle the East."

[*Chapter Headings: The Naulahka*]

Take my word for it, the silliest woman can manage a clever man; but it needs a very clever woman to manage a fool.

[*Three and – an Extra*]

Primo Levi, Italian scientist and writer

To be considered stupid and to be told so is more painful than being called gluttonous, mendacious, violent, lascivious, lazy, cowardly: every weakness, every vice, has found its defenders, its rhetoric, its ennoblement and exaltation, but stupidity hasn't.

[*Other People's Trades* 1985]

Abraham Lincoln, 1809–65, 16th president of the United States

You can fool some of the people all of the time, and all of the people some of the time, but you cannot fool all of the people all the time.

[Attributed 1856]

Better to remain silent and be thought a fool than to speak out and remove all doubt.

[Attributed]

W[illiam] Somerset Maugham, 1874–1965, English novelist

Most people are such fools that it is really no great compliment to say that a man is above the average.

[*A Writer's Notebook* 1949]

John Milton, 1608–74, English poet

Sweet bird, that shunn'st the noise of folly,
Most musical, most melancholy.

[*Il Penseroso* 1645]

Hence vain, deluding joys,
The brood of folly without father bred.

[*Ibid*]

Into a Limbo large and broad, since called
The Paradise of Fools, to few unknown.

[*Paradise Lost* 1667]

Lady Mary Wortley Montagu, 1689–1762, English writer

I enjoy vast delight in the folly of mankind; and, God be praised, that is an inexhaustible source of entertainment.

[Letter 1725]

Thomas Moore, 1779–1852, Irish poet

My only books
Were woman's looks,
And folly's all they've taught me.

[*Irish Melodies* 1801–34: *The Time I've lost in wooing*]

P[atrick] J[ake] O'Rourke, 1947– , American satirist

Seriousness is stupidity sent to college.

[*Give War a Chance* 1992]

Edgar Allan Poe, 1809–49, American writer

I have great faith in fools: – self-confidence my friends will call it.

[*Marginalia* 1844–9]

Alexander Pope, 1688–1744, English poet

Some have at first for Wits then Poets past,
Turn'd Critics next, and prov'd plain fools at last.

[*Essay on Criticism* 1711]

Good-nature and good-sense must ever join;
To err is human, to forgive, divine.

[*Ibid*]

Pride, the never-failing vice of fools.

[*Ibid*]

For fools admire, but men of sense approve.

[*Ibid*]

For fools rush in where angels fear to tread.

[*Ibid*]

For forms of government let fools contest;
What'er is best administer'd is best:
For modes of faith let graceless zealots fight;
He can't be wrong whose life is in the right:
In faith and hope the world will disagree,
But all mankind's concern is charity.

[*Essay on Man* 1732–4]

Fired that the house reject him, "'Sdeath! I'll print it,
And shame the fools.

[*Epistle to Dr Arbuthnot* 1735]

No creature smarts so little as a fool.

[*Ibid*]

Damn with faint praise, assent with civil leer,
And, without sneering, teach the rest to sneer;
Willing to wound, and yet afraid to strike,
Just hint a fault, and hesitate dislike;
Alike reserved to blame, or to commend,
A timorous foe, and a suspicious friend;
Dreading e'en fools, by flatterers besieged,
And so obliging, that he ne'er obliged.

[*Ibid*]

Helen Rowland, 1875–1950, American writer
A fool and her money are soon courted.

[*A Guide to Men* 1922]

Bertrand [Arthur William] Russell, 3rd Earl Russell, 1872–1970, English philosopher
The average man's opinions are much less foolish than they would be if he thought for himself.

[*The Autobiography of Bertrand Russell* 1969]

[Johann Christoph] Friedrich von Schiller, 1759–1805, German poet
Mit der Dummheit kämpfen Götter selbst vergebens.
(Against stupidity the gods themselves struggle in vain.)

[*Die Jungfrau von Orleans* (*The Maid of Orleans*) 1801]

William Shakespeare, 1564–1616, English dramatist
Lord, what fools these mortals be!

[*A Midsummer Night's Dream* 3 1595–6]

But love is blind and lovers cannot see
The pretty follies that themselves commit.

[*The Merchant of Venice* 2 1596–7]

I know thee not, old man: fall to thy prayers;
How ill white hairs become a fool and jester!

[*King Henry IV, Part II* 5 1597–8]

If thou remember'st not the slightest folly
That ever love did make thee run into,
Thou hast not loved.

[*As You Like It* 2 1598–1600]

Call me not fool till heaven hath sent me fortune.

[*Ibid*]

My lungs began to crow like chanticleer,
That fools should be so deep-contemplative,
And I did laugh sans intermission
An hour by his dial.

[*Ibid*]

I had rather have a fool to make me merry than experience to make me sad.

[*Ibid* 4]

The fool doth think he is wise, but the wise man knows himself to be a fool.

[*Ibid* 5]

He uses his folly like a stalking-horse and under the presentation of that he shoots his wit.

[*Ibid*]

Be absolute for death; either death or life
Shall thereby be the sweeter.
Reason thus with life:
If I do lose thee, I do lose a thing
That none but fools would keep: a breath thou art,
Servile to all the skyey influences.

[*Measure for Measure* 3 1604–5]

We make guilty of our disasters the sun, the moon, and the stars; as if we were villains by necessity, fools by heavenly compulsion.

[*King Lear* 1 1605–6]

Life's but a walking shadow, a poor player
That struts and frets his hour upon the stage
And then is heard no more: it is a tale
Told by an idiot, full of sound and fury,
Signifying nothing.

[*Macbeth* 5 1605–6]

So true a fool is love that in your will,
Though you do any thing, he thinks no ill.

[*Sonnets* 52 1609]

And art made tongue-tied by authority,
And folly doctor-like controlling skill,
And simple truth miscall'd simplicity,
And captive good attending captain ill.

[*Ibid* 66]

William Shenstone, 1714–63, English gardener and poet
A fool and his words are soon parted; a man of genius and his money.

[*Essays on Men and Manners: On Reserve*]

Sir Richard Steele, 1672–1729, Anglo-Irish essayist
No woman of spirit thinks a man hath any respect for her 'till he hath plaid the fool in her service.

[*The Lover* 1714]

William Temple, 1881–1944, English prelate and Archbishop of Canterbury.
If a man is going to be a villain, in heaven's name let him remain a fool.

[*Mens Creatrix*]

190

Henry David Thoreau, 1817–62, American naturalist and writer
Any fool can make a rule
And any fool will mind it.

[Journals 1906]

Thomas Tusser, c.1524–1580, English agriculturalist and writer
A fool and his money be soon at debate.

[*Five Hundred Points of Good Husbandry*]

Samuel Warren, 1807–77, English physician, lawyer and writer
There is probably no man living, though ever so great a fool, that cannot do *something* or other well.

[*Ten Thousand a Year* 1840–41]

Oscar [Fingall O'Flahertie Wills] Wilde, 1854–1900, Irish writer
There is no sin except stupidity.

[*Intentions: The Critic as Artist* 1891]

Thornton [Niven] Wilder, 1897–1975, American playwright
There's nothing like mixing with woman to bring out all the foolishness in a man of sense.

[*The Matchmaker* 1954]

But there comes a moment in everybody's life when he must decide whether he'll live among human beings or not – a fool among fools or a fool alone.

[*Ibid.*]

John Wilmot, 2nd Earl of Rochester, 1647–80, English poet
Here lies our sovereign lord the King
Whose word no man relies on,
Who never said a foolish thing,
Nor ever did a wise one.

[Epitaph for Charles II]

Thomas Woodrow Wilson, 1856–1924, 28th president of the United States
The best way to silence any friend of yours whom you know to be a fool is to induce him to hire a hall.

[Speech 1916]

William Butler Yeats, 1865–1939, Irish poet
If Folly link with Elegance
No man knows which is which,
Said the man in the golden breastplate
Under the old stone Cross.

[*The Old Stone Cross* 1938]

Friends and Friendship

Henry [Brooks] Adams, 1838–1918, American historian

A friend in power is a friend lost.

[*The Education of Henry Adams* 1907]

Friends are born not made.

[*Ibid*]

Anonymous

If you have one true friend, you have more than your share.

[Proverb]

Old friends and old wine are best.

[Proverb]

Friends are like fiddle-strings; they must not be screwed too tight.

[Proverb]

Friendship is friendship, but accounts must be kept.

[Proverb]

Aristotle, 384–322BC, Greek philosopher

The perfect friendship is that between good men, alike in their virtue.

[*The Nicomachean Ethics c.* 340BC]

When men are friends there is no need of justice between them, but though they be just they still need friendship.

[*Ibid*]

Without friends no one would choose to live, though he had all other goods.

[*Ibid*]

What is a friend? A single soul dwelling in two bodies.

[In Diogenes Laertius' *Lives of Eminent Philosophers*]

We should wish to behave to our friends as we would wish our friends to behave to us.

[*Ibid*]

Francis Bacon, Baron Verulam of Verulam and Viscount of St Albans, 1561–1626, English philosopher

The worst solitude is to be destitute of sincere friendship.

[*De Augmentis Scientiarum* 1623]

[Joseph] Hilaire [Pierre] Belloc, 1870–1953, English writer
From quiet homes and first beginning,
Out to the undiscovered ends,
There's nothing worth the wear of winning,
But laughter and the love of friends.

[*Dedicatory Ode*]

The Bible
A friend loveth at all times, and a brother is born for adversity.

[*Proverbs* 17:17]

A man that hath friends must show himself friendly; and there is a friend that sticketh closer
than a brother.

[*Ibid* 18:24]

Greater love hath no man than this, that a man lay down his life for his friends.

[*John* 15:13]

A faithful friend is a strong defence: and he that hath found such a one hath found a treasure.

[*Ecclesiasticus* 6:14]

A faithful friend is the medicine of life.

[*Ibid* 6:16]

Forsake not an old friend; for the new is not comparable to him; a new friend is as new wine;
when it is old, thou shalt drink it with pleasure.

[*Ibid* 9:10]

Ambrose [Gwinett] Bierce, 1842–1914, American writer
Acquaintance: a person whom we know well enough to borrow from, but not well enough to
lend to. A degree of friendship called slight when its object is poor or obscure, and intimate
when he is rich or famous.

[*The Devil's Dictionary* 1906]

Friendless: having no favours to bestow. Destitute of fortune. Addicted to utterance of truth
and common sense.

[*Ibid*]

While your friend holds you affectionately by both your hands you are safe, for you can watch
both his.

[*Ibid*]

William Blake, 1757–1827, English poet and artist
I was angry with my friend
I told my wrath, my wrath did end.
I was angry with my foe;
I told it not, my wrath did grow.

[*Songs of Experience: A Poison Tree* 1794]

Nicholas Breton, c.1545–c.1626. English poet
I wish my deadly foe no worse
Than want of friends, and empty purse.

[*A Farewell to Town*]

George Bryan ["Beau"] Brummell, 1778–1840, English man of fashion
[Of the Prince of Wales] Who's your fat friend?

Jean de La Bruyère, 1645–96, French moralist
In friendship we see only those faults that may injure our friends; in love we see only those that may injure ourselves.

[*Caractères* 1688]

Edward [George Earle Lytton] Bulwer-Lytton, 1st Baron, 1803–73, English statesman and writer
Whatever the number of a man's friends, there will be times in his life when he has one too few; but if he has only one enemy, he is lucky indeed if he has not one too many.

[*What Will He Do With It* 1858]

[Frank] Gelett Burgess, 1866–1951, American humorist
Love is only chatter,
Friends are all that matter.

[*Willy and the Lady*]

Robert Burns, 1759–96, Scottish poet
I want someone to laugh with me, someone to be grave with me, someone to please me and help my discrimination with his or her own remark, and at times, no doubt, to admire my acuteness and penetration.

[*Commonplace Book* 1787]

Should auld acquaintance be forgot,
And never brought to mind?
Should auld acquaintance be forgot,
And days o' auld lang syne.

[*Auld Lang Syne* 1788]

Byron, Lord George Gordon [Noel], 6th Baron Byron of Rochdale, 1788–1824, English poet
Friendship is Love without his wings.

[*Hours of Idleness*]

George Canning, 1770–1827, British statesman and writer
But of all plagues, good Heaven, thy wrath can send,
Save, save, oh save me from the candid friend!

[*New Morality*]

Willa Cather, 1876–1947, American author
Only solitary men know the full joy of friendship. Others have their family; but to a solitary and an exile his friends are everything.

[*Shadows on the Rock* 1931]

Susannah Centlivre, c.1667–1723, English dramatist
Friendship's a noble name, 'tis love refined.

[*The Stolen Heiress* 1715]

George Chapman, c.1559–1634, English dramatist
Trust not a reconciled friend, for good turns cannot blot out old grudges.

[*Alphonsus* 1654]

Anton [Pavlovoch] Chekhov, 1860–1904, Russian author and playwright
A woman can become a man's friend only in the following stages – first an acquaintance, next a mistress, and only then a friend.

[*Uncle Vanya* 1896]

Charles Churchill, 1731–64, English churchman and poet
[Of Dr Johnson and his dictionary]
He for subscribers baits his hook,
And takes your cash; but where's the book?
No matter where; wise fear, you know,
Forbids the robbing of a foe;
But what, to serve our private ends,
Forbids the cheating of our friends?

[*The Ghost* 1762]

Marcus Tullius Cicero, 106–43BC, Roman statesman
Friendship can exist only where men harmonize in their views of things human and divine.

[*De Amicitia c.*50BC]

A friend is, as it were, a second self.

[*Ibid*]

Samuel Taylor Coleridge, 1772–1834, English poet
Alas! they had been friends in youth;
But whispering tongues can poison truth;
And constancy lives in realms above;
And life is thorny, and youth is vain.

[*Christabel* 1816]

Charles Caleb Colton, c.1780–1832, English writer
Friendship often ends in love; but love, in friendship – never.

[*Lacon* 1820]

If you want enemies, excel others; if you want friends, let others excel you.
[*Ibid*]

Confucius [K'ung fu-tzu], 551–479BC, Chinese philosopher
Have no friends not equal to yourself.

[*Analects c.*500BC]

There are three friendships that are advantageous, and three that are injurious. Friendship with the upright; friendship with the sincere; and friendship with the man of much observation; these are advantages. Friendship with the man of specious airs; friendship with the insinuatingly soft; and friendship with the glib-tongued; these are injurious.

[*Ibid*]

Abraham Cowley, 1618–67, English writer and Poet
Ah, yet, ere I descend to th' grave
May I a small house, and a large garden have!
And a few friends, and many books, both true,
Both wise, and both delightful too!

[*The Wish*]

William Cowper, 1731–1800, English poet
How sweet, how passing sweet, is solitude!
But grant me still a friend in my retreat,
Whom I may whisper – solitude is sweet.

[*Retirement* 1782]

I would not enter on my list of friends
(Tho' grac'd with polish'd manners and fine sense,
Yet wanting sensibility) the man
Who needlessly sets foot on a worm.

[*The Task: The Winter Walk at Noon* 1785]

Abbé Jacques Delille, 1738–1813, French poet
Fate chooses our relatives, we choose our friends.

[*Malheur et Pitié* 1803]

Charles [John Huffam] Dickens, 1812–70, English novelist
What is the odds so long as the fire of soul is kindled at the taper of conwiviality, and the wing of friendship never moults a feather!

[*The Old Curiosity Shop* 1841]
Fan the sinking flame of hilarity with the wing of friendship; and pass the rosy wine.

[*Ibid*]
Wery glad to see you, indeed, and hope our acquaintance may be a long 'un, as the gen'l'm'n said to the fi' pun' note.

[*Pickwick Papers* 1836–7]

Benjamin Disraeli, 1st Earl of Beaconsfield, 1804–81, British statesman and novelist
There is a magic in the memory of a schoolboy friendship; it softens the heart, and even affects the nervous system of those who have no heart.

[George] Norman Douglas, 1868–1952, English novelist
To find a friend one must close one eye; to keep him – two.

[*An Almanac*]

John Dryden, 1631–1700, English dramatist
In friendship false, implacable in hate,
Resolved to ruin or to rule the state.

[*Absalom and Achitophel* 1681]

Be kind to my remains; and O defend,
Against your judgment, your departed friend.

[*Epistle to Mr Congreve*]

Richard Edwards, c.1523–1566, English poet
The falling out of faithful friends renewing is of love.

[*Amantium Irae*]

George Eliot [Mary Ann Evans], 1819–80, English novelist
Friendships begin with liking or gratitude – roots that can be pulled up.

[*Daniel Deronda* 1874–6]

Ralph Waldo Emerson, 1803–82, American writer
A friend is a person with whom I may be sincere. Before him, I may think aloud.

[*Essays: Friendship* 1841]

196

The only reward of virtue is virtue; the only way to have a friend is to be one.

[*Ibid*]

I do then with my friends as I do with my books. I would have them where I can find them, but I seldom use them.

[*Ibid*]

Jean de La Fontaine, 1621–95, French poet
Nothing is so dangerous as an ignorant friend; a wise enemy is much better.

[*Fables* 1671]

Benjamin Franklin, 1706–90, American scientist and philosopher
There are three faithful friends – an old wife, an old dog, and ready money.

[*Poor Richard's Almanac* 1738]

A brother may not be a friend, but a friend will always be a brother.

[*Ibid* 1752]

Oliver Goldsmith, 1728–74, Irish-born English writer
Friendship is a disinterested commerce between equals; love, an abject intercourse between tyrants and slaves.

[*The Good-Natured Man* 1768]

[On David Garrick]
He cast off his friends, as a huntsman his pack,
For he knew when he pleas'd he could whistle them back.

[*Retaliation* 1774]

Thomas Gray, 1716–71, English poet
A fav'rite has no friend.

[*Ode on the Death of a Favourite Cat* 1748]

Julius Charles Hare, 1795–1855, and Augustus William Hare, 1792–1834, English writers
We never know the true value of friends. While they live we are too sensitive of their faults: when we have lost them we only see their virtues.

[*Guesses at Truth* 1827]

William Hazlitt, 1778–1830, English essayist
I like a friend the better for having faults that one can talk about.

[*Plain Speaker* 1826]

Robert Herrick, 1591–1674, English poet and churchman
Wilt thou my true friend be?
Then love not mine, but me.

[*Hesperides* 1648]

E[dgar] W[atson] Howe, 1853–1937, American writer
When we lose a friend we die a little.

[*The Indignations of E. W. Howe* 1933]

Thomas Jefferson, 1743–1826, 3rd president of the United States
I find as I grow older that I love those most whom I loved first.

[Letter 1787]

An injured friend is the bitterest of foes.

[*French Treaties Opinion* 1793]

I never considered a difference of opinion in politics, in religion, in philosophy, as cause for withdrawing from a friend.

[Letter 1800]

Peace, commerce, and honest friendship with all nations – entangling alliances with none.

[First Inaugural Address 1801]

I find friendship to be like wine, raw when new, ripened with age, the true old man's milk and restorative cordial.

[Letter 1811]

Dr Samuel Johnson, 1709–84, English lexicographer

If a man does not make new acquaintance as he advances through life, he will soon find himself left alone. A man, sir, should keep his friendship in constant repair.

[1755. In Boswell's *Life of Samuel Johnson* 1791]

Always, Sir, set a high value on spontaneous kindness. He whose inclination prompts him to cultivate your friendship of his own accord, will love you more than one whom you have been at pains to attach to you.

[1781. In *Ibid*]

The endearing elegance of female friendship.

[*Rasselas* 1759]

Friendship is not always the sequel of obligation.

[*James Thomson*]

Ben[jamin] Jonson, 1572–1637, English poet

True happiness
Consists not in the multitude of friends,
But in the worth and choice.

[*Cynthia's Revels* 1600]

Brian Keenan, 1950– , Irish teacher and writer

I remember every moment of my time alone, my time with John and with those other captives. And I remember how we first met, our relationship, the kinds of needs I had of John and he of me. And how we sought always to give and take, thinking always of the other. And as I review it all, all that wonder, I see his face stare at mine. I had watched this man grow, become full and in his fullness enrich me.

[*An Evil Cradling* 1992]

Paul de Kock, 1793–1871, French writer

The best way to keep your friends is to never borrow from them and never lend them anything.

[*Homme aux trois culottes* 1830]

Walter Savage Landor, 1775–1864, English writer

No friendship is so cordial or so delicious as that of girl for girl; no hatred so intense and immovable as that of woman for woman.

[*Imaginary Conversations* 1824]

Henry Wadsworth Longfellow, 1807–82, American poet

And the song, from beginning to end, I found again in the heart of a friend.

[*The Arrow and the Song*]

Sir Thomas Malory, *fl.* 1470, English writer

[Lancelot] Thou wert the truest friend to thy lover that ever bestrad horse; and thou wert the truest lover of a sinful man that ever loved woman; and thou wert the kindest man that ever struck with sword; and thou wert the goodliest person that ever came among press of knights; and thou wert the meekest man and the gentlest that ever ate in hall among ladies; and thou wert the sternest knight to thy mortal foe that ever put spear in the rest.

[*Morte D'Arthur*]

W[illiam] Somerset Maugham, 1874–1965, English novelist
My dear, she's been my greatest friend for fifteen years. I know her through and through and I tell you that she hasn't got a single redeeming quality.

[*Our Betters*]

George Louis Palmella Busson Du Maurier, 1834–96, English artist and novelist
I have no talent for making new friends, but oh, such a genius for fidelity to old ones.

[*Peter Ibbetson* 1891]

Mary McCarthy, 1912–89, American writer
Friendship . . . is essential to intellectuals. You can date the evolving life of a mind, like the age of a tree, by the rings of friendship formed by the expanding central trunk.

[*How I Grew 1987*]

Albert Midlane, 1825–1909, writer of hymns
There's a Friend for little children
Above the bright blue sky,
A Friend who never changes,
Whose love can never die.

Spike [Terence Alan] Milligan, 1918–2002, Irish comedian and writer
Money couldn't buy friends but you got a better class of enemy.

[*Puckoon* 1963]

Marylin Monroe [Norma Jean Mortenson], 1926–62, American film actress
Diamonds are a girl's best friend.

[Song title, Leo Robin and Jule Styne 1949]

Ovid [Publius Ovidius Naso], 43BC–AD18, Roman poet
The vulgar estimate friends by the advantage to be derived from them.

[*Epistulae ex Ponto c.*AD5]

Blaise Pascal, 1623–62, French mathematician and writer
I lay it down as a fact that if all men knew what others say of them, there would not be four friends in the world.

[*Pensées* 1670]

William Penn, 1644–1718, English founder of Pennsylvania
A true friend unbosoms freely, advises justly, assists readily, adventures boldly, takes all patiently, defends courageously, and continues a friend unchangeably.

[*Some Fruits of Solitude* 1693]

Edgar Allan Poe, 1809–49, American writer
My best friend would be the man who would blow my brains out with a pistol.

[On his deathbed]

Alexander Pope, 1688–1744, English poet
Histories are more full of examples of the fidelity of dogs than of friends.

[Letter 1709]

True friendship's laws are by this rule exprest,
Welcome the coming, speed the parting guest.

[Homer's Odyssey 1725–6]

In action faithful, and in honour clear;
Who broke no promise, served no private end,
Who gained no title, and who lost no friend.

[Moral Essays: To Mr Addison 1731–5]

Thou wert my guide, philosopher, and friend.

[Essay on Man 1732–4]

Damn with faint praise, assent with civil leer,
And, without sneering, teach the rest to sneer;
Willing to wound, and yet afraid to strike,
Just hint a fault, and hesitate dislike;
Alike reserved to blame, or to commend,
A timorous foe, and a suspicious friend.

[Epistle to Dr Arbuthnot 1735]

There is nothing that is meritorious but virtue and friendship; and, indeed friendship itself is only a part of virtue.

[On his deathbed, 1744]

François, Duc de La Rochefoucauld, 1613–80, French writer
It is more ignominious to mistrust our friends than to be deceived by them.

[Reflections, or Sentences and Moral Maxims 1665]

We always like those who admire us; we do not always like those whom we admire.

[Ibid]

Dante Gabriel Rossetti, 1828–82, English poet
Was it a friend or foe that spread these lies?
Nay, who but infants question in such wise?
'Twas one of my most intimate enemies.

[Fragment]

George Santayana, 1863–1952, Spanish-American philosopher
Friends are generally of the same sex, for when men and women agree, it is only in their conclusions; their reasons are always different.

[The Life of Reason 1905]

John Selden, 1584–1654, English antiquary and politician
Old friends are best. King James used to call for his old shoes; they were easiest for his feet.

[Table Talk: Friends 1689]

Seneca, c.4BC–AD65, Roman philosopher
Friendship always benefits; love sometimes injures.

[Epistolae ad Lucilium c. AD63]

William Shakespeare, 1564–1616, English dramatist
I count myself in nothing else so happy
As in a soul remembering my good friends.

[King Richard II 2 1595–6]

FRIENDS AND FRIENDSHIP

Our plot is as good a plot as ever was laid; our friends true and constant; a good plot, good friends, and full of expectation; an excellent plot, very good friends.

[*King Henry IV, Part I* 2 1597–8]

Call you that backing of your friends? A plague upon such backing.

[*Ibid*]

Yet the first bringer of unwelcome news
Hath but a losing office, and his tongue
Sounds ever after as a sullen bell,
Remember'd tolling a departed friend.

[*King Henry IV, Part II* 1 1597–8]

Friendship is constant in all other things,
Save in the office and affairs of love:
Therefore all hearts in love use their own tongues;
Let every eye negotiate for itself
And trust no agent.

[*Much Ado About Nothing* 2 1598–1600]

Most friendship is feigning, most loving mere folly.

[*As You Like It* 2 1598–1600]

He that wants money, means and content is without three good friends.

[*Ibid* 3]

Let me have men about me that are fat;
Sleek-headed men and such as sleep o' nights.

[*Julius Caesar* 1 1598–1600]

Friends, Romans, countrymen, lend me your ears;
I come to bury Caesar, not to praise him.
The evil that men do lives after them;
The good is oft interred with their bones.

[*Ibid* 3]

A friendly eye could never see such faults.

[*Ibid*]

A friend should bear his friend's infirmities,
But Brutus makes mine greater than they are.

[*Ibid*]

Those friends thou hast, and their adoption tried,
Grapple them to thy soul with hoops of steel.

[*Hamlet* 1 1600–1601]

And that which should accompany old age,
As honour, love, obedience, troops of friends.

[*Macbeth* 5 1605–6]

Wishing me like to one more rich in hope,
Featur'd like him, like him with friends possess'd,
Desiring this man's art and that man's scope,
With what I most enjoy contented least.

[*Sonnets* 29 1609]

But if the while I think on thee, dear friend,
All losses are restored and sorrows end.

[*Ibid*]

Percy Bysshe Shelley, 1792–1822, English poet
When a man marries, dies or turns Hindoo,
His best friends hear no more of him.

[Letter to Maria Gisborne]

Sydney Smith, 1771–1845, English churchman
Madam, I have been looking for a person who disliked gravy all my life; let us swear eternal friendship.

[Lady Holland's *Memoir* 1855]

Sophocles, c.496–c.406BC, Greek poet
An enemy should be hated only so far as one may be hated who may one day be a friend.

[*Ajax c.*450BC]

He who throws away a friend is as bad as he who throws away his life.

[*Oedipus Tyrannus c.*450BC]

Robert Southey, 1774–1843, English poet
[Written in his library]
My days among the Dead are past;
Around me I behold,
Where'er these casual eyes are cast,
The mighty minds of old,
My never-failing friends are they,
With whom I converse day by day.

[*My Days among the Dead are Past*]

Robert Louis [Balfour] Stevenson, 1850–94, Scottish novelist and poet
To keep a few friends, but these without capitulation – above all, on the same grim condition, to keep friends with himself – here is a task for all that a man has of fortitude and delicacy.

[*Across the Plains: A Christmas Sermon*]

Give us grace and strength to forbear and to persevere. Give us courage and gaiety and the quiet mind, spare us to our friends, soften to us our enemies.

[*Ibid: Prayer*]

Jonathan Swift, 1667–1745, Irish-born English writer
We are so fond of one another, because our ailments are the same.

[*Journal to Stella* 1711]

Algernon Charles Swinburne, 1837–1909, English poet
I shall never be friends again with roses.

[*The Triumph of Time* 1866]

[Vernon] James Taylor, 1948– , American singer and songwriter
You've got a friend.

[Song title 1970]

Alfred, Lord Tennyson, 1809–92, English poet
He makes no friend who never made a foe.

[*Idylls of the King: Lancelot and Elaine* 1859–85]

Mark Twain [Samuel Langhorne Clemens], 1835–1910, American writer
The holy passion of Friendship is of so sweet and steady and loyal and enduring a nature that it will last through a whole lifetime, if not asked to lend money.

[*Pudd'nhead Wilson* 1894]

202

Gore [Eugene Luther] Vidal, 1925– , American novelist and critic
Whenever a friend succeeds, a little something in me dies.
[In the *Sunday Times* September 16 1973]

Leonardo da Vinci, 1452–1519, Italian artist
Reprove a friend in secret, but praise him before others.
[*Notebooks c.*1500]

George Washington, 1732–99, 1st president of the United States
Be courteous to all, but intimate with few, and let those few be well tried before you give them your confidence. True friendship is a plant of slow growth, and must undergo and withstand the shocks of adversity before it is entitled to the appellation.
[Letter 1783]

Simone Weil, 1909–43, French essayist and philosopher
Learn to reject friendship, or rather the dream of friendship. To want friendship is a great fault. Friendship ought to be a gratuitous joy, like the joys afforded by art, or life (like aesthetic joys).
[*First and Last Notebooks: The Pre-War Notebook* 1970]

Walt[er] Whitman, 1819–92, American poet
I no doubt deserved my enemies, but I don't believe I deserved my friends.
[In Bradford's *Biography and the Human Heart*]

Cornelius Whur, 1782–1853, English churchman
Will not a beauteous landscape bright –
Or music's soothing sound,
Console the heart – afford delight,
And throw sweet peace around?
They may, but never comfort lend
Like an accomplished female friend.
[*Village Musings: The Female Friend*]

Oscar [Fingall O'Flahertie Wills] Wilde, 1854–1900, Irish writer
I choose my friends for their good looks, my acquaintances for their characters, and my enemies for their brains.
[*The Picture of Dorian Gray* 1891]

[Adeline] Virginia Woolf, 1882–1941, English novelist and critic
I have lost friends, some by death . . . others through sheer inability to cross the street.
[*The Waves* 1931]

William Wycherley, c.1640–1716, English dramatist
Ceremony and great professing renders friendship as much suspect as it does religion.
[*The Plain Dealer c.*1674]

203

Edward Young, 1683–1765, English churchman and poet
Friendship's the wine of life.

[*Night Thoughts* 1742]

God and Religion

Abdallah Ibn Tumart, *fl.* c. 1112–1140, North African Islamic leader
Time does not contain Him, nor space hold Him. No intelligence can grasp Him, nor imagination figure Him. Nothing is like Him. But still He hears and sees all things.
[Tauhid or *Confession of Faith c.*1140]

Sarah Flower Adams, 1805–48, English poet
Nearer, my God, to Thee,
Nearer to Thee!
E'en though it be a cross
That raiseth me.

[Nearer, my God, to Thee]

Joseph Addison, 1672–1719, English essayist
The spacious firmament on high,
With all the blue ethereal sky,
And spangled heavens, a shining frame,
Their great Original proclaim.

[Ode]

Cecil Frances Alexander, 1818–95, English poet
All things bright and beautiful,
All creatures great and small,
All things wise and wonderful,
The Lord God made them all.

[All Things Bright and Beautiful]

Woody Allen [Allen Stewart Konisberg], 1935– , American writer, actor and film director
How can I believe in God when just last week I got my tongue caught in the roller of an electric typewriter?
[Without Feathers, 1976]

Henri Frederic Amiel, 1821–81, Swiss writer
Every life is a profession of faith, and exercises an inevitable and silent influence.
[Journal 1852]

A belief is not true because it is useful.
[Ibid 1876]

Sir Kingsley Amis, 1922–95, English novelist and poet
He was of the faith chiefly in the sense that the church he currently did not attend was Catholic.

[*One Fat Englishman*, 1963]

Lancelot Andrewes, 1555–1626, English theologian and bishop
The nearer the Church the further from God.

[Sermon]

Anonymous
They who worship God merely for fear, would worship the devil should he appear.

[Proverb]

The danger past, and God forgotten.

[Proverb]

Matthew Arnold, 1822–88, English poet and critic
But as on some far northern strand,
Thinking of his own Gods, a Greek
In pity and mournful awe might stand
Before some fallen Runic stone –
For both were faiths, and both are gone.

[*The Grande Chartreuse*]

Thomas Arnold, 1795–1842, English schoolmaster
My object will be, if possible, to form Christian men, for Christian boys I can scarcely hope to make.

[Letter 1828]

Sir Jacob Astley, 1579–1652, English soldier
O Lord, thou knowest how busy I must be this day; if I forget thee, do not thou forget me.

[At the Battle of Edgehill, 1642]

St Augustine of Hippo, 354–430, Christian philosopher
We can know what God is not, but we cannot know what he is.

[*De Trinitate c* 410]

There is no salvation outside the church.

[*De Bapt.*]

Francis Bacon, Baron Verulam of Verulam and Viscount of St Albans, 1561–1626, English philosopher
A little philosophy inclineth man's mind to atheism, but depth in philosophy bringeth men's minds about to religion.

[*Essays: Of Atheism*]

Walter Bagehot, 1826–77, English economist and journalist
The whole history of civilization is strewn with creeds and institutions which were invaluable at first, and deadly afterwards.

[*Physics and Politics* 1872]

So long as there are earnest believers in the world, they will always wish to punish opinions, even if their judgment tells them it is unwise, and their conscience that it is wrong.

[*Literary Studies* 1879]

GOD AND RELIGION

James Baldwin, 1924–87, American writer
If we do not now dare everything, the fulfillment of that prophecy, recreated from the Bible in song by a slave, is upon us: *God gave Noah the rainbow sign, No more water, the fire next time!*
[*The Fire Next Time* 1963]

Honoré de Balzac, 1799–1850, French novelist
I believe in the incomprehensibility of God.
[Letter 1837]

Sir J[ames] M[atthew] Barrie, 1860–1937, Scottish playwright
If it's heaven for climate, it's hell for company.
[*The Little Minister* 1891]

Brendan Behan, 1923–64, Irish playwright
Pound notes is the best religion in the world.
[*The Hostage* 1959]

Arthur Christopher Benson, 1862–1925, English writer and academic
Land of Hope and Glory, Mother of the Free,
How shall we extol thee, who are born of thee?
Wider still and wider shall thy bounds be set;
God, who made thee mighty, make thee mightier yet.
[*Land of Hope and Glory*]

Sir John Betjeman, 1906–84, English poet
And girls in slacks remember Dad,
And oafish louts remember Mum,
And sleepless children's hearts are glad,
And Christmas morning bells say "Come!"
Even to shining ones who dwell
Safe in the Dorchester Hotel,
And is it true? And is it true,
This most tremendous tale of all,
Seen in a stained-glass window's hue,
A Baby in an ox's stall?
[*A Few Late Chrysanthemums: Christmas* 1954]

The Bible
Then your eyes shall be opened, and ye shall be as gods, knowing good and evil.
[*Genesis* 3:5]
The Lord God of your fathers, the God of Abraham, the God of Isaac, and the God of Jacob.
[*Exodus* 3:15]
Be strong and of good courage; be not afraid, neither be thou dismayed: for the Lord thy God is with thee, whithersoever thou goest.
[*Joshua* 1:9]
The Lord gave, and the Lord hath taken away; blessed be the name of the Lord.
[*Job* 1:21]
I know that my redeemer liveth, and that he shall stand at the latter day upon the earth.
[*Ibid* 19:25–26]
The Lord is my shepherd; I shall not want. He maketh me to lie down in green pastures: he leadeth me beside the still waters. He restoreth my soul: he leadeth me in the paths of

207

righteousness for his name's sake. Yea, though I walk through the valley of the shadow of death, I will fear no evil: for thou art with me; thy rod and thy staff they comfort me.

[*Psalms* 23:1–6]

God is our refuge and strength, a very present help in trouble.

[*Ibid* 46:1]

I will lift up mine eyes unto the hills, from whence cometh my help. My help cometh from the Lord, which made heaven and earth. He will not suffer thy foot to be moved: he that keepeth thee will not slumber. Behold, he that keepeth Israel shall neither slumber nor sleep. The Lord is thy keeper: the Lord is thy shade upon the right hand. The sun shall not smite thee by day, nor the moon by night. The Lord shall preserve thee from all evil: he shall preserve thy soul. The Lord shall preserve thy going out and thy coming in from this time forth, and even for evermore.

[*Ibid* 121:1–8]

God is in heaven, and thou upon earth: therefore let thy words be few.

[*Ecclesiastes* 5:2]

Let us hear the conclusion of the whole matter: Fear God, and keep his commandments: for this is the whole duty of man.

[*Ibid* 12:13]

Blessed are the poor in spirit: for theirs is the kingdom of heaven. Blessed are they that mourn: for they shall be comforted. Blessed are the meek: for they shall inherit the earth. Blessed are they which do hunger and thirst after righteousness: for they shall be filled. Blessed are the merciful: for they shall obtain mercy. Blessed are the pure in heart: for they shall see God. Blessed are the peacemakers: for they shall be called the children of God.

[*Matthew* 5:3–9]

Be ye therefore perfect, even as your Father which is in heaven is perfect.

[*Ibid* 5:48]

After this manner therefore pray ye: Our Father which art in heaven, Hallowed be thy name. Thy kingdom come. Thy will be done in earth, as it is in heaven. Give us this day our daily bread. And forgive us our debts, as we forgive our debtors. And lead us not into temptation, but deliver us from evil. For thine is the kingdom, and the power, and the glory, for ever. Amen.

[*Ibid* 6:9–13]

Thou art Peter, and upon this rock I will build my church; and the gates of hell shall not prevail against it. And I will give unto thee the keys of the kingdom of heaven.

[*Ibid* 16:18–19]

Verily I say unto you, Except ye be converted, and become as little children, ye shall not enter into the kingdom of heaven.

[*Ibid* 18:3]

For where two or three are gathered together in my name, there am I in the midst of them.

[*Ibid* 18:20]

With men this is impossible; but with God all things are possible.

[*Ibid* 19:26]

For many are called, but few are chosen.

[*Ibid* 22:14]

The sabbath was made for man, and not man for the sabbath.

[*Mark* 2:27]

Glory to God in the highest, and on earth peace, good will toward men.

[*Luke* 2:14]

Likewise joy shall be in heaven over one sinner that repenteth, more than over ninety and nine just persons, which need no repentance.

[*Ibid* 15:7]

In the beginning was the Word, and the Word was with God, and the Word was God.

[John 1:1]

Thomas, because thou has seen me, thou hast believed: blessed are they that have not seen, and yet have believed.

[Ibid 20:29]

Then Peter opened his mouth, and said, Of a truth I perceive that God is no respecter of persons: But in every nation he that feareth him, and worketh righteousness, is accepted with him.

[Acts 10:34–35]

If God be for us, who can be against us?

[Romans 8:31]

For I am persuaded, that neither death, nor life, nor angels, nor principalities, nor powers, nor things present, nor things to come, nor height, nor depth, nor any other creature, shall be able to separate us from the love of God which is in Christ Jesus our Lord.

[Ibid 8:38–39]

Avenge not yourselves, but rather given place unto wrath: for it is written, vengeance is mine; I will repay, saith the Lord.

[Ibid 12:19–21]

And the peace of God, which passeth all understanding, shall keep your hearts and minds through Christ Jesus.

[Philippians 4:7]

Whatsoever things are true, whatsoever things are honest, whatsoever things are just, whatsoever things are pure, whatsoever things are lovely, whatsoever things are of good report; if there be any virtue, and if there be any praise, think on these things.

[Ibid 4:8]

I have fought a good fight, I have finished my course, I have kept the faith.

[2 Timothy 4:7]

Now faith is the substance of things hoped for, the evidence of things not seen.

[Hebrews 11:1]

God is love; and he that dwelleth in love dwelleth in God, and God in him.

[1 John 4:16]

I am Alpha and Omega, the beginning and the ending, saith the Lord, which is, and which was, and which is to come, the Almighty.

[Revelation 1:8]

William Blake, 1757–1827, English poet and artist
I will not cease from mental fight,
Nor shall my sword sleep in my hand,
Till we have built Jerusalem
In England's green and pleasant land.

[Milton preface]

A robin redbreast in a cage
Puts all Heaven in a rage.

[Auguries of Innocence 1805]

William Bradford, c.1590–1657, English-born American statesman
Thus out of small beginnings greater things have been produced by His hand that made all things of nothing, and gives being to all things that are; and, as one small candle may light a thousand, so the light here kindled hath shone unto many, yea in some sort to our whole nation.

[Of Plymouth Plantation 1620–47]

Emily Jane Brontë, 1818–48, English novelist and poet
No coward soul is mine,
No trembler in the world's storm-troubled sphere:
I see Heaven's glories shine,
And faith shines equal, arming me from fear.

[*Last Lines* 1845]

Vain are the thousand creeds
That move men's hearts: unutterably vain;
Worthless as withered weeds.

[*Ibid*]

He was, and is yet, most likely, the wearisomest, self-righteous pharisee that ever ransacked a Bible to rake the promises to himself and fling the curses on his neighbours.

[*Wuthering Heights* 1847]

Cecil Browne, American businessman
But not so odd
As those who choose
A Jewish God
But spurn the Jews.

[*Reply to William Norman Ewer (see page 214)*]

Sir Thomas Browne, 1605–82, English physician
Persecution is a bad and indirect way to plant religion.

[*Religio Medici* 1643]

Robert Browning, 1812–89, English poet
All we have gained then by our unbelief
Is a life of doubt diversified by faith,
For one of faith diversified by doubt:
We called the chess board white – we call it black.

[*Bishop Blougram's Apology*]

If once we choose belief, on all accounts
We can't be too decisive in our faith.

[*Ibid*]

I show you doubt, to prove that faith exists.

[*Ibid*]

There may be heaven; there must be hell;
Meantime, there is our earth here – well!

[*Time's Revenges*]

In youth I looked to these very skies,
And probing their immensities,
I found God there.

[*Christmas Eve* 1850]

Ah, but a man's reach should exceed his grasp,
Or what's a heaven for?

[*Andrea del Sarto* 1855]

Edmund Burke, 1729–97, Irish-born English political writer
Politics and the pulpit are terms that have little agreement. No sound ought to be heard in the church but the healing voice of Christian charity.

[*Reflections on the Revolution in France* 1790]

Robert Burns, 1759–96, Scottish poet
They never sought in vain that sought the Lord aright.

[*The Cottar's Saturday Night* 1786]

O Thou, who in the heavens does dwell,
Who, as it pleases best Thysel',
Sends ane to heaven, and ten to hell,
A' for Thy glory,
And no for ony gude or ill
They've done afore Thee!

[*Holy Willie's Prayer*]

Ah, Tam! ah, Tam! thou'll get thy fairin!
In hell they'll roast thee like a herrin!

[*Tam o' Shanter*]

Robert Burton, 1577–1640, English churchman and writer
One religion is as true as another.

[*The Anatomy of Melancholy* 1621]

Roger, Comte de Bussy-Rabutin, 1618–93, French soldier
As you know, God is usually on the side of the big squadrons and against the small ones.

[Letter 1677]

Samuel Butler, 1835–1902, English writer
An apology for the Devil: it must be remembered that we have heard only one side of the case. God has written all the books.

[*Note Books c.*1890]

An honest God's the noblest work of man.

[*Further Extracts from the Note-Books*]

Byron, Lord George Gordon [Noel], 6th Baron Byron of Rochdale, 17881824, English poet
"Whom the gods love die young" was said of yore.

[*Don Juan* 1819–24]

Jane Montgomery Campbell, 1817–78, English writer
We plough the fields, and scatter
The good seed on the land,
But it is fed and watered
By God's almighty hand.

[*We Plough the Fields*]

Thomas Carlyle, 1795–1881, Scottish historian and writer
If Jesus Christ were to come today, people would not even crucify him. They would ask him to dinner, and hear what he had to say, and make fun of it.

[In D.A. Wilson's *Carlyle at his Zenith*]

The three great elements of modern civilization, Gunpowder, Printing, and the Protestant Religion.

[*Critical and Miscellaneous Essays: State of German Literature*]

William Herbert Carruth, 1859–1924, American poet
Some call it Evolution,
And others call it God.

[*Each in his own Tongue*]

211

Charles V (Charles the Wise), 1338–80, king of France
I speak Spanish to God, Italian to women, French to men, and German to my horse.

[Attributed]

Marcus Tullius Cicero, 106–43BC, Roman statesman
Nature herself has imprinted on the minds of all the idea of a God.

[*De Natura Deorum* 45B]

Arthur Hugh Clough, 1819–61, English poet
And almost everyone when age,
Disease, or sorrows strike him,
Inclines to think there is a God,
Or something very like Him.

[*Dipsychus*]

Thou shalt have one God only; who
Would be at the expense of two?

[*The Latest Decalogue* 1862]

Samuel Taylor Coleridge, 1772–1834, English poet
He prayeth best, who loveth best
All things both great and small;
For the dear God who loveth us,
He made and loveth all.

[*The Ancient Mariner* 1798]

He who begins by loving Christianity better than Truth will proceed by loving his own sect or church better than Christianity, and end by loving himself better than all.

[*Aids to Reflection. Moral and Religious Aphorisms*]

Charles Caleb Colton, c.1780–1832, English writer
Men will wrangle for religion; write for it; fight for it; die for it; anything but – live for it.

[*Lacon* 1820]

Etienne Bonnot de Condillac, 1715–80, French philosopher
The most perfect idea of God that we can form in this life is that of an independent, unique, infinite, external, omnipotent, immutable, intelligent and free First Cause, whose power extends over all things.

[*Traité des animaux* 1755]

Sir Noel [Pierce] Coward, 1899–1973, English actor and playwright
Life without faith is an arid business.

[*Blithe Spirit* 1941]

William Cowper, 1731–1800, English poet
Oh! for a closer walk with God.

[*Olney Hymns* 1]

Charles Robert Darwin, 1809–82, English naturalist
The assumed instinctive belief in God has been used by many persons as an argument for His existence. But this is a rash argument, as we should thus be compelled to believe in the existence of many cruel and malignant spirits, only a little more powerful than man; for the belief in them is far more general than in a beneficent Deity.

[*The Descent of Man* 1871]

GOD AND RELIGION

Clarence Shepard Day, 1874–1935, American writer
Apart from a few odd words in Hebrew, I took it for granted that God had never spoken anything but the most dignified English.

[Life With Father 1935]

Daniel Defoe, 1660–1731, English novelist
Wherever God erects a house of prayer,
The Devil always builds a chapel there;
And 'twill be found, upon examination,
The latter has the largest congregation.

[The True-Born Englishman 1701]

And of all plagues with which mankind are curst,
Ecclesiastic tyranny's the worst.

[Ibid]

René Descartes, 1596–1650, French philosopher
Our idea of God implies necessary and eternal existance; the manifest conclusion then is that God does exist.

[Principles of Philosophy 1644]

Charles [John Huffam] Dickens, 1812–70, English novelist
"God bless us every one!" said Tiny Tim.

[A Christmas Carol 1843]

Diogenes, 412–323BC, Cynic philosopher
I do not know whether there are gods, but there ought to be.

[In Tertullian's Ad Nationes]

John Dryden, 1631–1700, English dramatist
Yet dull religion teaches us content;
But when we ask it where that blessing dwells,
It points to pedant colleges and cells.

[The Conquest of Granada 1670]

In pious times, ere priestcraft did begin,
Before polygamy was made a sin.

[Absalom and Achitophel 1681]

Gods they had tried of every shape and size
That godsmiths could produce or priests devise.

[Ibid]

So over-violent or over-civil
That every man with him was God or Devil.

[Ibid]

Did wisely from expensive sins refrain
And never broke the Sabbath but for gain.

[Ibid]

But since men will believe more than they need;
And every man will make himself a creed,
In doubtful questions 'tis the safest way
To learn what unsuspected ancients say.

[Religio Laic]

William Dunbar, c.1456–c.1513, Scottish priest and poet
All love is lost but upon God alone.

[*The Merle and the Nightingale*]

Albert Einstein, 1879–1955, German-born mathematical physicist
Science without religion is lame, religion without science is blind.

[*Out of My Later Years* 1950]

Henry Havelock Ellis, 1859–1939, English psychologist
God is an unutterable Sigh in the Human Heart, said the old German mystic. And therewith said the last word.

[*Impressions and Comments*]

The whole religious complexion of the modern world is due to the absence from Jerusalem of a lunatic asylum.

[*Ibid*]

Ralph Waldo Emerson, 1803–82, American philosopher
Shove Jesus and Judas equally aside.

[*Essays, First Series: Self-Reliance* 1841]

I like the silent church before the sevice begins, better than any preaching.

[*Ibid*]

For every Stoic was a Stoic; but in Christendom where is the Christian?

[*Ibid*]

You shall have joy, or you shall have power, said God; you shall not have both.

[*Journal*, October 1842]

Demonology is the shadow of theology.

[*Demonology* 1877]

The Americans have little faith. They rely on the power of the dollar.

[*Nature, Addresses and Lectures: Man the Reformer*]

Empedocles, d.c.430BC, Greek philosopher
The nature of God is a circle of which the centre is everywhere and the circumference is nowhere.

[Attributed]

Epicurus, c 341–270BC, Greek philosopher
It is folly for a man to pray to the gods for that which he has the power to obtain for himself.

[*Vatican Sayings*]

William Norman Ewer, 1885–1976, British journalist
How odd
Of God
To choose
The Jews.

[*How Odd* (see Cecil Browne's reply page 210)]

Anne Frank, 1929–45, German-Jewish diarist
What *one* Christian does is his own responsibilty, what *one* Jew does is thrown back at all Jews.

[*The Diary of a Young Girl* 1947]

Sigmund Freud, 1856–1939, Austrian psychiatrist
Religion is an attempt to get control over the sensory world, in which we are placed, by means of the wish-world, which we have developed inside us as a result of biological and psychological necessities.

[*New Introductory Lectures on Psychoanalysis* 1932]

Christopher [Harris] Fry, 1907– , English poet and playwright
Who should question then
Why we lean our bicycle against a hedge
And go into the house of God?

[*The Boy with a Cart*]

Thomas Gainsborough, 1727–88, English artist
We are all going to heaven, and Van Dyck is of the company.

[Last words]

Stephen William Hawking, 1942– , English physicist
Why does the universe go to all the bother of existing? Is the unified theory so compelling that it brings about its own existence? Or does it need a creator, and, if so, does he have any other effect on the universe? And who created him?

[*A Brief History of Time* 1988]

[Christian Johann] Heinrich Heine, 1797–1856, German poet
Christianity is an idea, and as such is indestructible and immortal, like every idea.

[*History of Religion and Philosophy in Germany* 1834]

People in those old times had convictions; we moderns only have opinions. And it needs more than a mere opinion to erect a Gothic cathedral.

[*Franzosische Bühne* (*The French Stage*) 1837]

When people talk about a wealthy man of my creed, they call him an Israelite; but if he is poor they call him a Jew.

[MS Papers]

Joseph Heller, 1923–1999, American novelist
Good God, how much reverence can you have for a Supreme Being who finds it necessary to include such phenomena as phlegm and tooth-decay in His divine system of Creation?

[*Catch-22* 1961]

W[illiam] E[rnest] Henley, 1849–1903, English writer
Out of the night that covers me,
Black as the pit from pole to pole,
I thank whatever gods may be
For my unconquerable soul.

[*Echoes: Invictus*]

Henry II, 1133–89, king of England
[On Thomas à Becket] Will no one free me of this turbulent priest?

[Attributed]

Joe Hill [Joseph Hillstrom], 1879–1915, Swedish-born American labour leader
You will eat, bye and bye,
In that glorious land above the sky,

(Way up high).

215

Work and pray, live on hay,
You'll get pie in the sky when you die
(That's a lie).

[*The Preacher and the Slave*]

Hippocrates, *c.*460–*c.*377BC, Greek physician

Prayer indeed is good, but while calling on the gods a man should himself lend a hand.

[*Regimen*]

John Haynes Holmes, 1879–1964, American churchman

Priests are no more necessary to religion than politicians to patriotism.

[*The Sensible Man's View of Religion* 1933]

If Christians were Christians, there would be no anti-Semitism. Jesus was a Jew. There is nothing that the ordinary Christian so dislikes to remember as this awkward historical fact.

[*Ibid*]

Eric Hoffer, 1902–83, American philosopher and dockworker

To know a person's religion we need not listen to his profession of faith but must find his brand of intolerance.

[*The Passionate State of Mind* 1955]

Homer, *fl.* 9th century BC, Greek poet

But verily these things lie on the knees of the gods.

[*Iliad*]

Thomas Hood, 1799–1845, English poet

I remember, I remember,
The fir trees dark and high;
I used to think their slender tops
Were close against the sky:
It was a childish ignorance,
But now 'tis little joy
To know I'm farther off from heav'n
Than when I was a boy.

[*I remember, I remember*]

Gerard Manley Hopkins, 1844–89, English priest and poet

Glory be to God for dappled things.

[*Poems: Pied Beauty* 1918]

The world is charged with the grandeur of God.

[*Ibid: God's Grandeur*]

I am all at once what Christ is, since he was what I am, and
This Jack, joke, poor potsherd, patch, matchwood, immortal diamond,
Is immortal diamond.

[*Ibid: That Nature is a Heraclitean Fire*]

St Ignatius of Loyola, 1491–1556, Spanish founder of the Jesuit Order

A sound mind in a sound body is the most useful instrument wherewith to serve God.

[Letter to Francis Borgia *c.*1548]

GOD AND RELIGION

William Ralph Inge, 1860–1954, English churchman
The modern town-dweller has no God and no Devil; he lives without awe, without admiration, without fear.

[Outspoken Essays: Our Present Discontents]

Robert G[reen] Ingersoll, 1833–99, American lawyer
We, too, have our religion, and it is this:
Help for the living, hope for the dead.

[Address at a child's grave]

An honest God is the noblest work of man.

[Gods]

William James, 1842–1910, American philosopher
We can act *as if* there were a God; feel *as if* we were free; consider Nature *as if* she were full of special designs; lay plans *as if* we were to be immortal; and we find then that these words do make a genuine difference in our moral life.

[The Varieties of Religious Experience 1902]

Douglas William Jerrold, 1803–57, English writer
Religion's in the heart, not in the knees.

[The Devil's Ducat]

John Paul I [Albino Luciani], 1912–78, Italian pope
He is Father. Even more, God is Mother, who does not want to harm us.

[Blessing, Rome, 1978]

Dr Samuel Johnson, 1709–84, English lexicographer
To be of no church is dangerous. Religion, of which the rewards are distant, and which is animated only by Faith and Hope, will glide by degrees out of the mind, unless it be invigorated and reimpressed by external ordinances, by stated calls to worship, and the salutary influence of example

[Lives of the English Poets: Milton 1779–81]

Thomas à Kempis [Thomas Hemerken], c.1379–1471, German religious writer
Man proposes but God disposes.

[Of the Imitation of Christ c.1415–24]

Martin Luther King Jr, 1929–68, American churchman and civil rights activist
I just want to do God's will. And He's allowed me to go to the mountain. And I've looked over, and I've seen the promised land . . . So I'm happy tonight. I'm not worried about anything. I'm not fearing any man.

[Speech, 3 April 1968, the evening before his assassination]

Rudyard Kipling, 1865–1936, English writer
The tumult and the shouting dies;
The Captains and the Kings depart;
Still stands Thine ancient sacrifice,
An humble and a contrite heart,
Lord God of Hosts, be with us yet,
Lest we forget – lest we forget!

[Recessional]

The Koran
There is no God but God.

[III]

William Lamb, 2nd Viscount Melbourne, 1779–1848, English statesman
Things have come to a pretty pass when religion is allowed to invade the sphere of private life.
[Attributed]

James Russell Lowell, 1819–91, American editor and poet
An' you've gut to git up airly
Ef you want to take in God.
[*The Bigelow Papers* 1862]
Puritanism, believing itself quick with the seed of religious liberty, laid, without knowing it,
the egg of democracy.
[*Literary Essays: New England Two Centuries Ago* 1870–90]

Robert Lowry, 1826–99, American churchman
Yes, we'll gather at the river,
The beautiful, the beautiful river,
Gather with the saints at the river
That flows from the throne of God.

[*Shall we gather at the River?*]

Martin Luther, 1483–1546, German religious reformer
I cannot and I will not recant anything, for to go against conscience is neither right nor safe.
Here I stand. I cannot do otherwise. God help me. Amen.
[Speech at the Diet of Worms 1521]
A mighty fortress is our God.

[*Ein' feste Burg* 1529]

Thomas Babington Macaulay, 1st Baron Macaulay, 1800–1859, English historian
[On the Roman Catholic church] She may still exist in undiminished vigour when some
traveller from New Zealand shall, in the midst of a vast solitude, take his stand on a broken
arch of London Bridge to sketch the ruins of St Paul's.
[On Leopold von Ranke's
History of the Popes 1840]

André Malraux, 1901–76, French writer
The genius of Christianity is to have proclaimed that the path to the deepest mystery is the
path of love.
[*Anti-Memoirs* 1967]

Christopher Marlowe, 1564–93, English dramatist
I count religion but a childish toy,
And hold there is no sin but ignorance.

[*The Jew of Malta* 1589]

Karl Marx, 1818–83, German philosopher
Religion is the sigh of the oppressed creature, the feeling of a heartless world and the soul of
soulless circumstances. It is the opium of the people.
[*Critique of the Hegelian Philosophy of Right* 1843]

218

GOD AND RELIGION

John Milton, 1608–74, English poet
O welcome, pure-eyed Faith, white-handed Hope,
Thou hovering angel girt with golden wings.

[*Comus* 1634]

Avenge, O Lord, thy slaughtered Saints, whose bones
Lie scattered on the Alpine mountains cold;
Ev'n them who kept thy truth so pure of old,
When all our Fathers worshipped Stocks and Stones.

[*Sonnet: On the late Massacre at Piedmont*]

God doth not need
Either man's work or His own gifts; who best
Bear His mild yoke, they serve Him best: His state
Is kingly. Thousands at his bidding speed
And post o'er Land and Ocean without rest:
They also serve who only stand and wait.

[*Ibid: On His Blindness*]

New Presbyter is but old Priest writ large.

[*Ibid*: *On the New forcers of Conscience under the Long Parliament*]

What in me is dark
Illumine, what is low raise and support;
That to the highth of this great argument
I may assert eternal Providence,
And justify the ways of God to men.

[*Paradise Lost* 1668]

The mind is its own place, and in itself
Can make a heav'n of hell, a hell of heav'n.

[*Ibid*]

Better to reign in hell, than serve in heav'n.

[*Ibid*]

Long is the way
And hard, that out of hell leads up to light.

[*Ibid*]

A heaven on earth.

[*Ibid*]

Just are the ways of God,
And justifiable to men;
Unless there be who think not God at all.

[*Samson Agonistes* 1671]

Michel [Eyquem] de Montaigne, 1533–92, French essayist
Man cannot make a worm, yet he will make gods by the dozen.

[*Essays* 1580]

Pablo Neruda [Ricard Eliecer Neftali Reyes], 1904–73, Chilean poet and diplomat
Poetry is a deep inner calling in man; from it came liturgy, the psalms, and also the content of religions.

[*Memoirs* 1974]

BOOK OF QUOTATIONS

Reinhold Niebuhr, 1892–1971, American religious thinker
God give us grace to accept with serenity the things that cannot be changed, courage to change the things which should be changed, and the wisdom to distinguish the one from the other.

[*The Serenity Prayer* 1934]

Friedrich Wilhelm Nietzsche, 1844–1900, German philosopher and poet
We deny that God is God.

[*The Antichrist* 1888]

Novalis [Friedrich Leopold von Hardenberg], 1772–1801, German poet
[On Spinoza] *Gott-trunkener Mensch.*
A God-intoxicated man.

Joe Orton [Joe Kingsley], 1933–67, English actor and playwright
God is a gentleman. He prefers blondes.

[*Loot* 1966]

Ovid [Publius Ovidius Naso], 43BC–AD18, Roman poet
There is a god within us, and we glow when he stirs us.

[*Fasti c.*AD5]

John Owen, c.1560–1622, Welsh epigrammatist
God and the doctor we alike adore
But only when in danger, not before;
The danger o'er, both are alike requited,
God is forgotten, and the doctor slighted.

[*Epigrammata* 1606–13]

Thomas Paine, 1737–1809, English political writer
Every religion is good that teaches man to be good.

[*The Rights of Man* 1791]

The only idea man can affix to the name of God is that of a first cause, the cause of all things. Incomprehensible and difficult as it is for a man to conceive what a first cause is, he arrives at the belief of it from the tenfold greater difficulty of disbelieving it.

[*The Age of Reason* 1794]

Thomas Parnell, 1679–1718, Irish-born English poet
Remote from man, with God he passed the days,
Prayer all his business, all his pleasure praise.

[*The Hermit* 1721]

Blaise Pascal, 1623–62, French mathematician and writer
Men never do evil so completely and cheerfully as when they do it from religious conviction.

[*Pensées* 1670]

Wendell Phillips, 1811–84, American orator and reformer
One on God's side is a majority.

[Speech 1859]

William Pitt, 1st Earl of Chatham, 1708–78, British statesman
We have a Calvinistic creed, a Popish liturgy, and an Arminian clergy.

[Speech in the House of Lords 1770]

220

Alexander Pope, 1688–1744, English poet
Some to church repair
Not for the doctrine, but the music there.

[*Essay on Criticism* 1711]

Laugh where we must, be candid where we can;
But vindicate the ways of God to man.

[*An Essay on Man* 1732]

Who sees with equal eye as God of all,
A hero perish or a sparrow fall,
Atoms or systems into ruin hurl'd,
And now a bubble burst, and now a world.

[*Ibid*]

Hope springs eternal in the human breast:
Man never is, but always to be blest.

[*Ibid*]

Men would be Angels, Angels would be Gods,
Aspiring to be Gods, if Angels fell,
Aspiring to be Angels, Men rebel.

[*Ibid*]

Nor God alone in the stall calm we find;
He mounts the storm, and walks upon the wind.

[*Ibid*]

A Wit's a feather, and a Chief a rod;
An honest Man's the noblest work of God.

[*Ibid*]

To rest, the cushion and soft dean invite,
Who never mentions hell to ears polite.

[*Ibid*]

Ernest Renan, 1823–92, French historian
Religion is not a popular error; it is a great instinctive truth, sensed by the people, expressed by the people.

[*Les Apôtres* 1866]

O Lord, if there is a Lord, save my soul, if I have a soul.

[*Prière d'un Sceptique*]

Jean Paul Richter, 1763–1825, German novelist
The Infinite has written its name on the heavens in shining stars, and on the earth in tender flowers.

[*Hesperus* 1795]

[Johann Christoph] Friedrich von Schiller, 1759–1805, German poet
Freude, schöner Götterfunken,
Tochter aus Elysium,
Wir betreten feuertrunken,
Himmlische, dein Heiligtum.
O Joy, lovely gift of the gods, daughter of Paradise, divinity, we are inspired as we approach our sanctuary.

[*An die Freude* (set to music by Beethoven in his Ninth Symphony)]

Time consecrates;
And what is grey with age becomes religion.

[*Die Piccolomini*]

Arthur Schopenhauer, 1788–1860, German philosopher
Faith is like love: it cannot be forced.

[*Parerga und Paralipomena* 1851]

Sir Walter Scott, 1771–1832, Scottish novelist
That day of wrath, that dreadful day,
When heaven and earth shall pass away.

[*The Lay of the Last Minstrel: Hymn for the Dead* 1805]

When Israel, of the Lord beloved,
Out of the land of bondage came,
Her fathers' God before her moved,
An awful guide in smoke and flame.

[*Ivanhoe: Rebecca's Hymn* 1819]

Charles Louis de Secondat, Baron de Montesquieu, 1689–1755, French philosopher
If triangles had a god, he would have three sides.

[*Lettres Persanes* 1721]

William Shakespeare, 1564–1616, English dramatist
Down, down to hell; and say I sent thee thither.

[*King Henry VI, Part III* 5 1591]

The God of my idolatry.

[*Romeo and Juliet* 2 1594–5]

God made him, and therefore let him pass for a man.

[*The Merchant of Venice* 1 1596–7]

What damned error, but some sober brow
Will bless it and approve it with a text?

[*Ibid* 3]

Now I, to comfort him, bid him a' should not think of God; I hoped there was no need to trouble himself with any such thoughts yet.

[*King Henry V* 2 1598–1600]

All hell shall stir for this.

[*Ibid* 5]

He wears his faith but as the fashion of his hat.

[*Much Ado About Nothing* 1 1598–1600]

There are no tricks in plain and simple faith.

[*Julius Caesar* 4 1598–1600]

Do not, as some ungracious pastors do,
Show me the steep and thorny way to heaven;
Whiles, like a puff'd and reckless libertine,
Himself the primrose path of dalliance treads.

[*Hamlet* 1 1600–1601]

Angels and ministers of grace defend us!
Be thou a spirit of health or goblin damn'd,
Bring with thee airs from heaven or blasts from hell.

[*Ibid*]

There are more things in heaven and earth, Horatio,
Than are dreamt of in your philosophy.

[*Ibid*]

My words fly up, my thoughts remain below:
Words without thoughts never to heaven go.

[*Ibid* 3]

Our remedies oft in ourselves do lie,
Which we ascribe to heaven: the fated sky
Gives us free scope, only doth backward pull
Our slow designs when we ourselves are dull.

[All's Well That Ends Well 1 1601–1603]

You are one of those that will not serve God, if the devil bid you.

[Othello 1 1604–5]

As flies to wanton boys, are we to gods;
They kill us for their sport.

[King Lear 4 1605–6]

The gods are just, and of our pleasant vices
Make instruments to plague us.

[Ibid 5]

There's husbandry in heaven;
Their candles are all out.

[Ibid 2]

Heaven is above all yet; there sits a judge
That no king can corrupt.

[King Henry VIII 3 1613]

Had I but served my God with half the zeal
I served my king, he would not in mine age
Have left me naked to mine enemies.

[Ibid]

George Bernard Shaw, 1856–1950, Irish playwright

There is only one religion, though there are a hundred versions of it.

[Plays Unpleasant preface 1898]

Beware of the man whose god is in the skies.

[Man and Superman: *Maxims for Revolutionists* 1903]

In heaven an angel is nobody in particular.

[Ibid]

O God that madest this beautiful earth, when will it be ready to receive Thy saints? How long, O Lord, how long?

[St Joan 1923]

Must then a Christ perish in torment in every age to save those that have no imagination?

[Ibid: epilogue]

Fulton John Sheen, 1895–1979, American bishop

An atheist is a man who has no invisible means of support.

[In Look 1955]

Percy Bysshe Shelley, 1792–1822, English poet

Kings, priests, and statesmen, blast the human flower
Even in its tender bud; their influence darts
Like subtle poison through the bloodless veins
Of desolate society.

[Queen Mab 1813]

Earth groans beneath religion's iron age
And priests dare babble of a God of peace
Even whilst their hands are red with guiltless blood.

[Ibid]

From the dust of creeds outworn.

[*Prometheus Unbound* 1818–19]

The world's great age begins anew,
The golden years return,
The earth doth like a snake renew
Her winter weeds outworn;
Heaven smiles, and faiths and empires gleam,
Like wrecks of a dissolving dream.

[*Hellas* 1821]

Hell is a city much like London –
A populous and a smoky city.

[*Peter Bell the Third*]

Philip Henry Sheridan, 1831–88, American general
If I owned Texas and Hell, I would rent out Texas and live in Hell.
[Remark to officers, Texas, 1855]

Sydney Smith, 1771–1845, English churchman
As the French say, there are three sexes – men, women, and clergymen.

[In Lady Holland's *Memoir* 1855]

Philip Dormer Stanhope, 4th Earl of Chesterfield, 1694–1773, English statesman
Religion is by no means a proper subject of conversation in a mixed company.

[Letter to his godson, undated]

Laurence Sterne, 1713–68, English churchman and writer
Whenever a man talks loudly against religion, – always suspect that it is not his reason, but his passions which have got the better of his creed.

[*Tristram Shandy* 1760]

The excellency of this text is that it will suit any sermon, – and of this sermon, – that it will suit any text.

[*Ibid*]

"God tempers the wind," said Maria, "to the shorn lamb."

[*A Sentimental Journey* 1768]

Robert Louis [Balfour] Stevenson, 1850–94, Scottish novelist and poet
Mankind was never so happily inspired as when it made a cathedral.

[*An Inland Voyage* 1878]

Every man is his own doctor of divinity in the last resort.

[*Ibid*]

[Johan] August Strindberg, 1849–1912, Swedish dramatist
To search for God and to find the Devil – that is what happened to me.

[*Inferno* 1897]

Jonathan Swift, 1667–1745, Irish-born English writer
We have just enough religion to make us hate, but not enough to make us love one another.

[*Thoughts on Various Subjects; from Miscellanies* 1711]

Algernon Charles Swinburne, 1837–1909, English poet
Yea, is not even Apollo, with hair and harpstring of gold,
A bitter God to follow, a beautiful God to behold?

[*Hymn to Proserpine* 1866]

From too much love of living,
From hope and fear set free,
We thank with brief thanksgiving
Whatever gods may be
That no life lives for ever;
That dead men rise up never;
That even the weariest river
Winds somewhere safe to sea.

[*The Garden of Proserpine*]

Alfred, Lord Tennyson, 1809–92, English poet
Kind hearts are more than coronets,
And simple faith than Norman blood.

[*Lady Clara Vere de Vere*]

The Gods themselves cannot recall their gifts.

[*Tithonus* 1833]

There lives more faith in honest doubt,
Believe me, than in half the creeds.

[*In Memoriam* 1850]

One God, one law, one element,
And one far off divine event,
To which the whole creation moves.

[*Ibid*]

The old order changeth, yielding place to new,
And God fulfils himself in many ways,
Lest one good custom should corrupt the world.

[*Idylls of the King: The Passing of Arthur* 1859–85]

If thou shouldst never see my face again,
Pray for my soul. More things are wrought by prayer
Than this world dreams of.

[*Ibid*]

For so the whole round earth is every way
Bound by gold chains about the feet of God.

[*Ibid*]

Sink me the ship, Master Gunner – sinker her, split her in twain!
Fall into the hands of God, not into the hands of Spain!

[*The Revenge*]

Tertullian, c.160–c.230, Roman Christian theologian
One man's religion neither harms nor helps another man.

[*Ad Scapulam*]

It is certainly no part of religion to compel religion.

[*Ibid*]

William Makepeace Thackeray, 1811–63, English novelist
'Tis not the dying for a faith that's so hard, Master Harry – every man of every nation has
done that – 'tis the living up to it that is difficult.

[*The History of Henry Esmond* 1852]

James Thomson, 1700–1748, Scottish poet
An elegant sufficiency, content
Retirement, rural quiet, friendship, books,
Ease and alternate labour, useful life,
Progressive virtue, and approving Heaven!

[*The Seasons: Spring* 1726–30]

A little, round, fat, oily man of God.

[*The Castle of Indolence* 1848]

Sojourner Truth [Isabella Van Wagener], 1797–1883, American abolitionist
Where did your Christ come from? From God and a woman! Man had nothing to do with him.

[Speech 1851]

John Tyndall, 1820–93, Irish-born physicist
Superstition may be defined as constructive religion which has grown incongruous with intelligence.

[*Fragments of Science: Science and Man*]

Virgil *or* Vergil [Publius Vergilius Maro], 70–19BC, Roman poet
The will of the gods was otherwise.

[*Aeneid*]

Voltaire [François Marie Arouet], 1694–1778, French philosopher and writer
I have never made but one prayer to God, a very short one: "O Lord, make my enemies ridiculous." And God granted it.

[Letter 1767]

Si Dieu n'existait pas, il faudrait l'inventer.
(If God did not exist, it would be necessary to invent him.)

[*Epitre à l'auteur du nouveau livre des trois imposteurs* 1769]

God is always on the side of the heaviest battalions.

[Letter 1770]

Alice [Malsenior] Walker, 1944– , American novelist and poet
When I found out I thought that God was white, and a man, I lost interest.

[*The Color Purple* 1982]

Isaac Watts, 1674–1748, English poet and hymn-writer
Our God, our help in ages past,
Our hope for years to come,
Our shelter from the stormy blast,
And our eternal home.

[*Psalm 90*]

Katherine Whitehorn, 1926– , English journalist
We were discussing the possibility of making one of our cats Pope recently, and we decided that the fact that she was not Italian and was female, made the third point, that she was a cat, quite irrelevant.

[In *The Observer*]

Walt[er] Whitman, 1819–92, American poet
I say the whole earth and all the stars in the sky are for religion's sake.

[*Leaves of Grass: Starting from Paumanok* 1855–92]

226

Ella Wheeler Wilcox, 1850–1919, American poet
So many gods, so many creeds,
So many paths that wind and wind,
When just the art of being kind
Is all this sad world needs.

[The World's Need]

Oscar [Fingall O'Flahertie Wills] Wilde, 1854–1900, Irish writer
We are each our own devil, and we make
This world our hell.

[The Duchess of Padua 1891]

Religions die when they are proved to be true. Science is the record of dead religions.

[Phrases and Philosophies for the Use of the Young: Chameleon 1894]

When the gods wish to punish us they answer our prayers.

[An Ideal Husband]

Thomas Wolsey, c.1475–1530, English churchman and politician
Had I served my God as diligently as I have served the king, He would not have given me over
in my grey hairs.

[On the day of his death]

[Adeline] Virginia Woolf, 1882–1941, English novelist and critic
I read the book of Job last night–I don't think God comes well out of it.

[Letter to Lytton Strachey]

William Wordsworth, 1770–1850, English poet
Plain living and high thinking are no more:
The homely beauty of the good old cause
Is gone; our peace, our fearful innocence,
And pure religion breathing household laws.

[Sonnet: O Friend! I know not which Way I must look]

Great God! I'd rather be
A pagan suckled in a creed outworn.

[Sonnet: The World is too much with us]

Our birth is but a sleep and a forgetting:
The soul that rises with us, our life's star,
Hath had elsewhere its setting,
And cometh from afar:
Not in entire forgetfulness,
And not in utter nakedness,
But trailing clouds of glory do we come
From God, who is our home:
Heaven lies about us in our infancy!

[Ode on Intimations of Immortality]

Thomas Russell Ybarra, 1880–1971,
A Christian is a man who feels
Repentance on a Sunday
For what he did on Saturday
And is going to do on Monday.

[The Christian]

William Butler Yeats, 1865–1939, Irish poet
And god stands winding His lonely horn,
And time and the world are ever in flight;
And love is less kind than the grey twilight,
And hope is less dear than the dew of the morn.

[*Into the Twilight* 1893]

Edward Young, 1683–1765, English churchman and poet
A God all mercy, is a God unjust.

[*Night Thoughts* 1742–5]

Government and Politics

Fisher Ames, 1758–1808, American politician
A monarchy is a merchantman which sails well, but will sometimes strike on a rock, and go to the bottom; a republic is a raft which will never sink, but then your feet are always in the water.

[Speech in the House of Representatives 1795]

Anonymous
It doesn't matter who you vote for. The government always gets in.

[Graffiti]

Aristophanes, c.448–c.388BC, Greek playwright
You have all the characteristics of a popular politician: a horrible voice, bad breeding, and a vulgar manner.

[*Knights c.*424BC]

Aristotle, 384–322BC, Greek philosopher
A democracy is a government in the hands of men of low birth, no property, and vulgar employments.

[*Politics c.*322BC]

Man is by nature a political animal.

[*Ibid*]

Clement Richard Attlee, 1st Earl Attlee, 1883–1967, British statesman
Democracy means government by discussion, but it is only effective if you can stop people talking.

[*Anatomy of Britain*]

Francis Bacon, Baron Verulam of Verulam and Viscount of St Albans, 1561–1626, English philosopher
It is as hard and severe a thing to be a true politician as to be truly moral.

[*The Advancement of Learning* 1605]

Russell Wayne Baker, 1925– , American columnist
The dirty work at political conventions is almost always done in the grim hours between midnight and dawn. Hangmen and politicians work best when the human spirit is at its lowest ebb.

[*The Sayings of Poor Russell* in *Harpers* 1972]

Mikhail Aleksandrovich Bakunin, 1814–76, Russian revolutionary
Even in the purest democracies, such as the United States and Switzerland, a privileged minority stands against the vast enslaved majority.

[*Dieu et l'état* 1871]

August Bebel, 1840–1913, German politician
All political questions, all matters or right, are at bottom only questions of might.

[Speech in the Reichstag 1871]

[Enoch] Arnold Bennett, 1867–1931, English Novelist
Every Briton is at heart a Tory – especially every British Liberal.

[*Journal*, 1929]

Aneurin Bevan, 1897–1960, British politician
We know what happens to people who stay in the middle of the road. They get run over.

[In *The Observer* 1953]

Ambrose [Gwinett] Bierce, 1842–1914, American writer
Elector: one who enjoys the sacred privilege of voting for the man of another man's choice.

[*The Devil's Dictionary* 1906]

Politics: a strife of interests masquerading as a contest of principles. The conduct of public affairs for private advantage.

[*Ibid*]

[Prince] Otto [Edward Leopold] von Bismarck, Duke of Lauenburg, 1815–98, Prussian statesman
Politics is the doctrine of the possible, the attainable.

[Speech 1863]

Sir William Blackstone, 1723–80, English lawyer
That the king can do no wrong, is a necessary and fundamental principle of the English constitution.

[*Commentaries*]

Tony [Anthony Charles Lynton] Blair, 1953– , British politician
Education, education and education!

[Speech, Labour Party conference 1996]

There is no greater honour than to serve you as prime minister and you have given us tonight an historic moment for the Labour Party.

[Election victory speech June 2001]

Henry Peter Brougham, Baron Brougham and Vaux, 1778–1868, British law reformer
In my mind, he was guilty of no error, he was chargeable with no exaggerations, he was betrayed by his fancy into no metaphor, who once said, that all we see about us, Kings, Lords, and Commons, the whole machinery of the State, all the apparatus of the system, and its varied workings, end in simply bringing twelve good men into a box.

[*The Present State of the Law* 1828]

Pearl S[ydenstricker] Buck, 1892–1973, American writer
People on the whole are very simple-minded, in whatever country one finds them. They are so simple as to take literally, more often than not, the things their leaders tell them.

[*What America Means to Me* 1944]

Samuel Dickinson Burchard, 1812–91, American churchman
We are Republicans, and don't propose to leave our party and identify ourselves with the party whose antecedents have been Rum, Romanism, and Rebellion.

[Speech 1884]

[John] Anthony Burgess [Wilson], 1917– 93, English-born novelist and critic
The U.S. Presidency is a Tudor monarchy plus telephones.

[In *Writers at Work* 1977]

Edmund Burke, 1729–97, Irish-born English political writer
Your representative owes you, not his industry only, but his judgment; and he betrays instead of serving you if he sacrifices it to your opinion.

[Speech 1774]

Government is a contrivance of human wisdom to provide for human wants. Men have a right that these wants should be provided for by this wisdom.

[*Reflections on the Revolution in France* 1790]

Kings will be tyrants from policy, when subjects are rebels from principle.

[*Ibid*]

Robert Burns, 1759–96, Scottish poet
Princes and lords are but the breath of kings,
"An honest man's the noblest work of God."

[*The Cottar's Saturday Night* 1785]

Kings may be blest, but Tam was glorious,
O'er a' the ills o' life victorious.

[*Tam o' Shanter* 1791]

John Byrom, 1692–1763, English poet
God bless the King! – I mean the Faith's Defender;
God bless (no harm in blessing) the Pretender!
But who Pretender is, or who is King –
God bless us all! – that's quite another thing.

[*To an Officer of the Army*]

Byron, Lord George Gordon [Noel], 6th Baron Byron of Rochdale, 1788–1824, English poet
When a proposal is made to emancipate or relieve, you hesitate, you deliberate for years, you temporize and tamper with the minds of men; but a death-bill must be passed off-hand, without a thought of the consequences.

[Maiden speech in the House of Lords, 1812]

The impression of Parliament upon me was that its members are not formidable as speakers, but very much so as an audience.

[*Detached Thoughts* 1921]

Cicero himself, and probably the Messiah, could never have alter'd the vote of a single Lord of the Bedchamber or Bishop.

[*Ibid*]

John Caldwell Calhoun, 1782–1850, American statesman
The very essence of a free government consists in considering offices as public trusts, bestowed for the good of the country, and not for the benefit of an individual or a party.

[Speech 1835]

231

Albert Camus, 1913–60, Algerian-born French philosopher and novelist

Fascism . . . represents the exaltation of the executioner by the executioner . . . Russian Communism . . . represents the exaltation of the executioner by the victim. The former never dreamed of liberating all men, but only of liberating the few by subjugating the rest. The latter, in its most profound principle, aims at liberating all men by provisionally enslaving them all.

[*The Rebel* 1951]

All modern revolutions have ended in a reinforcement of the power of the State.

[*The Rebel* 1951]

Thomas Carlyle, 1795–1881, Scottish historian and writer

He who first shortened the labour of copyists by device of *Moveable Types* was disbanding hired armies, and cashiering most Kings and Senates, and creating a whole new democratic world: he had invented the art of printing.

[*Sartor Resartus* 1833–4]

What is the end of government? To suppress all noise and disturbance, whether of Puritan preaching, Cameronian psalm-singing, thieves'-riot, murder, arson, or what noise soever, and – be careful that supplies do not fail!

[*Past and Present* 1843]

Jimmy [James Earl] Carter, 1924– , 39th president of the United States

All I want is the same thing you want. To have a nation with a government that is as good and honest and decent and competent and compassionate and as filled with love as are the American people.

[Speech 1976]

G[ilbert] K[eith] Chesterton, 1874–1936, English writer

Democracy means government by the uneducated, while aristocracy means government by the badly educated.

[In the *New York Times* 1931]

You can never have a revolution in order to establish a democracy. You must have a democracy in order to have a revolution.

[*Tremendous Trifles*]

Shirley Chisholm, 1924– , American politician

It is a great honour to be chosen as the nation's first black congresswoman. As a United States Representative in Washington, I intend to represent all the people – the blacks, the whites, the men, the women, especially the youth. There are many new ideas abroad in this country and I intend to speak for these ideas. And my voice will be heard.

Winston [Leonard Spencer] Churchill, 1874–1965, British statesman

Politics are almost as exciting as war, and quite as dangerous. In war you can only be killed once, but in politics many times.

[Remark 1920]

It has been said that democracy is the worst form of government, except for all those other forms that have been tried from time to time.

[Speech in the House of Commons 1947]

[On political skill] The ability to foretell what is going to happen tomorrow, next week, next month, and next year. And to have the ability afterwards to explain why it didn't happen.

[In Bill Adler's *The Churchill Wit*]

Henry Clay, 1777–1852, American statesman
Sir, I would rather be right than be President.

[Speech 1850]

Stephen Grover Cleveland, 1837–1908, 22nd and 24th president of the United States
Your every voter, as surely as your chief magistrate, exercises a public trust.

[Inaugural address 1885]

Bill [William Jefferson] Clinton, 1946– , 42nd president of the United States
[On President Nixon] If a president of the United States ever lied to the American people, he should resign.

[In *Arkansas Democratic Gazette* August 6 1974]

Confucius [K'ung fu-tzu], 551–479BC, Chinese philosopher
An oppressive government is more to be feared than a tiger.

[*Analects c.*500BC]

In a country well governed, poverty is something to be ashamed of. In a country badly governed, wealth is something to be ashamed of.

[*Ibid*]

Calvin Coolidge, 1872–1933, 30th president of the United States
The governments of the past could fairly be characterized as devices for maintaining in perpetuity the place and position of certain privileged classes . . . The Government of the United States is a device for maintaining in perpetuity the rights of the people, with the ultimate extinction of all privileged classes.

[Speech 1924]

James Fenimore Cooper, 1789–1851, American novelist
Contact with the affairs of state is one of the most corrupting of the influences to which men are exposed.

[*The American Democrat* 1838]

Richard [Howard Stafford] Crossman, 1907–74 British politician
The Civil Service is profoundly deferential – "Yes, Minister! No, Minister! If you wish it, Minister!"

[*The Diaries of a Cabinet Minister 1964–70*]

John Emerich Edward Dalberg, 1st Baron Acton, 1834–1902, English historian
Power tends to corrupt, and absolute power corrupts absolutely. Great men are almost always bad men . . . There is no worse heresy than that the office sanctifies the holder of it.

[Letter to Bishop Creighton 1887]

Charles [John Huffam] Dickens, 1812–70, English novelist
Your sister is given to government.

[*Great Expectations* 1860–61]

Joan Didion, 1934– , American novelist
To believe in "the greater good" is to operate, necessarily, in a certain ethical suspension. Ask anyone committed to a Marxist analysis how many angels on the head of a pin, and you will be asked in return to never mind the angels, tell me who controls the production of pins.

[*The White Album* 1979]

Diogenes, 412–323BC, Cynic philosopher

The foundation of every state is the education of its youth.

[In Stobaeus' *Florilegium*]

Benjamin Disraeli, 1st Earl of Beaconsfield, 1804–81, British statesman

No Government can be long secure without a formidable Opposition.

[*Coningsby* 1844]

Conservatism discards Prescription, shrinks from Principle, disavows Progress; having rejected all respect for antiquity, it offers no redress for the present, and makes no preparation for the future.

[*Ibid*]

A sound Conservative government . . . Tory men and Whig measures.

[*Ibid*]

A Conservative government is an organized hypocrisy.
[Speech in the House of Commons1845]
I believe that without party Parliamentary government is impossible.

[Speech 1872]

Permissive legislation is the characteristic of a free people.

[Speech in the House of Commons1875]

John Dryden, 1631–1700, English dramatist

For politicians neither love nor hate.

[*Absalom and Achitophel* 1681]

A man so various that he seem'd to be
Not one, but all mankind's epitome:
Stiff in opinions, always in the wrong,
Was everything by starts and nothing long;
But in the course of one revolving moon,
Was chymist, fiddler, statesman, and buffoon.

[*Ibid*]

Albert Einstein, 1879–1955, German-born mathematical physicist

The State is made for man, not man for the State.

[*The World As I See It*]

Elizabeth I, 1533–1603, queen of England and Ireland

I know I have the body of a weak and feeble woman, but I have the heart and stomach of a king, and of a king of England too.

[Speech 1588]

Ralph Waldo Emerson, 1803–82, American writer

Politics is a deleterious profession, like some poisonous handicrafts. Men in power have no opinions, but may be had cheap for any opinion, for any purpose.

[*The Conduct of Life* 1860]

Gerald R[udolph] Ford, 1913– , 38th president of the United States

I believe that truth is the glue that holds government together, not only our government but civilization itself.

[Speech, Washington August 1974]

Charles Frankel, 1917–79, American academic
Whatever happens in government could have happened differently, and it usually would have been better if it had.

[High on Foggy Bottom 1969]

Benjamin Franklin, 1706–90, American scientist and philosopher
In rivers and bad governments the lightest things swim at the top.

[Poor Richard's Almanack 1754]

Milton Friedman, 1912– , American economist
Governments never learn. Only people learn.

[In *The Observer* 1980]

The government solution to a problem is usually as bad as the problem.

[Attributed]

John Kenneth Galbraith, 1908– , Canadian-born American economist
Politics is not the art of the possible. It consists in choosing between the disastrous and the unpalatable.

[Ambassador's Journal 1969]

Mohandas Karamchand ("Mahatma") Gandhi, 1869–1948, Indian political leader
Men say I am a saint losing himself in politics. The fact is that I am a politician trying my hardest to become a saint.

John Gay, 1685–1732, English poet and playwright
That politician tops his part,
Who readily can lie with art:
The man's proficient in his trade;
His power is strong, his fortune's made.

[Fables 1738]

Sir William Schwenck Gilbert, 1836–1911, English librettist
When I was a lad I served a term
As office boy to an Attorney's firm.
I cleaned the windows and I swept the floor,
And I polished up the handle of the big front door.
I polished up that handle so carefullee
That now I am the ruler of the Queen's Navee!

[HMS Pinafore 1878]

I always voted at my party's call,
And I never thought of thinking for myself at all.

[Ibid]

Politics we bar,
They are not our bent;
On the whole we are
Not intelligent.

[Princess Ida 1884]

Isaac Goldberg, 1887–1938, American critic
Diplomacy is to do and say
The nastiest thing in the nicest way.

[The Reflex]

235

Oliver Goldsmith, 1728–74, Irish-born English writer
[On Edmund Burke]
Here lies our good Edmund, whose genius was such,
We scarcely can praise it, or blame it too much;
Who, born for the Universe, narrow'd his mind,
And to party gave up what was meant for mankind.

[*Retaliation* 1774]

Though equal to all things, for all things unfit,
Too nice for a statesman, too proud for a wit:
For a patriot, too cool; for a drudge, disobedient;
And too fond the *right* to pursue the *expedient*.

[*Ibid*]

Alexander Hamilton, 1755–1804, American statesman
Why has government been instituted at all? Because the passions of men will not conform to the dictates of reason and justice without restraint.

[*The Federalist* 1788]

Thomas Hardy, 1840–1928, English novelist and poet
When shall the softer, saner politics,
Whereof we dream, have play in each proud land?

[*Departure*]

Georg Wilhelm Friedrich Hegel, 1770–1831, German philosopher
But what experience and history teach is this, that peoples and government have never learned anything from history.

[*The Philosophy of History* 1832]

Richard Hooker, 1554–1600, English theologian
He that goeth about to persuade a multitude, that they are not so well governed as they ought to be, shall never want attentive and favourable hearers.

[*Laws of Ecclesiastical Polity* 1594]

David Hume, 1711–76, Scottish philosopher and writer
Nothing appears more surprising to those who consider human affairs with a philosophical eye, than the easiness with which the many are governed by the few.

[*Essays Moral and Political* 1741–2]

Andrew Jackson, 1767–1845, 7th president of the United States
One man with courage makes a majority.

[Saying]

Thomas Jefferson, 1743–1826, 3rd president of the United States
Those who bear equally the burdens of government should equally participate of its benefits.
[Address to Lord Dunmore 1775]
I hold it, that a little rebellion, now and then, is a good thing, and as necessary in the political world as storms in the physical.

[Letter 1787]
A bill of rights is what the people are entitled to against every government on earth, general or particular and what no just government should refuse or rest on inference.

[*Ibid*]
I have no ambition to govern men. It is a painful and thankless office.

[*Ibid* 1796]

Politics is such a torment that I would advise every one I love not to mix with it.

[*Ibid* 1800]

The care of human life and happiness, and not their destruction, is the first and only legitimate object of good government.

[To the Republican citizens of Washington County, Maryland, 1809]

Dr Samuel Johnson, 1709–84, English lexicographer

Why, Sir, most schemes of political improvement are very laughable things.

[In Boswell's *Life of Samuel Johnson* 1791]

"Junius," fl. 1769–72 [?Sir Philip Francis, 1740–1818, British civil servant]

The right of election is the very essence of the constitution.

[Letter in the *Public Advertiser* 1769]

Is this the wisdom of a great minister? or is it the ominous vibration of a pendulum?

[*Ibid*]

There is a holy mistaken zeal in politics as well as in religion. By persuading others, we convince ourselves.

[*Ibid*]

John Fitzgerald Kennedy, 1917–63, 35th president of the United States

Those who make peaceful revolution impossible, make violent revolution inevitable.

[Address to diplomats 1962]

John Maynard Keynes, 1st Baron Keynes of Tilton, 1883–1946, English economist

This *long run* is a misleading guide to current affairs. In the *long run* we are all dead. Economists set themselves too easy, too useless a task if in tempestuous seasons they can only tell us that when the storm is long past the ocean is flat again.

[*A Tract on Monetary Reform*]

Neil Gordon Kinnock, 1942– , British politician

If Margaret Thatcher wins – I warn you not to be ordinary. I warn you not to be young. I warn you not to fall ill. I warn you not to get old.

[Speech on the eve of the General Election June 7 1983]

Rudyard Kipling, 1865–1936, English writer

If you can talk with crowds and keep your virtue,
Or walk with Kings – nor lose the common touch.

[*If –*]

Nikolai Lenin [Vladimir Ilyich Ulyanov], 1870–1924, Russian revolutionary leader

We must hate – hatred is the basis of Communism. Children must be taught to hate their parents if they are not Communists.

[Speech 1923]

Leo XIII [Gioacchino Pecci], 1810–1903, Italian pope

The right to rule is not necessarily bound up with any special mode of government. It may take this form or that, provided only that it be of a nature to ensure the general welfare.

[*Immortale Dei* 1885]

Abraham Lincoln, 1809–65, 16th president of the United States

No man is good enough to govern another man without that other's consent.

[Speech 1854]

The ballot is stronger than the bullet.

[*Ibid* 1856]

I believe this government cannot endure permanently half-slave and half-free. I do not expect the Union to be dissolved . . . but I do expect it will cease to be divided.

[*Ibid* 1858]

As I would not be a slave, so I would not be a master. This expresses my idea of democracy. Whatever differs from this, to the extent of the difference, is no democracy.

[Said while vice-president 1858]

Louis XIV, 1638–1715, king of France
L'Etat, c'est moi.
(I am the State.)

[Attributed]

James Russell Lowell, 1819–91, American editor and poet
He's been true to *one* party – an' thet is himself.

[*The Bigelow Papers:* 1862]

Democracy gives every man
The right to be his own oppressor.

[*Ibid*]

Thomas Babington Macaulay, 1st Baron Macaulay, 1800–1859, English historian
Then none was for a party;
Then all were for the State;
Then the great man helped the poor,
And the poor man loved the great:
Then lands were fairly portioned;
Then spoils were fairly sold;
The Romans were like brothers
In the brave days of old.

[*Lays of Ancient Rome: Horatius* 1842]

Timid and interested politicians think much more about the security of their seats than about the security of their country.
[Speech in the House of Commons 1842]
In every age the vilest specimens of human nature are to be found among demagogues.

[*History of England* 1855]

Niccolo Machiavelli, 1469–1527, Italian political philosopher
All well-governed states and wise princes have taken care not to reduce the nobility to despair, nor the people to discontent.

[*The Prince* 1513]

Mao Tse-Tung, 1893–1976, Chinese revolutionary leader
We Communists are like seeds and the people are like the soil. Wherever we go, we must unite with the people, take root and blossom among them.

[*Quotations from Chairman Mao* 1966]

Joseph Marie, Comte de Maistre, 1754–1821, French writer
Toute nation a le gouvernement qu'elle merite.
(Every nation has the government it deserves.)

[Letter from Russia 1811]

Don[ald Robert Perry] Marquis, 1878–1937, American novelist, playwright and poet
the bees got their
governmental system settled
millions of years ago
but the human race is still
groping.

[*archy and mehitabel* 1927]

Karl Marx, 1818–83, German philosopher
From each according to his ability, to each according to his needs.

[*Critique of the Gotha Programme* 1875]

Karl Marx and Friedrich Engels, 1820–95, German philosopher
In this sense, the theory of the Communists may be summed up in the single sentence:
Abolition of private property.

[*The Communist Manifesto* 1848]

Philip Massinger, 1583–1640, English dramatist
He that would govern others, first should be
The master of himself.

[*The Bondman* 1624]

H[enry] L[ouis] Mencken, 1880–1956, American critic and writer
Democracy is the theory that the common people know what they want, and deserve to get it
good and hard.

[*A Book of Burlesques* 1920]

John Stuart Mill, 1806–73, English philosopher
The worth of a state, in the long run, is the worth of the individuals composing it.

[*On Liberty* 1859]

Thomas Moore, 1779–1852, Irish poet
The minds of some of our own statesmen, like the pupil of the human eye, contract
themselves the more, the strong light there is shed upon them.

[*Corruption and Intolerance* preface]

Jawaharlal Nehru, 1889–1964, Indian statesman
The forces of a capitalist society, if left unchecked, tend to make the rich richer and the poor
poorer.

[*Credo*]

George Orwell [Eric Arthur Blair], 1903–50, English novelist and critic
All animals are equal, but some animals are more equal than others.

[*Animal Farm* 1945]

James Otis, 1725–83, American political leader
Taxation without representation is tyranny.

[Attributed 1763]

William Tyler Page, 1868–1942,
I believe in the United States of America as a government of the people, by the people, for
the people; whose just powers are derived from the consent of the governed; a democracy in a
republic; a sovereign nation of many sovereign states; a perfect union, one and inseparable;

established upon those principles of freedom, equality, justice and humanity for which American patriots sacrificed their lives and fortunes. I therefore believe it is my duty to my country to love it, to support its constitution, to obey its laws, to respect its flag, and to defend it against all enemies.

[*The American's Creed*]

Thomas Paine, 1737–1809, English politicial writer
Society in every state is a blessing, but government, even in its best state, is but a necessary evil; in its worst state, an intolerable one.

[*Common Sense* 1776]

Society performs for itself almost everything which is ascribed to government.

[*The Rights of Man* 1791]

Cyril Northcote Parkinson, 1909–93, English political scientist
Men enter local politics as a result of being unhappily married.

[*Parkinson's Law, The Pursuit of Progress*]

William Penn, 1644–1718, English founder of Pennsylvania
Any government is free to the people under it where the laws rule and the people are a party to the laws.

[*Frame of Government* 1682]

No system of government was ever so ill devised that, under proper men, it wouldn't work well enough.

[*Some Fruits of Solitude* 1693]

Let the people think they govern and they will be governed.

[*Ibid*]

Wendell Phillips, 1811–84, American orator and reformer
Governments exist to protect the rights of minorities. The loved and the rich need no protection, they have many friends and few enemies.

[Speech 1860]

Politicians are like the bones of a horse's foreshoulder – not a straight one in it.

[*Ibid* 1864]

William Pitt, 1st Earl of Chatham, 1708–78, British statesman
The poorest man may in his cottage bid defiance to all the forces of the Crown. It may be frail – its roof may shake – the wind may blow through it – the storm may enter – the rain may enter – but the King of England cannot enter – all his force dares not cross the threshold of the ruined tenement.

[In Lord Brougham's *Statesmen in the Time of George III* 1839]

Plato, c.428–348BC, Greek philosopher
Democracy . . . is a charming form of government, full of variety and disorder, and dispensing a kind of quality to equals and unequals alike.

[*The Republic c.*370BC]

The rulers of the State are the only ones who should have the privilege of lying, either at home or abroad; they may be allowed to lie for the good of the State.

[*Ibid*]

Our object in the construction of the state is the greatest happiness of the whole, and not that of any one class.

[*Ibid*]

Alexander Pope, 1688–1744, English poet

Party-spirit, which at best is but the madness of many for the gain of a few.

[Letter 1714]

Coffee, which makes the politician wise,
And see through all things with his half-shut eyes.

[*The Rape of the Lock* 1714]

The right divine of kings to govern wrong.

[*The Dunciad* 1728]

Statesman, yet friend to truth! of soul sincere.

[*Moral Essays: To Mr Addison* 1731–5]

Michael Portillo, 1953– , British Conservative politician

Compassion is an essential ingredient in Conservatism.

[Speech, Conservative Party conference 1997]

Sir Charles Pratt, 1st Earl Camden, 1714–94, English lawyer and statesman

The British parliament has no right to tax the Americans . . . Taxation and representation are inseparably united. God hath joined them: no British parliament can put them asunder. To endeavour to do so is to stab our very vitals.

[Speech in the House of Lords 1765]

Ronald Wilson Reagan, 1911– , 40th president of the United States

I used to say that politics was the second oldest profession, and I have come to know that it bears a gross similarity to the first.

[Said while running for the presidency 1979]

Will[iam Penn Adair] Rogers, 1879–1935, American humorist

The more you read and observe about this Politics thing, the more you've got to admit that each party's worse than the other. The one that's out always looks the best.

[*The Illiterate Digest* 1924]

Franklin Delano Roosevelt, 1882–1945, 32nd president of the United States

In the field of world policy I would dedicate this nation to the policy of the good neighbour.

[Inaugural address 1933]

Theodore Roosevelt, 1858–1919, 26th president of the United States

The best executive is the one who has sense enough to pick good men to do what he wants done, and self-restraint enough to keep from meddling with them while they do it.

Jean Jacques Rousseau, 1712–78, Swiss-born French philosopher

If there were a nation of gods they would be governed democratically, but so perfect a government is not suitable to men.

[*The Social Contract* 1762]

John Ruskin, 1819–1900, English art critic and writer

Government and co-operation are in all things the laws of life; anarchy and competition, the laws of death.

[*Unto This Last* 1860]

The first duty of government is to see that people have food, fuel, and clothes. The second, that they have means of moral and intellectual education.

[*Fors Clavigera* 1876]

Anwar al-Sadat, 1918–81, president of Egypt
There can be hope only for a society which acts as one big family, and not as many separate ones.

[*In Search of Identity* 1978]

Sir Walter Scott, 1771–1832, Scottish novelist
When we had a king, and a chancellor, and parliament men o' our ain, we could aye pebble them wi' stanes when they werna guid bairns, but naebody's nails can reach the length o' Lunnon.

[*Malachi Malagrowther* 1826]

Charles Louis de Secondat, Baron de Montesquieu, 1689–1755, French philosopher
When a government lasts a long while, it deteriorates by insensible degrees.

[*The Spirit of the Laws* 1748]

The deterioration of every government begins with the decay of the principles on which it was founded.

[*Ibid*]

All things human have their ends, and some day England will lose its liberty, and perish. It will perish when its legislative power becomes more corrupt than its executive power.
[*Ibid*]

Sir John Robert Seeley, 1834–95, English historian
[On the English] We seem as it were to have conquered and peopled half the world in a fit of absence of mind.

[*The Expansion of England* 1883]

History is past politics and politics present history.

[*The Growth of British Policy* 1895]

John Selden, 1584–1654, English antiquary and politician
A King is a thing men have made for their own sakes, for quietness' sake. Just as in a family one man is appointed to buy the meat.

[*Table Talk: Of a King* 1689]

There is not anything in the world so much abused as this sentence, *Salus populi suprema lex esto* (Let public safety be the supreme law).

[*Ibid: People*]

They that govern most make least noise.

[*Ibid: Power*]

William Shakespeare, 1564–1616, English dramatist
His greatness weigh'd, his will is not his own;
For he himself is subject to his birth:
He may not, as unvalued persons do,
Carve for himself; for on his choice depends
The safety and the health of this whole state.

[*Hamlet* 1 1600–1601]

Something is rotten in the state of Denmark.

[*Ibid*]

Soft you; a word or two before you go.
I have done the state some service, and they know 't.
No more of that. I pray you, in your letters,
Speak of me as I am; nothing extenuate,
Nor set down aught in malice.

[*Othello* 5 1605–5]

Get thee glass eyes;
And, like a scurvy politician, seem
To see the things thou dost not.

[*King Lear* 4 1605–6]

George Bernard Shaw, 1856–1950, Irish playwright

Democracy substitutes election by the incompetent many for appointment by the corrupt few.

[*Man and Superman: Maxims for Revolutionists* 1903]

An all-night sitting in a theatre would be at least as enjoyable as an all-night sitting in the House of Commons, and much more useful.

[*St Joan* preface 1923]

Percy Bysshe Shelley, 1792–1822, English poet

My name is Ozymandias, king of kings:
Look on my works, ye Mighty, and despair!

[*Ozymandias* 1818]

Richard Brinsley Sheridan, 1751–1816, English dramatist

No scandal about Queen Elizabeth, I hope?

[*The Critic* 1779]

James Shirley, 1596–1666, English dramatist

The glories of our blood and state
Are shadows, not substantial things;
There is no armour against fate;
Death lays his icy hand on kings.

[*The Contention of Ajax and Ulysses* 1659]

Socrates, c.469–399BC, Greek philosopher

If I had engaged in politics, O men of Athens, I should have perished long ago, and done no good either to you or myself.

[In Plato's *Apology of Socrates* 399BC]

Alexander Solzhenitsyn, 1918– , Russian novelist

The Western world has lost its civil courage, both as a whole and separately, in each country, each government, each political party, and of course in the United Nations.

[*The Exhausted West* 1978]

I have spent all my life under a Communist regime, and I will tell you that a society without any objective legal scale is a terrible one indeed. But a society with no other scale but the legal one is not quite worthy of man either.

[*Ibid*]

Herbert Spencer, 1820–1903, English philosopher

The Republican form of government is the highest form of government; but because of this it requires the highest type of human nature – a type nowhere at present existing.

[*Essays: The Americans* 1891]

Benedict (or Baruch) Spinoza, 1632–77, Dutch philosopher

To give aid to every poor man is far beyond the reach and power of every man . . . Care for the poor is incumbent on society as a whole.

[*Ethics* 1677]

Robert Louis [Balfour] Stevenson, 1850–94, Scottish novelist and poet

These are my politics: to change what we can; to better what we can; but still to bear in mind that man is but a devil weakly fettered by some generous beliefs and impositions; and for no word however sounding, and no cause however just and pious, to relax the stricture of these bonds.

[*The Dynamiter: Epilogue of the Cigar Divan*]

Politics is perhaps the only profession for which no preparation is thought necessary.

[*Familiar Studies of Men and Books: Yoshida-Torajiro* 1882]

Joseph Story, 1779–1845, American judge

A new race of men is springing up to govern the nation; they are the hunters after popularity, men ambitious, not of the honour so much as of the profits of office – the demagogues, whose principles hang laxly upon them, and who follow not so much what is right as what leads to a temporary vulgar applause.

[*Commentaries on the Constitution of the United States* 1833]

Jonathan Swift, 1667–1745, Irish-born English writer

Politics, as the word is understood, are nothing but corruptions.

[*Thoughts on Various Subjects* 1706]

And he gave it for his opinion, that whoever could make two ears of corn or two blades of grass to grow upon a spot of ground where only one grew before, would deserve better of mankind, and do more essential service to his country than the whole race of politicians put together.

[*Gulliver's Travels: Voyage to Brobdingnag* 1726]

Norman Tebbit, 1931– , British politician

My father. . . didn't riot. He got on his bike and looked for work and he kept looking till he found it.

[Speech, Conservative Party conference 1981]

Alfred, Lord Tennyson, 1809–92, English poet

A land of settled government,
A land of just and old renown,
Where freedom slowly broadens down
From precedent to precedent.

[*You Ask Me Why*]

Authority forgets a dying king.

[*Idylls of the King: The Passing of Arthur* 1859–85]

Tertullian, c.160–c.230, Roman Christian theologian

Nothing is more foreign to us Christians than politics.

[*The Christian's Defence c.*215]

Margaret Hilda Thatcher, Baroness Thatcher of Kesteven, 1925– , British politician

No woman in my time will be Prime Minister or Chancellor or Foreign Secretary – not the top jobs. Anyway, I wouldn't want to be Prime Minister, you have to give yourself 100 per cent.

[In *The Sunday Telegraph* 1969]

In politics if you want anything said, ask a man. If you want anything done, ask a woman.

[In *People* September 15 1975]

You turn if you want to. The lady's not for turning.

[Speech 1980]

James Grover Thurber, 1894–1961, American humorist
You can fool too many of the people too much of the time.

[*The Thurber Carnival* 1945]

If you can't stand the heat, get out of the kitchen.

[*Mr Citizen* 1960]

Harry S. Truman, 1884–1972, 33rd president of the United States
I never gave them hell. I just tell the truth and they think it's hell.

[1956]

Barbara W[ertheim] Tuchman, 1912–89, American historian
No more distressing moment can ever face a British government than that which requires it to come to a hard and fast and specific decision.

[*The Guns of August* 1962]

Mark Twain [Samuel Langhorne Clemens], 1835–1910, American writer
The radical invents the views. When he has worn them out the conservative adopts them.

[*Notebook*]

William Henry Vanderbilt, 1821–85, American financier
When I want to buy up any politicians I always find the anti-monopolists the most purchasable. They don't come so high.

[In the *Chicago Daily News* 1882]

Willard Duncan Vandiver, 1854–1932, American politician
I come from a state that raises corn and cotton and cockleburs and Democrats, and frothy eloquence neither convinces me nor satisfies me. I am from Missouri. You have got to show me.

[Speech 1899]

Voltaire [François Marie Arouet], 1694–1778, French philosopher and writer
Democracy seems suitable only to a very little country.

[*Philosophical Dictionary* 1764]

The pleasure of governing must certainly be exquisite if we may judge from the vast numbers who are eager to be concerned with it.

[*Ibid*]

In general, the art of government consists in taking as much money as possible from one class of citizens to give to the other.

[*Ibid*]

Horace Walpole, 4th Earl of Orford, 1717–97, English writer
I do not admire politicians; but when they are excellent in their way, one cannot help allowing them their due.

[Letter 1763]

Artemus Ward [Charles Farrar Browne], 1834–67, American humorist

My pollertics, like my religion, bein of a exceedin accommodatin character.

[*Artemus Ward, His book* 1862]

I'm not a politician and my other habits air good.

[*Ibid: Fourth of July Oration*]

Daniel Webster, 1782–1852, American statesman

The people's government made for the people, made by the people, and answerable to the people.

[Speech in the Senate 1830]

John Webster, c.1580–c.1632, English dramatist

A politician imitates the Devil, as the Devil imitates a cannon: wheresoever he comes to do mischief, he comes with his backside towards you.

[*The White Devil* 1612]

H[erbert] G[eorge] Wells, 1866–1946, English writer

The world may discover that all its common interests are being managed by one concern, while it still fails to realize that a world government exists.

[*A Short History of the World* 1922]

Sir [James] Harold Wilson, Baron of Rievaulx, 1915–1995, English Labour politician and prime minister

A week is a long time in politics

[Remark 1964]

Tom [Thomas Kennerly] Wolfe, 1931– , American journalist and novelist

It is very comforting to believe that leaders who do terrible things are, in fact, mad. That way, all we have to do is make sure we don't put psychotics in high places and we've got the problem solved.

[*In Our Time*, 1980]

William Wordsworth, 1770–1850, English poet

The gold old rule
Sufficeth them, the simple plan,
That they should take, who have the power,
And they should keep who can.

[*Rob Roy's Grave*]

William Butler Yeats, 1865–1939, Irish poet

A statesman is an easy man,
He tells his lies by rote.

[*The Old Stone Cross* 1938]

So stay at home and drink your beer
And let the neighbours vote,
Said the man in the golden breastplate
Under the old stone cross.

[*Ibid*]

Happiness

Aeschylus, 525–456BC, Greek poet
Who, save the gods, can be happy all life long?

[*Agamemnon c.*490BC]

Anonymous
Content lodges oftener in cottages than in palaces.

[Proverb]

Happiness does not notice the passing of time.

[Proverb]

Jean Anouilh, 1910–87, French dramatist
There will always be a lost dog somewhere that will prevent me from being happy.

[*La Sauvage* 1947]

Aristotle, 384–322BC, Greek philosopher
Happiness may be defined as good fortune joined to virtue, or as independence, or as a life that is both agreeable and secure, or as plenty of property and slaves, with the capacity to get more.

[*Rhetoric c.*322BC]

St Augustine of Hippo, 354–430, Christian philosopher
Here we are called happy when we have peace, such little peace as can be had in a good life; but that happiness, in comparison with our final happiness, is altogether misery.

[*The City of God* 427]

Jane Austen, 1775–1817, English novelist
Perfect happiness, even in memory, is not common.

[*Emma* 1816]

Why not seize the pleasure at once? How often is happiness destroyed by preparation, foolish preparation!

[*Ibid*]

Honoré de Balzac, 1799–1850, French novelist
So long as there are differences between one moment of pleasure and another a man can go on being happy with the same woman.

[*The Physiology of Marriage* 1830]

Jeremy Bentham, 1748–1832, English philosopher
The sad truth is that it is the greatest happiness of the greatest number that is the measure of right and wrong.

[Fragment of Government 1776]

José Bergamin, 1895–1983, Spanish writer
Happiness is always a coincidence.

[The Rocket and the Stars 1923]

Paul [Tristan] Bernard, 1866–1947, French writer
To live happily with other people one should ask of them only what they can give.

[L'Enfant Prodigue du Vesinet 1921]

The Bible
Where there is no vision, the people perish: but he that keepeth the law, happy is he.

[Proverbs 29:18]

Wherefore are all they happy that deal very treacherously?

[Jeremiah 12:1]

Wilfred Scawen Blunt, 1840–1922, English poet
He who has once been happy is for aye
Out of destruction's reach.

[Esther]

Ancius Manlius Severinus Boethius, c.475–524, Roman statesman and philosopher
At every blow of fate, the cruellest kind of misfortune is to have been happy.

[De Consolatione Philosophiae]

Nothing is miserable unless you think it so; conversely, every lot is happy if you are content with it.

[Ibid]

Sir Thomas Browne, 1605–82, English physician
To enjoy true happiness we must travel into a very far country, and even out of ourselves.

[Christian Morals c.1680]

Robert Browning, 1812–89, English poet
Make us happy and you make us good.

[The Ring and the Book 1869]

Byron, Lord George Gordon [Noel], 6th Baron Byron of Rochdale, 1788–1824, English poet
There comes
For ever something between us and what
We deem our happiness.

[Sardanapalus 1821]

Happiness was born a twin.

[Don Juan 1819–24]

Then the few whose spirits float above the wreck of happiness
Are driven o'er the shoals of guilt or ocean of excess:
The magnet of their course is gone, or only points in vain
The shore to which their shiver'd sail shall never stretch again.

[Stanzas for Music]

248

Lewis Carroll [Charles Lutwidge Dodgson], 1832–92, English mathematician and writer
[The Cheshire Cat] This time it vanished quite slowly, beginning with the end of the gail, and ending which the grin, which remained some time after the rest of it had gone.

[*Alice's Adventures in Wonderland* 1865]

Miguel de Cervantes [Saavedra], 1547–1616, Spanish dramatist and poet
I would do what I pleased; and doing what I pleased, I should have my will; and having my will, I should be contented; and when one is contented, there is no more to be desired; and when there is no more to be desired, there is an end of it.

[*Don Quixote* 1615]

G[ilbert] K[eith] Chesterton, 1874–1936, English writer
Happiness is a mystery like religion, and should never be rationalised.

[*Heretics*]

Charles Caleb Colton, c.1780–1832, English writer
Happiness is much more equally divided than some of us imagine.

[*Lacon* 1820]

He that thinks himself the happiest man, really is so.

[*Ibid*]

Pierre Corneille, 1606–84, French dramatist
We never enjoy perfect happiness; our most fortunate successes are mingled with sadness; some anxieties always perplex the reality of our satisfaction.

[*The Cid* 1636]

Dante [Alighieri], 1265–1321, Italian poet
Nessun maggior dolore,
Che ricordarsi del tempo felice
Nella miseria.
No greater sorrow than to recall in our misery the time when we were happy.

[*The Divine Comedy: Inferno*]

Charles [John Huffam] Dickens, 1812–70, English novelist
In came Mrs Fezziwig, one vast substantial smile.

[*A Christmas Carol* 1843]

John Dryden, 1631–1700, English dramatist
Happy the man, and happy he alone,
He, who can call today his own:
He who, secure within, can say,
Tomorrow do thy worst, for I have lived today.

[*Imitation of Horace* 1865]

George Eliot [Mary Ann Evans], 1819–80, English novelist
The happiest women, like the happiest nations, have no history.

[*The Mill on the Floss* 1860]

Ralph Waldo Emerson, 1803–82, American writer
To fill the hour – that is happiness.

[*Essays, First Series: Experience* 1841]

Gustave Flaubert, 1821–80, French novelist
The only way to be happy is to shut yourself up in art, and count everything else as nothing.

[Letter 1845]

Bernard le Bovier de Fontenelle, 1657–1757, French writer
To be happy one must have a good stomach and a bad heart.

[*Dialogues des morts* 1683]

Anne Frank, 1929–45, German-Jewish diarist
Whoever is happy will make others happy too. He who has courage and faith will never perish in misery!

[*The Diary of a Young Girl* 1952]

Benjamin Franklin, 1706–90, American scientist and philosopher
Be in general virtuous, and you will be happy.

[On Early Marriages]

Human felicity is produced not so much by great pieces of good furtune that seldom happen, as by little advantages that occur every day.

[*Autobiography* 1798]

Théophile Gautier, 1811–72, French writer
Happiness is white and pink.

[*Caprices et zigzags* 1845]

John Gay, 1685–1732, English poet and playwright
How happy could I be with either,
Were t'other dear charmer away!

[*The Beggar's Opera* 1728]

Happy as a king.

[*A New Song of New Similes*]

Thomas Gray, 1716–71, English poet
Yet ah! why should they know their fate?
Since sorrow never comes too late,
And happiness too swiftly flies.

[*Ode on a Distant Prospect of Eton College* 1747]

Nathaniel Hawthorne, 1804–64, American novelist
Happiness in this world, when it comes, comes incidentally. Make it the object of pursuit, and it leads us a wild-goose chase, and is never attained. Follow some other object, and very possibly we may find that we have caught happiness without dreaming of it.

[*American Notebooks* November 1852]

William Hazlitt, 1778–1830, English essayist
So have I loitered my life away, reading books, looking at pictures, going to plays, hearing, thinking, writing on what pleased me best. I have wanted only one thing to keep me happy, but wanting that have wanted everything.

[*Winterslow: My First Acquaintance with Poets*]

HAPPINESS

James Hogg ("The Ettrick Shepherd"), 1770–1835, Scottish poet and novelist
Bird of the wilderness,
Blithesome and cumberless,
Sweet be thy matin o'er moorland and lea!
Emblem of happiness,
Blest is thy dwelling place –
O to abide in the desert with thee!

[*The Skylark*]

Thomas Hood, 1799–1845, English poet
There is ev'n a happiness
That makes the heart afraid.

[*To Melancholy c.*1830]

Horace [Quintus Horatius Flaccus], 65BC–8BC, Roman poet
If thou art sound in stomach, side, and feet, the riches of a king will add nothing to thy happiness.

[*Epistles c.*19BC]

Frank McKinney ("Kin") Hubbard, 1868–1930, American humorist
It's pretty hard to tell what does bring happiness; poverty and wealth have both failed.

[*Abe Martin's Broadcast*]

Francis Hutcheson, 1694–1746, Scottish philosopher
That action is best, which procures the greatest happiness for the greatest numbers.

[*Inquiry into the Original of our Ideas of Beauty and Virtue* 1720]

Aldous [Leonard] Huxley, 1894–1963, English writer
Happiness is like coke – something you get as a by-product in the process of making something else.

[*Point Counter Point* 1928]

Happiness is a hard master – particularly other people's happiness.

[*Brave New World* 1932]

Henrik Ibsen, 1828–1906, Norwegian dramatist
What right have we to happiness.

[*Ghosts* 1881]

Take the life-lie away from the average man and straight away you take away his happiness.

[*The Wild Duck* 1884]

William James, 1842–1910, American philosopher
Happiness, like every other emotional state, has blindness and insensibility to opposing facts given it as its instinctive weapon for self-protection against disturbance.

[*The Varieties of Religious Experience* 1902]

Richard Jefferies, 1848–87, English naturalist and writer
If only we could persuade ourselves to be quiescent when we are happy.

[*The Open Air* 1885]

Thomas Jefferson, 1743–1826, 3rd president of the United States
We hold these truths to be self-evident – that all men are created equal; that they are endowed by their Creator with certain unalienable rights; that among these are life, liberty, and the pursuit of happiness.

[*The Declaration of Independence* 1776]

He is happiest of whom the world says least, good or bad.

[Letter to John Adams 1786]

It is neither wealth nor splendour, but tranquility and occupation, which give happiness.

[Letter 1788]

Dr Samuel Johnson, 1709–84, English lexicographer
There is nothing which has yet been contrived by man, by which so much happiness is produced as by a good tavern or inn.

[1776. In Boswell's *Life of Samuel Johnson* 1791]

Immanuel Kant, 1724–1804, German philosopher
Happiness is not an ideal of reason but of imagination.

[*Fundamental Principles of the Metaphysics of Ethics* 1785]

John Keats, 1795–1821, English poet
Wherein lies happiness? In that which becks
Our ready minds to fellowship divine,
A fellowship with essence.

[*Endymion* 1818]

Rudyard Kipling, 1865–1936, English writer
And those that were good shall be happy: they shall sit in a golden chair;
They shall splash at a ten-league canvas with brushes of comet's hair.

[*When Earth's Last Picture is Painted*]

Georg Christoph Lichtenberg, 1742–99, German scientist and writer
A long happiness loses by its mere length.

[*Reflections* 1799]

Karl Marx, 1818–83, German philosopher
The first requisite for the happiness of the people is the abolition of religion.

[*A Criticism of the Hegelian Philosophy of Right* 1844]

H[enry] L[ouis] Mencken, 1880–1956, American critic and writer
The only really happy people are married women and single men.

[Attributed]

John Stuart Mill, 1806–73, English philosopher
Unquestionably, it is possible to do without happiness; it is done involuntarily by nineteen-twentieths of mankind.

[*Utilitarianism* 1863]

Ask yourself whether you are happy, and you cease to be so.

[*Autobiography* 1873]

John Milton, 1608–74, English poet
And feel that I am happier than I know.

[*Paradise Lost* 1668]

Molière [Jean-Baptiste Poquelin], 1622–73, French playwright
Unbroken happiness is a bore: it should have ups and downs.

[*Les fourberies de Scapin* 1671]

Lady Mary Wortley Montagu, 1689–1762, English writer
One would suffer a great deal to be happy.

[Letter 1759]

Dame Iris Murdoch, 1919–99, English novelist and philosopher
Happiness is a matter of one's most ordinary everyday mode of consciousness being busy and lively and unconcerned with self. To be damned is for one's ordinary everyday mode of consciousness to be unremitting agonising preoccupation with self.

[*The Nice and the Good* 1968]

Napoleon I [Napoleon Bonaparte], 1769–1821, emperor of France
All men have the same share of happiness.

[To Gaspard Gourgand at St Helena, 1817]

Friedrich Wilhelm Nietzsche, 1844–1900, German philosopher and poet
What trifles make for happiness! The sound of a bagpipe!

[*The Twilight of the Idols* 1889]

Edgar Allan Poe, 1809–49, American writer
Man's real life is happy, chiefly because he is ever expecting that it soon will be so.

[*Marginalia* 1844–9]

Alexander Pope, 1688–1744, English poet
O happiness! our being's end and aim!
Good, pleasure, ease, content! whate'er thy name:
That something still which prompts th' eternal sigh,
For which we bear to live, or dare to die.

[*Essay on Man* 1732–4]

Publilius Syrus, *fl.* 1st century BC, Roman writer
No man is happy unless he believes he is.

[*Sententiae c.*50BC]

Francis Quarles, 1592–1644, English poet
The way to bliss lies not on beds of down,
And he that has no cross deserves no crown.

[*Esther* 1621]

Jean Paul Richter, 1763–1825, German novelist
In the child happiness dances; in the man, at most, it only smiles or weeps.

[*Levana* 1807]

François, Duc de La Rochefoucauld, 1613–80, French writer
We are more interested in making others believe we are happy than in trying to be happy ourselves.

[*Reflections, or Sentences and Moral Maxims* 1665]

The happiness or unhappiness of men depends no less upon their dispositions than on their fortunes.

[*Ibid*]

We are never so happy, nor so unhappy, as we think we are.

[*Ibid*]

It is a kind of happiness to know to what extent we may be unhappy.

[*Ibid*]

Bertrand [Arthur William] Russell, 3rd Earl Russell, 1872–1970, English philosopher

The secret of happiness is this: let your interests be as wide as possible, and let your reactions to the things and persons that interest you be as far as possible friendly rather than hostile.

[*The Conquest of Happiness* 1930]

George Santayana, 1863–1952, Spanish-American philosopher

Happiness is the only sanction of life; where happiness fails, existence remains a mad and lamentable experiment.

[*The Life of Reason* 1905]

Charles Monroe Schulz, 1922–2000, American cartoonist

Happiness Is a Warm Puppy.

[Book title 1962]

Thomas Shadwell, c.1642–1692, English dramatist

No man is happy but by comparison.

[*The Virtuoso* 1676]

William Shakespeare 1564–1616, English dramatist

O, how bitter a thing it is to look into happiness through another man's eyes.

[*As You Like It* 5 1598–1600]

George Bernard Shaw, 1856–1950, Irish playwright

We have no more right to consume happiness without producing it than to consume wealth without producing it.

[*Candida* 1898]

A lifetime of happiness! No man alive could bear it: it would be hell on earth.

[*Man and Superman* 1903]

Richard Brinsley Sheridan, 1751–1816, English dramatist

'Tis now six months since Lady Teazle made me the happiest of men – and I've been the most miserable dog ever since.

[*The School for Scandal* 1777]

Sydney Smith, 1771–1845, English churchman

This great spectacle of human happiness.

[*Essays: Waterton's Wanderings* 1877]

Tobias [George] Smollett, 1721–71, Scottish novelist and surgeon

If there be such a thing as true happiness on earth, I enjoy it.

[*Roderick Random*]

Alexander Solzhenitsyn, 1918– , Russian novelist

A man is happy so long as he chooses to be happy and nothing can stop him.

[*Cancer Ward* 1968]

Herbert Spencer, 1820–1903, English philosopher

No one can be perfectly free till all are free; no one can be perfectly moral till all are moral; no one can be perfectly happy till all are happy.

[*Social Statics* 1851]

Robert Louis [Balfour] Stevenson, 1850–94, Scottish novelist and poet

There is no duty we so much underrate as the duty of being happy.

[*Virginibus Puerisque* 1881]

The world is so full of a number of things,
I'm sure we should all be as happy as kings.

[*A Child's Garden of Verses* 1885]

If I have faltered more or less
In my great task of happiness;
If I have moved among my race
And shown no glorious morning face;
If beams from happy human eyes
Have moved me not; if morning skies,
Books, and my food, and summer rain
Knocked on my sullen heart in vain: –
Lord, thy most pointed pleasure take
And stab my spirit broad awake.

[*Underwoods: The Celestial Surgeon* 1887]

Thomas Stephen Szasz, 1920– , American psychiatrist

Happiness is an imaginary condition, formerly often attributed by the living to the dead, now usually attributed by adults to children, and by children to adults.

[*The Second Sin: Emotions* 1973]

Alfred, Lord Tennyson, 1809–92, English poet

This is truth the poet sings,
That a sorrow's crown of sorrow is remembering happier things.

[*Locksley Hall* 1842]

Evelyn [Arthur St John] Waugh, 1903–66, English writer

I can't quite explain it, but I don't believe one can ever be unhappy for long provided one does just exactly what one wants to and when one wants to.

[*Decline and Fall* 1928]

Richard Whateley, 1787–1863, English archbishop of Dublin

Happiness is no laughing matter.

[*Apophthegms*]

Walt[er] Whitman, 1819–92, American poet

The sun and stars that float in the open air;
The apple-shaped earth, and we upon it –
surely the drift of them is something grand!
I do not know what it is, except that it is grand,
and that it is happiness.

[*Carol of Occupations* 1855]

Oscar [Fingall O'Flahertie Wills] Wilde, 1854–1900, Irish writer

Pleasure is the only thing to live for. Nothing ages like happiness.

[*An Ideal Husband* 1895]

Mary Wollstonecraft, 1759–97, English writer
True happiness must arise from well-regulated affections, and an affection includes a duty.

[*A Vindication of the Rights of Women* 1792]

William Wordsworth, 1770–1850, English poet
Happy is he, who caring not for Pope,
Consul, or King, can sound himself to know
The destiny of Man, and live in hope.

[*Sonnets Dedicated to Liberty*]

Not in Utopia–subterranean fields,–
Or some secreted island, Heaven knows where!
But in the very world, which is the world
Of all of us,–the place where, in the end
We find our happiness, or not at all!

[*The Prelude*]

Sir Henry Wotton, 1568–1639, English diplomat and poet
How happy is he born and taught
That serveth not another's will;
Whose armour is his honest thought,
And simple truth his utmost skill!

[*The Character of a Happy Life*]

William Butler Yeats, 1865–1939, Irish poet
While on the shop and street I gazed
My body of a sudden blazed;
And twenty minutes more or less
It seemed, so great my happiness,
That I was blessèd and could bless

[*Vacillation* 1932]

Yevgeni Aleksandrovich Yevtushenko, 1933– , Russian poet
Who never knew the price of happiness will not be happy.

[*Babi Yar* 1962]

Health and Medicine

Joseph Addison, 1672–1719, English essayist
Health and cheerfulness mutually beget each other.

[*The Spectator* 1712]

Aeschylus, 525–456BC, Greek poet
There is a limit to the best of health: disease is always a near neighbour.

[*Agamemnon c.*490BC]

Alexander the Great, 356–323BC, king of Macedonia
I die by the help of too many physicians.

[Said on his deathbed]

Henri Frédéric Amiel, 1821–81, Swiss writer
In health there is freedom. Health is the first of all liberties.

[*Journal* 1866]

Anonymous
Health is not valued till sickness comes.

[Proverb]

God heals, and the doctor takes the fee.

[Proverb]

Francis Bacon, Baron Verulam of Verulam and Viscount of St Albans, 1561–1626, English philosopher
The remedy is worse than the disease.

[*Essays: Of Seditions and Troubles*]

St Benedict, c.480–c.547, Italian monk
Before all, and above all, attention shall be paid to the care of the sick, so that they shall be served as if they were Christ Himself.

[*The Rule of St Benedict c.*529]

The Bible
A merry heart doeth good like a medicine: but a broken spirit drieth the bones.

[*Proverbs* 17:22]

Dead flies cause the ointment of the apothecary to send forth a stinking savour.

[*Ecclesiastes* 10:1]

Be not slow to visit the sick.

[*Ecclesiasticus* 7:35]

Health and good estate of body are above all gold.

[*Ibid* 30:15]

Honour a physician with the honour due unto him for the uses which ye may have of him: for the Lord hath created him.

[*Ibid* 38:1]

The Most High hath created medicines out of the earth, and a wise man will not abhor them.

[*Ibid* 38:4]

He that sinneth before his Maker, let him fall into the hand of the physician.

[*Ibid* 38:15]

Jean de La Bruyère, 1645–96, French moralist
A long illness between life and death makes death a comfort both to those who die and to those who remain.

[*Caractères* 1688]

James Bryce, Viscount Bruce, 1838–1922, British historian
Medicine is the only profession that labours incessantly to destroy the reason for its own existence.

[Said in New York 1914]

Art Buchwald, 1925– , American journalist
"Dr Peters said it was one of the best operations he had ever seen."
"So it was, except that you cut off the wrong leg."

[*I Never Danced in the White House* 1973]

[John] Anthony Burgess [Wilson], 1917– 93, English-born novelist and critic
Doctors leave it to Nature to cure in her own time, but they take the credit.

[*Nothing Like the Sun*]

William [Seward] Burroughs, 1914–97, American novelist
A paranoid is a man who knows a little of what is going on.

[*Friends* 1970]

Thomas Carlyle, 1795–1881, Scottish historian and writer
I am always sick; I am sicker and worse in body and mind, a little, for the present; but it has no deep significance.

[Letter to Emerson 1836]

Jean Martin Charcot, 1825–93, French pathologist
The condition of the patient is only an accident in the history of the disease.

[*De l'expectation en médecine* 1857]

Anton [Pavlovoch] Chekhov, 1860–1904, Russian author and playwright
When a lot of remedies are suggested for a disease, that means it can't be cured.

[*The Cherry Orchard* 1 1904]

Marcus Tullius Cicero, 106–43BC, Roman statesman
Because all the sick do not recover, therefore medicine is no art.

[*De Natura Deorum* 45BC]

Arthur Hugh Clough, 1819–61, English poet
Thou shall not kill; but need'st not strive
Officiously to keep alive.

[*The Latest Decalogue* 1862]

Mary Baker Glover Eddy, 1821–1910, American founder of Christian Science
Health is not a condition of matter, but of mind.

[*Science and Health* 1908]

Ralph Waldo Emerson, 1803–82, American writer
A person seldom falls sick, but the bystanders are animated with a faint hope that he will die.

[*The Conduct of Life: Considerations By the Way* 1860]

George Formby 1904–61, English entertainer
Auntie Maggie's Remedy
It's guaranteed never to fail
Now that's the stuff that will do the trick
It's sold at every chemist for one and a kick.

[Song: *Auntie Maggie's Remedy*]

Benjamin Franklin, 1706–90, American scientist and philosopher
He's the best physician that knows the worthlessness of the most medicines.

[*Poor Richard's Almanack* 1733]

Be not sick too late, nor well too soon.

[*Ibid* 1734]

Oliver Goldsmith, 1728–74, Irish-born English writer
Sweet Auburn, loveliest village of the plain,
Where health and plenty cheered the labouring swain.
Where smiling spring its earliest visit paid,
And parting summer's lingering blooms delayed.

[*The Deserted Village* 1770]

And in that town a dog was found,
As many dogs there be,
Both mongrel, puppy, whelp, and hound,
And curs of low degree.

[*Elegy on the Death of a Mad Dog* 1776]

The dog, to gain some private ends,
Went mad and bit the man.

[*Ibid*]

The man recover'd of the bite,
The dog it was that died.

[*Ibid*]

Samuel Goldwyn, 1882–1974, Polish-born American film producer
Anybody who goes to see a psychiatrist ought to have his head examined.

[Attributed]

Joseph Heller, 1923–1999, American novelist
Hungry Joe collected lists of fatal diseases and arranged them in alphabetical order so that he could put his finger without delay on any one he wanted to worry about.

[*Catch-22* 1961]

Herophilus, *fl.* 4th century BC, Greek anatomist
To lose one's health renders science null, art inglorious, strength unavailing, wealth useless, and eloquence powerless.

[*Fragment c.*300BC]

Hippocrates, *c.*460–*c.*377BC, Greek physician
Healing is a matter of time, but it is sometimes also a matter of opportunity.

[*Precepts*]

Natural forces within us are the true healers of disease.

[*Aphorisms c.*400BC]

The art of medicine consists in three things: the disease, the patient, and the physician. The patient must combat the disease along with the physician.

[*Ibid*]

Wherever the art of medicine is loved, there also is love of humanity.

[*Ibid*]

Oliver Wendell Holmes, 1809–94, American physician and writer
Insanity is often the logic of an accurate mind overtaxed.

[*The Autocrat of the Breakfast Table* 1858]

I firmly believe that if the whole *materia medica*, as now used, could be sunk to the bottom of the sea, it would be all the better for mankind – and all the worse for the fishes.

[Address to the Massachusetts Medical Society 1860]

Thomas Henry Huxley, 1825–95, English biologist
The only medicine for suffering, crime, and all the other woes of mankind, is wisdom.

[*Science and Education* 1868]

There is the greatest practical benefit in making a few failures early in life.

[*On Medical Education* 1870]

Eugene Ionesco, 1912–94, Romanian-born French playwright
All doctors are charlatans. And all their patients too.

[*The Bald Prima Donna* 1956]

Thomas Jefferson, 1743–1826, 3rd president of the United States
Health is worth more than learning.

[Letter 1790]

Dr Samuel Johnson, 1709–84, English lexicographer
Disease generally begins that equality which death completes.

[*The Rambler* 1750]

How few of his friends' houses would a man choose to be at when sick.

[1783. In Boswell's *Life of Samuel Johnson* 1791]

R[onald] D[avid] Laing, 1927–89, Scottish psychiatrist
Schizophrenia cannot be understood without understanding despair.

[*The Divided Self*]

Charles Lamb, 1775–1834, English essayist
What have I gained by health? Intolerable dullness. What by early hours and moderate meals? A total blank.

[Letter to Wordsworth 1830]

Baron Gottfried Wilhelm von Leibnitz, 1646–1716, German philosopher
I often say a great doctor kills more people than a great general.

[Attributed]

Henry Wadsworth Longfellow, 1807–82, American poet
Forth then issued Hiawatha,
Wandered eastward, wandered westward,
Teaching men the use of simples
And the antidotes for poisons,
And the cure of all diseases.

[*The Song of Hiawatha* 1855]

Martin Luther, 1483–1546, German religious reformer
'Tis wonderful how God has put such excellent physic in mere muck; we know by experience
that swine's dung stints the blood; horse's serves for the pleurisy; man's heals wounds and
black blotches; asses' is used for the bloody flux, and cow's with preserved roses serves for
epilepsy, or for convulsions of children.

[*Table-Talk* 1569]

William James Mayo, 1861–1939, American physician
The aim of medicine is to prevent disease and prolong life, the ideal of medicine is to
eliminate the need of a physician.

[*National Education Association: Proceedings and Addresses* 1928]

A[lan] A[lexander] Milne, 1882–1956, English writer
Christopher Robin
Had wheezles
And sneezles,
They bundled him
Into
His bed.

[*Now We are Six* 1927]

Molière [Jean-Baptiste Poquelin], 1622–73, French playwright
Nearly all men die of their medicines, not of their diseases.

[*Le malade imaginaire* 1673]

Henri de Mondeville, 1260–1320, French physician
Keep up the spirits of your patient with the music of the viol and the psaltery, or by forging
letters telling of the death of his enemies, or (if he be a cleric) by informing him that he has
been made a bishop.

[*Treatise on Surgery* 1316]

Christopher [Darlington] Morley, 1890–1957, American writer
A human being: an ingenious assembly of portable plumbing.

[*Human Being* 1932]

Napoleon I [Napoleon Bonaparte], 1769–1821, emperor of France
Medicines are fit only for old people.

[To Barry E. O'Meara at St Helena 1816]

You medical people will have more lives to answer for in the other world than even we
generals.

[*Ibid* 1817]

Sir William Osler, 1849–1919, Canadian physician
The desire to take medicine is perhaps the greatest feature which distinguishes men from animals.

[*Science and Immortality* 1904]

Ovid [Publius Ovidius Naso], 43BC–AD18, Roman poet
Time is the best medicine.

[*Remedia amoris c.*10]

Laurence Johnston Peter, 1919–90, Canadian-born American educator
Psychiatry enables us to correct our faults by confessing our parents' shortcomings.

[*The Peter Principle* 1977]

Plato, c.428–348BC, Greek philosopher
Medicine may be regarded generally as the knowledge of the loves and desires of the body, and how to satisfy them or not.

[*Symposium c.*360BC]

Matthew Prior, 1664–1721, English diplomat and poet
Cured yesterday of my disease,
I died last night of my physician.

[*The Remedy Worse than the Disease* 1714]

You tell your doctor that y' are ill,
And what does he do but write a bill?

[*Alma* 1718]

Publilius Syrus, *fl.* 1st century BC, Roman writer
That sick man does badly who makes his physician his heir.

[*Sententiae c.*50BC]

A bad patient makes a cruel physician.

[*Ibid*]

Francis Quarles, 1592–1644, English poet
Physicians of all men are most happy; What success soever they have, the world proclaimeth, and what fault they commit, the earth covereth.

[*Hieroglyphics on the Life of Man* 1646]

François Rabelais, c.1494–c.1553, French physician and satirist
Without health life is not life; it is not living life. Without health life is only a state of langour and an image of death.

[*Pantagruel* 1533]

François, Duc de La Rochefoucauld, 1613–80, French writer
It is a boresome disease to try to keep health by following too strict a regimen.

[*Reflections, or Sentences and Moral Maxims* 1665]

Seneca, c.4BC–AD65, Roman philosopher
It is part of the cure to wish to be cured.

[*Phaedra c.*60]

William Shakespeare, 1564–1616, English dramatist
With the help of a surgeon, he might yet recover, and prove an ass.

[*A Midsummer Night's Dream* 5 1595–6]

262

For there was never yet philosopher
That could endure the toothache patiently.

[*Much Ado About Nothing* 5 1598–1600]

William Shenstone, 1714–63, English gardener and poet
Health is beauty, and the most perfect health is the most perfect beauty.

[*Of Men and Manners* 1764]

Robert Louis [Balfour] Stevenson, 1850–94, Scottish novelist and poet
You doctors have a serious responsibility. You call a man from the gates of death, you give
health and strength once more to use or abuse. But for your kindness and skill, this would
have been my last book, and now I am in hopes that it will be neither my last nor my best.

[Inscribed in a copy of *Travels with a Donkey* given to his physician 1879]

The Talmud, c.200
A physician who demands no fee is worth none.

[*Baba Kamma*]

James Thomson, 1700–1748, Scottish poet
Health is the vital principle of bliss.

[*The Castle of Indolence* 1748]

Henry David Thoreau, 1817–62, American naturalist and writer
Measure your health by your sympathy with morning and Spring.

[*Journal* 25 February 1859]

Paul Valéry, 1871–1945, French poet
The purpose of psychology is to give us a completely different idea of the things we know
best.

[*Tel Quel* 1943]

Leonardo da Vinci, 1452–1519, Italian artist
Strive to preserve your health; and in this you will the better succeed in proportion as you
keep clear of the physicians, for their drugs are a kind of alchemy concerning which there are
no fewer books than there are medicines.

[*Notebooks c.*1500]

Oscar [Fingall O'Flahertie Wills] Wilde, 1854–1900, Irish writer
One knows so well the popular idea of health. The English country gentleman galloping after
a fox – the unspeakable in full pursuit of the uneatable.

[*A Woman of No Importance* 1893]

Human Nature

Joseph Addison, 1672–1719, English essayist
There is nothing which we receive with so much reluctance as advice.

[*The Spectator* 24 May 1711]

Anonymous
Monday's child is fair of face,
Tuesday's child is full of grace,
Wednesday's child is full of woe,
Thursday's child has far to go,
Friday's child is loving and giving,
Saturday's child works hard for a living,
And the child that is born on the Sabbath day
Is bonny, and blithe, and good and gay.

Aristotle, 384–322BC, Greek philosopher
The high-minded man does not bear grudges, for it is not the mark of a great soul to remember injuries, but to forget them.

[*The Nicomachean Ethics c.* 340BC]

At his best man is the noblest of all animals; separated from law and justice, he is the worst.

[*Politics c.* 322BC]

St Augustine of Hippo, 354–430, Christian philosopher
He that is good is free, though he be a slave; he that is evil is a slave, though he be a king.

[*The City of God* 427]

An earthly animal, but worthy of Heaven.

[*Ibid*]

Sir A[lfred] J[ules] Ayer, 1910–89, English philosopher
Why should you mind being wrong if someone can show you that you are?

[In *The Sunday Times* 1962]

P[hineas] T[aylor] Barnum, 1810–91, American showman
There's a sucker born every minute.

[Attributed]

Simone de Beauvoir, 1908–86, French writer
It is not in giving but in risking life that man is raised above the animal; that is why superiority has been accorded in humanity not to the sex that brings forth but to that which kills.

[*The Second Sex* 1949–50]

HUMAN NATURE

Carl Lotus Becker, 1873–1945, American historian
The significance of man is that he is that part of the universe that asks the question, What is the significance of Man? He alone can stand apart imaginatively and, regarding himself and the universe in their eternal aspects, pronounce a judgment: the significance of man is that he is insignificant and is aware of it.

[*Progress and Power* 1935]

Henry Ward Beecher, 1813–87, American preacher
The cynic is one who never sees a good quality in a man, and never fails to see a bad one. He is the human owl, vigilant in darkness, and blind to light, mousing for vermin, and never seeing noble game.

[*Proverbs from Plymouth Pulpit* 1870]

The Bible
So God created man in his own image, in the image of God created he him; male and female created he them.

[*Genesis* 1:27]

Ambrose [Gwinett] Bierce, 1842–1914, American writer
Absurdity: a statement of belief manifestly inconsistent with one's own opinion.

[*The Devil's Dictionary* 1906]

William Blake, 1757–1827, English poet and artist
No bird soars too high, if he soars with his own wings.

[*The Marriage of Heaven and Hell: Proverbs of Hell* 1791]

James H. Boren, 1925– , American bureaucrat
When in doubt, mumble; when in trouble, delegate; when in charge, ponder.

[In P. Dickson's *The Official Rules* 1972]

Omar Nelson Bradley, 1893–1981, American general
We have grasped the mystery of the atom and rejected the Sermon on the Mount.

[Armistice Day Address 1948]

Robert Browning, 1812–89, English poet
Love, hope, fear, faith – these make humanity;
These are its sign and note and character.

[*Paracelsus* 1835]

Georg Büchner [Karl Georg Büchner], 1813–37, German dramatist
Every man's a chasm. It makes you dizzy when you look down it.

[*Woyzeck*, 1879]

Art Buchwald, 1925– , American journalist
People are broad-minded. They'll accept the fact that a person can be an alcoholic, a dope fiend, a wife beater and even a newspaperman, but if a man doesn't drive, there's something wrong with him.

[*Have I Ever Lied to You?* 1968]

Edmund Burke, 1729–97, Irish-born English political writer
When bad men combine, the good must associate; else they will fall one by one, an unpitied sacrifice in a contemptible struggle.

[*Thoughts on the Cause of the Present Discontents* 1770]

The only thing necessary for the triumph of evil is for good men to do nothing.

[Attributed]

Samuel Butler, 1835–1902, English writer
The advantage of doing one's praising for oneself is that one can lay it on so thick and exactly in the right places.

[*The Way of All Flesh* 1903]

Albert Camus, 1913–60, Algerian-born French philosopher and novelist
Man is the only creature who refuses to be what he is.

[*The Rebel* 1951]

Miguel de Cervantes [Saavedra], 1547–1616, Spanish dramatist and poet
Every man is as Heaven made him, and sometimes a great deal worse.

[*Don Quixote* 1615]

Colley Cibber, 1671–1757, English playwright
As good be out of the world as out of the fashion.

[*Love's Last Shift* 1696]

Charles Caleb Colton, c. 1780–1832, English writer
Imitation is the sincerest of flattery.

[*Lacon* 1820–22]

He that is good will infallibly become better, and he that is bad will as certainly become worse; for vice, virtue and time are three things that never stand still.

[*Ibid*]

Confucius [K'ung fu-tzu], 551–479BC, Chinese philosopher
The nature of men is always the same; it is their habits that separate them.

[*Analects c.* 500BC]

Charles Robert Darwin, 1809–82, English naturalist
The main conclusion of this work, namely, that man is descended from some lowly organised form, will, I regret to think, be highly distasteful to many. But there can hardly be a doubt that we are descended from barbarians.

[*The Descent of Man* 1871]

René Descartes, 1596–1650, French philosopher
Good sense is of all things in the world the most equally distributed, for everybody thinks he is so well supplied with it, that even those most difficult to please in all other matters never desire more of it than they already possess.

[*Le Discours de la Méthode* 1637]

Destouches (Philippe Néricault), 1680–1754, French dramatist
Those not present are always wrong.

[*L'Obstacle Imprevu* 1717]

Charles [John Huffam] Dickens, 1812–70, English novelist
A wonderful fact to reflect upon, that every human creature is constituted to be that profound secret and mystery to every other.

[*A Tale of Two Cities* 1859]

Subdue your appetites, my dears, and you've conquered human nature.

[*Nicholas Nickleby* 1839]

J[ames] P[atrick] Donleavy, 1926– , Irish author
I got disappointed in human nature as well and gave it up because I found it too much like my own.

[*A Fairy Tale of New York*, 1960]

Margaret Drabble, 1939– , English novelist
Perhaps the rare and simple pleasure of being seen for what one is compensates for the misery of being it.

[*A Summer Bird Cage* 1963]

Georges Duhamel (Denis Thevenin), 1884–1966, French writer
Error is the rule. Truth is an accident of error.

[*Le notaire du Havre*]

Lawrence [George] Durrell, 1912–90, English novelist
We are the children of our landscape; it dictates behaviour and even thought in the measure to which we are responsive to it.

[*Justine* 1957]

Clifton Fadiman, 1904– , American writer
Experience teaches you that this man who looks you straight in the eye, particularly if he adds a firm handshake, is hiding something.

[*Enter, Conversing*]

William Faulkner, 1897–1962, American novelist
He is immortal, not because he alone among creatures has an inexhaustible voice, but because he has a soul, a spirit capable of compassion, sacrifice and endurance.

[Nobel Speech 1949]

W.C. Fields (William Claude Dunkinfield), 1879–1946, American actor
I am free of all prejudice. I hate everyone equally.

[Attributed]

E[dward] M[organ] Forster, 1879–1970, English novelist
I don't think I understand people very well. I only know whether I like or dislike them.

[*A Passage to India* 1924]

Anne Frank, 1929–1945, German-Jewish diarist
In spite of everything I still believe that people are really good at heart.

[*The Diary of a Young Girl* 1947]

Sigmund Freud, 1856–1939, Austrian psychiatrist
I have found little that is "good" about human beings on the whole. In my experience most of them are trash, no matter whether they publicly ascribe to this or that ethical doctrine or to none at all.

[Letter October 9 1918. In *The Letters of Sigmund Freud and Oscar Pfister* 1963]

Betty [Naomi] Friedan, 1921– , American feminist
It is easier to live through someone else than to become complete yourself.

[*The Feminine Mystique* 1963]

267

Edward Gibbon, 1737–94, English historian
History. . . is indeed little more than the register of the crimes, follies, and misfortunes of mankind.

[*Decline and Fall of the Roman Empire* 1776–88]

Oliver Goldsmith, 1728–74, Irish-born English writer
All his faults are such that one loves him still the better for them.

[*The Good-Natured Man* 1768]

Thomas Gray, 1716–71, English poet
Too poor for a bribe, and too proud to importune,
He had not the method of making a fortune.

[*On His Own Character* 1761]

[Henry] Graham Greene, 1904–91, English novelist
In human relations kindness and lies are worth a thousand truths.

[*The Heart of the Matter* 1948]

Dag Hammarskjöld, 1905–61, Swedish secretary general of the UN
Only he deserves power who every day justifies it.

[*Markings*]

Never look down to test the ground before taking your next step: only he who keeps his eye fixed on the far horizon will find his right road.

[*Ibid*]

Ernest [Miller] Hemingway, 1899–1961, American novelist
I know only that what is moral is what you feel good after and what is immoral is what you feel bad after.

[*Death in the Afternoon* 1932]

Homer, *fl* 9th century BC, Greek poet
Of all the creatures that creep and breathe on the earth there is none more wretched than man.

[*Iliad c.* 800BC]

Dr Samuel Johnson, 1709–84, English lexicographer
A man of genius has been seldom ruined but by himself.

[21 December 1762. In Boswell's *Life of Samuel Johnson* 1791]

Humanity is very uniform.

[*Taxation No Tyranny* 1775]

Carl Gustav Jung, 1875–1961, Swiss psychiatrist
A man who has not passed through the inferno of his passions has never overcome them.

[*Memories, Dreams, Reflections* 1962]

Rudyard Kipling, 1865–1936, English writer
Horrible, hairy, human.

[*The Truce of the Bear* 1898]

Charles Lamb, 1775–1834, English essayist
The human species, according to the best theory I can form of it, is composed of two distinct races, the men who borrow, and the men who lend.

[*Essays of Elia*: *The Two Races of Men*, 1823]

Frederick Langbridge, 1849–1923, English writer
Two men look out through the same bars:
One sees the mud, and one the stars.

[*A Cluster of Quiet Thoughts* 1896]

Leo XIII (Gioacchino Pecci), 1810–1903, Italian pope
Humanity must remain as it is.

[*Quadragesimo anno* 15 May 1931]

C[live] S[taples] Lewis, 1898–1963, English writer
The safest road to Hell is the gradual one – the gentle slope, soft underfoot, without sudden turnings, without milestones, without signposts.

[*The Screwtape Letters* 1941]

Arnold Lobel, 1933– , American writer
When the need is strong, there are those who will believe anything.

[*Fables* 1980]

John Locke, 1632–1704, English philosopher
New opinions are always suspected, and usually opposed, without any other reason but because they are not already common.

[*Essay Concerning Human Understanding* 1690]

Marcus Aurelius [Antoninus] [Marcus Annius Verus] AD121–80, Roman emperor
Let us put an end, once for all, to this discussion of what a good man should be–and be one.

[*Meditations c.*170]

Martial (Marcus Valerius Martialis), c.40–c.104, Roman poet
Conceal a flaw, and the world will imagine the worst.

[*Epigrams*]

W[illiam] Somerset Maugham, 1874–1965, English novelist
Like all weak men he laid an exaggerated stress on not changing one's mind.

[*Of Human Bondage* 1915]

I've always been interested in people, but I've never liked them.

[In *The Observer* 1949]

I'll give you my opinion of the human race in a nutshell . . . Their heart's in the right place, but their head is a thoroughly inefficient organ.

[*The Summing Up 1938*]

H[enry] L[ouis] Mencken, 1880–1956, American critic and writer
Conscience is the inner voice that warns us that someone might be looking.

[*A Mencken Chrestomathy* 1949]

An idealist is one who, on noticing that a rose smells better than a cabbage, concludes that it will also make better soup.

[In Alistair Cooke's *The Vintage Mencken* 1955]

George Augustus Moore, 1852–1933, Anglo-Irish novelist
Humanity is a pigsty where liars, hypocrites and the obscene in spirit congregate.

[*Confessions of a Young Man* 1888]

If you are a good man you want a bad one to convert; if you are a bad man you want a bad one to go out on a spree with.

[*Ibid*]

Desmond [John] Morris, 1928– , English ethnologist and writer

He is proud of the fact that he has the biggest brain of all the primates, but attempts to conceal the fact that he also has the biggest penis.

[*The Naked Ape* 1967]

Ben Okri, 1959– , Nigerian novelist and poet

A man's greatest battles are the ones he fights within himself.

[*Flowers and Shadows* 1980]

George Orwell [Eric Arthur Blair], 1903–50, English novelist and critic

The high sentiments always win in the end, the leaders who offer blood, toil, tears and sweat always get more out of their followers than those who offer safety and a good time. When it comes to the pinch, human beings are heroic.

[*Collected Essays: The Art of Donald McGill* 1961]

Blaise Pascal, 1623–1662, French mathematician and writer

Curiosity is only vanity. Most frequently we wish not to know, but to talk. We would not take a sea voyage for the sole pleasure of seeing without hope of ever telling.

[*Pensées* 1670]

Octavio Paz, 1914– 98, Mexican poet

Solitude lies at the lowest depth of the human condition. Man is the only being who feels himself to be alone and the only one who is searching for the Other.

[*The Labyrinth of Solitude* 1950]

[Lloyd] Logan Pearsall Smith, 1865–1946, American-born English writer

How awful to reflect that what people say of us is true.

[*Afterthoughts* 1931]

Plato, c. 428–348BC, Greek philosopher

Man is a tame, a domesticated animal.

[*Laws c.*360BC]

Pliny the Elder, AD23–79, Roman naturalist

Man is the only animal that knows nothing, and can learn nothing without being taught. He can neither speak nor walk nor eat, nor do anything at the prompting of nature, but only weep.

[*Natural History* 77]

Lions do not fight with one another; serpents do not attack serpents, nor do the wild monsters of the deep rage against their like. But most of the calamities of man are caused by his fellow man.

[*Ibid*]

Alexander Pope, 1688–1744, English poet

Some praise at morning what they blame at night.
But always think the last opinion right.

[*An Essay on Criticism* 1711]

I never knew any man in my life who could not bear another's misfortunes perfectly like a Christian.

[*Thoughts on Various Subjects* 1727]

Hope springs eternal in the human breast:
Man never is, but always to be blest.

[*An Essay on Man* 1733–4]

Publilius Syrus, *fl.* 1st century BC, Roman writer
Familiarity breeds contempt.

Thomas Brackett Reed, 1839–1902, American legislator
For the ordinary business of life an ounce of habit is worth a pound of intellect.
[Speech at Bowdoin College, Maine, 1902]

François, Duc de La Rochefoucauld, 1613–80, French writer
Nothing is rarer than true good nature; they who are reputed to have it are generally only pliant and weak.
[*Reflections, or Sentences and Moral Maxims* 1665]
If we had no faults of our own, we would not take so much pleasure in noticing those of others.
[*Ibid*]

Bertrand [Arthur William] Russell, 3rd Earl Russell, 1872–1970, English philosopher
Next to enjoying ourselves, the next greatest pleasure consists in preventing others from enjoying themselves, or, more generally, in the acquisition of power.
[*Sceptical Essays: The Recrudescence of Puritanism*]
Men who are unhappy, like men who sleep badly, are always proud of the fact.
[In *The Faber Book of Aphorisms* 1964]

Franz [Peter] Schubert, 1797–1828, Austrian composer
Let us take men as they are, not as they ought to be.
[*Diary* 16 June 1816]

Charles Monroe Schulz, 1922–2000, American cartoonist
I love mankind, it's people I can't stand.
[*Go Fly a Kite, Charlie Brown*]

Seneca, c.4BC–AD65, Roman philosopher
Man is a social animal.
[*De Beneficiis c.*63]

Man is a reasoning animal.
[*Epistolae ad Lucilium c.*63]

To err is human. (*Humanum est errare.*)
[*Quaestiones Naturales c.*63]

William Shakespeare, 1564–1616, English dramatist
'Tis time to fear when tyrants seem to kiss.
[*Pericles* 1:2:79 1608–9]

3rd fisherman: Master, I marvel how the fishes live in the sea.
1st fisherman: Why, as men do a-land; the great ones eat up the little ones.
[*Ibid* 2:1:29]

Richard Brinsley Sheridan, 1751–1816, English dramatist
Certainly nothing is unnatural that is not physically impossible.
[*The Critic* 1779]

Vittorio De Sica, 1902–74, Italian film director
Moral indignation is in most cases 2 percent moral, 48 percent indignation and 50 percent envy.
[*The Observer* 1961]

Sophocles, c.496–c.406BC, Greek poet

There are many wonderful things in nature, but the most wonderful of all is man.

[*Antigone c.* 450BC]

Benedict (*or* Baruch) Spinoza, 1632–77, Dutch philosopher

Surely human affairs would be far happier if the power in men to be silent were the same as that to speak. But experience more than sufficiently teaches that men govern nothing with more difficulty than their tongues.

[*Ethics* 1677]

It may easily come to pass that a vain man may become proud and imagine himself pleasing to all when he is in reality a universal nuisance.

[*Ibid*]

Man is a social animal.

[*Ethics* 1677]

John [Ernst] Steinbeck, 1902–68, American novelist

Man, unlike anything organic or inorganic in the universe, grows beyond his work, walks up the stairs of his concepts, emerges ahead of his accomplishments.

[*The Grapes of Wrath* 1939]

Jonathan Swift, 1667–1745, Irish-born English writer

Satire is a sort of glass, wherein beholders do generally discover everybody's face but their own.

[*The Battle of the Books* 1704]

Alfred, Lord Tennyson, 1809–92, English poet

His honour rooted in dishonour stood,
And faith unfaithful kept him falsely true.

[*Elaine* 1859]

Terence (Publius Terentius Afer), c.190–c.159BC, Roman poet

I am a man; and nothing human is foreign to me.
(*Homo sum; humani nihil a me alienum puto*)

[*Heauton Timoroumenos c.* 160BC]

Ivan Sergeyevich Turgenev, 1818–83, Russian novelist

A man's capable of understanding . . . how the aether vibrates, and what's going on in the sun – but how any other man can blow his nose differently from him, that he's incapable of understanding.

[*Fathers and Sons* 1862]

Mark Twain (Samuel Langhorne Clemens), 1835–1910, American writer

Man is the only animal that blushes. Or needs to.

[*Following the Equator* 1897]

The fact that man knows right from wrong proves his *intellectual* superiority to the other creatures; but the fact that he can *do* wrong proves his *moral* inferiority to any creature that *cannot*.

[*What is Man?* 1906]

Sir Jan Laurens Van der Post, 1906–96, South African-born writer

Human beings are perhaps never more frightening than when they are convinced beyond doubt that they are right.

[*The Lost World of the Kalahari* 1958]

Leonardo da Vinci, 1452–1519, Italian artist
Man and the animals are merely a passage and channel for food, a tomb for other animals, a haven for the dead, giving life by the death of others, a coffer of corruption.

[*Notebooks c.* 1500]

Voltaire [François Marie Arouet], 1694–1778, French philosopher and writer
The secret of being a bore is to tell everything.

[*Sept Discours en Vers sur L'Homme* 1738]

If this is the best of possible worlds, what then are the others?

[*Candide* 1759]

Optimism, said Candide, is a mania for maintaining that all is well when things are going badly.

[*Ibid*]

Horace Walpole, 4th Earl of Oxford, 1717–97, English writer
It is charming to totter into vogue.

[Letter 1765]

The world is a comedy to those that think, a tragedy to those that feel.

[*Ibid* 1776]

H[erbert] G[eorge] Wells, 1866–1946, English writer
The Highly Fashionable and the Absolutely Vulgar are but two faces of the common coin of humanity.

[*Select Conversations with an Uncle*]

E[lwyn] B[rooks] White, 1899–1985, American humorist
As long as there is one upright man, as long as there is one compassionate woman, the contagion may not spread and the scene is not desolate. Hope is the thing that is left us in a bad time.

[Letter 1973]

Katharine Whitehorn, 1926– , English journalist
I am firm. You are obstinate. He is a pig-headed fool.

[In *The Observer* 1974]

A good listener is not someone who has nothing to say. A good listener is a good talker with a sore throat.

[*Ibid*]

Walt[er] Whitman, 1819–92, American poet
And I will show of male and female that either is but the equal of the other.

[*Leaves of Grass: Starting from Paumanok* 1855–92]

Oscar [Fingal O'Flahertie Wills] Wilde, 1854–1900, Irish writer
A cynic is a man who knows the price of everything, and the value of nothing.

[*Lady Windermere's Fan* 1892]

Experience is the name everyone gives to their mistakes.

[*Ibid*]

John Wilmott, 2nd Earl of Rochester, 1647–80, English poet
Women and men of wit are dangerous tools,
And ever fatal to admiring fools.

[*A Satire Against Mankind*]

[Adeline] Virginia Woolf, 1882–1941, English novelist and critic

It is in our idleness, in our dreams, that the submerged truth sometimes comes to the top.

[*A Room of One's Own* 1929]

William Wordsworth, 1770–1850, English poet

The still, sad music of humanity.

[*Tintern Abbey* 1798]

Frank Lloyd Wright, 1869–1959, American architect

An expert is a man who has stopped thinking. Why should he think? He is an expert.

[In *The Daily Express* 1959]

Give me the luxuries of life and I will willingly do without the necessities.

[Quoted in his obituary]

Love

Anonymous

Love is as warm among cottagers as courtiers.

[*Proverb*]

There is more pleasure in loving than in being beloved.

[*Proverb*]

Jean Anouilh, 1910–87, French dramatist

Oh, love is real enough, you will find it some day, but it has one arch-enemy – and that is life.

[*Ardèle* 1948]

Matthew Arnold, 1822–88, English poet and critic

Is it so small a thing
To have enjoy'd the sun,
To have liv'd light in the spring,
To have lov'd, to have thought, to have done.

[*Empedocles on Etna* 1852]

W[ystan] H[ugh] Auden, 1907–73, English-born poet

I'll love you, dear, I'll love you
Till China and Africa meet,
And the river jumps over the mountain
And the salmon sing in the street.
I'll love you till the ocean
Is folded and hung up to dry
And the seven stars go squawking
Like geese about the sky.

[*As I Walked Out One Evening*]

He was my North, my South, my East, my West,
My working week and my Sunday rest,
My noon, my midnight, my talk, my song;
I thought that love would last for ever: I was wrong.

[*Another Time: Funeral Blues* 1940]

St Augustine of Hippo, 354–430, Christian philosopher

Da mihi castitatem et continentiam, sed noli modo.
Give me chastity and continence, but not yet.

[*Confessions* 397]

275

Jane Austen, 1775–1817, English novelist
All the privilege I claim for my own sex . . . is that of loving longest, when existence or when hope is gone.

[*Persuasion* 1815–16]

Francis Bacon, Baron Verulam of Verulam and Viscount of St Albans, 1561–1626, English philosopher
They do best who, if they cannot but admit Love, yet make it keep quarter; and sever it wholly from their serious affairs and actions of life: for if it checke once with Business, it troubleth men's Fortunes, and maketh men, that they can no wayes be true to their own ends.

[*Essays: Of Love*]

Honoré de Balzac, 1799–1850, French novelist
It is easier to be a lover than a husband for the simple reason that it is more difficult to be witty every day than to say pretty things from time to time.

[*The Physiology of Marriage* 1830]

To kill the emotions and so live to an old age, or to accept the martyrdom of our passions and die young is our doom.

[*La Peau de chagrin* 1831]

Sir J[ames] M[atthew] Barrie, 1860–1937, Scottish playwright
Let no one who loves be called altogether unhappy. Even love unreturned has its rainbow.

[*The Little Minister* 1891]

Francis Beaumont, 1584–1616, and John Fletcher, 1579–1625, English dramatists
Kiss till the cow comes home.

[*The Scornful Lady* 1616]

Sir [Henry] Max[imilian] Beerbohm, 1872–1956, English writer
Women who love the same man have a bitter kind of freemasonry.

[*Zuleika Dobson* 1912]

Aphra Behn, 1640–89, English playwright
Love ceases to be a pleasure when it ceases to be a secret.

[*The Lover's Watch: Four o'clock*]

Georges Bernanos, 1888–1948, French writer
Hell is not to love any more, madame. Not to love any more!

[*The Diary of a Country Priest* 1936]

Louis de Bernières, 1954– , English author
Love is a temporary madness, it erupts like volcanoes and then subsides. And when it subsides you have to make a decision. You have to work out whether your roots have so entwined that it is inconceivable that you should ever part.

[*Captain Corelli's Mandolin* 1994]

Sir John Betjeman, 1906–84, English poet
Love-thirty, love-forty, oh! weakness of joy,
The speed of a swallow; the grace of a boy,
With carefullest carelessness, gaily you won,
I am weak from your loveliness, Joan Hunter Dunn.

[*John Betjeman's Collected Poems: A Subaltern's Love-Song* 1958]

And the scent of her wrap, and the words never said,
And the ominous, ominous dancing ahead.
We sat in the car-park till twenty to one
And now I'm engaged to Miss Joan Hunter Dunn.

[*Ibid*]

The Bible
And Jacob served seven years for Rachel; and they seemed unto him but a few days, for the love he had to her.

[*Genesis* 29:20]

I am distressed for thee, my brother Jonathan: very pleasant hast thou been unto me: thy love to me was wonderful, passing the love of women.

[*2 Samuel* 1:26]

Let him kiss me with the kisses of his mouth.

[*Song of Solomon* 1:2]

He brought me to the banqueting house, and his banner over me was love. Stay me with flagons, comfort me with apples: for I am sick of love.

[*Ibid* 2:4–5]

My beloved is mine, and I am his: he feedeth among the lilies.

[*Ibid* 2:16]

Set me as a seal upon thine heart, as a seal upon thine arm: for love is strong as death; jealousy is cruel as the grave; the coals thereof are coals of fire, which hath a most vehement flame.

[*Ibid* 8:6–7]

A new commandment I give unto you, That ye love one another; as I have loved you, that ye also love one another.

[*John* 13:34]

Love worketh no ill to his neighbour: therefore love is the fulfilling of the law.

[*Romans* 13:10]

Though I speak with the tongues of men and of angels, and have not charity, I am become as sounding brass, or a tinkling cymbal. And though I have the gift of prophecy, and understand all mysteries, and all knowledge; and though I have all faith, so that I could remove mountains, and have not charity, I am nothing.

[*1 Corinthians* 13:1–2]

There is no fear in love; but perfect love casteth out fear.

[*1 John* 4:18]

To have and to hold from this day forward, for better for worse, for richer for poorer, in sickness and in health, to love and to cherish, till death us do part, according to God's holy ordinance: and thereto I plight thee my troth.

[*Book of Common Prayer: Betrothal*]

Ambrose [Gwinett] Bierce, 1842–1914, American writer
Love: a temporary insanity curable by marriage or by removal of the patient from the influences under which he incurred the disorder. This disease, like caries and many other ailments, is prevalent only among civilized races living under artificial conditions; barbarous nations breathing pure air and eating simple food enjoy immunity from its ravages. It is sometimes fatal, but more frequently to the physician than to the patient.

[*The Devil's Dictionary* 1906]

Women in love are less ashamed than men. They have less to be ashamed of.

[*Ibid*]

Josh Billings [Henry Wheeler Shaw], 1818–85, American humorist
Love is like measles: you can get it only once, and the later in life it occurs the tougher it is.
[Lecture 1885]

William Blake, 1757–1827, English poet and artist
What is it that men in women do require?
The lineaments of gratified desire.
What is it women do in men require?
The lineaments of gratified desire.

[*Notebooks: What Is It* 1793]

Never seek to tell thy love,
Love that never told can be;
For the gentle wind does move
Silently, invisibly.

[*Songs of Experience: Love's Secret* 1794]

Love seeketh not itself to please,
Nor for itself hath any care,
But for another gives its ease,
And builds a heaven in hell's despair.

[*Songs of Experience: The Clod and the Pebble* 1794]

Ancius Manlius Severinus Boethius, c.475–524, Roman statesman and philosopher
Who can give a law to lovers? Love is a greater law unto itself.
[*De Consolatione Philosophiae*]

Francis William Bourdillon, 1852–1921, English writer
The mind has a thousand eyes,
And the heart but one;
Yet the light of a whole life dies,
When love is done.

[*Light* or *Among the Flowers* 1878]

Nicholas Breton, c.1545–c.1626, English poet
Much ado there was, God wot;
He would love, and she would not.

[*Phillida and Coridon*]

Robert Bridges, 1844–1930, English poet
So sweet love seemed that April morn,
When first we kissed beside the thorn,
So strangely sweet, it was not strange
We thought that love could never change.

[*So Sweet Love Seemed*]

Emily Jane Brontë, 1818–48, English novelist and poet
Riches I hold in light esteem
And love I laugh to scorn;
And lust of fame was but a dream,
That vanished with the morn.

[*The Old Stoic*]

LOVE

Sweet Love of youth, forgive if I forget thee
While the World's tide is bearing me along:
Sterner desires and darker hopes beset me,
Hopes which obscure but cannot do thee wrong.

[*Remembrance*]

Rupert Chawner Brooke, 1887–1915, English poet
And I shall find some girl perhaps,
And a better one than you,
With eyes as wise, but kindlier,
And lips as soft, but true
And I dare say she will do.

[*The Chilterns*]

I thought when love for you died,
I should die. It's dead.
Alone, mostly strangely, I live on.

[*The Life Beyond*]

Leave the sick hearts that honour could not move
And half-men, and their dirty songs and dreary,
And all the little emptiness of love.

[*Peace*]

Thomas Brown, 1663–1704, English writer
I do not love you, Dr Fell,
But why I cannot tell;
But this I know full well,
I do not love you, Dr Fell.

[Translation of an epigram by Martial]

Elizabeth Barrett Browning, 1806–61, English poet
Unless you can muse in a crowd all day
On the absent face that fixed you;
Unless you can love, as the angels may,
With the breadth of heaven betwixt you;
Unless you can dream that his faith is fast,
Through behoving and unbehoving;
Unless you can die when the dream is past –
Oh, never call it loving!

[*A Woman's Shortcomings*]

And a voice said in mastery while I strove, . . .
"Guess now who holds thee?" – "Death," I said. But, there,
The silver answer rang, . . . "Not Death, but Love."

[*Sonnets from the Portuguese* 1850]

279

If thou must love me, let it be for nought
Except for love's sake only. Do not say
"I love her for her smile . . . her look . . . her way
Of speaking gently, . . . for a trick of thought
That falls in well with mine, and certes brought
A sense of pleasant ease on such a day" –
For these things in themselves, Beloved, may
Be changed, or change for thee.
But love me for love's sake, that evermore
Thou mayst love on, through love's eternity.

[*Ibid*]

How do I love thee? Let me count the ways.
I love thee to the length and depth and height
My soul can reach, when feeling out of sight
For the ends of Being and ideal Grace.
I love thee to the level of every day's
Most quiet need, by sun and candlelight.
I love thee with the breath,
Smiles, tears, of all my life! – and, if God choose,
I shall but love thee better after death.

[*Ibid*]

Whoever lives true life, will love true love.

[*Aurora Leigh* 1857]

Robert Browning, 1812–89, English poet
She should never have looked at me,
If she meant I should not love her!

[*Cristina*]

Nay but you, who do not love her,
Is she not pure gold, my mistress?

[*Song*]

Only I discern –
Infinite passion, and the pain
Of finite hearts that yearn.

[*Two in the Campagna* 1855]

God be thanked, the meanest of his creatures
Boasts two soul-sides, one to face the world with,
One to show a woman when he loves her.

[*One Word More*]

O lyric Love, half angel and half bird
And all a wonder and a wild desire.

[*The Ring and the Book* 1868–9]

Edmund Burke, 1729–97, Irish-born English political writer
To tax and to please, no more than to love and to be wise, is not given to men.

[Speech 1774]

Robert Burns, 1759–96, Scottish poet
My love she's but a lassie yet.

[Title of a song]

What can a young lassie do wi' an auld man?

[Title of a song]

280

LOVE

Ae fond kiss and then we sever.

[*Ae Fond Kiss*]

But to see her was to love her,
Love but her, and love for ever.

[*Ibid*]

Had we never lov'd sae kindly,
Had we never lov'd sae blindly,
Never met – or never parted,
We had ne'er been broken-hearted.

[*Ibid*]

To see her is to love her,
And love but her for ever;
For Nature made her what she is,
And never made anither!

[*Bonnie Lesley*]

]Whistle, and I'll come to ye, my lad.

[Title of a song]

O, my luve is like a red red rose,
That's newly sprung in June.
O my luve's like the melodie
That's sweetly play'd in tune.

[*A Red Red Rose*]

To be overtopped in anything else I can bear: but in the tests of generous love I defy all
mankind.

[Letter to Clarinda]

Samuel Butler, 1835–1902, English writer

God is Love, I dare say. But what a mischievous devil Love is.

[*Note Books c.* 1890]

To live is like love, all reason is against it, and all healthy instinct for it.

[*Ibid*]

'Tis better to have loved and lost than never to have lost at all.

[*The Way of All Flesh* 1903]

Byron, Lord George Gordon [Noel], 6th Baron Byron of Rochdale, 1788–1824, English poet

A thousand hearts beat happily; and when
Music arose with its voluptuous swell,
Soft eyes look'd love to eyes which spake again,
And all went merry as a marriage bell;
But hush! hark! a deep sound strikes like a rising knell!

[*Childe Harold's Pilgrimage* 1818]

Here's a sight to those who love me,
And a smile to those who hate;
And, whatever sky's above me,
Here's a heart for every fate.

[*To Thomas Moore*]

Merely innocent flirtation.
Not quite adultery, but adulteration.

[*Don Juan* 1819–24]

A little while she strove, and much repented,
And whispering "I will ne'er consent" – consented.

[*Ibid*]

Man's love is of man's life a thing apart,
'Tis woman's whole existence.

[*Ibid*]

Alas! the love of women! it is known
To be a lovely and a fearful thing.

[*Ibid*]

In her first passion woman loves her lover,
In all the others all she loves is love.

[*Ibid*]

What men call gallantry, and gods adultery,
Is much more common where the climate's sultry.

[*Ibid*]

So, we'll go no more a-roving
So late into the night,
Though the heart be still as loving,
And the moon be still as bright.

[*So, We'll Go No More a-Roving*]

Mrs Patrick Campbell, 1865–1940, English actress
I don't mind where people make love, so long as they don't do it on the street and frighten the horses.

[Attributed]

Marriage is the result of the longing for the deep, deep peace of the double bed after the hurly-burly of the chaise longue.

[*Ibid*]

Thomas Campbell, 1777–1844, Scottish poet
Better be courted and jilted
Than never be courted at all.

[*The Jilted Nymph*]

Thomas Campion, 1567–1620, English poet, musician, and doctor
Never love unless you can
Bear with all the faults of man.

[*Never Love*]

Thomas Carew, c.1594–1640, English diplomat and poet
He that loves a rosy cheek,
Or a coral lip admires;
Or from star-like eyes doth seek
Fuel to maintain his fires:
As old Time makes these decay
So his flames must waste away.

[*Disdain Returned*]

Then fly betimes, for only they
Conquer Love, that run away.

[*Conquest by Flight*]

Julia Fletcher Carney, 1823–1908, American teacher
Little deeds of kindness, little words of love,
Help to make earth happy, like the heaven above.

[*Little Things*]

Lewis Carroll [Charles Lutwidge Dodgson], 1832–92, English mathematician and writer
And the moral of that is – "Oh, 'tis love, 'tis love that makes the world go round."

[*Alice's Adventures in Wonderland* 1865]

Gaius Valerius Catullus, c.87–c.54BC, Roman poet
Give me a thousand kisses, then a hundred, then another thousand, then a second hundred, then yet another thousand, then a hundred.

[*Carmin*]

But a woman's words to a lusting lover
Should be written in wind and running water.

[*Ibid*]

Geoffrey Chaucer, c.1340–1400, English poet
Love is blind.

[*The Canterbury Tales: The Merchant's Tale* c.1387]

Wostow nat wel the olde clerkes sawe,
That "who shal yeve a lovere any lawe?"
Love is a gretter lawe, by my pan,
Than may be yeve to any erthely man.

[*Ibid*: *The Knight's Tale*]

John Cheever, 1912–82, American novelist
The deep joy we take in the company of people with whom we have just recently fallen in love is undisguisable.

[*The Stories of John Cheever: The Bus to St James* 1978]

Hartley Coleridge, 1796–1849, English writer
She is not fair to outward view
As many maidens be;
Her loveliness I never knew
Until she smiled on me.
O then I saw her eye was bright,
A well of love, a spring of light.

[*Song: She is not Fair*]

Samuel Taylor Coleridge, 1772–1834, English poet
All thoughts, all passions, all delights,
Whatever stirs this mortal frame,
All are but ministers of Love,
And feed his sacred flame.

[*The Devil's Thoughts* 1799]

And to be wroth with one we love
Doth work like madness in the brain.

[*Christabel* 1816]

A person once said to me that he could make nothing of love, except that it was friendship accidently combined with desire. Whence I concluded that he had never been in love. For what shall we say of the feeling which a man of sensibility has towards his wife with her baby at her breast? How pure from sensual desire! yet how different from friendship'

[*Table-Talk* 1830]

William Congreve, 1670–1729, English dramatist
Heav'n has no rage like love to hatred turn'd,
Nor Hell a fury like a woman scorn'd.

[*The Mourning Bride* 1697]

If there's delight in love, 'tis when I see
That heart, which others bleed for, bleed for me.

[*The Way of the World* 1700]

Eliza Cook, 1818–89, English poet
I love it, I love it; and who shall dare
To chide me from loving that old armchair?

[*The Old Armchair* 1837]

Frances Crofts Cornford, 1886–1960, English poet
O why do you walk through the fields in gloves,
Missing so much and so much?
O fat white woman whom nobody loves,
Why do you walk through the fields in gloves?

[*To a Fat Lady Seen from a Train* 1915]

Abraham Cowley, 1618–67, English writer and poet
Love in her sunny eyes doth basking play;
Love walks the pleasant mazes of her hair;
Love does on both her lips for ever stray,
And sows and reaps a thousand kisses there:
In all her outward parts love's always seen;
But oh! he never went within.

[*The Change*]

William Cowper, 1731–1800, English poet
England, with all thy faults I love thee still,
My country!

[*The Task: The Timepiece* 1785]

Richard Crashaw, c.1612–1649, English poet
Love, thou art absolute sole Lord
Of life and death.

[*Hymne to Sainte Theresa*]

Dante [Alighieri], 1265–1321, Italian poet
L'amor che move il sole e l'altre stelle.
The love that moves the sun and the other stars.

[*The Divine Comedy: Paradise*]

Charles [John Huffam] Dickens, 1812–70, English novelist
As it is, I don't think I can do with anythin' under a female markis. I might keep up with a young 'ooman o' large property as hadn't a title, if she made wery fierce love to me. Not else.

[*Pickwick Papers* 1836–7]

284

LOVE

Benjamin Disraeli, 1st Earl of Beaconsfield, 1804–81, British statesman and novelist

The magic of first love is our ignorance that it can ever end.

[*Henrietta Temple* 1837]

We are all born for love; it is the principle of existence and its only end.

[*Sybil* 1845]

John Donne, c.1571–1631, English poet

For God's sake hold your tongue and let me love.

[*The Canonization*]

Twice or thrice had I loved thee,
Before I knew thy face or name;
So in a voice, so in a shapeless flame,
Angels affect us oft, and worship'd be.

[*Aire and Angels*]

Just such disparitie
As is twixt Aire and Angels' puritie,
'Twixt women's love and men's will ever be.

[*Ibid*]

All other things, to their destruction draw,
Only our love hath no decay;
This, no tomorrow hath, nor yesterday,
Running it never runs from us away,
But truly keeps his first, last, everlasting day.

[*The Anniversarie*]

Come live with me, and be my love,
And we will some new pleasures prove
Of golden sands, and christall brooks,
With silken lines, and silver hooks.

[*The Baite*]

Love built on beauty, soon as beauty, dies.

. [*Elegy 2: The Anagram*]

Here take my picture; though I bid farewell,
Thine, in my heart, where my soul dwells, shall dwell.

[*Elegy 5: His Picture*]

Temper, O fair love, love's impetuous rage,
Be my true mistress still, not my feigned page.
How happy were our sires in ancient times,
Who held plurality of loves no crime.

[*Elegy 17*]

Licence my roving hands, and let them go,
Before, behind, between, above, below.
O my America! my new-found-land,
My kingdom, safeliest when with one man mann'd.

[*Elegy 19: To his Mistress Going to Bed*]

Full nakedness! All joys are due to thee,
As souls unbodied, bodies uncloth'd must be,
To taste whole joys.

[*Ibid*]

Love, all alike, no season knows, nor clime,
Nor hours, days, months, which are the rags of time.

[*The Sunne Rising*]

John Drinkwater, 1882–1937, English writer
And not a girl goes walking
Along the Cotswold lanes
But knows men's eyes in April
Are quicker than their brains.

[*Cotswold Love*]

John Dryden, 1631–1700, English dramatist
Love's the noblest frailty of the mind.

[*The Indian Emperor* 1667]

Pains of love be sweeter far
Than all other pleasures are.

[*Tyrannic Love* 1669]

Love the sense of right and wrong confounds.

[*Palamon and Arcite* 1699]

Edward VIII, 1894–1972, king of Great Britain and Northern Ireland
At long last, I am able to say a few words of my own . . . Until now it has not been constitu-
tionally possible for me to speak. I have found it impossible to carry the heavy burden of
responsibility and to discharge my duties as king as I would wish to do without the help and
support of the woman I love.

[Radio broadcast on his abdication,11 December 1936]

Ralph Waldo Emerson, 1803–82, American writer
All mankind love a lover.

[*Essays: Love* 1841]

Epictetus, c.AD50–c.120, Greek philosopher
Chastise your passions, that they may not chastise you.

[*Encheiridion c.*ll0]

George Farquhar, 1678–1707, Irish playwright
Money is the sinews of love, as of war.

[*Love and a Bottle* 1698]

How a little love and good company improves a woman.

[*The Beaux' Stratagem* 1707]

Charming women can true converts make,
We love the precepts for the teacher's sake.

[*The Constant Couple* 1699]

Henry Fielding, 1707–54, English novelist
The devil take me, if I think anything but love to be the object of love.

[*Amelia* 1752]

Love and scandal are the best sweeteners of tea.

[*Love in Several Masques*1728]

Jean de La Fontaine, 1621–95, French poet
Ah, love, love! When thou seizeth us we may well say, Goodbye, prudence!

[*Fables* 1668]

Sigmund Freud, 1856–1939, Austrian psychiatrist
The credulity of love is the most fundamental source of authority.

[*Collected Works*]

LOVE

Christopher [Harris] Fry, 1907– , English poet and playwright
Oh, the unholy mantrap of love!

[*The Lady's not for Burning*1949]

John Gay, 1685–1732, English poet and playwright
She who has never lov'd, has never liv'd.

[*The Captives*]

Then nature rul'd, and love, devoid of art,
Spoke the consenting language of the heart.

[*Dione*]

Sir William Schwenck Gilbert, 1836–1911, English librettist
So I fell in love with a rich attorney's
Elderly ugly daughter.

[*Trial by Jury* 1875]

Time was when Love and I were well acquainted.

[*The Sorcerer* 1877]

Twenty love-sick maidens we,
Love-sick all against our will.

[*Patience* 1881]

It's a song of a merryman, moping mum,
Whose soul was sad, and whose glance was glum,
Who sipped no sup, and who craved no crumb,
As he sighed for the love of a ladye.

[*The Yeomen of the Guard* 1888]

Oliver Goldsmith, 1728–74, Irish-born English writer
The hawthorn bush, with seats beneath the shade,
For talking age and whisp'ring lovers made.

[*The Deserted Village* 1770]

The bashful virgin's sidelong looks of love,
The matron's glance that would those looks reprove.

[*Ibid*]

Robert von Ranke Graves, 1895–1985, English poet
O Love, be fed with apples while you may,
And feel the sun and go in royal array,
A smiling innocent on the heavenly causeway.

[*Sick Love*]

Thomas Gray, 1716–71, English poet
The bloom of young desire and purple light of love.

[*The Progress of Poesy* 1757]

Bright-eyed Fancy, hovering o'er,
Scatters from her pictured urn
Thoughts that breathe and words that burn.

[*Ibid*]

Fitz-Greene Halleck, 1790–1867, American poet
None knew thee but to love thee,
Nor named thee but to praise.

[*On the Death of Joseph Rodman Drake*]

Thomas Hardy, 1840–1928, English novelist and poet

A lover without indiscretion is no lover at all.

[*The Hand of Ethelberta* 1876]

O the opal and the sapphire of that wandering western sea,
And the woman riding high above with bright hair flapping free–
The woman whom I loved so, and who loyally loved me.

[*Beeny Cliff*]

Nathaniel Hawthorne, 1804–64, American novelist

Selfishness is one of the qualities apt to inspire love. This might be thought out at great length.

[*American Note-Books* 1840]

Georg Wilhelm Friedrich Hegel, 1770–1831, German philosopher

We may affirm absolutely that nothing great in the world has been accomplished without passion.

[*The Philosophy of History* 1832]

Cincinnatus Heine [Joaquin Miller], 1839–1913, American poet

Love well who will, love wise who can,
But love, be loved.

[*With Walker in Nicaragua* 1871]

Ernest [Miller] Hemingway, 1899–1961, American novelist

Love is something that hangs up behind the bathroom door and smells of Lysol.

[*To Have and Have Not*]

Edward Herbert, 1st Baron Herbert of Cherbury, 1583–1648, English soldier and philosopher

O that our love might take no end
Or never had beginning took!

[*An Ode upon a Question moved, Whether Love should continue for ever?*]

For where God doth admit the fair.
Think you that he excludeth Love?

[*Ibid*]

George Herbert, 1593–1633, English poet

Love is swift of foot;
Love's a man of war,
And can shoot,
And can hit from far.

[*Discipline*]

Robert Herrick, 1591–1674, English poet and churchman

A sweet disorder in the dress
Kindles in clothes a wantonness.

[*Hesperides: Delight in Disorder* 1648]

Bid me to live, and I will live
Thy Protestant to be:
Or bid me love, and I will give
A loving heart to thee.

[*Ibid: To Anthea, who may command him any Thing*]

All love, all liking, all delight
Lies drowned with us in endless night.

[Ibid: Corinna's Going a-Maying]

Thomas Hobbes, 1588–1679, English political philosopher
Desire and love are the same thing; save that by desire we always signify the absence of the object; by love, most commonly the presence of the same.

[Leviathan 1651]

Passions unguided are for the most part mere madness.

[Ibid]

James Hogg, ("The Ettrick Shepherd"), 1770–1835, Scottish poet and novelist
My love she's but a lassie yet.

[Title of song]

O, love, love, love; Love is like a dizziness;
It winna let a poor body gang about his business!

[Love is Like a Dizziness]

E[dgar] W[atson] Howe, 1853–1937, American writer
If a woman doesn't chase a man a litte, she doesn't love him.

[Sinner Sermons 1926]

Victor [Marie] Hugo, 1802–85, French novelist and poet
The supreme happiness of life is the conviction that we are loved.

[Les Misérables 1862]

Herman Hupfield, 1894–1951, American songwriter
You must remember this,
A kiss is still a kiss,
A sigh is just a sigh;
The fundamental things apply,
As time goes by.

[Song: *As Time Goes By*, in *Casablanca* 1942]

James I, 1394–1437, king of Scotland
So far I fallen was in loves dance,
That suddenly my wit, my countenance,
My heart, my will, my nature, and my mind
Was changit right clean in another kind.

[The Kingis Quair]

Thomas Jefferson, 1743–1826, 3rd president of the United States
The happiest moments my heart knows are those in which it is pouring forth its affections to a few esteemed characters.

[Letter 1786]

Jerome K[lapka] Jerome, 1859–1927, English humorous writer
Love is like the measles; we all have to go through it.

[Idle Thoughts of an Idle Fellow: On Being in Love 1886]

Douglas William Jerrold, 1803–57, English writer
Love's like the measles – all the worse when it comes late in life.

[A Philanthropist]

Dr Samuel Johnson, 1709–84, English lexicographer
Love is the wisdom of the fool and the folly of the wise.

[Johnsonian Miscellanies]

James [Augustine Aloysius] Joyce, 1882–1941, Irish writer and poet
Whatever else is unsure in this stinking dunghill of a world, a mother's love is not.

[A Portrait of the Artist as a Young Man 1916]

Carl Gustav Jung, 1875–1961, Swiss psychiatrist
Where love rules, there is no will to power; and where power predominates, there love is lacking. The one is the shadow of the other.

[The Psychology of the Unconscious 1943]

John Keats, 1795–1821, English poet
O what can ail thee, Knight-at-arms,
Alone and palely loitering;
The sedge has wither'd from the lake,
And no birds sing.

[La Belle Dame Sans Merci 1819]

La belle Dame sans Merci
Hath thee in thrall!

[Ibid]

Love in a hut, with water and a crust,
Is – Love, forgive us! – cinders, ashes, dust;
Love in a palace is perhaps at last
More grievous torment than a hermit's fast.

[Lamia 1819]

For ever wilt thou love, and she be fair!

[Ode on a Grecian Urn 1819]

And there shall be for thee all soft delight
That shadowy thought can win,
A bright torch, and a casement ope at night,
To let the warm Love in!

[Ode to Psyche 1819]

John Philip Kemble, 1757–1823, English actor
Perhaps it was right to dissemble your love,
But – Why did you kick me downstairs?

[The Panel]

Henry King, 1592–1669, English bishop
We that did nothing study but the way
To love each other, with which thoughts the day
Rose with delight to us, and with them set,
Must learn the hateful art, how to forget.

[The Surrender]

Sir Harry Lauder, 1870–1950, Scottish comic singer
I love a lassie, a bonnie Hieland lassie.

[Song title]

LOVE

D[avid] H[erbert] Lawrence, 1885–1930, English novelist and poet

Love is the great Asker.

[*End of Another Home Holiday*]

T[homas] E[dward] Lawrence, 1888–1935, English soldier and writer

I loved you, so I drew these tides of men into my hands and wrote my will across the sky in stars.

[Dedication, *The Seven Pillars of Wisdom* 1926]

John [Winston] Lennon, 1940–80, English pop singer and songwriter

We've got this gift of love, but love is like a precious plant. You can't just accept it and leave it in the cupboard or just think it's going to get on by itself. You've got to keep watering it. You've got to really look after it and nurture it.

[Television broadcast, 1969]

Henry Wadsworth Longfellow, 1807–82, American poet

There is nothing holier, in this life of ours, than the first consciousness of love – the first fluttering of its silken wings.

[*Hyperion* 1839]

As unto the bow the cord is,
So unto the man is woman;
Though she bends him, she obeys him,
Though she draws him, yet she follows:
Useless each without the other!

[*The Song of Hiawatha: Hiawatha's Wooing* 1855]

Richard Lovelace, 1618–57/8, English poet

I could not love thee, Dear, so much
Lov'd I not Honour more.

[*To Lucasta, Going to the Wars* 1649]

Hugh MacDiarmid [Christopher Murray Grieve], 1892–1978, Scottish poet

Wheesht, wheesht, my foolish hert,
For weel ye ken
I widna ha'e ye stert
Auld ploys again.

[*Wheesht, Wheesht*]

Marcus Aurelius [Antoninus] [Marcus Annius Verus] AD121–80, Roman emperor It is man's peculiar duty to love even those who wrong him.

[*Meditations c.*170]

Edwin Markham, 1852–1940, American poet

He drew a circle that shut me out –
Heretic, rebel, a thing to flout.
But Love and I had the wit to win:
We drew a circle that took him in.

[*Outwitted*]

Christopher Marlowe, 1564–93, English dramatist
Was this the face that launch'd a thousand ships
And burnt the topless towers of Ilium?
Sweet Helen, make me immortal with a kiss.

[*Dr Faustus* 1588]

O, thou art fairer than the evening air
Clad in the beauty of a thousand stars.

[*Ibid*]

Thou hast committed –
Fornication: but that was in another country;
and besides, the wench is dead.

[*The Jew of Malta* 1589]

It lies not in our power to love, or hate,
For will in us is over-rul'd by fate.

[*Hero and Leander* 1598]

Where both deliberate, the love is slight;
Whoever loved that loved not at first sight?

[*Ibid*]

Come live with me, and be my love,
And we will all the pleasures prove
That hills and valleys, dales and fields,
Woods or steepy mountain yields.

[*The Passionate Shepherd to His Love* 1599]

Martial [Marcus Valerius Martialis], c.ad 42–c.102, Roman epigrammatist
Non amo te, Sabidi, nec possum dicere quare:
Hoc tantum Possum dicere. non amo te.
(I do not love you, Sabidius, and I cannot say why: this only I can say, I do not love you.)

[*Epigrams*]

Andrew Marvell, 1621–78, English poet and politician
My Love is of a birth as rare
As 'tis for object strange and high:
It was begotten by despair
Upon Impossibility.

[*The Definition of Love* 1650–52]

As Lines so Loves *oblique* may well
Themselves in every Angle greet:
But ours so truly Paralel,
Though infinite can never meet.

[*Ibid*]

Groucho [Julius Henry] Marx, 1895–1977, American comedian
Send two dozen roses to Room 424 and put "Emily, I love you" on the back of the bill.

[*A Night in Casablanca* film 1946]

H[enry] L[ouis] Mencken, 1880–1956, American critic and writer
To be in love is merely to be in a state of perpetual anaesthesis – to mistake an ordinary young man for a Greek god or an ordinary young woman for a goddess.

[*Prejudices* 1919–27]

George Meredith, 1828–1909, English writer
Kissing don't last: cookery do!

[*The Ordeal of Richard Feverel* 1859]

To plod on and still keep the passion fresh.

[*The Egoist* 1879]

She whom I love is hard to catch and conquer,
Hard, but O the glory of the winning were she won!

[*Love in the Valley* 1883]

Edna St Vincent Millay, 1892–1950, American poet
And if I loved you Wednesday,
Well, what is that to you?
I do not love you Thursday –
So much is true.

[*Thursday*]

And, "One thing there's no getting by –
I've been a wicked girl," said I;
"But if I can't be sorry, why,
I might as well be glad!"

[*The Penitent* 1920]

Alice Duer Miller, 1874–1942, American writer and poet
When a woman like that whom I've seen too much
All of a sudden drops out of touch,
Is always busy and never can
Spare you a moment, it means a man.

[*Forsaking all others*]

John Milton, 1608–74, English poet
But headlong joy is ever on the wing,
In Wintry solstice like the shortn'd light
Soon swallow'd up in dark and long out-living night.

[*The Passion* 1630]

To whom the angel with a smile that glow'd
Celestial rosy red, love's proper hue.

[*Paradise Lost* 1667]

And calm of mind all passion spent.

[*Samson Agonistes* 1671]

Molière [Jean-Baptiste Poquelin], 1622–73, French playwright
On est aisement dupé par ce qu'on aime.
We are easily duped by those we love.

[*Le Tartuffe* 1664]

George Augustus Moore, 1852–1933, Anglo-Irish novelist
All reformers are bachelors.

[*The Bending of the Bough*]

Thomas Moore, 1779–1852, Irish poet
No, the heart that has truly lov'd never forgets,
But as truly loves on to the close,
As the sunflowers turns on her god, when he sets,
The same look which she turn'd when he rose.

[*Irish Melodies: Believe me, if all those endearing Young Charms* 1801–34]

The time I've lost in wooing,
In watching and pursuing
The light, that lies
In woman's eyes
Has been my heart's undoing.

[*Ibid: The Time I've lost in wooing*]

And to know, when far from the lips we love,
We've but to make love to the lips we are near.

[*Ibid: 'Tis Sweet to Think*]

But there's nothing half so sweet in life
As love's young dream.

[*Ibid: Love's Young Dream*]

Then awake! – the heavens look bright, my dear,
'Tis never too late for delight, my dear,
And the best of all ways
To lengthen our days,
Is to steal a few hours from the night, my dear!

[*Ibid: The Young May Moon*]

William Morris, 1834–96, English artist, novelist and poet
Love is enough, though the world be a-waning,
And the woods have no voice but the voice of complaining,
Though the sky be too dark for dim eyes to discover
The gold-cups and daisies fair blooming thereunder.

[*Love Is Enough* 1872]

Van [George Ivan] Morrison, 1945– , Irish singer and songwriter
Have I told you lately that I love you
Have I told you there's no-one above you
Fill my heart with gladness
Take away my sadness
Ease my troubles, that's what you do.

[Song: *Have I Told You Lately* 1989]

Wolfgang Amadeus Mozart, 1756–91, Austrian composer
We poor, common folk must take wives whom we love and who love us.

[Letter to his father 1778]

Napoleon I [Napoleon Bonaparte], 1769–1821, emperor of France
I have never loved anyone for love's sake, except, perhaps Josephine – a little.

[To Gaspard Gourgaud, St Helena, 1817]

Friedrich Wilhelm Nietzsche, 1844–1900, German philosopher and poet
In revenge, as in love, woman is always more barbarous than man.

[*Beyond Good and Evil* 1886]

LOVE

Woman likes to believe that love can achieve anything. It is her peculiar superstition.

[*Ibid*]

Love is the state in which man sees things most decidedly as they are not.

[*The Antichrist* 1888]

Thomas Otway, 1652–85, English dramatist
O woman! lovely woman! Nature made thee
To temper man: we had been brutes without you;
Angels are painted fair, to look like you;
There's in you all that we believe of heaven –
Amazing brightness, purity, and truth,
Eternal joy, and everlasting love.

[*Venice Preserv'd* 1682]

Dorothy [Rothschild] Parker, 1893–1967, American writer
Four be the things I'd been better without:
Love, curiosity, freckles, and doubt.

[*Enough Rope: Inventory* 1926]

Life is a glorious cycle of song
A medley of extemporania,
And love is a thing that can never go wrong
And I am Marie of Rumania.

[*Comment*]

Blaise Pascal, 1623–62, French mathematician and writer
Le coeur a ses raisons que la raison ne connait point.
The heart has its reasons, of which reason knows nothing.

[*Pensées* 1670]

Octavio Paz, 1914–98 , Mexican poet
Love is an attempt at penetrating another being, but it can only succeed if the surrender is mutual.

[*The Labyrinth of Solitude* 1950]

Thomas Love Peacock, 1785–1866, English essayist and poet
Love is to be avoided because marriage is at best a dangerous experiment.

[*Gryll Grange* 1861]

Plato, c.428–348BC, Greek philosopher
At the touch of love everyone becomes a poet.

[*Symposium c.*360BC]

Edgar Allan Poe, 1809–49, American writer
I was a child and she was a child,
In this kingdom by the sea,
But we loved with a love that was more than love –
I and my Annabel Lee –
With a love that the winged seraphs of heaven
Coveted her and me.

[*Annabel Lee* 1849]

Alexander Pope, 1688–1744, English poet

Where'er you walk, cool gales shall fan the glade,
Trees, where you sit, shall crowd into a shade:
Where'er you tread, the blushing flowers shall rise
And all things flourish where you turn your eyes.

[Pastorals: Summer 1709]

How loved, how honour'd once, avails thee not,
To whom related, or by whom begot.

[Elegy to the Memory of an Unfortunate Lady 1717]

Love, free as air, at sight of human ties,
Spreads his light wings, and in a moment flies.

[Eloisa to Abelard 1717]

And love th' offender, yet detest th' offence.

[Ibid]

What reason weaves, by passion is undone.

[Essay on Man 1732–4]

The ruling passion, be it what it will,
The ruling passion conquers reason still.

[Moral Essays 1731–5]

Ezra [Loomis] Pound, 1855–1972, American poet

As a bathtub lined with white porcelain,
When the hot water gives out or goes tepid,
So is the slow cooling of our chivalrous passion,
O my much praised but-not-altogether satisfactory lady.

[The Bath Tub]

Sextus Propertius, c. 50BC–c.AD16, Roman poet

Love is fostered by confidence and constancy; he who is able to give much is able also to love much.

[Elegies c.20BC]

Jean [Baptiste] Racine, 1639–99, French dramatist

Ce n'est plus une ardeur dans mes veines cachée;
C'est Vénus toute entière a sa proie attachée.
It is no longer a passion hidden in my veins; it is Venus' very self fastened on her prey.

[Phèdre 1677]

Sir Walter Raleigh, c.1552–1618, English explorer and poet

If all the world and love were young,
And truth in every shepherd's tongue,
These pretty pleasures might me move
To live with thee, and be thy love.

[The Nymph's Reply to the Passionate Shepherd]

Silence in love betrays more woe
Than words, though ne'er so witty!

[The Silent Lover]

So the heart be right, it is no matter which way the head lieth.

[Said at his execution]

LOVE

Sir Walter Alexander Raleigh, 1861–1922, English academic
I wish I loved the Human Race;
I wish I loved its silly face;
I wish I liked the way it walks;
I wish I liked the way it talks;
And when I'm introduced to one
I wish I thought *What Jolly Fun!*

[*Laughter from a Cloud*]

Ernest Percival Rhys, 1859–1946, Welsh writer
Wales England wed; so I was bred. 'Twas merry London gave me breath.
I dreamt of love, and fame; I strove. But Ireland taught me love was best.

[*An Autobiography*]

Jean Paul Richter, 1763–1825, German novelist
Love diminishes the delicacy of women and increases that of men.

[*Titan* 1803]

François, Duc de La Rochefoucauld, 1613–80, French writer
One can find women who have never had a love affair, but it is rare to find a woman who has had only one.

[*Reflections, or Sentences and Moral Maxims* 1665]

True love is like ghosts, which everybody talks about but few have seen.

[*Ibid*]

The pleasure of love is in loving. We are happier in the passion we feel than in that we arouse.

[*Ibid*]

Samuel Rogers, 1763–1855, English poet
Oh. she was good as she was fair!
None – none on earth above her!
As pure in thought as angels are,
To know her was to love her.

[*Jacqueline*]

John Ruskin, 1819–1900, English art critic and writer
Trust thou thy Love: if she be proud, is she not sweet?
Trust thou thy Love: if she be mute, is she not pure?
Lay thou thy soul full in her hands, low at her feet;
Fail, Sun and Breath! – yet, for they peace, she shall endure.

[*Trust Thou Thy Love*]

Bertrand [Arthur William] Russell, 3rd Earl Russell, 1872–1970, English philosopher
To fear love is to fear life, and those who fear life are already three parts dead.

[*Marriage and Morals* 1929]

Antoine de Saint-Exupéry, 1900–1944, French aviator and writer
It is only with the heart that one can see rightly; what is essential is invisible to the eye.

[*The Little Prince* 1943]

George Savile, 1st Marquis of Halifax, 1633–95, English statesman
Love is a passion that hath friends in the garrison.

[*Advice to a Daughter* 1688]

Alexander Scott, c.1525–c.1584, Scottish poet
Luve is ane fervent fire,
Kendillit without desire:
Short plesour, lang displesour,
Repentance is the hire.

[*Lo! What it is to Luve*]

Sir Walter Scott, 1771–1832, Scottish novelist and poet
In peace, Love tunes the shepherd's reed;
In war, he mounts the warrior's steed;
In halls, in gay attire is seen;
In hamlets, dances on the green.
Love rules the court, the camp, the grove,
And men below, and saints above;
For love is heaven, and heaven is love.

[*The Lay of the Last Minstrel* 1805]

Her blue eyes sought the west afar,
For lovers love the western star.

[*Ibid*]

True love's the gift which God has given
To man alone beneath the heaven.

[*Ibid*]

It is the secret sympathy,
The silver link, the silken tie,
Which heart to heart, and mind to mind,
In body and in soul can bind.

[*Ibid*]

So faithful in love, and so dauntless in war,
There never was knight like the young Lochinvar.

[*Marmion: Lochinvar* 1808]

For a laggard in love, and a dastard in war,
Was to wed the fair Ellen of brave Lochinvar.

[*Ibid*]

O Woman! in our hours of ease,
Uncertain, coy, and hard to please,
And variable as the shade
By the light quivering aspen made;
When pain and anguish wring the brow
A ministering angel thou!

[*Ibid*]

Erich Segal, 1937– , American author and filmwriter
Love means never having to say you're sorry.

[*Love Story* film 1970]

Thomas Shadwell, c.1642–1692, English dramatist
'Tis the way of all flesh.

[*The Sullen Lovers* 1668]

Every man loves what he is good at.

[*A True Widow*]

LOVE

William Shakespeare, 1564–1616, English dramatist

She is a woman, therefore may be woo'd;
She is a woman, therefore may be won;
She is Lavinia, therefore must be loved.

[Titus Andronicus 2 1593–4]

Love comforteth like sunshine after rain,
But Lust's effect is tempest after sun;
Love's gentle spring doth always fresh remain,
Lust's winter comes ere summer half be done:
Love surfeits not, Lust like a glutton dies;
Love is all truth, Lust full of forged lies.

[Venus and Adonis 1593]

O, how this spring of love resembleth
The uncertain glory of an April day!

[The Two Gentlemen of Verona 1 1594–5]

A lover's eyes will gaze an eagle blind;
A lover's ear will hear the lowest sound.

[Love's Labour's Lost 4 1594–5]

And when Love speaks, the voice of all the gods
Make heaven drowsy with the harmony.

[Ibid]

A pair of star-cross'd lovers.

[Romeo and Juliet prologue 1594–5]

And in this state she gallops night by night
Through lovers' brains, and then they dream of love.

[Ibid]

See, how she leans her cheek upon her hand!
O that I were a glove upon that hand,
That I might touch that cheek!

[Ibid]

O Romeo, Romeo! wherefore art thou Romeo?

[Ibid]

What's in a name? that which we call a rose
By any other name would smell as sweet.

[Ibid]

At lovers' perjuries,
They say, Jove laughs.

[Ibid]

O, swear not by the moon, the inconstant moon,
That monthly changes in her circled orb,
Lest that thy love prove likewise variable.

[Ibid]

Love goes toward love, as schoolboys from their books,
But love from love, toward school with heavy looks.

[Ibid]

How silver-sweet sound lovers' tongues by night,
Like softest music to attending ears!

[Ibid]

Spread thy close curtain, love-performing night,
That runaways' eyes may wink, and Romeo
Leap to these arms, untalk'd of and unseen.

[Ibid 3]

Give me my Romeo; and, when he shall die,
Take him and cut him out in little stars,
And he will make the face of heaven so fine
That all the world will be in love with night
And pay no worship to the garish sun.

[*Ibid*]

For aught that I could ever read,
Could ever hear by tale or history,
The course of true love never did run smooth.

[*A Midsummer Night's Dream* 1 1595–6]

O hell! to choose love by another's eyes.

[*Ibid*]

Love looks not with the eyes, but with the mind;
And therefore is wing'd Cupid painted blind.

[*Ibid*]

Yet mark'd I where the bolt of Cupid fell:
It fell upon a little western flower,
Before milk-white, now purple with love's wound,
And maidens call it love-in-idleness.

[*Ibid* 2]

The lover, all as frantic,
Sees Helen's beauty in a brow of Egypt.

[*Ibid* 5]

But love is blind and lovers cannot see
The pretty follies that themselves commit.

[*The Merchant of Venice* 2 1596–7]

I am bewitched with the rogue's company. If the rascal have not given me medicines to make me love him, I'll be hanged.

[*King Henry IV, Part I* 2 1597–8]

Is it not strange that desire should so many years outlive performance?

[*King Henry IV, Part II* 2 1597–8]

Speak low, if you speak love.

[*Much Ado About Nothing* 2 1598–1600]

Sigh no more, ladies, sigh no more,
Men were deceivers ever,
One foot on sea and one on shore,
To one thing constant never.

[*Ibid*]

Shall quips and sentences and these paper bullets of the brain awe a man from the career of his humour? No, the world must be peopled. When I said I would die a bachelor, I did not think I should live till I were married.

[*Ibid*]

Taming my wild heart to thy loving hand.

[*Ibid* 3]

We that are true lovers run into strange capers.

[*As You Like It* 2 1598–1600]

And then the lover,
Sighing like furnace, with a woeful ballad
Made to his mistress' eyebrow.

[*Ibid*]

LOVE

If ever, – as that ever may be near, –
You meet in some fresh cheek the power of fancy,
Then shall you know the wounds invisible
That love's keen arrows make.

[Ibid 3]

Down on your knees,
And thank heaven, fasting, for a good man's love.

[Ibid]

Dead shepherd, now I find thy saw of might,
"Who ever loved that loved not at first sight?"

[Ibid quoting Marlowe, see above]

No sooner met but they looked, no sooner looked but they loved, no sooner loved but they
sighed, no sooner sighed but they asked one another the reason, no sooner knew the reason
but they sought the remedy.

[Ibid 5]

It was a lover and his lass,
With a hey, and a ho, and a hey nonino,
That o'er the green corn-field did pass
In the spring time, the only pretty ring time,
When birds do sing, hey ding a ding, ding:
Sweet lovers love the spring.

[Ibid]

O mistress mine, where are you roaming?
O, stay and hear; your true love's coming,
That can sing both high and low:
Trip no further, pretty sweeting;
Journeys end in lovers meeting,
Every wise man's son doth know.

[Twelfth Night 2 1598–1600]

Love sought is good, but given unsought is better.

[Ibid 3]

Though last, not least in love.

[Julius Caesar 3 1598–1600]

When love begins to sicken and decay,
It useth an enforced ceremony.

[Ibid 4]

Doubt thou the stars are fire;
Doubt that the sun doth move;
Doubt truth to be a liar;
But never doubt I love.

[Hamlet 2 1600–1601]

Ophelia: 'Tis brief, my lord.
Hamlet: As woman's love.

[Ibid 3]

To be wise and love
Exceeds man's might.

[Troilus and Cressida 3 1601–3]

Love all, trust a few,
Do wrong to none: be able for thine enemy
Rather in power than use, and keep thy friend
Under thy own life's key: be check'd for silence,
But never tax'd for speech.

[All's Well That Ends Well 1 1601–3]

'Twere all one
That I should love a bright particular star
And think to wed it, he is so above me.

[Ibid]

The hind that would be mated by the lion
Must die for love.

[Ibid]

Take, O, take those lips away
That so sweetly were forsworn;
And those eyes, the break of day,
Lights that do mislead the morn:
But my kisses bring again, bring again;
Seals of love, but seal'd in vain, seal'd in vain.

[Measure for Measure 4 1604–5]

Your daughter and the Moor are now making the beast with two backs.

[Othello 1 1604–5]

I will a round unvarnish'd tale deliver
Of my whole course of love.

[Ibid]

She thank'd me,
And bade me, if I had a friend that loved her,
I should but teach him how to tell my story,
And that would woo her. Upon this hint I spake:
She loved me for the dangers I had pass'd,
And I loved her that she did pity them.
This only is the witchcraft I have used.

[Ibid]

But I do love thee! and when I love thee not,
Chaos is come again.

[Ibid 3]

Then must you tell
Of one that loved not wisely but too well;
Of one not easily jealous, but being wrought
Perplex'd in the extreme.

[Ibid 5]

There's beggary in the love that can be reckon'd.

[Antony and Cleopatra 1 1606–7]

If thou and nature can so gently part,
The stroke of death is as a lover's pinch
Which hurts, and is desired.

[Ibid 5]

LOVE

Fear no more the lightning-flash,
Nor the all-dreaded thunder-stone;
Fear not slander, censure rash;
Thou hast finish'd joy and moan;
All lovers young, all lovers must
Consign to thee, and come to dust.

[*Cymbeline* 4 1609–10]

So true a fool is love that in your will,
Though you do any thing, he thinks no ill.

[*Sonnets* 52]

Love's not Time's fool, though rosy lips and cheeks
Within his bending sickle's compass come.

[*Ibid* 16]

I think there is not half a kiss to choose
Who loves another best.

[*The Winter's Tale* 4 1610–11]

Ferdinand: Here's my hand.
Miranda: And mine, with my heart in't.

[*The Tempest* 3 1611–12]

Love thyself last: cherish those hearts that hate thee.

[*King Henry VIII* 3 1613]

George Bernard Shaw, 1856–1950, Irish playwright
When we want to read of the deeds that are done for love, whither do we turn? To the murder
column.

[*Three Plays for Puritans*: preface 1901]

You think that you are Ann's suitor; that you are the pursuer and she the pursued; that it is
your part to woo, to persuade, to prevail, to overcome. Fool: it is you who are the pursued, the
marked-down quarry, the destined.

[*Man and Superman* 1903]

Percy Bysshe Shelley, 1792–1822, English poet
I never was attached to that great sect,
Whose doctrine is, that each one should select
Out of the crowd a mistress or a friend,
And all the rest, though fair and wise, commend
To cold oblivion.

[*Epipsychidion* 1821]

True Love in this differs from gold and clay,
That to divide is not to take away.

[*Ibid*]

Fame is love disguised.

[*Ibid*]

The wise want love; and those who love want wisdom;
And all best things are thus confused to ill.

[*Prometheus Unbound* 1820]

All love is sweet,
Given or returned. Common as light is love,
And its familiar voice wearies not ever.
They who inspire it as most fortunate,
As I am now; but those who feel it most
Are happier still.

[*Ibid*]

For love, and beauty, and delight,
There is no death, no change.

[*The Sensitive Plant*]

Nothing in the world is single;
All things by a law divine
In one spirit meet and mingle.
Why not I with thine.

[*Love's Philosophy*]

Richard Brinsley Sheridan, 1751–1816, English dramatist
An oyster may be crossed in love!

[*The Critic* 1779]

Sir Philip Sidney, 1554–86, English soldier, statesman and poet
My true love hath my heart and I have his,
By just exchange one for the other given.

[*Arcadia* 1581]

Sydney Smith, 1771–1845, English churchman
How can a bishop marry? How can he flirt? The most he can say is, "I will see you in the vestry after service."

[In Lady Holland's *Memoirs* 1855]

Sophocles, c.496–c.406BC, Greek poet
Love, unconquered in battle.

[*Antigone*]

Thomas Southerne, 1660–1746, Anglo-Irish dramatist
Pity's akin to love.

[*Oroonoko* 1695]

Edmund Spenser, c.1552–1599, English poet
So let us love, dear love, like as we ought,
– Love is the lesson which the Lord us taught.

[*Amoretti* 1595]

One day I wrote her name upon the sand
But came the waves and washed it away:
Again I wrote it with a second hand
But came the tide, and made my pains his prey.

[*Ibid*]

Open the temple gates unto my love,
Open them wide that she may enter in.

[*Epithalamion* 1595]

Ah! when will this long weary day have end,
And lend me leave to come unto my love?

[*Ibid*]

LOVE

Fierce wars and faithful loves shall moralize my song.

[*The Faerie Queen* 1590–6]

And all for love, and nothing for reward.

[*Ibid*]

Philip Dormer Stanhope, 4th Earl of Chesterfield, 1694–1773, English statesman
Women are much more like each other than men: they have, in truth, but two passions, vanity and love.

[*Letters to His Son* 1749]

Sir Richard Steele, 1672–1729, Anglo-Irish essayist
Women dissemble their passions better than men, but men subdue their passions better than women.

[*The Lover* 1714]

Laurence Sterne, 1713–68, English churchman and writer
Love, an' please your Honour, is exactly like war, in this; that a soldier, though he has escaped three weeks complete o' Saturday night, – may, nevertheless, be shot though his heart on Sunday morning.

[*Tristram Shandy* 1760]

I had an affair with the moon, in which there was neither sin nor shame.

[*A Sentimental Journey* 1768]

Having been in love with one princess or another almost all my life, and I hope I shall go on so, till I die, being firmly persuaded, that if I ever do a mean action, it must be in some interval betwixt one passion and another.

[*Ibid*]

Robert Louis [Balfour] Stevenson, 1850–94, Scottish novelist and poet
The friendly cow, all red and white,
I love with all my heart:
She gives me cream with all her might
To eat with apple-tart.

[*A Child's Garden of Verses* 1855]

Sir John Suckling, 1609–41, English poet
I prithee send me back my heart,
Since I cannot have thine:
For if from yours you will not part,
Why then shouldst thou have mine?

[*Song*]

Why so pale and wan, fond lover?
Prithee, why so pale?
Will, when looking well can't move her,
Looking ill prevail?

[*Algaura* 1638]

Out upon it, I have loved
Three whole days together
And am like to love three more,
If it prove fair weather.

[*A Poem with the Answer*]

'Tis love in love that makes the sport.

[*Sonnet*]

Alfred, Lord Tennyson, 1809–92, English poet
Dower'd with the hate of hate, the scorn of scorn,
The love of love.

[*The Poet*]

In the Spring a livelier iris changes on the burnish'd dove;
In the Spring a young man's fancy lightly turns to thoughts of love.

[*Locksley Hall* 1842]

He will hold thee, when his passion shall have spents its novel force,
Something better than his dog, a little dearer than his horse.

[*Ibid*]

Man is the hunter; woman is his game.

[*The Princess* 1847]

'Tis better to have loved and lost
Than never to have loved at all.

[*In Memoriam* 1850]

O that 'twere possible
After long grief and pain
To find the arms of my true love
Round me once again.

[*Maud* 1855]

To me
He is all fault who hath no fault at all:
For who loves me must have a touch of earth.

[*Idylls of the King: Lancelot and Elaine* 1859–85]

Sweet is true love though given in vain, in vain;
And sweet is death who puts an end to pain.

[*Ibid*]

We needs must love the highest when we see it.

[*Ibid: Guinevere*]

Terence [Publius Terentius Afer], c.195–159BC, Roman poet
Amantium irae amoris integratio est.
The quarrels of lovers are the renewal of love.

[*Heauton Timoroumenos*]

William Makepeace Thackeray, 1811–63, English novelist
Some cynical Frenchman has said that there are two parties to a love transaction; the one who loves and the other who condescends to be so treated.

[*Vanity Fair* 1847–8]

'Tis strange what a man may do, and a woman yet think him an angel.

[*The History of Henry Esmond* 1852]

Frederic Herbert Trench, 1865–1923, Irish poet
Come let us make love deathless, thou and I.

[*To Ardilia*]

Anthony Trollope, 1815–82, English novelist
There is no happiness in love, except at the end of an English novel.

[*Barchester Towers* 1857]

Those who have courage to love should have courage to suffer.

[*The Bertrams* 1859]

306

LOVE

Archbishop Desmond [Mpilo] Tutu, 1931– , South African churchman
Nothing is too much trouble for love.

[In Maomi Tutu's*The Words of Desmond Tutu* 1989]

Royall Tyler, 1757–1826, American writer
The chains of love are never so binding as when the links are made of gold.

[*The Contrast* 1790]

Miguel de Unamuno [y Jugo], 1864–1936, Spanish philosopher.
It is sad not be loved, but it is much sadder not to be able to love.

[*To a Young Writer*]

Sir John Vanburgh, 1664–1726, English dramatist and architect
I viewed her with a world of admiration, but not one glance of love.

[*The Relapse* 1696]

Sir Laurens Jan Van der Post, 1906–96, South African-born writer
Of all man's inborn dispositions there is none more heroic than the love in him. Everything else accepts defeat and dies, but love will fight no-love every inch of the way.

[*Flamingo Feather* 1955]

Virgil *or* Vergil [Publius Vergilius Maro], 70–19BC, Roman poet
Omnia vincit amor: et nos cedamus amori.
Love conquers all: and we succumb to love.

[*Eclogues* 37BC]

William Walsh, 1663–1708. English poet
And sadly reflecting
That a lover forsaken
A new love may get,
But a neck when once broken
Can never be set.

[*The Despairing Lover*]

Rowland Watkyns, *fl.* 1662, English writer
I love him not; but shew no reason can
Wherefore, but this, *I do not love the man.*

[*Flamma sine Fumo,* or *Poems without Fictions: Antipathy*]

Thomas Watson, c.1557–92, English poet
Love is a sour delight, a sugared grief,
A living death, an ever-dying life,
A breach of reason's law.

[*Hecatompathia* 1582]

Iaaac Watts, 1674–1748, English poet and hymn-writer
But, children, you should never let
Such angry passions rise;
Your little hands were never made
To tear each other's eyes.

[*Divine Songs for the use of Children* 1715]

Evelyn [Arthur St John] Waugh, 1903–66, English writer

She admitted that love was a thing one could grow to be fond of after a time, like smoking a pipe.

[Vile Bodies 1930]

Mae West, 1892–1980, American entertainer

It's not the men in my life that counts – it's the life in my men.

[I'm no Angel 1933]

William Whitehead, 1715–85, English poet

Yes, I'm in love, I feel it now,
And Celia has undone me!
And yet I'll swear I can't tell how
The pleasing plague stole on me.

[The Je ne sais quoi]

George John Whyte-Melville, 1721–78, Scottish writer

We always believe our first love is our last, and our last love our first.

[Katerfelto]

Oscar [Fingall O'Flahertie Wills] Wilde, 1854–1900, Irish writer

There is always something ridiculous about the passions of people whom one has ceased to love.

[The Picture of Dorian Grey1891]

Those who are faithful know only the trivial side of love; it is the faithless who know love's tragedies.

[Ibid]

Each passion being loth
For love's own sake to leave the other's side
Yet killing love by staying.

[The Burden of Itys]

To love oneself is the beginning of a lifelong romance, Phipps.

[An Ideal Husband 1895]

Yet each man kills the thing he loves,
By each let this be heard,
Some do it with a bitter look,
Some with a flattering word.
The coward does it with a kiss,
The brave man with a sword!

[The Ballad of Reading Gaol 1898]

Some kill their love when they are young
And some when they are old;
Some strangle with the hands of Lust,
Some with the hands of Gold:
The kindest use a knife, because
The dead so soon grow cold.

[Ibid]

LOVE

Some love too little, some too long,
Some sell, and others buy;
Some do the deed with many tears,
And some without a sigh;
For each man kills the thing he loves,
Yet each man does not die.

[*Ibid*]

John Wilmot, 2nd Earl of Rochester, 1647–80, English poet

I cannot change, as others do,
Though you unjustly scorn,
Since that poor swain that sights for you,
For you alone was born;
No, Phillis, no, your heart to move
A surer way I'll try –
And to revenge my slighted love
Will still love on, and die.

[*Constancy*]

Alas! 'tis sacred jealousy,
Love raised to an extreme:
The only proof 'twixt her and me
We love, and do not dream.

[*The Mistress*]

William Wordsworth, 1770–1850, English poet

What fond and wayward thoughts will slide
Into a lover's head! –
"O mercy!" to myself I cried,
"If Lucy should be dead!"

[*Strange Fits of Passion have I known*]

And you must love him, ere to you
He will seem worthy of your love.

[*A Poet's Epitaph*]

She gave me eyes, she gave me ears;
And humble cares, and delicate fears;
A heart, the fountain of sweet tears;
And love, and thought, and joy.

[*The Sparrow's Nest*]

William Butler Yeats, 1865–1939, Irish Poet

Danger no refuge holds, and war no peace,
For him who hears love sing and never cease.

[*The Rose of Battle* 1892]

Never give all the heart, for love
Will hardly seem worth thinking of
To passionate women if it seem
Certain, and they never dream
That it fades out from kiss to kiss.

[*Never Give all the Heart* 1905]

In middle life
They take a kiss for what a kiss is worth,
And let the dream go by.

[*The Shadowy Waters* 1906]

And she and I
Shall light upon a place in the world's core,
Where passion grows to be a changeless thing.

[*Ibid*]

There is not one among you that made love
By any other means. You call it passion,
Consideration, generosity;
But it was all deceit, and flattery
To win a woman in her own despite,
For love is war, and there is hatred in it.

[*Ibid*]

Do you not know
How great a wrong it is to let one's thought
Wander a moment when one is in love?

[*Ibid*]

He might have had my sister,
My cousins by the score,
But nothing satisfied the fool
But my dear Mary Moore,
None other knows what pleasures man
At table or in bed.
What shall I do for pretty girls
Now my old bawd is dead?

[*John Kinsella's Lament for Mrs Mary Moore* 1938]

The Media

Anonymous

No news is good news.

[Proverb]

Jean Anouilh, 1910–87, French dramatist

Have you noticed that life, real honest to goodness life, with murders, and catastrophes and fabulous inheritances, happens almost exclusively in newspapers?

[*The Rehearsal*]

W[ystan] H[ugh] Auden, 1907–73, English-born poet

What the mass media offer is not popular art, but entertainment which is intended to be consumed like food, forgotten, and replaced by a new dish.

[*The Dyer's Hand: The Poet and the City*]

Stanley Baldwin, 1st Earl Baldwin of Bewdley, 1867–1947, British statesman

What the proprietorship of these papers is aiming at is power, and power without responsibility – the prerogative of the harlot throughout the ages.

[On the press barons, Lords Beaverbrook and Rothermere]

Cristobal Balenciaga, 1895–1972, Spanish-born French fashion designer

If you want publicity – add a touch of vulgarity.

[In *The Sunday Telegraph* 1968]

[Enoch] Arnold Bennett, 1867–1931, English novelist

Journalists say a thing that they know isn't true in the hope that if they keep on saying it long enough it *will* be true.

[*The Title*]

The Bible

As cold waters to a thirsty soul, so is good news from a far country.

[*Proverbs* 25:25]

[Mark] James [Walter] Cameron, 1911–85, Scottish-born journalist

The press can only be a mirror – albeit a distorting mirror, according to its politics or the smallness of its purpose – but it rarely lies because it dare not.

[In *The Listener* 1979]

Eric Cantona, 1966– , French footballer
[On press interest in his court appearance for assault] When the seagulls follow the trawler, it is because they think sardines will be thrown into the sea.

[In the *Independent* April 1995]

G[ilbert] K[eith] Chesterton, 1874–1936, English writer
And the faith of the poor is faint and partial,
And the pride of the rich is all for sale,
And the chosen heralds of England's Marshal
Are the sandwich-men of the *Daily Mail*.

[*A Song of Defeat*]

Cyril Connolly, 1903–74, English writer
Literature is the art of writing something that will be read twice; journalism what will be grasped at once.

[*Enemies of Promise* 1938]

Alan Coren, 1938– , English humorist
Television is more interesting than people. If it were not, we should have people standing in the corners of our rooms.

Sir Noel [Pierce] Coward, 1899–1973, English actor and playwright
Television is for appearing on, not looking at.

[Attributed]

Quentin Crisp, 1908–99, English eccentric and writer
If any reader of this book is in the grip of some habit of which he is deeply ashamed, I advise him not to give way to it in secret but to do it on television. No one will pass him by with averted gaze on the other side of the street. People will cross the road at the risk of losing their own lives in order to say "We saw you on the telly."

[*How to Become a Virgin* 1981]

Charles Anderson Dana, 1819–97, American newspaper editor
When a dog bites a man that is not news, but when a man bites a dog that is news.

[*What is News?* in the *New York Sun* 1882]

[George] Norman Douglas, 1868–1952, English novelist
You can tell the ideals of a nation by its advertisements.

[*South Wind* 1917]

T[homas] S[tearns] Eliot, 1888–1965, American-born English poet
[Television] is a medium of entertainment which permits millions of people to listen to the same joke at the same time, and yet remain lonesome.

[In *The New York Post* 1963]

Harold Evans, 1928– , English-born journalist
A headline is not an act of journalism, it is an act of marketing.

[*Sunday Times* 1981]

Henry Fielding, 1707–54, English novelist
A newspaper, which consists of just the same number of words, whether there be any news in it or not . . . may, likewise, be compared to a stagecoach, which performs constantly the same course, empty as well as full.

[*Tom Jones* 1749]

David [Parradine] Frost, 1939– , English television personality
Television is an invention that permits you to be entertained in your living room by people you wouldn't have in your home.

[*David Frost Revue* CBS TV 1971]

Sir James Goldsmith, 1933–97, English businessman
Gossip columnists are diseases, like flu. Everyone is subject to them.

[In *Time* 1978]

Samuel Goldwyn, 1882–1974, Polish-born American film producer
Why should people go out and pay money to see bad films when they can stay at home and see bad television for nothing?

[In *The Observer* 1956]

Frederic William Goudy, 1865–1947, American type designer
I am the voice of today, the herald of tomorrow . . . I am the leaden army that conquers the world – I am TYPE.

[*The Type Speaks*]

[Henry] Grahame Greene, 1904–91, English novelist
Media is a word that has come to mean bad journalism.

[*Ways of Escape* 1981]

Frank McKinney ("Kin") Hubbard, 1868–1930 American humorist
Editor: a person employed by a newspaper whose business it is to separate the wheat from the chaff and to see that only the chaff is printed.

[*A Thousand and One Epigrams*]

Richard Ingrams, 1937– , English journalist
Children watch too much television not only because indolent parents allow them to, but because the standard of most programmes is pitched at their level.

[In *The Observer* 1977]

My own motto is publish and be sued.

[BBC Radio, May 4, 1977]

Mick [Michel Philip] Jagger, 1943– , English rock singer
It's really difficult to get out of gossip columns once you've got in.

Clive [Vivian Leopold] James, 1939– , Australian broadcaster and writer
A TV programme can never be worse than its viewers; for the more stupid it is, the more stupid they are to watch it.

[In *The Observer* 1980]

Anyone who is afraid of what he thinks television does to the world is probably just afraid of the world.

[*Glued to the Box* 1983]

The greatest risk to the television critic is bedsores.

[*Ibid*]

Thomas Jefferson, 1743–1826, 3rd president of the United States
Were it left to me to decide whether we should have a government without newspapers or newspapers without a government, I should not hesitate for a moment to prefer the latter.

[1787]

Where the press is free and every man able to read, all is safe.

[Letter 1816]

Lyndon Baines Johnson, 1908–73, 36th president of the United States
Reporters are puppets. They simply respond to the pull of the most powerful strings.

Pauline Kael, 1919–2001, American film critic
The words "Kiss Kiss Bang Bang" which I saw on an Italian movie poster are perhaps the briefest statement imaginable of the basic appeal of the movies.

[*Kiss Kiss Bang Bang* 1968]

Rudyard Kipling, 1865–1936, English writer
King over all he children of pride
Is the Press – the Press – the Press!

[*The Press*]

Ernie Kovacs, 1919–62, American comedian
Television – a medium. So called because it is neither rare nor well done.

[In Halliwell's *The Filmgoer's Book of Quotes* 1973]

Louis Kronenberger, 1904–80, American critic
It is the gossip columnist's business to write about what is none of his business.

[*The Cart and the Horse* 1964]

Dorothea Lange, 1895–1965, American photographer
While there is perhaps a province in which the photograph can tell us nothing more than what we see with our own eyes, there is another in which it proves to us how little our eyes permit us to see.

Fran Lebowitz, 1951– , American journalist and writer
Educational television should be absolutely forbidden. It can only lead to unreasonable disappointment when your child discovers that the letters of the alphabet do not leap out of books and dance around with royal-blue chickens.

[*Metropolitan Life* 1978]

Walter Lippmann, 1889–1974, American journalist
In order to avoid the embarrassment of calling a spade a spade, newspapermen have agreed to talk about the credibility gap. This is a polite euphemism for deception.

[1967]

George Lois, 1931– , American advertising executive
Most advertising is absolutely awful, easily forgotten, invisible garbage. *That's* why most advertising is ignored.

[*The Art of Advertising* 1977]

Lord Longford [Francis Aungier Pakenham], 7th Earl of Longford, 1905–2001, English politician
On the whole I would not say that our Press is obscene. I would say that it trembles on the brink of obscenity.

[In the *Observer* 1963]

Anita Loos, 1893–1981, American writer
If we have to kiss Hollywood goodbye, it may be with one of those tender, old-fashioned, seven-second kisses as exchanged between two people of the opposite sex with all their clothes on.

[In *New York Herald Tribune* 1974]

[Herbert] Marshall McLuhan, 1911–80, Canadian educator
The medium is the message. This is merely to say that the personal and social consequences of any medium . . . result from the new scale that is introduced into our affairs by each extension of ourselves or by any new technology.

[*Understanding Media* 1964]

Advertising is the greatest art form of the twentieth century.

[*Advertising Age*]

Norman Mailer, 1923– , American novelist and essayist
Once a newspaper touches a story, the facts are lost forever, even to the protagonists.

[*The Presidential Papers* 1963]

Groucho [Julius Henry] Marx, 1895–1977, American comedian
I find television very educational. Every time someone switches it on I go into another room and read a good book.

[*The Groucho Papers*]

George Mason, 1725–92, American revolutionary
The freedom of the press is one of the great bulwarks of liberty, and can never be restrained but by despotic governments.

[*Virginia Bill of Rights* 1776]

Margaret Mead, 1901–78, American anthropologist
For the first time the young are seeing history being made before it is censored by their elders.

Sir Yehudi Menuhin, 1916–99, American-born British violinist
Whenever I see a newspaper, I think of the poor trees. As trees they provide beauty, shade and shelter, but as paper all they provide is rubbish.

[1970]

Arthur Miller, 1915– , American playwright
A good newspaper, I suppose, is a nation talking to itself.

[In the *Observer* November 26 1961]

Slobodan Milosevic, 1941– , Serbian politician
In the West, we see a complete media darkness where it comes to Yugoslavia, because world global networks have been assigned the task of being an instrument of war and of disinforming the public.

[Address to U.N. War Crimes Tribunal February 14 2002]

John Milton, 1608–74, English poet
For evil news rides post, while good news waits.

[*Samson Agonistes* 1671]

Malcolm Muggeridge, 1903–90, English journalist
Television was not invented to make human beings vacuous, but is an emanation of their vacuity.

[*Tread Softly For You Tread on My Jokes* 1966]

[Keith] Rupert Murdoch, 1931– , Australian-born American media entrepreneur
British journalism will not suffer from a little less alcohol.

[In the *Sydney Morning Herald* February 8 1989]

Newsweek Magazine
Almost from the moment the horror occurred, television changed. It was no longer a small box containing entertainment, news, and sports; suddenly, it was a window opening onto violently unpredictable life in Washington and Dallas, where a President had been assassinated.

[Following the assassination of President John F Kennedy, 1963]

Lord Northcliffe [Alfred Charles William Harmsworth, 1st Viscount Northcliffe], 1865–1922, English newspaper proprietor
It is hard news that catches the readers. Features hold them.

[In T. Clarke's *My Northcliffe Diary*]

[On journalism] A profession whose business it is to explain to others what it personally does not understand.

Adolph Simon Ochs, 1858–1935, American publisher
All the news that's fit to print.

[Motto of the *New York Times*]

David [MacKenzie] Ogilvie, 1911– , English-born American advertising executive
The consumer is not a moron. She is *your wife*. And she is grown up.

[In *New York Herald Tribune* 1956]

John [Henry] O'Hara, 1905–70, American novelist
Hot lead can be almost as effective coming from a linotype as from a firearm.

[Introduction to *The Portable F. Scott Fitzgerald* 1945]

George Orwell [Eric Arthur Blair], 1903–50, English novelist and critic
Advertising is the rattling of a stick inside a swill bucket.

Wendell Phillips, 1811–84, American orator and reformer
We live under a government of men and morning newspapers.

[Address: The Press]

Theodore Roosevelt, 1858–1919, 26th president of the United States
The men with the muck-rake are often indispensable to the well-being of society, but only if they know when to stop raking the muck.

[Address 1906]

C[harles] P[restwich] Scott, 1846–1932, English newspaper editor
The newspaper is of necessity something of a monopoly, and its first duty is to shun the temptations of monopoly. Its primary office is the gathering of news. At the peril of its soul it must see that the supply is not tainted. Neither in what it gives, nor in what it does not give,

nor in the mode of presentation, must the unclouded face of truth suffer wrong. Comment is free but facts are sacred.

[In the *Manchester Guardian* 1926]

Television? The word is half Latin and half Greek. No good can come of it.

[Attributed]

William Shakespeare 1564–1616, English dramatist
Here are a few of the unpleasant'st words
That ever blotted paper.

[*The Merchant of Venice* 3 1596–7]

Yet the first bringer of unwelcome news
Hath but a losing office, and his tongue
Sounds ever after as a sullen bell,
Remember'd tolling a departed friend.

[*King Henry IV, Part II* 1 1597–8]

The nature of bad news infects the teller.

[*Antony and Cleopatra* 1 1606–7]

Though it be honest, it is never good
To bring bad news.

[*Ibid* 5]

Richard Brinsley Sheridan, 1751–1816, English dramatist
The newspapers! Sir, they are the most villainous – licentious – abominable – infernal – Not that I ever read them – no – I make it a rule never to look into a newspaper.

[*The Critic* 1779]

H[arry] Allen Smith, 1907–76, American humorist
Some performers on television appear to be horrible people, but when you finally get to know them in person, they turn out to be even worse.

[*Let the Crabgrass Grow* 1960]

Susan Sontag, 1933– , American critic and writer
Reality has come to seem more and more like what we are shown by cameras.

[*Photography Unlimited* in the *New York Review of Books* 1977]

Sir Tom Stoppard [Thomas Straussler], 1937– , Czech-born British dramatist
I'm with you on the free press. It's the newspapers I can't stand.

[*Night and Day* 1 1978]

The media. It sounds like a convention of spiritualists.

[*Night and Day* 1 1978]

Gore [Eugene Luther] Vidal, 1925– , American novelist and critic
The aim of so much journalism is to exploit the moral prejudices of the reader, to say nothing of those of the proprietor.

[In *Nova* 1969]

Voltaire [François Marie Arouet], 1694–1778, French philosopher and writer
In the case of news, we should always wait for the sacrament of confirmation.

Barbara Ward, 1914–81, English economist
The modern world is not given to uncritical admiration. It expects its idols to have feet of clay, and can be reasonably sure that press and camera will report their exact dimensions.

[In *Saturday Review* 1961]

Evelyn [Arthur St John] Waugh, 1903–66, English writer
News is what a chap who doesn't care much about anything wants to read.

[*Scoop* 1938]

Fay Weldon, 1933– , English novelist
Go to work on an egg.

[Advertising slogan]

Katherine Whitehorn, 1926– , English journalist
My brother cuts the time it takes to read a newspaper by skipping everything in the future tense, and it's amazing what he doesn't miss.

[*Sunday Best: Never Never Land*]

Oscar [Fingall O'Flahertie Wills] Wilde, 1854–1900, Irish writer
As for modern journalism, it is not by business to defend it. It justifies its own existence by the great Darwinian principle of the survival of the vulgarest.

[*Intentions: The Critic as Artist* 1891]

There is much to be said in favour of modern journalism. By giving us the opinions of the uneducated, it keeps us in touch with the ignorance of the community.

[*Ibid*]

The Lords Temporal say nothing, the Lords Spiritual have nothing to say, and the House of Commons has nothing to say and says it. We are dominated by Journalism.

[*The Soul of Man under Socialism* 1891]

Billy [Samuel] Wilder, 1906– , Austrian-born American film director
Television is . . . a twenty-one inch person. I'm delighted with it, because it used to be that films were the lowest form of art. Now we've got something to look down on.

[In Leslie Halliwell's *Filmgoer's Book of Quotes* 1973]

William Butler Yeats, 1865–1939, Irish poet
A journalist makes up his lies
And takes you by the throat.

[*The Old Stone Cross* 1938]

Money and Wealth

John Quincy Adams, 1767–1848, 6th president of the United States
The extremes of opulence and want are more remarkable, and more constantly obvious, in this country than in any other that I ever saw.

[*Diary* 1816]

Abbé Leonor Jean d'Allainval, c.1700–1753, French writer
L'embarrases des richesses.
(The embarrassment of riches.)

[Title of play 1726]

Woody Allen [Allen Stewart Konigsberg], 1935– , American writer, actor and film director
Money is better than poverty, if only for financial reasons.

[*Without Feathers* 1972]

Martin Amis, 1949– , English writer
Making lots of money – it's not that hard, you know. It's overestimated. Making money is a breeze. You watch.

[*Money* 1984]

Anonymous
It's the same the whole world over;
It's the poor that gets the blame,
It's the rich that gets the pleasure.
Isn't it a blooming shame?

[*She Was Poor But She Was Honest*]

If you put nothing into your purse, you can take nothing out.

[Proverb]

Money, like manure, does no good till it is spread.

[Proverb]

Aristotle, 384–322BC, Greek philosopher
Men are divided between those who are as thrifty as if they would live forever, and those who are as extravagant as if they were going to die the next day.

[In Diogenes Laertius' *Lives and Opinions of Eminent Philosophers*]

The character which results from wealth is that of a prosperous fool.

[*Rhetoric c.*322BC]

Jane Austen, 1775–1817, English novelist

An annuity is a very serious business; it comes over and over every year, and there is no getting rid of it.

[*Sense and Sensibility* 1811]

Francis Bacon, Baron Verulam of Verulam and Viscount of St Albans, 1561–1626, English philosopher

And money is like muck, not good except it be spread.

[*Essays: Of Seditions and Troubles*]

Riches are for spending.

[*Essays: Of Expense*]

Of great riches, there is no real use, except it be in distribution; the rest is but conceit.

[*Essays: Of Riches*]

Walter Bagehot, 1826–77, English economist and journalist

Poverty is an anomaly to rich people. It is very difficult to make out why people who want dinner do not ring the bell.

[*Literary Studies* 1879]

Maurice Baring, 1874–1945, English writer

If you would know what the Lord God thinks of money, you have only to look at those to whom he gives it.

[In Dorothy Parker's *Writers at Work* 1958]

Aphra Behn, 1640–89, English playwright

Money speaks sense in a language all nations understand.

[*The Rover*]

Edward Bellamy, 1850–98, American writer

An American credit card . . . is just as good in Europe as American gold used to be.

[*Looking Backward, 2000–1887* 1888]

[Joseph] Hilaire [Pierre] Belloc, 1870–1953, English writer

I'm tired of Love: I'm still more tired of Rhyme.
But Money gives me pleasure all the time.

[*Epigrams: Fatigue*]

Jack Benny, 1894–1974, American comedian

I don't want to tell you how much insurance I carry with the Prudential, but all I can say is: when I go, they go.

[Attributed]

The Bible

A good name is rather to be chosen than great riches, and loving favour rather than silver and gold.

[*Proverbs* 22:1]

Wilt thou set thine eyes upon that which is not? for riches certainly make themselves wings; they fly away as an eagle toward heaven.

[*Ibid* 23:5]

It is easier for a camel to go through the eye of a needle, than for a rich man to enter into the kingdom of God.

[*Matthew* 19:24]

For the love of money is the root of all evil.

[*1 Timothy* 6:10]

William Jennings Bryan, 1860–1925, American statesman
We will answer their demand for a gold standard by saying to them: You shall not press down upon the brow of labour this crown of thorn. You shall not crucify mankind upon a cross of gold.

[Speech 1896]

Samuel Butler, 1612–80, English poet
What makes all doctrines plain and clear?
About two hundred pounds a year.
And that which was prov'd true before,
Prove false again? Two hundred more.

[*Hudibras* 1664]

Samuel Butler, 1835–1902, English writer
It has been said that the love of money is the root of all evil. The want of money is so quite as truly.

[*Erewhon* 1872]

All progress is based upon a universal innate desire on the part of every organism to live beyond its income.

[*Note Books c.*1890]

Byron, Lord George Gordon [Noel], 6th Baron Byron of Rochdale, 1788–1824, English poet
Ready money is Aladdin's lamp.

[*Don Juan* 1819–24]

Thomas Carlyle, 1795–1881, Scottish historian and writer
But the world is an old woman, and mistakes any gilt farthing for a gold coin; whereby being often cheated, she will thenceforth trust nothing but the common copper.

[*Sartor Resartus* 1833–4]

Aristocracy of the money bag.

[*History of the French Revolution* 1837]

Cash payment is not the sole nexus of man with man.

[*Past and Present* 1843]

Andrew Carnegie, 1835–1919, Scottish-born American industrialist
Surplus wealth is a sacred trust which its possessor is bound to administer in his lifetime for the good of the community.

[*The Gospel of Wealth* in *North American Review* 1889]

The man who dies . . . rich dies disgraced

[*Ibid*]

Such, in my opinion, is the true Gospel concerning Wealth, obedience to which is destined some day to solve the problem of the Rich and the Poor, and to bring "Peace on earth, among men Good will."

[*Ibid*]

Miguel de Cervantes [Saavedra], 1547–1616, Spanish dramatist and poet
That which costs little is less valued.

[*Don Quixote* 1615]

Coco [Gabrielle] Chanel, 1883–1970, French dress designer
There are people who have money and people who are rich.

[Attributed]

Sir Winston [Leonard Spencer] Churchill, 1874–1965, British statesman
Saving is a very fine thing. Especially when your parents have done it for you.

[Attributed]

William Cobbet, 1763–1835, English political reformer
To be poor and independent is very nearly an impossibility.

[*Advice to Young Men* 1829]

Confucius [K'ung fu-tzu], 551–479BC, Chinese philosopher
When wealth is centralized, the people are dispersed; when wealth is distributed the people are brought together.

[*Analects c.*500BC]

William Cowper, 1731–1800, English poet
He found it inconvenient to be poor.

[*Charity* 1782]

Charles [John Huffam] Dickens, 1812–70, English novelist
Annual income twenty pounds, annual expenditure nineteen nineteen six, result happiness. Annual income twenty pounds, annual expenditure twenty pounds ought and six, result misery.

[*David Copperfield* 1849–50]

Benjamin Disraeli, 1st Earl of Beaconsfield, 1804–81, British statesman and novelist
"Two nations; between whom there is no intercourse and no sympathy; who are as ignorant of each other's habits, thoughts, and feelings, as if they were dwellers in different zones or inhabitants of different planets; who are formed by a different breeding, are fed by a different food, are ordered by different manners, and are not governed by the same laws." "You speak of – " said Egremont, hesitatingly. "The rich and the poor."

[*Sybil* 1845]

John Dryden, 1631–1700, English dramatist
Bankrupt of life, yet prodigal of ease.

[*Absalom and Achitophel* 1681]

In squandering wealth was his peculiar art;
Nothing went unrewarded but desert.
Beggared by fools whom still he found too late,
He had his jest, and they had his estate.

[*Ibid*]

Ralph Waldo Emerson, 1803–82, American writer
Poeple say law but they mean wealth.

[*Journals* 1839]

Can anybody remember when the times were not hard and money not scarce?

[*Society and Solitude: Works and Days* 1870]

Frederick William Faber, 1814–63, English churchman
Small things are best;
Grief and unrest
To rank and wealth are given;
But little things
On little wings
Bear little souls to heaven.

[*Written in a Little Lady's Little Album*]

George Farquhar, 1678–1707, Irish playwright
Money is the sinews of love, as of war.

[*Love and a Bottle* 1698]

My Lady Bountiful.

[*The Beaux' Stratagem* 1707]

'Tis still my maxim, that there is no scandal like rags, nor any crime so shameful as poverty.

[*Ibid*]

Henry Fielding, 1707–54, English novelist
Money will say more in one moment than the most eloquent lover can in years.

[*The Miser* 1733]

F[rancis] Scott [Key] Fitzgerald, 1896–1940, American novelist
Her voice is full of money.

[*The Great Gatsby* 1925]

Let me tell you about the very rich. They are different from you and me. They possess and enjoy early, and it does something to them, makes them soft where we are hard, and cynical where we are trustful, in a way that, unless you were born rich, it is very difficult to understand.

[*All the Sad Young Men : The Rich Boy* 1926]

Gustave Flaubert, 1821–80, French novelist
Of all the icy blasts that blow on love, a request for money is the most chilling and havoc-breaking.

[*Madame Bovary* 1857]

Benjamin Franklin, 1706–90, American scientist and philosopher
Nothing but money is sweeter than honey.

[*Poor Richard's Almanack* 1735]

Many a man would have been worse if his estate had been better.

[*Ibid* 1751]

If you would know the value of money, go and try to borrow some; for he that goes a-borrowing goes a-sorrowing.

[*Ibid* 1754]

Creditors have better memories than debtors.

[*Ibid*]

In this world nothing can be said to be certain, except death and taxes.

[Letter 1789]

A man is sometimes more generous when he has but a little money than when he has plenty, perhaps thro' fear of being thought to have but little.

[*Autobiography* 1798]

A bargain is something you have to find a use for once you have bought it.

[Attributed]

323

Henry George, 1839–97, American economist
So long as all the increased wealth which modern progress brings goes but to build up great fortunes, to increase luxury and make sharper the contrast between the House of Have and the House of Want, progress is not real and cannot be permanent.

[*Progress and Poverty* 1879]

J[ean] Paul Getty, 1892–1976, American financier
The meek shall inherit the earth but *not* its mineral rights.

[Attributed]

If you can actually count your money then you are not really a rich man.

[In Bernard Levin's *The Pendulum Years*]

[Gibran] Kahlil Gibran, 1883–1931, Syrian-American writer
You give but little when you give of your possessions. It is when you give of yourself that you truly give.

[*The Prophet: On Giving* 1923]

Sir William Schwenck Gilbert, 1836–1911, English librettist
Now that's the kind of king for me –
He wished all men as rich as he,
So to the top of every tree
Promoted everybody.

[*The Gondoliers* 1889]

Oliver Goldsmith, 1728–74, Irish-born English writer
Ill fares the land, to hast'ning ills a prey,
Where wealth accumulates, and men decay:
Princes and lords may flourish, or may fade;
A breath can make them, as a breath has made;
But a bold peasantry, their country's pride,
When once destroy'd, can never be supplied.

[*The Deserted Village* 1770]

His best companions, innocence and health;
And his best riches, ignorance of wealth.

[*Ibid*]

A man he was to all the country dear,
And passing rich with forty pounds a year.

[*Ibid*]

Thomas Gray, 1716–71, English poet
Let not ambition mock their useful toil,
Their homely joys, and destiny obscure;
Nor grandeur hear with a disdainful smile,
The short and simple annals of the poor.

[*Elegy Written in a Country Churchyard* 1851]

O. Henry [William Syndey Porter], 1862–1910, American writer
Whenever he saw a dollar in another man's hand he took it as a personal grudge, if he couldn't take it any other way.

[*The Octopus Marooned*]

Lester Townsend ("Bob") Hope, 1904– , English-born American comedian
A bank is a place that will lend you money if you can prove that you don't need it.
[In Alan Harrington's *Life in the Crystal Palace*]

Horace [Quintus Horatius Flaccus], 65BC–8BC, Roman poet
Make money, money, honestly if you can; if not, by any means at all, make money.
[*Epistles*]
Why should I exchange my Sabine valley for wealth that brings more troubles.
[*Ibid*]
A poor man surrounded by riches.
[*Ibid*]

E[dgar] W[atson] Howe, 1853–1937, American writer
A man is usually more careful of his money than he is of his principles.
[*Ventures in Common Sense*]
Inherited wealth is a big handicap to happiness. It is as certain death to ambition as cocaine is to morality.
[*The Blessing of Business* 1918]

Henry James, 1843–1916, American-born English writer
Money's a horrid thing to follow, but a charming thing to meet.
[*The Portrait of a Lady*, 1881]

Thomas Jefferson, 1743–1826, 3rd president of the United States
Money, and not morality, is the principle of commercial nations.
[Letter 1810]

Dr Samuel Johnson, 1709–84, English lexicographer
There are few ways in which a man can be more innocently employed than in getting money.
[1775. In Boswell's *Life of Samuel Johnson* 1791]
No man but a blockhead ever wrote except for money.
[1776. In *Ibid*]
[On his edition of Shakespeare] Sir, I have two very cogent reasons for not printing any list of subscribers; – one, that I have lost all the names, – the other, that I have spent all the money.
[1781. In *Ibid*]
It is better to *live* rich than to *die* rich.
[In *Ibid*]

Juvenal [Decimus Junius Juvenalis], c.AD40–c.136, Roman satirist
Nothing is more intolerable than a wealthy woman.
[*Satires c.*110]

John Fitzgerald Kennedy, 1917–63, 35th president of the United States
If a free society cannot help the many who are poor, it cannot save the few who are rich.
[Inaugural address 1961]

D[avid] H[erbert] Lawrence, 1885–1939, English novelist and poet
Money is our madness, our vast collective madness.
[*Money Madness*]

Edward Lear, 1812–88, English writer and artist
The Owl and the Pussy-Cat went to sea
In a beautiful pea-green boat,
They took some honey, and plenty of money,
Wrapped up in a five-pound note.

[*The Owl and the Pussy-Cat* 1871]

[Walter Valentino] Liberace, 1919–87, American pianist
[To critics] What you said hurt me very much. I cried all the way to the bank.

[1954]

James Russell Lowell, 1819–91, American editor and poet
I don't care how hard money is
Ez long ez mine's paid punctooal.

[*The Pious Editor's Creed*]

I *don't* believe in princerple,
But O, I *du* in interest.

[*Ibid*]

John James Robert Manners, 7th Duke of Rutland, 1818–1906, English politician
Let wealth and commerce, laws and learning die,
But leave us still our old nobility.

[*England's Trust*]

Christopher Marlowe, 1564–93, English dramatist
Infinite riches in a little room.

[*The Jew of Malta* 1589]

John Milton, 1608–74, English poet
Let none admire
That riches grow in hell; that soil may best
Deserve the precious bane.

[*Paradise Lost* 1667]

Riches are needless then, both for themselves,
And for the reason why they should be sought,
To gain a Sceptre, oftest better miss'd.

[*Paradise Regained* 1671]

Edward Moore, 1712–57, English dramatist and poet
I am rich beyond the dreams of avarice.

[*The Gamester* 1753]

Henry More, 1614–87, English philosopher
It is good for a man to have that wherewith he may live well and happily.

[*Enchiridion Ethicum* 1667]

Malcolm Muggeridge, 1903–90, English journalist
About money and sex it is impossible to be truthful ever, one's ego is too involved.

[In *The Observer* 1968]

George Orwell [Eric Arthur Blair], 1903–50, English novelist and critic
Within certain limits it is actually true that the less money you have, the less you worry.

[*Down and Out in Paris and London* 1933]

MONEY AND WEALTH

Thomas Love Peacock, 1785–1866, English essayist and poet
Respectable means rich, and decent means poor. I should die if I heard my family called decent.

[*Crotchet Castle* 1831]

Samuel Pepys, 1633–1703, English diarist
This morning came home my fine camlet cloak, with gold buttons, and a silk suit, which cost me much money, and I pray God to make me able to pay for it.

[*Diary* 1 July 1660]

But it is pretty to see what money will do.

[*Diary* 1667]

Titus Maccius Plautus, c.250–184BC, Roman poet
You must spend money, if you wish to make money.

[*Asinaria*]

Joan [Violet] Robinson, 1903–83, English economist
Owning capital is not a productive activity.

[*An Essay on Marxian Economics*]

Theodore Roosevelt, 1858–1919, 26th president of the United States
Probably the greatest harm done by vast wealth is the harm that we of moderate means do ourselves when we let the vices of envy and hatred enter deep into our own natures.

[Speech 1902]

Jean Jacques Rousseau, 1712–78, Swiss-born French philosopher
Money is the seed of money, and the first guinea is sometimes more difficult to acquire than the second million.

[*Discours sur l'origine de l'inegalité* 1755]

John Ruskin, 1819–1900, English art critic and writer
Whereas it has long been known and declared that the poor have no right to the property of the rich, I wish it also to be known and declared that the rich have no right to the property of the poor.

[*Unto This Last* 1860]

Bertrand [Arthur William] Russell, 3rd Earl Russell, 1872–1970, English philosopher
It is preoccupation with possession, more than anything else, that prevents men from living freely and nobly.

[*Principles of Social Reconstruction* 1917]

Sir Walter Scott, 1771–1832, Scottish novelist
If such there breathe, go, mark him well;
For him no Minstrel raptures swell;
High though his titles, proud his name,
Boundless his wealth as wish can claim;
Despite those titles, power, and pelf,
The wretch, concentred all in self,
Living, shall forfeit fair renown,
And, doubly dying, shall go down
To the vile dust, from whence he sprung,
Unwept, unhonour'd, and unsung.

[*The Lay of the Last Minstrel* 1805]

William Shakespeare, 1564–1616, English dramatist
Saint-seducing gold.

[*Romeo and Juliet* 1 1594–5]

I hate him for he is a Christian,
But more for that in low simplicity
He lends out money gratis and brings down
The rate of usance here with us in Venice.

[*The Merchant of Venice* 1 1596–7]

There is some ill a-brewing towards my rest,
For I did dream of money-bags tonight.

[*Ibid* 2]

You take my house when you do take the prop
That doth sustain my house; you take my life
When you do take the means whereby I live.

[*Ibid* 4]

He is well paid that is well satisfied.

[*Ibid*]

Bell, book, and candle shall not drive me back,
When gold and silver becks me to come on.

[*King John* 3 1596–7]

Neither a borrower nor a lender be;
For loan oft loses both itself and friend,
And borrowing dulls the edge of husbandry.
This above all: to thine own self be true,
And it must follow as the night the day,
Thou canst not then be false to any man.

[*Hamlet* 1 1600–1601]

Percy Bysshe Shelley, 1792–1822, English poet
The harmony and happiness of man
Yields to the wealth of nations.

[*Queen Mab* 1813]

Wealth is a power usurped by the few, to compel the many to labour for their benefit.

[*Ibid* notes]

Adam Smith, 1723–90, Scottish philosopher
It is the highest impertinence and presumption, therefore, in kings and ministers to pretend to watch over the economy of private people, and to restrain their expense . . . They are themselves always, and without exception, the greatest spendthrifts in society. Let them look well after their own expense, and they may safely trust private people with theirs.

[*The Wealth of Nations* 1776]

[Lloyd] Logan Pearsall Smith, 1865–1946, American-born English writer
The wretchedness of being rich is that you live with rich people.

[*Afterthoughts* 1931]

William Somerville, 1675–1742, English poet
Let all the learned say what they can,
'Tis ready money makes the man.

[*Ready Money* 1727]

328

Henry St John, Viscount Bolingbroke, 1678–1751, English statesman

All our wants, beyond those which a very moderate income will supply, are purely imaginary.

[Letter to Swift 1719]

Philip Dormer Stanhope, 4th Earl of Chesterfield, 1694–1773, English politician

I knew once a very covetous, sordid fellow, who used to say, "Take care of the pence, for the pounds will take care of themselves."

[*Letters to His Son* 1747]

Alfred, Lord Tennyson, 1809–92, English poet

Ring out old shapes of foul disease;
Ring out the narrowing lust of gold;
Ring out the thousands wars of old,
Ring in the thousand years of peace.

[*In Memoriam* 1850]

Margaret Hilda Thatcher, Baroness Thatcher of Kesteven, 1925– , British politician

No one would remember the Good Samaritan if he'd only had good intentions. He had money as well.

[In *The Observer* 1980]

Henry David Thoreau, 1817–62, American naturalist and writer

Superfluous wealth can buy superfluities only.

[*Walden, or Life in the Woods* 1854]

That man is the richest whose pleasures are the cheapest.

[*Journal* 11 March 1856]

Mark Twain [Samuel Langhorne Clemens], 1835–1910, American writer

Few of us can stand prosperity. Another man's, I mean.

[*Pudd'nhead Wilson* 1894]

There are two times in a man's life when he should not speculate: when he can't afford it, and when he can.

[*Following the Equator* 1897]

Virgil *or* Vergil [Publius Vergilius Maro], 70–19BC, Roman poet

Auri sacra fames.
(Accursed hunger for gold.)

[*Aeneid*]

Artemus Ward [Charles Farrar Browne], 1834–67, American humorist

Let us all be happy and live within our means, even if we have to borrow the money to do it with.

[*Natural History*]

George Washington, 1732–99, 1st president of the United States

It is not a custom with me to keep money to look at.

[Letter 1780]

H[erbert] G[eorge] Wells, 1866–1946, English writer

I don't 'old with Wealth. What *is* Wealth? Labour robbed out of the poor.

[*Autocracy of Mr Parham*]

329

Oscar [Fingall O'Flahertie Wills] Wilde, 1854–1900, Irish writer

If property had simply pleasures, we could stand it; but its duties make it unbearable. In the interest of the rich we must get rid of it.

[The Soul of Man under Socialism 1891]

We are often told that the poor are grateful for charity. Some of them are, no doubt, but the best amongst the poor are never grateful. They are ungrateful, discontented, disobedient, and rebellious. They are quite right to be so.

[Ibid]

As for the virtuous poor, one can pity them, of course, but one cannot possibly admire them. They have made private terms with the enemy, and sold their birthright for very bad pottage.

[Ibid]

To recommend thrift to the poor is both grotesque and insulting. It is like advising a man who is starving to eat less.

[Ibid]

Tennessee Williams [Thomas Lanier Williams], 1911–83, American playwright

You can be young without money, but you can't be old without it.

[Cat on a Hot Tin Roof 1955]

The Natural World

Alfonso the Wise [Alfonso X], 1221–84, king of Castile and Leon
Had I been present at the Creation, I would have given some useful hints for the better ordering of the universe.

[Attributed]

Anonymous
Red sky at night, shepherd's delight: red sky at morning, shepherd's warning.

[Proverb]

If the frog and mouse quarrel,the kite will see them agreed.

[Proverb]

Apollonius of Tyana, 3BC–c.AD97, Greek philosopher
God made the beauties of nature like a child playing in the sand.

[Attributed]

St Augustine, 354–430, Christian philosopher
All nature is good.

[*Of Continence c.* 425]

Francis Bacon, Baron Verulam of Verulam and Viscount of St Albans, 1561–1626, English philosopher
God Almighty first planned a garden; and indeed it is the purest of human pleasures.

[*Essays of Gardens* 1625]

Nature cannot be ordered about, except by obeying her.

[*Novum Oganum: Of natural philosophy*]

Walter Bagehot, 1826–77, English economist and journalist
Taken as a whole, the universe is absurd.

[*Literary Studies* 1879]

Henry Ward Beecher, 1813–87, American preacher
Flowers are the sweetest things that God ever made, and forgot to put a soul into.

[*Life Thoughts*, 1858]

Ludwig van Beethoven, 1770–1827, German composer
Nature has an etiquette all her own.

[Letter 1812]

The Bible

For to him that is joined to all the living there is hope: for a living dog is better than a dead lion.

[*Ecclesiastes* 9:4]

The wolf also shall dwell with the lamb, and the leopard shall lie down with the kid; and the calf and the young lion and the fatling together; and a little child shall lead them.

[*Isaiah* 11:6]

Surely in vain the net is spread in the sight of any bird.

[*Proverbs* 1:17]

Go to the ant, thou sluggard; consider her ways, and be wise.

[*Ibid* 6:6]

There be three things which are too wonderful for me, yea, four which I know not: The way of an eagle in the air; the way of a serpent upon a rock; they way of a ship in the midst of the sea; and they way of a man with a maid.

[*Ibid* 30:18–19]

The wind bloweth where it listeth, and thou hearest the sound thereof, but canst not tell whence it cometh, and whither it goeth: so is everyone that is born of the Spirit.

[*John* 3:8]

Consider the lilies of the field, how they grow; they toil not, neither do they spin: And yet I say unto you, That even Solomon in all his glory was not arrayed like one of these.

[*Matthew* 6:28–29]

William Blake, 1757–1827, English poet and artist

Little Lamb, who made thee?
Dost thou know who made thee?
Gave thee life, and bid thee feed,
By the stream and o'er the mead;
Gave thee clothing of delight,
Softest clothing, woolly, bright;
Gave thee such a tender voice,
Making all the vales rejoice?

[*Songs of Innocence: The Lamb* 1789]

Tyger! Tyger! burning bright
In the forests of the night,
What immortal hand or eye
Could frame they fearful symmetry?

[*Ibid: The Tyger* 1794]

When the stars threw down their spears,
And water'd heaven with their tears,
Did he smile his work to see?
Did he who made the Lamb make thee?

[*Ibid*]

A robin redbreast in a cage
Puts all Heaven in a rage.

[*Auguries of Innocence* 1805]

332

A dog starv'd at his master's gate
Predicts the ruin of the State,
A horse misus'd upon the road
Calls to Heaven for human blood.
Each outcry of the hunted hare
A fibre from the brain does tear,
A skylark wounded in the wing,
A cherubim does cease to sing.

[*Ibid*]

He who shall hurt the little wren
Shall never be belov'd by men.
He who the ox to wrath has mov'd
Shall never be by woman lov'd.

[*Ibid*]

Robert Browning, 1812–89, English poet

Any nose
May ravage with impunity a rose.

[*Sordello* 1840]

Rats!
They fought the dogs and killed the cats,
And bit the babies in the cradles,
And ate the cheeses out of the vats,
And licked the soup from the cooks' own ladles,
Split open the kegs of salted sprats,
Made nests inside men's Sunday hats,
And even spoiled the women's chats
By drowning their speaking
With shrieking and squeaking
In fifty different sharps and flats.

[*The Pied Piper of Hamelin* 1842]

That's the wise thrush; he sings each song twice over,
Lest you should think he never could recapture
The first fine careless rapture!

[*Home-Thoughts from Abroad*]

Bill [William] Bryson, 1951– , American travel writer

Woods are not like other spaces. To begin with they are cubic. Their trees surround you, loom over you, press in from all sides. They make you feel small and confused and vulnerable, like a small child lost in a crowd of strange legs.

[*A Walk in the Woods* 1997]

333

Byron, Lord George Gordon [Noel], 6th Baron Byron of Rochdale, 1788–1824, English poet
Near this spot
Are deposited the remains of one
Who possessed beauty without vanity,
Strength without insolence,
Courage without ferocity,
And all the virtues of man without his vices.
This praise, which would be unmeaning flattery
If inscribed over human ashes,
Is but a just tribute to the memory of
Boatswain, a dog.

[Epitaph for a dog buried at Newstead Abbey 1808]

There is a pleasure in the pathless woods,
There is a rapture on the lonely shore,
There is society, where none intrudes,
By the deep sea and music in its roar:
I love not man the less, but Nature more,
From these our interviews, in which I steal
From all I may be, or have been before,
To mingle with the Universe, and feel
What I can ne'er express, yet cannot all conceal.

[Childe Harold's Pilgrimage 1818]

Roy Campbell, 1901–57, South African poet
Giraffes! – a People who live between the earth and skies,
Each in his lone religious steeple,
Keeping a lighthouse with his eyes.

[Dreaming Spires]

G[ilbert] K[eith] Chesterton, 1874–1936, English writer
When fishes flew and forests walked
And figs grew upon thorn,
Some moment when the moon was blood
Then surely I was born.

[The Donkey]

With monstrous head and sickening cry
And ears like errant wings,
The devil's walking parody
On all four-footed things.

[Ibid]

Fools! For I also had my hour;
One far fierce hour and sweet:
There was a shout about my ears,
And palms before my feet.

[Ibid]

Marcus Tullius Cicero, 106–43BC, Roman statesman
Those things are better which are perfected by nature than those which are finished by art.

[De Natura Deorum 45BC]

Thomas Cole, 1801–48, American painter
Over all, rocks, wood, and water, brooded the spirit of repose, and the silent energy of nature stirred the soul to its inmost depths.

[*Essay on American Scenery* 1835]

George Colman, 1732–94, English playwright
Give a dog an ill name and hang him.

[*Polly Honeycombe* 1760]

Salvador Dali, 1904–89, Spanish artist
The only animals I really like are the rhinoceros and fillet of sole.

[In *TV Times* 1973]

Charles Robert Darwin, 1809–82, English naturalist
I agree with Agassiz that dogs possess something very like a conscience.

[*The Descent of Man*, 1871]

Bob Dylan (Robert Zimmerman), 1941– , American singer
You don't need a weatherman to know which way the wind blows.

[*Subterranean Homesick Blues* 1965]

Ralph Waldo Emerson,1803–82, American writer
There is not chance, and no anarchy, in the universe. All is system and gradation. Every god is there sitting in his sphere.

[*The Conduct of Life* 1860]

Nature is an endless combination and repetition of very few laws. She hums the old well-known air through innumerable variations.

[*History* 1841]

Nature has made up her mind that what cannot defend itself shall not be defended.

[*Ibid*]

Flying Hawk, 1852–1931, Oglala Sioux chief
The tepee is much better to live in: always clean, warm in winter, cool in summer; easy to move . . . Indians and animals know better how to live than white men; nobody can be in good health if he does not have all the time fresh air, sunshine, and good water.

[Said in his old age]

Robert [Lee] Frost, 1874–1963, American poet
How many times it thundered before Franklin took the hint! How many apples feel on Newton's head before he took the hint! Nature is always hinting at us. It hints over and over again. And suddenly we take the hint.

[*Comment*]

Johann Wolfgang von Goethe, 1749–1832, German poet and playwright
Nature goes her own way, and all that to us seems an exception is really according to order.

[*Conversations with Eckerman* 1824]

Dorothy Frances Gurney,1858–1932, English poet
The kiss of the sun for pardon,
The song of the birds for mirth,
One is nearer God's Heart in a garden
Than anywhere else on earth.

[*God's Garden*]

Thomas Hobbes, 1588–1679, English philosopher
There be beasts that, at a year old, observe more, and pursue that which is for their good more prudently, than a child can do at ten.

[*Leviathan* 1651]

William Henry Hudson, 1841–1922, Argentinian-born English writer
I . . . thanked the Author of my being for the gift of that wild forest, those green mansions where I had found so great a happiness.

[*Green Mansions* 1904]

Ted [Edward James] Hughes, 1930–98, English poet
Pike, three inches long, perfect
Pike in all parts, green tigering the gold.
Killers from the egg: the malevolent aged grin.
They dance on the surface among the flies.

[*Pike*]

Thomas Henry Huxley, 1825–95, English biologist
For every man the world is as fresh as it was at the first day, and as full of untold novelties for him who has the eyes to see them.

[*A Liberal Education* 1868]

P[hyllis] D[]orothy] James [*née* White], Baroness James of Holland Park, 1920– , English novelist
A man who lives with nature is used to violence and is companionable with death. There is more violence in an English hedgerow than in the meanest streets of a great city.

[*Devices and Desires*, 1989]

James [Augustine Aloysius] Joyce, 1882–1941, Irish writer and poet
The snotgreen sea. The scrumtightening sea.

[*Ulysses* 1922]

Juvenal [Decimus Junius Juvenalis], c.AD60–c.136, Roman satirist
Never does nature say one thing and wisdom another.

[*Satires* 128]

Charles Lamb, 1775–1834, English essayist
I must confess that I am not romance-hit about nature. The earth, the sea, and sky (when all is said) is but as a house to dwell in.

[Letter 1800]

Baron Gottfried Wilhelm von Leibnitz, 1646–1716, German philosopher
In nature there can never be two beings that are exactly alike.

[*The Monadology*, 1714]

There is nothing uncultivated, nothing sterile, nothing dead in the universe; there is no chaos, no confusion except in appearance.

[*Ibid*]

Carolus Linnaeus [Carl von Linné], 1707–78, Swedish botanist
Nature does not proceed by leaps.

[*Philosophia Botanica* 1750]

If a tree dies, plant another in its place.

[Written above the door to his bedroom]

Jack London [John Griffith Chaney], 1876–1916, American writer
The aim of life was meat. Life itself was meat. Life lived on life. There were the eaters and the eaten. The law was: EAT OR BE EATEN.

[*White Fang* 1905]

Fear! – that legacy of the Wild which no animal may escape nor exchange for pottage.

[*Ibid*]

George Macdonald, 1824–1905, Scottish novelist and poet
A bird knows nothing of gladness,
Is only a song machine.

[*A Book of Dreams c.*1860]

Marya Mannes, 1904–90, American journalist
The earth we abuse and the living things we kill will, in the end, take their revenge; for in exploiting their presence we are diminishing our future.

[*More in Anger*]

Margaret Mead,1901–78, American anthropologist
The overwhelming importance of the atmosphere means that there are no longer any frontiers to defend against pollution, attack, or propaganda. It means, further, that only by a deep patriotic devotion to one's country can there be a hope of the kind of protection of the whole planet, which is necessary for the survival of the people of other countries.

[*Culture and Commitment* 1970]

George Meredith, 1828–1909, English poet and novelist
For singing till his heaven fills,
'Tis love of earth that he instills,
And ever winging up and up,
Our valley is his golden cup,
And he the wine which overflows
To lift us with him as he goes.

[*The Lark Ascending* 1881]

Spike [Terence Alan] Milligan, 1918–2002, Irish comedian and writer
"God, that sun's hot," said Watson.
"Then don't touch it," said McGonagall.

[*William MacGonagall – Freefall*]

Desmond John Morris, 1928– , English ethnologist and writer
There are one hundred and ninety-three living species of monkeys and apes. One hundred and ninety-two of them are covered with hair. The exception is a naked ape self-named *Homo sapiens*.

[*The Naked Ape* 1967]

John Muir, 1838–1914, Scottish-born American naturalist
The clearest way into the Universe is through a forest wilderness.

[*John of the Mountains* 1938]

In God's wilderness lies the hope of the world – the great fresh unblighted, unredeemed wilderness.

[*Alaska Fragment* 1890]

Ogden Nash, 1902–71, American humorous writer

The cow is of the bovine ilk;
One end is moo, the other, milk.

[*The Cow*]

I marvel at thee, Octopus;
If I were thou, I'd call me Us.

[*The Octopus*]

Cardinal John Henry Newman, 1801–90, English churchman and poet

Living Nature, not dull Art
Shall plan my ways and rule my heart.

[*Nature and Art* 1868]

Julius [Kambarage] Nyerere, 1922–99, president of Tanzania

The survival of our wildlife is a matter of grave concern to all of us in Africa. These wild creatures amid the wild places they inhabit are not only important as a source of wonder and inspiration but are an integral part of our natural resources and of our future livelihood and well-being.

[*The Arusha Declaration* 1961]

Ohiyesa [Charles Alexander Eastman], 1858–1939, Santee Dakota Indian

Nearness to nature . . . keeps the spirit sensitive to impressions not commonly felt, and in touch with unseen powers.

[*The Soul of the Indian* 1911]

P[atrick] J[ake] O'Rourke, 1947– , American satirist

If our desire to preserve the environment is real, then we should make that preservation provide economic benefits. Some people will baby-sit nature for purely altruistic reasons, but don't bet the red cockaded woodpecker on everybody doing it.

[*All the Trouble in the World: Saving the Earth* 1994]

If we lose the rain forest, we'll lose the earth's principal source of prom corsages.

[*Ibid: Evironment*]

George Orwell [Eric Arthur Blair], 1903–50, English novelist and critic

Four legs good, two legs bad.

[*Animal Farm* 1945]

Alexander Pope, 1688–1744, English poet

All are but parts of one stupendous whole,
Whose body Nature is, and God the soul.

[*Essay on Man* 1732–4]

Slave to no sect, who takes no private road,
But looks through nature up to nature's God.

[*Ibid*]

Theodore Roosevelt, 1858–1919, 26th president of the United States

To waste, to destroy, our natural resources, to skin and exhaust the land instead of using it so as to increase its usefulness, will result in undermining in the days of our children the very prosperity which we ought by right to hand down to them amplified and developed.

[Message to Congress 1907]

Anwar al-Sadat, 1918–81, president of Egypt
Land is immortal, for it harbours the mysteries of creation.

[*In Search of Identity* 1978]

A man's village is his peace of mind.

[*Ibid*]

Charles Louis de Secondat, Baron de Montesquieu, 1689–1755, French philosopher
The lower animals have not the high advantages that we have, but they have something that we lack. They know nothing of our hopes, but they also know nothing of our fears; they are subject to death as we are, but they are not aware of it; most of them are better able to take care of themselves than we are, and they make a less evil use of their passions.

[*The Spirit of the Laws* 1748]

Seneca, c.4BC–AD65, Roman philosopher
Naturam mutare difficile est.
It is difficult to change nature.

[*De Ira c.*43]

William Shakespeare, 1564–1616, English dramatist
I know a bank where on the wild thyme blows,
Where ox-lips, and the nodding violet grows
Quite over-canopied with luscious woodbine,
With sweet musk-roses, and with eglantine.

[*A Midsummer Night's Dream* 2 1595–6]

Daffodils,
That come before the swallow dares, and take
The winds of March with beauty.

[*The Winter's Tale* 4 1610]

Isaac Bashevis Singer, 1904–91, American Yiddish novelist
What nature delivers to us is never stale. Because what nature creates has eternity in it.
[In the *New York Times Magazine* 1978]

Alexander Smith, 1829–67, Scottish poet
Nature never quite goes along with us. She is sombre at weddings, sunny at funerals, and she frowns on ninety-nine out of a hundred picnics.

[*Dreamthorp* 1863]

It is curious, pathetic almost, how deeply seated in the human heart is the liking for gardens and gardening.

[*Ibid*]

Herbert Spencer, 1820–1903, English philosopher
The behaviour of men to the lower animals, and their behaviour to each other, bear a constant relationship.

[*Social Statics* 1851]

Adlai E[wing] Stevenson, 1900–65, American statesman
Nature is neutral. Man has wrested from nature the power to make the world a desert or to make the deserts bloom. There is no evil in the atom; only in men's souls.

[Speech 1952]

Alfred, Lord Tennyson, 1809–92, English poet
Nature red in tooth and claw.

[*In Memoriam* 1850]

I chatter, chatter, as I flow,
To join the brimming river,
For men may come and men may go,
But I go on forever.

[*The Brook* 1887]

James Thomson, 1700–1748, Scottish poet
Behold the merry minstrels of the morn,
The swarming songsters of the careless grove,
Ten thousand throats that, from the flowering thorn,
Hymn their good God and carol sweet of love.

[*The Castle of Indolence* 1748]

Henry David Thoreau, 1817–62, American naturalist
The Indian . . . stands free and unconstrained in Nature, is her inhabitant and not her guest, and wears her easily and gracefully. But the civilized man has the habits of the house. His house is a prison.

[*Journal* 1841]

We need the tonic of wildness . . . We can never have enough of nature.

[*Walden, or Life in the Woods* 1854]

Stewart Lee Udall, 1920– , U.S. Secretary of the Interior
The most common trait of all primitive peoples is a reverence for the life-giving earth, and the native American shared this elemental ethic: the land was alive to his loving touch, and he, its son, was brother to all creatures. His feelings were made visible in medicine bundles and dance rhythms for rain, and all of his religious rites and land attitudes savored the inseparable world of nature and God, the master of Life. During the long Indian tenure the land remained undefiled save for scars no deeper than the scratches of cornfield clearings or the farming canals of the Hohokams on the Arizona desert.

[*The Quiet Crisis* 1963]

Leonardo da Vinci, 1452–1519, Italian artist
Nature never breaks her own laws.

[*Notebooks c.* 1500]

Voltaire [François Marie Arouet], 1694–1778, French philosopher and writer
Men argue, nature acts.

[*Philosophical Dictionary* 1764]

Animals have these advantages over man: they never hear the clock strike, they die without any idea of death, they have no theologians to instruct them, their last moments are not disturbed by unwelcome and unpleasant ceremonies, their funerals cost them nothing, and no one starts lawsuits over their wills.

[Letter 1769]

Edmund Waller, 1606–87, English poet
To man, that was in th' evening made,
Stars gave the first delight;
Admiring, in the gloomy shade,
Those little drops of light.

[*An Apology for Having Loved Before* 1664]

Isaac Watts, 1674–1748, English poet and hymn-writer
Let dogs delight to bark and bite,
For God hath made them so;
Let bears and lions growl and fight,
For 'tis their nature to.

[Song]

Walt[er] Whitman, 1819–92, American poet
I could turn and live awhile with the animals . . . they are so placid and self-contained,
I stand and look at them sometimes half the day long.
They do not sweat and whine about their condition,
They do not lie awake in the dark and weep for their sins,
They do not make me sick discussing their duty to God,
Not one is dissatisfied . . . not one is demented with the mania of knowing things,
Not one kneels to another nor to his kind that lived thousands of years ago,
Not one is respectable or industrious over the whole earth.

[*Leaves of Grass : Song of Myself* 1855]

Give me the splendid silent sun with all his beams full-dazzling.

[*Leaves of Grass: Give Me The Splendid Sun*]

Whereto answering, the sea,
Delaying not, hurrying not,
Whispered me through the night, and very plainly before daybreak,
Lisped to me the low and delicious word death.

[*Ibid: Out of the Cradle Endlessly Rocking*]

Mary Wollstonecraft, 1759–97, English writer
It is the preservation of the species, not of individuals, which appears to be the design of Deity
throughout the whole of nature.

[*Letters written in Sweden, Norway and Denmark* 1796]

William Wordsworth, 1770–1850, English poet
The holy time is quiet as a nun
Breathless with adoration.

[*It is a Beauteous Evening* 1807]

And 'tis my faith that every flower
Enjoys the air it breathes.

[*Lines Written in Early Spring*]

Travel and Travelling

Henry [Brooks] Adams, 1838–1918, American historian
The less a tourist knows, the fewer mistakes he need make, for he will not expect himself to explain ignorance.

[*The Education of Henry Adams* 1907]

George Ade, 1866–1944, American humorist, writer and dramatist
The time to enjoy a European tour is about three weeks after you unpack.

[*Forty Modern Fables* 1901]

Anonymous
Travel makes makes a wise man better, but a fool worse.

[Proverb]

Neil Alden Armstrong, 1930– , American astronaut
Houston, Tranquility Base here – the Eagle has landed.

[Radio message from Apollo 11 moon landing, July 21 1969]

Francis Bacon, Baron Verulam of Verulam and Viscount of St Albans, 1561–1626, English philosopher
Travel, in the younger sort, is a part of education; in the elder, a part of experience. He that travelleth into a country before he hath some entrance into the language, goeth to school, and not to travel.

[*Essays: Of Travel* 1597]

Giuseppe Baretti, 1719–89, Italian-born English critic
Travellers . . . seem to have no other purpose by taking long journeys but to procure themselves the pleasure of railing at everything they have seen or heard.

[*An Account of the Manners and Customs of Italy* 1768]

Sir Thomas Beecham, 1879–1961, English conductor
I have recently been all round the world and have formed a very poor opinion of it.

Doromont de Belloy, 1727–75, French dramatist
The more foreigners I saw, the more I loved my homeland.

[*Le Siège de Calais* 1765]

Ambrose [Gwinett] Bierce, 1842–1914, American writer
Passport: a document treacherously inflicted upon a citizen going abroad, exposing him as an alien and pointing him out for special reprobation and outrage.

[*The Devil's Dictionary* 1906]

Richard Braithwaite, 1588–1673, English writer
Travellers, poets and liars are three words all of one significance.
[*The English Gentleman* 1631]

Bill [William] Bryson, 1951– , American travel writer
What *is* it about this town? I've blown more intelligent life into a handkerchief.
[*A Walk in the Woods* 1997]

Fanny Burney [Frances, Madame d'Arblay], 1752–1840, English writer
Travelling is the ruin of all happiness. There's no looking at a building here after seeing Italy.
[*Cecilia* 1782]

Charles Stuart Calverley [Blayds], 1831–84, English poet
For king-like rolls the Rhine,
And the scenery's divine,
And the victuals and the wine
Rather good.
[*Dover to Munich*]

Albert Camus, 1913–60, Algerian-born French philosopher and novelist
There is no pleasure in travelling, and I look upon it more as an occasion for spiritual testing.
[*Notebooks* 1939–44]

Lewis Carroll [Charles Lutwidge Dodgson], 1832–92, English mathematician and writer
But the principal failing occurred in the sailing,
And the Bellman, perplexed and distressed,
Said he *had* hoped, at least, when the wind blew due East,
That the ship would *not* travel due West!
[*The Hunting of the Snark* 1867]

Charles II, 1630–85, king of England, Scotland and Ireland
Brother, I am too old to go again to my travels.
[Attributed]

Samuel Taylor Coleridge, 1772–1834, English poet
From whatever place I write you will expect that part of my "Travels" will consist of excursions in my own mind.
[*Satyrane's Letters* 1809]

In Xanadu did Kubla Khan
A stately pleasure-dome decree:
Where Alph, the sacred river ran
Through caverns measureless to man
Down to a sunless sea.
[*Kubla Khan* 1816]

Don DeLillo, 1936– , American novelist
Tourism is the march of stupidity.
[*The Names* 1982]

René Descartes, 1596–1650, French philosopher
Travelling is almost like talking with men of other centuries.
[*Le Discours de la Méthode* 1637]

Benjamin Disraeli, 1st Earl of Beaconsfield, 1804–81, British statesman and novelist
Travel teaches toleration.

[*Contarini Fleming* 1832]

Ralph Waldo Emerson, 1803–82, American writer
The least change in our point of view gives the whole world a pictorial air. A man who seldom rides needs only to get into a coach and traverse his own town, to turn the street into a puppet-show.

[*Nature* 1836]

It is for want of self-culture that the superstition of travelling, whose idols are Italy, England, Egypt, retains its fascination for all educated Americans.

[*Essays: Self-Reliance* 1841]

The difference between landscape and landscape is small, but there is a great difference in the beholders.

[*Nature* 1844]

All educated Americans, first or last, go to Europe.

[*The Conduct of Life: Culture* 1860]

George Farquhar, 1678–1707, Irish playwright
Captain is a good travelling name, so I take it.

[*The Beaux' Stratagem* 1707]

Benjamin Franklin, 1706–90, American scientist and philosopher
Travelling is one way of lengthening life, at least in appearance.

[Letter 1767]

André [Paul Guillaume] Gide, 1869–1951, French novelist
One doesn't discover new lands without consenting to lose sight of the shore for a very long time.

[*The Counterfeiters*]

Carlo Goldoni, 1707–93, Italian dramatist
A wise traveller never despises his own country.

[*Pamela Nubile* 1757]

Kenneth Grahame, 1859–1932, English writer
The poetry of motion! The *real* way to travel! The *only* way to travel! Here today – in next week tomorrow! Villages skipped, towns and cities jumped – always somebody else's horizon!

[*The Wind in the Willows* 1908]

[Henry] Grahame Greene, 1904–91, English novelist
When a train pulls into a great city I am reminded of the closing moments of an overture.

[*Travels with My Aunt* 1969]

William Hazlitt, 1778–1830, English essayist
I should like to spend the whole of my life travelling, if I could anywhere borrow another life to spend at home.

[*Table Talk* 1824]

Ernest [Miller] Hemingway, 1899–1961, American novelist
If you are lucky enough to have lived in Paris as a young man, then wherever you go for the rest of your life, it stays with you, for Paris is a moveable feast.

[*A Moveable Feast* 1964]

O. Henry [William Syndey Porter], 1862–1910, American writer
The true adventurer goes forth aimless and uncalculating to meet and greet an anknown fate.
A fine example was the Prodigal Son – when he started back home.
[*The Green Door*]

Homer, *fl.* 9th century BC, Greek poet
There is nothing worse for mortals than a wandering life.
[*Odyssey c.*800BC]

Horace [Quintus Horatius Flaccus], 65–8BC, Roman poet
Not bound to swear allegiance to any master, wherever the wind takes me I travel as a visitor.
[*Epistles*]

A[lfred] E[dward] Housman, 1859–1936, English poet and scholar
O suitably attired in leather boots
Head of a traveller, wherefor seeking whom
Whence by what way how purposed art thou come
To this well-nightingaled vicinity?
My object in enquiring is to know
But if you happen to be deaf and dumb
And do not understand a word I say,
Nod with your hand to signify as much.
[*Fragment of a Greek Tragedy* 1883]

James Henry Leigh Hunt, 1784–1859, English poet and essayist
Travelling in the company of those we love is home in motion.
[*The Indicator* 1821]

Thomas Jefferson, 1743–1826, 3rd president of the United States
Travelling. This makes men wiser, but less happy.
[Letter 1787]

Dr Samuel Johnson, 1709–84, English lexicographer
A man who has not been in Italy, is always conscious of an inferiority, from his not having seen what it is expected a man should see. The grand object of travelling is to see the shores of the Mediterranean.
[1776. In Boswell's *Life of Samuel Johnson* 1791]
The use of travelling is to regulate imagination by reality, and, instead of thinking how things may be, to see them as they are.
[In Mrs Piozzi's *Anecdotes* 1786]

Juvenal [Decimus Junius Juvenalis], c.AD60–c.136, Roman satirist
Travel light and you can sing in the robber's face.
[*Satires*]

John Keats, 1795–1821, English poet
Much have I travell'd in the realms of gold,
And many goodly states and kingdoms seen.
[*On First Looking into Chapman's Homer*]

Jack Kerouac [Jean Louis Lebris de Kerouac], 1922–1969, American novelist
Do you know there's a road that goes down to Mexico and all the way to Panama? – and maybe and maybe all the way to the bottom of South America where the Indians are seven

feet tall and eat cocaine on the mountainside? Yes! You and I, Sal, we'd dig the whole world with a car like this because, man, the road must eventually lead to the whole world. Ain't nowhere else it can go, – right?

[*On the Road*, 1957]

The Road is life.

[*Ibid*]

Rudyard Kipling, 1865–1936, English writer
Down to Gehenna or up to the Throne,
He travels the fastest who travels alone.

[*The Story of the Gadsbys* 1890]

Pull out, pull out, on the Long Trail – the trail that is always new.

[*The Long Trail*]

And what should they know of England who only England know?

[*The English Flag*]

Katherine Mansfield [Katherine Mansfield Beauchamp], 1888–1923, New Zealand writer
Whenever I prepare for a journey I prepare as though for death. Should I never return, all is in order.

[*Journal*]

Walter John de la Mare, 1873–1956, English poet
"Is there anybody there?" said the Traveller,
Knocking on the moonlit door.

[*The Listeners* 1912]

John Edward Masefield, 1878–1967, English poet
I must go down to the seas again, to the lonely sea and the sky,
And all I ask is a tall ship and a star to steer her by.

[*Sea-Fever* 1902]

Quinquireme of Nineveh from distant Ophir
Rowing home to haven in sunny Palestine.

[*Cargoes* 1910]

Dirty British coaster with a salt-caked smoke stack,
Butting through the Channel in the mad March days.

[*Ibid*]

Herman Melville, 1819–91, American novelist
I love to sail forbidden seas, and land on barbarous coasts.

[*Moby Dick* 1851]

Edna St Vincent Millay, 1892–1950, American poet
My heart is warm with the friends I make,
And better friends I'll not be knowing;
Yet there isn't a train I wouldn't take,
No matter where it's going.

[*Travel* 1921]

Spike [Terence Alan] Milligan, 1918–2002, Irish comedian and writer
By midday in Colombo, the heat is so unbearable that the streets are empty save for thousands of Englishmen taking mad dogs for walks.

[*A Dustbin of Milligan*]

Sidney Joseph Perelman, 1904–79, American humorist
The whistle shrilled, and in a moment I was chugging out of Grand Central Station. . . I had chugged only a few feet when I realized I had left without the train, so I had to run back and wait for it to start.

[*Strictly from Hunger*]

Publilius Syrus, *fl.* 1st century BC, Roman writer
A pleasant companion reduces the length of the journey.

[*Sententiae c.*50BC]

Jonathan Raban, 1942– , English travel writer
In an underdeveloped country don't drink the water, in a developed country, don't breathe the air.

[In *Reader's Digest* 1976]

Gene Roddenberry, 1921–91 American television writer and producer.
Space – the final frontier. These are the voyages of the starship *Enterprise*. Its five-year mission: to explore strange new worlds, to seek out new life and new civilizations, to boldy go where no man has gone before.

[*Star Trek* television series 1966–69]

John Ruskin, 1819–1900, English art critic and writer
All travelling becomes dull in exact proportion to its rapidity.

[*Modern Painters* 1843–60]

Robert Falcon Scott, 1868–1912, English explorer
[Of the South Pole] Great God! This is an awful place!

[Journal entry 1912]

Seneca, c.4BC–AD65, Roman philosopher
Every change of scene is a delight.

[*Epistolae ad Lucilium c.*AD63]

William Shakespeare, 1564–1616, English dramatist
Ay, now am I in Arden; the more fool I; when I was at home, I was in a better place: but travellers must be content.

[*As You Like It* 2 1598–1600]

Farewell, Monsieur Traveller: look you lisp and wear strange suits, disable all the benefits of your own country, be out of love with your nativity, and almost chide God for making you the countenance you are, or I will scarce think you have swum in a gondola.

[*Ibid* 4]

Who would fardels bear,
To grunt and sweat under a weary life,
But that the dread of something after death,
The undiscover'd country from whose bourn
No traveller returns, puzzles the will
And makes us rather bear those ills we have
Than fly to others that we know not of?

[*Hamlet* 3 1600–1601]

No spurs the lated traveller apace
To gain the timely inn.

[*Macbeth* 3 1605–6]

O sir! you had then left unseen a wonderful piece of work which not to have been blessed withal would have discredited your travel.

[Anthony and Cleopatra 1 1606–7]

Why didst thou promise such a beauteous day
And make me travel forth without my cloak.

[Sonnets 34 1609]

George Bernard Shaw, 1856–1950, Irish playwright
The great advantage of a hotel is that it's a refuge from home life.

[You Never Can Tell 1898]

Percy Bysshe Shelley, 1792–1822, English poet
I met a traveller from an antique land
Who said: Two vast and trunkless legs of stone
Stand in the desert.

[Ozymandias 1818]

Philip Dormer Stanhope, 4th Earl of Chesterfield, 1694–1773, English statesman
Those who travel heedlessly from place to place, observing only their distance from each other, and attending only to their accommodation at the inn at night, set out fools, and will certainly return so.

[Letters to His Son 1747]

John [Ernst] Steinbeck, 1902–68, American novelist
A journey is like a marriage. The certain way to be wrong is to think you can control it.
[Travels with Charley: In Search of America 1962]

Laurence Sterne, 1713–68, English churchman and writer
A man should know something of his own country, too, before he goes abroad.
[Tristram Shandy 1765]

They order, said I, this matter better in France.
[A Sentimental Journey 1768]

As an English man does not travel to see English men, I retired to my room.
[Ibid]

I pity the man who can travel from Dan to Beersheba and cry, 'tis all barren.
[Ibid]

The whole circle of travellers may be reduced to the following Heads:
Idle Travellers,
Inquisitive Travellers,
Lying Travellers,
Proud Travellers,
Vain Travellers,
Splenetic Travellers,
Then follow The Travellers of Necessity,
The deliquent and felonious Traveller,
The unfortunate and innocent Traveller,
The simple Traveller,
And last of all (if you please)
The Sentimental Traveller.

[Sentimental Journey 1768]

Robert Louis [Balfour] Stevenson, 1850–94, Scottish novelist and poet
Let the blow fall soon or late,
Let what will be o'er me;
Give the face of earth around
And the road before me.
Wealth I seek not, hope nor love,
Nor a friend to know me;
All I seek, the heaven above
And the road before me.

[*Songs of Travel* 1896]

For my part, I travel not to go anywhere, but to go. I travel for travel's sake. The great affair is to move.

[*Travels with a Donkey; Cheylard and Luc* 1878]

To travel hopefully is a better thing than to arrive, and the true success is to labour.

[*Virginibus Puerisque: El Dorado* 1881]

Wealth I ask not, hope nor love,
Nor a friend to know me;
All I ask, the heaven above
And the road below me.

[*Songs of Travel: The Vagabond*]

Jonathan Swift, 1667–1745, Irish-born English writer
I always love to begin a journey on Sundays, because I shall have the prayers of the church, to preserve all that travel by land, or by water.

[*Polite Conversation* 1738]

The Talmud, c.200
Three things are weakening: fear, sin, and travel.

[*Gittin*]

John Taylor, 1580–1653, English poet
He that wants legs, feet, and brains, and wit
To be a traveller is most unfit.

[*A Short Relation of a Long Journey* 1652]

Alfred, Lord Tennyson, 1809–92, English poet
Sunset and evening star
Are one clear call for me!
And may there be no moaning of the bar
When I put out to sea.

[*Demeter and Other Poems: Crossing the Bar* 1889]

Paul Theroux, 1941– , American writer
Travel is glamorous only in retrospect.

[Quoted in the *Observer* October 7 1979.]

Extensive travelling induces a feeling of encapsulation, and travel, so broadening at first, contracts the mind.

[*The Old Patagonian Express* 1979]

Henry David Thoreau, 1817–62, American naturalist and writer
The man who goes alone can start today, but he who travels with another must wait till that other is ready.

[*Walden, or Life in the Woods* 1854]

William Trevor [Willian Trevor Cox], 1928– , Irish author and playwright
He travelled in order to come home.

[*Matilda's England* 1995]

Mark Twain [Samuel Langhorne Clemens], 1835–1910, American writer
It used to be a good hotel, but that proves nothing – I used to be a good boy.

[Letter to the Alta Californian, San Francisco, 1867]

To forget pain is to be painless; to forget care is to rid of it; to go abroad is to accomplish both.

[*Autobiography* 1924]

Anne Tyler, 1941– , America novelist
I've always thought a hotel ought to offer optional small animals . . . I mean a cat to sleep on your bed at night, or a dog of some kind to act pleased when you come in. You ever notice how a hotel room feels so lifeless?

[*The Accidental Tourist* 1985]

Sir Laurens Van der Post, 1906–96, South African-born writer
I have travelled so much because travel has enabled me to arrive at unknown places within my clouded self.

Sir John Vanburgh, 1664–1726, English dramatist and architect
The young fellows of this age profit no more by their going abroad than they do by their going to church.

[*The Relapse* 1696]

E[lwyn] B[rooks] White, 1899–1985, American humorist
Commuter – one who spends his life
In riding to and from his wife;
A man who shaves and takes a train,
And then rides back to shave again.

[*The Commuter* 1929]

William Carlos Williams, 1883–1963, American novelist and poet
Most of the beauties of travel are due to the strange hours we keep to see them.

[*Selected Poems: January Morning* 1949]

William Wordsworth, 1770–1850, English poet
I have travelled among unknown men
In lands beyond the sea;
Nor, England! did I know till then
What love I bore to thee.

[*I Travelled among Unknown Men* 1807]

He travelled here, he travelled there; –
But not the value of a hair
Was head or heart the better.

[*Peter Bell* 1819]

War and Peace

Muhammad Ali [Cassius Marcellus Clay], 1942– , American boxer
Keep asking me no matter how long –
On the war in Vietnam I sing this song –
I ain't got no quarrel with the Viet Cong.

[On the draft 1966]

Lewis Addison Armistead, 1817–63, American general
Give them the cold steel, boys!

[At the Battle of Gettysburg, 1863]

Bernard M[annes] Baruch, 1870–1965, American financier
Let us not be deceived – we are today in the midst of a cold war.

[To a Senate Committee 1948]

August Bebel, 1840–1913, German socialist politician
In the time of war, the loudest patriots are the greatest profiteers

[1870]

Menachem Begin, 1913–92, Israeli statesman
The ancient Jewish people gave the New World a vision of eternal peace, of universal disarmament, of abolishing the teaching and learning of war.

[At the signing of the peace treaty between Egypt and Israel, 1979]

[Joseph] Hilaire [Pierre] Belloc, 1870–1953, English writer
Pale Ebenezer thought it wrong to fight,
But Roaring Bill (who killed him) thought it right.

[*Epigrams: The Pacifist*]

Ruth Fulton Benedict 1887–1948, American anthropologist
If we justify war it is because all peoples always justify the traits of which they find themselves possessed.

Alan Bennett, 1934– , English playwright
I have never understood this liking for war. It panders to instincts already catered for within the scope of any respectable domestic establishment.

[*Forty Years On*]

Helmuth Karl Bernard, Count von Moltke, 1800–91, Prussian fieldmarshal
Everlasting peace is a dream, and not even a beautiful one.

[Letter 1880]

351

Sir John Betjeman, 1906–84, English poet
Gracious Lord, oh bomb the Germans,
Spare their women for Thy Sake,
And if that is not too easy
We will parden Thy Mistake.
But, gracious Lord, whate'er shall be,
Don't let anyone bomb me.

[John Betjeman's Collected Poems: In Westminster Abbey 1958]

The Bible
Peace be to you.

[Genesis 43:12]

How are the mighty fallen in the midst of battle! O Jonathan, thou wast slain in thine high places. I am distressed for thee, my brother Jonathan.

[2 Samuel 1:25]

How are the mighty fallen, and the weapons of war perished!

[Ibid 1:27]

Happy is the man that findeth wisdom, and the man that getteth understanding . . . Her ways are ways of pleasantness, and all her paths are peace.

[Proverbs 3:17]

Blessed are the peacemakers: for they shall be called the children of God.

[Matthew 5:9]

Put up again thy sword into his place: for all they that take the sword shall perish with the sword.

[Ibid 26:52]

Glory to God in the highest, and on earth peace, good will toward men.

[Luke 2:14]

Ambrose [Gwinett] Bierce, 1824–1914, American writer
Peace: in international affairs, a period of cheating between two periods of fighting.

[The Devil's Dictionary 1906]

Tony [Anthony Charles Linton] Blair, 1953– , British politician
This mass terrorism is the new evil in our world today. It is perpetrated by fanatics who are utterly indifferent to the sanctity of life and we, the democracies of this world, are going to have to come together and fight it together and eradicate this evil completely from our world.

[Speech following terrorist attacks on World Trade Centre, September 11 2001]

Omar Nelson Bradley, 1893–1981, American general
The wrong war, at the wrong place, at the wrong time, and with the wrong enemy.

[To a Senate inquiry into extending the Korean conflict into China, 1951]

Bertolt Brecht, 1898–1956, German dramatist and poet
On the wall in chalk is written
'They want war'
He who wrote it has already fallen.

[Collected Poems 1913–1956]

What they could do with round here is a good war. What else can you expect with peace running wild all over the place? You know what the trouble with peace is? No organization.

[Mother Courage and Her Children 1 1941]

George [Herbert Walker] Bush, 1924– , 41st president of the United States
War is never cheap or easy.

[Quoted in the *Observer* July 14 1991]

George W[illiam Herbert] Bush, 43rd president of the United States
Terrorist attacks can shake the foundations of our biggest buildings, but they cannot touch the foundation of America. These acts shatter steel, but they cannot dent the steel of American resolve.
America was targeted for attack because we're the brightest beacon for freedom and opportunity in the world. And no one will keep that light from shining.

[Speech on CNN following terrorist attacks on World Trade Centre, September 11 2001]

Byron, Lord George Gordon [Noel], 6th Baron Byron of Rochdale, 1788–1824, English poet
The Assyrian came down like the wolf on the fold,
And his cohorts were gleaming in purple and gold;
And the sheen of their spears was like stars on the sea,
When the blue wave rolls nightly on deep Gallilee.

[*Destruction of Sennacherib* 1815]

Sir Winston [Leonard Spencer] Churchill, 1874–1965 British statesman
Nothing in life is so exhilarating as to be shot at without result.

[*The Malakand Field Force* 1898]

I cannot forecast to you the action of Russia. It is a riddle wrapped in a mystery inside an enigma; but perhaps there is a key. That key is Russian national interest.

[Broadcast talk 1939]

I would say to the House, as I said to those who have joined this Government, "I have nothing to offer but blood, toil, tears and sweat."

[In the House of Commons, 13 May 1940]

We shall not flag or fail. We shall go on to the end, we shall fight in France, we shall fight on the seas and oceans, we shall fight with growing confidence and growing strength in the air, we shall defend our island, whatever the cost may be, we shall fight on the beaches, we shall fight on the landing grounds, we shall fight in the fields and in the streets, we shall fight in the hills; we shall never surrender.

[*Ibid* 4 June 1940]

Victory at all costs, victory in spite of all terror, victory however long and hard the road may be; for without victory there is no survival.

[*Ibid* 13 May 1940]

[On the Battle of Britain pilots] Never in the field of human conflict was so much owed by so many to so few.

[*Ibid* 20 August 1940]

Karl von Clausewitz, 1780–1831, Prussian general
War is the continuation of politics by other means.

[*On War* 1832]

War belongs, not to the Arts and Sciences, but to the province of social life.

[*Ibid*]

Confucius [K'ung fu-tzu], 551–479BC, Chinese philosopher
To lead an untrained people to war is to throw them away.

[*Analects c.* 500BC]

Ely Culbertson, 1893–1955, American bridge player
God and the politicians willing, the United States can declare peace upon the world, and win it.
[*Must We Fight Russia?* 1946]

Dwight D[avid] Eisenhower, 1890–1969, American general and 34th president of the United States
In preparing for battle I have always found that plans are useless, but planning is indispensable.
[Attributed]

Ferdinand Foch, 1851–1929, marshal of France
Mon centre cède, ma droite recule, situation excellente, j'attaque.
My centre is giving way, my right is pushed back, situation excellent, I am attacking.
[Message during the Battle of the Marne, 1914]

Benjamin Franklin, 1706–90, American scientist and philosopher
There never was a good war or a bad peace.
[Letter 1773]

Mohandas Karamchand ("Mahatma") Gandhi, 1869–1948, Indian political leader
What difference does it make to the dead, the orphans and the homeless, whether the mad destruction is wrought under the name of totalitarianism or the holy name of liberty and democracy?
[*Non-Violence in Peace and War* 1948]

John Gay, 1685–1732, English poet and playwright
Those who in quarrels interpose
Must often wipe a bloody nose.
[*Fables* 1727]

Oliver Goldsmith, 1728–74, Irish-born English writer
He who fights and runs away
May live to fight another day.
[*The Art of Poetry on a New Plan* 1761]

The first blow is half the battle.
[*She Stoops to Conquer* 1773]

Ulysses S[impson] Grant, 1822–85, 18th president of the United States
The art of war is simple enough. Find out where your enemy is. Get at him as soon as you can. Strike him as hard as you can and as often as you can, and keep moving on.
[*On the Art of War*]

William Frederic ("Bull") Hallsey, 1882–1959, American admiral
Our ships have been salvaged and are retiring at high speed toward the Japanese fleet.
[Radio message following claims that the American fleet had been sunk or was retiring, 1944]

Thomas Hardy, 1840–1928, English novelist and poet
Yes; quaint and curious war is!
You shoot a fellow down
You'd treat if met where any bar is,
Or help to half-a-crown.
[*The Man He Killed* 1902]

Mrs Felicia Dorothea Hemans, 1793–1835, English poet
The boy stood on the burning deck
Whence all but he had fled;
The flame that lit the battle's wreck
Shone round him o'er the dead.

[*Casabianca*]

Hesiod, *fl*. 8th century BC, Greek poet
Peace is a nursing mother to the land.

[*Works and Days* c.700BC]

Thomas Hobbes, 1588–1679, English philosopher
The first and fundamental law of nature . . . is to seek peace and follow it.

[*Leviathan* 1651]

Oliver Wendell Holmes, 1809–94, American physician and writer
The peaceful are the strong.

[*A Voice of the Loyal North* 1861]

Homer, *fl*. 9th century BC, Greek poet
Men would rather have their fill of sleep, love, singing and dancing than of war.

[*Iliad c*. 800BC]

Herbert [Clark] Hoover, 1874–1964, 31st president of the United States
Older men declare war. But it is youth that must fight and die.

[Speech 1944]

A[lfred] E[dward] Housman, 1859–1936, English poet and scholar
Here dead lie we because we did not choose
To live and shame the land from which we sprung.
Life, to be sure, is nothing much to lose;
But young men think it is, and we were young.

[*More Poems: Epigraph* 1936]

I did not lose my heart in summer's even,
When roses to the moonrise burst apart:
When plumes were under heel and lead was flying,
In blood and smoke and flame I lost my heart.

[*Ibid*]

I lost it to a soldier and a foeman,
A chap that did not kill me, but he tried;
That took the sabre straight and took it striking
And laughed and kissed his hand to me and died.

[*Ibid*]

Saddam Hussein, 1937– , Iraqi dictator
The mother of battles will be our battle of victory and our martyrdom.
[Speech before the Gulf War. In the *Times* January 7 1991]

Aldous [Leonard] Huxley, 1894–1936, English writer
The most shocking fact about war is that its victims and its instruments are individual human beings and that these individuals are condemned by the monstrous conventions of politics to murder or be murdered in quarrels not their own.

[*The Olive Tree* 1937]

355

Thomas Jefferson, 1743–1826, 3rd president of the United States
I think with the Romans of old, that the general of today should be a common soldier tomorrow, if necessary.

[Letter 1797]

John Paul II [Karol Wojtyla], 1920– , Polish pope
War should belong to the tragic past, in history. It should find no place on humanity's agenda for the future.

[Address at Coventry 1982]

[Gaius] Julius Caesar, c.100–44BC, Roman statesman
In war trivial causes produce momentous events.

[*The Gallic War* 51BC]

John Fitzgerald Kennedy, 1917–63, 35th president of the United States
Let us never negotiate out of fear, but let us never fear to negotiate.

[Inaugural address 1961]

Mankind must put an end to war or war will put an end to mankind.

[Address to the United Nations 1961]

Rudyard Kipling, 1865–1936, English writer
I went into a theatre as sober as could be,
They gave a drunk civilian room, but 'adn't none for me;
They sent me to the gallery or round the music-'alls,
But when it comes to fighting', Lord! they'll shove me in the stalls!
For it's Tommy this, an' Tommy that, an' "Tommy, wait outside";
But it's "Special train for Atkins" when the trooper's on the tide.

[*Barrack-Room Ballads* 1892]

For it's Tommy this, an' Tommy that, an' "Chuck himout, the brute!"
But it's "Saviour of 'is country" when the guns begin to shoot.

[*Ibid*]

Robert E[dward] Lee, 1807–70, American Confederate general
It is well that war is so terrible, or we should grow too fond of it.

[On seeing a Federal charge beaten back at Fredericksburg, December 1862]

John [Winston] Lennon, 1940–80, and Paul McCartney, 1942– , English pop singers and songwriters
Give Peace a Chance.

[Song title 1969]

Abraham Lincoln, 1809–65, 16th president of the United States
We have met on a great battlefield of that war. We have come to dedicate a portion of that field, as a final resting place for those who here gave their lives that the nation might live. It is altogether fitting and proper that we should do this. But in a larger sense we cannot dedicate – we cannot consecrate – we cannot hallow – this ground. The brave men, living and dead, who struggled here, have consecrated it far above our poor power to add or detract. The world will little note nor long remember what we say here, but it can never forget what they did here.

[*The Gettysburg Address* 1863]

Eric [Robert Russell] Linklater, 1899–1974, Scottish novelist
Kings had fallen and nations perished, armies had withered and cities been ruined for this and this alone: that poor men in stinking pubs might have great wealth of memory.

[*Magnus Merriman*]

Walter Lippmann, 1889–1974, American journalist
We must remember that in time of war what is said on the enemy's side of the front is always propaganda and what is said on our side of the front is truth and righteousness, the cause of humanity and a crusade for peace.

[1966]

Henry Wadsworth Longfellow, 1807–82, American poet
Buried was the bloody hatchet;
Buried was the dreadful war-club;
Buried were all war-like weapons,
And the war-cry was forgotten,
Then was peace among the nations.

[*The Song of Hiawatha*, 1855]

Martin Luther, 1483–1546, German religious reformer
War is the greatest plague that can afflict humanity; it destroys religion, it destroys states, it destroys families. Any scourge is preferable to it.

[1569. In Hazlitt's *Table Talk* 1821–2]

Dr John McCrae, 1872–1918, Canadian physician and poet
In Flanders fields the poppies blow
Between the crosses, row on row,
That mark our place.
If ye break faith with us who die
We shall not sleep, though poppies grow
In Flanders Fields.

[*In Flanders Fields* 1915]

Don McCullin, 1935– , English photographer
What's the point of getting killed if you've got the wrong exposure.

[*The Destruction Business* 1971]

Malcolm X [Malcolm Little], 1925–65, American black militant leader
You can't separate peace from freedom because no one can be at peace unless he has his freedom.

[*Malcolm X Speaks* 1965]

Mao Tse-Tung, 1893–1976, Chinese revolutionary leader
Politics is war without bloodshed, while war is politics with bloodshed.

[*Quotations from Chairman Mao* 1966]

Golda Meir [Goldie Mabovich], 1898–1978, Israeli stateswoman
I've never had to kill anyone. I'm not saying it with relief. There's no difference between one's killing and making decisions that will send others to kill.

Slobodan Milosevic, 1941– , Serbian politician
America crosses the globe to struggle against terrorism in Afghanistan, but to fight terrorism in the heart of your own country is considered to be a crime. Our defence was a heroic defence against the aggression of the NATO pact.
[Address to U.N. War Crimes Tribunal February 14 2002]

John Milton, 1608–74, English poet
No war, or battle's sound
Was heard the world around:
The idle spear and shield were hung up high.
[*On the Morning of Christ's Nativity* 1629]

Napoleon I [Napoleon Bonaparte], 1769–1821, emperor of France
What a beautiful fix we are in now: peace has been declared!
[After the Treaty of Amiens 1802]

Friedrich Wilhelm Nietzsche, 1844–1900, German philosopher and poet
The things necessary to Buddhism are a very mild climate, customs of great gentleness and liberality, and no militarism.
[*The Antichrist* 1888]

Richard Milhous Nixon, 1913–94, 37th president of the United States
The greatest honor history can bestow is the title of peacemaker. This honor now beckons America . . . This is our summons to greatness.
[Inaugural address 1969]

Frederick, Lord North, 2nd Earl of Guildford, 1732–92, British statesman
I do not know whether our generals will frighten the enemy, but I know they frighten me whenever I think of them.
[Attributed *c*.1776]

George Orwell [Eric Arthur Blair], 1903–50, English novelist and critic
War is war. The only good human being is a dead one
[*Animal Farm* 1945]

Wilfred Owen, 1893–1918, English poet
Dullness best solves
The tease and doubt of shelling,
And Chance's strange arithmetic
Comes simpler than the reckoning of their shilling.
They keep no check on armies' decimation.
[*Insensibility*]

Happy the soldier home, with not a notion
How somewhere, every dawn, some men attack,
And many sights are drained.
[*Ibid*]

What passing-bells for those who die as cattle?
Only the monstrous anger of the guns.
[*Anthem for Doomed Youth*]

Thomas Parnell, 1679–1718, Irish-born English poet
Lovely, lasting peace of mind,
Sweet delight of human kind.

[*Hymn to Contentment* 1721]

Polybius, c.203–120BC, Greek historian
A good general not only sees the way to victory; he also knows when victory is impossible.

[*Histories c*.125BC]

John Ruskin, 1819–1900, English art critic
You may either win your peace or buy it – win it, by resistance to evil; buy it, by compromise
with evil.

[*The Two Paths* 1859]

Sallust [Caius Sallustius Crispus] 86–c.34BC, Roman historian
It is always easy to begin a war, but very difficult to stop one, since its beginning and end are
not under the control of the same man. Anyone, even a coward, can commence a war, but it
can be brought to an end only with the consent of the victors.

[*Jugurtha*]

Siegfried Sassoon, 1886–1967, English poet
But death replied: "I choose him." So he went,
And there was silence in the summer night;
Silence and safety; and the veils of sleep.
Then, far away, the thudding of the guns.

[*The Death-Bed*]

William Shakespeare, 1564–1616, English dramatist
Once more into the breach, dear friends, once more:
Or close the wall up with our English dead!
In peace ther's nothing so becomes a man
As modest stillness and humility:
But when the blast of war blows in our ears,
Then imitate the action of the tiger;
Stiffen the sinews, summon up the blood,
Disguise fair nature with hard-favour'ed rage;
Then lend the eye a terrible aspect.

[*King Henry V* 3 1598–1600]

I see you stand like greyhounds in the slips,
Straining upon the start. The game's afoot:
Follow your spirit; and, upon this charge
Cry "God for Harry! England and Saint George!"

[*Ibid*]

Cry, "Havoc!" and let slip the dogs of war.

[*Julius Caesar* 1598–1600]

Let me have war, say I; it exceeds peace as far as day does night; it's spritely, waking, audible,
and full of vent. Peace is a very apoplexy, lethargy: mulled, deaf, sleep, insensible; a getter of
more bastard children than war's a destroyer of men.

[*Coriolanus* 5 1607–8]

If you have writ your annals true, 'tis there,
That, like an eagle in a dovecote, I
Flutter'd your Volscians in Corioli:
Alone I did it.

[*Ibid*]

William [Tecumseh] Sherman, 1820–91, American Unionist general
You cannot qualify war in harsher terms than I will. War is cruelty, and you cannot refine it.
[Letter 1864]
War is at best barbarism . . . Its glory is all moonshine. It is only those who have neither fired a shot nor heard the shrieks and groans of the wounded who cry aloud for blood, more vengeance, more desolation. War is hell.
[Attributed 1879]

Alfred, Lord Tennyson, 1809–92, English poet
The war-drum throbb'd no longer, and the battle-flags were furl'd
In the parliament of man, the federation of the world.
[*Locksley Hall* 1842]

Sir Peter [Alexander] Ustinov, 1921– , English playwright and actor
Generals are fascinating cases of arrested development – after all, at five we all of us wanted to be generals.
[In *The Illustrated London News* 1968]

Horace Walpole, 4th Earl of Orford, 1717–97, English writer
When will the world know that peace and propagation are the two most delightful things in it?
[Letter 1778]

George Washington, 1732–99, 1st president of the United States
There is nothing so likely to produce peace as to be well prepared to meet an enemy.
[Letter 1780]

Elie[zer] Weisel, 1928– , Romanian-born American writer and Auschwitz survivor.
Close your eyes and listen. Listen to the silent screams of terrified mothers, the prayers of anguished old men and women. Listen to the tears of children, Jewish children, a beautiful little girl among them, with golden hair, whose vulnerable tenderness has never left me. Look and listen as they quietly walk towards dark flames so gigantic that the planet itself seemed in danger.
[Speech to mark the fiftieth anniversary of the liberation of Auschwitz, January 27 1995]

Oscar [Fingal O'Flahertie Wills] Wilde, 1854–1900, Irish writer
As long as war is regarded as wicked, it will always have its fascination. When it is looked upon as vulgar, it will cease to be popular.
[*The Critic as Artist* 1891]

Gary Wills, 1934– , American journalist
Only the winners decide what were war crimes.
[*New York Times* 1975]

Thomas Woodrow Wilson, 1856–1924, 28th president of the United States
It must be a peace without victory. Only a peace between equals can last: only a peace, the very principle of which is eqality, and a common participation in a common benefit.

[Address to the Senate 1917]

Advice and Instruction

Douglas Adams, 1952–2001, English writer
Don't panic.

[*The Hitchhiker's Guide to the Galaxy* 1979]

Joseph Addison, 1672–1719, English essayist
There is not a more unhappy being than a superannuated idol.

[*The Spectator* 24 May 1711]

George Ade, 1866–1944, American humorist, writer and dramatist
Do unto yourself as your neighbours do unto themselves.

[*Hand-Made Fables*]

Nelson Algren, 1909–81, American novelist
Never play cards with a man called Doc. Never eat at a place called Mom's. Never sleep with a woman whose troubles are worse than your own. Never let nobody talk you into shaking another man's jolt. And never you cop another man's plea. I've tried 'em all and I know. They don't work.

[*A Walk on the Wild Side* 1956]

Anonymous
Be slow in choosing, but slower in change.

[Proverb]

Dig for Victory.

[British government poster, *c*.1940]

If you mock the lame, you will go so yourself in time.

[Proverb]

Say it with Flowers

[American advertising slogan, *c*. 1920]

George Asaf, 1880–1951, English songwriter
What's the use of worrying?
It never was worthwhile,
So, pack up your troubles in your old kitbag
And smile, smile, smile.

[Song: *Pack up your Troubles* 1915]

Richard Harris Barham, 1788–1845, English humorist
Never borrow a horse you don't know of a friend.

[*The Smuggler's Leap*]

Sir J[ames] M[atthew] Barrie, 1860–1937, Scottish playwright
Never ascribe to an opponent motives meaner than your own.

[*Courage* 1922]

Sir Arnold Bax, 1883–1953, English composer
One should try everything once, except incest and folk-dancing.

[*Farewell My Youth* 1943]

[John] Anthony Burgess [Wilson], 1917–93, English-born novelist and critic
The best thing to do, when you've got a dead body and it's your husband's on the kitchen floor, and you don't know what to do about it, is to make yourself a good strong cup of tea.

[*One Hand Clapping*]

Lewis Carroll [Charles Lutwidge Dodgson], 1832–92, English mathematician and writer
Off with his head!

[*Alice's Adventures in Wonderland* 1865]

Take care of the sense, and the sounds will take care of themselves.

[*Ibid*]

Thomas Carlyle, 1795–1881, Scottish historian and writer
Do the duty that lies nearest thee; which thou knowest to be a duty! The second duty will already become clearer.

[*Sartor Resartus*]

Charles I, 1600–49, King of England, Scotland and Ireland
Never make a defence or apology before you are accused.

[*Letter to Lord Wentworth*]

Sir Winston [Leonard Spencer] Churchill, 1874–1965]
And here I say to parents, especially wealthy parents, "Don't give your son money. As far as you can afford it, give him horses."

[*My Early Life* 1930]

Sir Noel [Pierce] Coward, 1899–1973, English actor and playwright
[On acting] Just know your lines and don't bump into the furniture.

[Attributed]

Phyllis Diller, 1917– , American writer and comedienne.
Never go to bed mad. Stay up and fight.

[*Phyllis Diller's Housekeeping Hints* 1966]

Finlay Peter Dunne ("Mr Dooley"), 1867–1936, American humorist
Don't jump on a man unless he's down.

[*Mr Dooley Remembers*]

Edward VIII, 1894–1972, King of Great Britain and Northern Ireland
Perhaps one of the only positive pieces of advice that I was ever given was that supplied by an old courtier who observed: "Only two rules really count. Never miss an opportunity to relieve yourself; never miss a chance to sit down and rest your feet."

[*A King's Story* 1951]

Oliver Goldsmith, 1728–74, Irish-born English writer
Ask me no questions, and I'll tell you no fibs.

[*She stoops to Conquer* 3 1773]

Edmund de Goncourt, 1822–96 and Jules de Goncourt, 1830–70, French novelists
Never speak of yourself to others; make them talk about themselves instead: therein lies the whole art of pleasing.

[*Idées et Sensations* 1866]

Joyce Grenfell, 1910–79, English actress and comedienne
George – don't do that.

[Catchphrase in comedy sketches]

Dag Hammarskjöld, 1905–1961, Swedish secretary general of the UN
Never let success hide its emptiness from you, achievement its nothingness, toil its desolation. And so . . . keep alive the incentive to push on further, that pain in the soul which drives us beyond ourselves . . . Do not look back. And do not dream about the future, either. It will neither give you back the past, nor satisfy your other daydreams.

[*Markings* 1965]

Frank McKinney ("Kin") Hubbard, 1868–1930 American humorist
The safest way to double your money is to fold it over and put it in your pocket.

David Hume, 1711–76, Scottish philosopher and writer
Be a philosopher, but, amidst all your philosophy, be still a man.

[*A Treatise of Human Nature* 1739–40]

Mick [Michael Philip] Jagger, 1943– , Keith Richards, 1943– , British rock musicians
You can't always get what you want
But if you try sometimes,
You just might find
You get what you need.

[Song: *You Can't Always Get What You Want*]

Dr Samuel Johnson, 1709–84, English lexicographer
The advice that is wanted is commonly unwelcome, and that which is not wanted is evidently impertinent.

[*The Piozzi Letters* 1788]

Erica Jong, 1942– , American writer and poet
Advice is what we ask for when we already know the answer but wish we didn't.

[*How to Save Your Own Life* 1977]

Charles Kingsley, 1819–75, English churchman and writer
Do noble things, not dream them all day long.

[*A Farewell*]

Stanislaw Jerzy Lec, 1909–66, Polish writer
When you jump for joy, beware that no-one moves the ground from beneath your feet.

[*Unkempt Thoughts* 1962]

ADVICE AND INSTRUCTION

James Russell Lowell, 1819–91, American editor and poet
Don't ever prophesy – unless ye know.

[*The Biglow Papers*]

George Lucas, 1944– , American filmmaker
Feel the Force!

[Obi-wan Kenobi (Alec Guiness) in *Star Wars* film 1977]

Robert Lynd, 1879–1949, Irish journalist and essayist
Never speak when you are angry. If you do you'll make the best speech you'll ever regret.

[*The Blue Lion* 1923]

Philip Massinger, 1583–1640, English dramatist
You must practise
The manners of the time, if you intend
To have favour from it.

[*The Unnatural Combat* 1]

W[illiam] Somerset Maugham, 1874–1965, English novelist
You can't learn too soon that the most useful thing about a principle is that it can always be sacrificed to expediency.

[*The Circle* 1]

Phyllis McGinley, 1905–78, American writer and poet
This is the gist of what I know:
Give advice and buy a foe.

[*The Love Letters of Phyllis McGinley*]

Arthur Miller, 1915– , American playwright
Never fight fair with a stranger, my boy. You'll never get out of the jungle that way.

[*Death of a Salesman* 1949]

Henry [Valentine] Miller, 1891–1980, American novelist
Do anything, but let it produce joy.

[*Tropic of Cancer* 1934]

A[lan] A[lexander] Milne, 1882–1926, English writer
Underneath the knocker there was a notice which said:
PLES RING IF AN RNSER IS REQIRD.
Underneath the bell-pull there was a notice which said:
PLES CNOKE IF AN RNSER IS NOT REQID.

[*Winnie the Pooh* 1926]

You must never go down to the end of the town if you don't go down with me.
[*When We Were Very Young: Disobedience* 1924]

Wilson Mizner, 1876–1933, American gambler
Be nice to people on your way up, because you'll meet them on your way down.

[Saying]

Lady Mary Wortley Montagu, 1689–1762, English writer
Be plain in dress, and sober in your diet;
In short, my deary! kiss me, and be quiet.

[*A Summary of Lord Lyttleton's Advice*]

Robin Morgan, 1941– , American feminist writer and poet
Don't accept rides from strange men,
and remember that all men are as strange as hell.

[Sisterhood is Powerful: Letter to a Sister Underground 1970]

William Morris, 1834–96, English artist, novelist and poet
If you want a golden rule that will fit everybody, this is it: Have nothing in your house that you
do not know to be useful, or believe to be beautiful.

[Hopes and Fears for Art 1882]

Napoleon I [Napoleon Bonaparte], 1769–1821, emperor of France
If you want a thing done well, do it yourself.

[Maxims]

Dorothy [Rothschild] Parker, 1893–1967, American writer
Early to bed, and you'll wish you were dead.

[The Little Hours]

Alexander Pope, 1688–1744, English poet
Do good by stealth, and blush to find it fame.

[Epilogue to the Satires]

François, Duc de La Rochefoucauld, 1613–80, French writer
Old people like to give good advice, as solace for no longer being able to provide bad
examples.

[Reflections, or Sentences and Moral Maxims 1665]

Theodore Roosevelt, 1858–1919, 26th president of the United States
Do not hit at all if it can be avoided, but never hit softly.

[Autobiography 1913]

J[oanne] K[athleen] Rowling, 1965– , English author
"Never trust something that can think for itself if you can't see where it keeps its brain!"

[Harry Potter and the Chamber of Secrets 1997]

Willie [William George] Rushton, 1937–96, English actor, writer and broadcaster
How to give up smoking. Stop putting cigarettes in your mouth and lighting them.

[Super Pig]

William Shakespeare, 1564–1616, English dramatist
This above all – to thine own self be true,
And it must follow, as the night the day,
Thou canst not then be false to any man.

[Hamlet 1 1600–1]

Give every man thy ear, but few thy voice;
Take each man's censure, but reserve thy judgement.

[Ibid]

Trust none.
For oaths are straws, men's faiths are wafer-cakes,
And hold-fast is the only dog, my duck.

[King Henry V 2 1598–1600]

Be just, and fear not:
Let all the ends thou aim'st at be thy country's,
Thy God's, and truth's.

[*King Henry VIII* 3 1613]

Gary [Sherman] Snyder, 1930– , American poet
Taste all, and hand the knowledge down.

[*Turtle Island: Ethnobotany* 1975]

Philip Dormer Stanhope, 4th Earl of Chesterfield, 1694–1773
Never put off till tomorrow what you can do today.

[Letter to his son February 5 1750]

Steven Stills, 1945– , American rock musician and songwriter
If you can't be with the one you love,
Love the one you're with.

[Song: *Love the One You're With*]

James Grover Thurber, 1894–1961, American humorist and cartoonist
Men of all degrees should form this prudent habit:
Never serve a rabbit stew before you catch the rabbit.

[*Further Fables of Our Time*]

Mark Twain [Samuel Langhorne Clemens], 1835–1910, American writer
Behold, the fool saith, "Put not all thine eggs in the one basket" – which is but a manner of saying, "Scatter your money and your attention," but the wise man saith, "Put all your eggs in the one basket and – *watch that basket.*"

[*Pudd'nhead Wilson* 1894]

Gore [Eugene Luther] Vidal, 1925– , American novelist and critic
Never miss a chance to have sex or appear on television.

[Attributed]

George Washington, 1732–99, 1st president of the United States of America
Associate yourself with men of good quality if you esteem your own reputation; for 'tis better to be alone than in bad company.

[*Rules of Civility*]

Irvine Welsh, 1958– , Scottish author
Choose us. Choose life. Choose mortgage payments; choose washing machines; choose cars; choose spitting oan a couch watching mind-numbing and spirit-crushing game shows, stuffing fuckin junk food intae yir mooth. Choose rotting away, pishing and shiteing yersel in a home, a total fuckin embarrassment tae the selfish, fucked-up brats ye've produced. Choose life.

[*Trainspotting* 1993]

Mae West, 1892–1980, American entertainer
I always say, keep a diary and some day it'll keep you.

[Attributed]

Oscar [Fingal O'Flahertie Wills] Wilde, 1854–1900, Irish writer
I always pass on good advice. It is the only thing to do with it. It is never any use to oneself.

[*An Ideal Husband* 1895]

Thornton [Niven] Wilder, 1897–1975, American playwright
Never support two weaknesses at the same time. It's your combination sinners – your lecherous liars and your miserly drunkards – who dishonour the vices and bring them into bad repute.

[*The Matchmaker* 3]

William Hale White [pseudonym Mark Rutherford], 1831–1944, English writer
Never say anything remarkable. It is sure to be wrong.

[*Last Pages from a Journal* 1915]

Ludwig Joseph Johann Wittgenstein, 1889–1951, Austrian-born British philosopher
Never stay up on the barren heights of cleverness, but come down into the green valleys of silliness.

[Journal entry 1948. In *Culture and Value* 1980]

Good, Evil and Morality

Samuel Alexander, 1859–1938, Australian philosopher

Evil is not . . . wholly evil; it is misplaced good.

[*Space, Time and Deity*]

Anonymous

Do good, reap good. Do evil, reap evil.

[Proverb]

To do good is like ascending a mountain; to do evil is as easy as following an avalanche.

[Chinese Proverb]

St Thomas Aquinas, 1225–74, Italian theologian

Evil denotes the Absence of Good. But it is not every absence of good that is called evil.

[*Summa Theologiae*]

Good and evil are essential differences of the act of the will. For good and evil pertain essentially to the will; just as truth and falsehood pertain to the reason, the act of which is distinguished essentially by the difference of truth and falsehood (according as we say that an opinion is true or false.) Consequently, good and evil volition are acts differing in species.

[*Ibid*]

Hannah Arendt, 1906–75, German-born American philosopher

The fearsome, word-and-thought-defying *banality of evil*.

[*Eichmann in Jerusalem* 1963]

W[ystan] H[ugh] Auden, 1907–73, English-born poet

Leave Truth to the police and us; we know the Good;
We build the Perfect City time shall never alter;
Our Law shall guard you always like a cirque of mountains.
Your ignorance keep off evil like a dangerous sea;
You shall be consummated in the General Will,
Your children innocent and charming as beasts.

[*Journey to a War: In Time of War* 1939]

I and the public know
What all schoolchildren learn,
Those to whom evil is done
Do evil in return.

[*Another Time:September 1, 1939*]

Charles Pierre Baudelaire, 1821–67, French poet

Evil is done without effort, naturally, it is the working of fate; good is always the product of an art.

[*L'Art Romantique* 1869]

What do I care that you are good? Be beautiful! and be sad!

[*Nouvelles Fleurs de Mal: Madrigal Triste* 1959]

Saul Bellow, 1915– , American writer

There are evils . . . that have the ability to survive identification and go on for ever . . . money, for instance, or war.

[*The Dean's December* 1982]

Sir Isaiah Berlin, 1907–97, British philosopher

Injustice, poverty, slavery, ignorance – these may be cured by reform or revolution. But men do not live only by fighting evils. They live by positive goals, individual and collective, a vast variety of them, seldom predictable, at times incompatible.

[*Four Essays on Liberty*]

The Bible

For he maketh his sun to rise on the evil and the good, and sendeth rain on the just and the unjust.

[*Matthew* 5:45]

Resist not evil: but whosoever shall smite thee on thy right cheek, turn to him the other also.

[*Matthew* 5:39]

Let us do evil, that good may come.

[*Romans* 3:8]

Beloved, follow not that which is evil, but that which is good. He that doeth good is of God: but he that doeth evil hath not seen God.

[*3 John* 12]

William Blake, 1757–1827, English poet and artist

He who would do good to another, must do it in Minute Particulars:
General Good is the plea of the scoundrel, hypocrite and flatterer.

[*Jerusalem* 1804–20]

Robert Oxton Bolt, 1924–95, English playwright

Morality's not practical. Morality's a gesture. A complicated gesture learned from books.

[*A Man for All Seasons* 2 1960]

Bertolt Brecht, 1898–1956, German dramatist and poet

The wickedness of the world is so great you have to run your legs off to avoid having them stolen from under you.

[*Threepenny Opera* 1928]

Robert Browning, 1812–89, English poet

And that's what all the blessed evil's for.

[*Bishop Bloughram's Apology*]

Jean de La Bruyère, 1645–96, French moralist

There exist some evils so terrible and some misfortunes so horrible that we dare not think of them . . . but if they happen to fall on us, we find ourselves stronger than we imagined, we grapple with our ill luck, and behave better than we expected we should.

[*Characters, or The Manners of the Age* 1688]

370

Edmund Burke, 1729–97, Irish-born English philosopher
The only thing necessary for the triumph of evil is for good men to do nothing.

[Attributed]

Robert Burns, 1759–96, Scottish poet
It's guid to be merry and wise,
It's guid to be honest and true,
It's guid to support Caledonia's cause,
And bide by the buff and the blue.

[*Here's a Health to Them That's Awa'*]

William Burroughs, 1914–97, American author
The face of "evil" is always the face of total need.

[*The Naked Lunch* 1962]

Albert Camus,1913–60, Algerian-born French philosopher and novelist
The rebel can never find peace. He knows what is good and, despite himself, does evil.

[*The Rebel* 1951]

John Cheever, 1912–82, American novelist
Wisdom we know is the knowledge of good and evil, not the strength to choose between the two.

[*Journals*]

G[ilbert] K[eith] Chesterton, 1874–1936, English writer
When some English moralists write about the importance of having character, they appear to mean only the importance of having a dull character.

[*Charles Dickens*]

Confucius [K'ung fu-tzu], 551–479BC, Chinese philosopher
True goodness springs from a man's own heart. All men are born good.

[*Analects*]

T[homas] S[tearns] Eliot, 1888–1965, American-born English poet
For every life and every act
Consequence of good and evil can be shown
And as in time results of many deeds are blended
So good and evil in the end become confounded.

[*Murder in the Cathedral*]

Henry Havelock Ellis, 1859–1939, English psychologist and writer
What we call morals is simply blind obedience to words of command.

[*The Dance of Life* 1923]

Ralph Waldo Emerson, 1803–82, American writer
In front of these sinister facts, the first lesson in history is the good of evil. Good is a good doctor, but Bad is sometimes a better.

[*The Conduct of Life* 1860]

Christopher [Harris] Fry, 1907– , English poet and playwright
We don't want to put ourselves wrong
With anything as positive as evil.

[*The Lady's Not for Burning* 1949]

Paul Gaugin, 1848–1903, French artist

Virtue, good and evil are nothing but words, unless one takes them apart in order to build something with them; they do not win their true meaning until one knows how to apply them.

[Intimate Journals]

[Henry] Grahame Greene, 1904–91, English novelist

Morality comes with the sad wisdom of age, when the sense of curiosity has withered.

[A Sort of Life 1971]

Thomas Hobbes, 1588–1679, English political philosopher

In sum, all actions and habits are to be esteemed good or evil by their causes and usefulness in reference to the commonwealth, and not by their mediocrity, nor by their being commended. For several men praise several customs, and, contrarily, what one calls vice, another calls virtue, as their present affections lead them.

[Behemoth]

Thomas Hood, 1799–1845, English poet

But evil is wrought by want of thought,
As well as want of heart!

[The Lady's Dream]

David Hume, 1711–76, Scottish philosopher and writer

Good and ill, both natural and moral, are entirely relative to human sentiment and affection.

[Essays, Moral and Political: The Sceptic]

Aldous [Leonard] Huxley, 1894–1963, English writer

Good is that which makes for unity; Evil is that which makes for separateness.

[Ends and Means]

Carl Gustav Jung, 1875–1961, Swiss psychiatrist

Man's psyche should be studied because we are the origin of all coming evil.
[Television interview 1959]

Franz Kafka, 1883–1924, Austrian writer

When one has once accepted and absorbed Evil, it no longer demands the unfitness of the means. The ulterior motives with which you absorb and assimilate Evil are not your own but those of Evil . . . Evil is whatever distracts. Evil knows of the Good, but Good does not know of Evil. Knowledge of oneself is something only Evil has. One means that Evil has is the dialogue . . . One cannot pay Evil in instalments – and one always keeps on trying to.

[The Blue Octavo Notebooks]

Immanuel Kant, 1724–1804, German philosopher

There is no possibility of thinking of anything at all in the world, or even out of it, which can be regarded as good without qualification, except a good will.

[Grounding for the Metaphysics of Morals 1785]

We do not need science and philosophy to know what we should do to be honest and good, yea, even wise and virtuous.

[Fundamental Principles of the Metaphysics of Ethics 1785]

Thomas à Kempis [Thomas Hemerken], c.1379–1471, German religious writer

Of the two evils, the lesser is always to be chosen.

[Of the Imitation of Christ c.1415–24]

Thomas Michael Keneally, 1935– , Australian novelist
For this is the story of the pragmatic triumph of good over evil, a triumph in eminently mea-
surable, statistical, unsubtle terms.
[Schindler's Ark: Prologue 1994]
Fatal human malice is the staple of narrators, original sin the mother-fluid of historians.
[Ibid]

Martin Luther King Jr, 1929–68, American churchman and civil rights activist
He who passively accepts evil is as much involved in it as he who helps to perpetrate it.
[Stride Towards Freedom 1964]

Rudyard Kipling, 1865–1936, English writer
Clear the land of evil, drive the road and bridge the ford.
[A Song of the English]

D[avid] H[erbert] Lawrence, 1885–1930, English novelist and poet
Morality which is based on ideas, or on an ideal, is an unmitigated evil.
[Fantasia of the Unconscious 1922]

Emmanuel Levinas, 1905–95, Lithuanian-born French philosopher
Evil is not a mystical principal that can be effaced by a ritual, it is an offence perpetrated on
man by man. No one, not even God, can substitute himself for the victim.
[Difficult Freedom: A Religion for Adults 1990]

John Milton, 1608–74, English poet
Of good and evil much they argued then,
Of happiness and final misery,
Passion and apathy, and glory and shame,
Vain wisdom all, and false philosophy.

[Paradise Lost 1667]

And out of good still to find means of evil.

[Ibid]

So farewell hope, and with hope farewell fear,
Farewell remorse: all good to me is lost;
Evil, be thou my good.

[Ibid]

Friedrich Wilhelm Nietzsche, 1844–1900, German philosopher and poet
Everything good is the transmutation of something evil; every god has a devil for a father.
[Fragment]
All the names of good and evil are parables: they do not declare, but only hint. Whoever
among you seeks knowledge of them is a fool.
[Thus Spake Zarathustra 1883–92]
Morality in Europe today is herd-morality.
[Beyond Good and Evil 1886]

Flannery O'Connor, 1925–64, American writer
Good and evil appear to be joined in every culture at the spine.
[Modern Manners]

Thomas Love Peacock, 1785–1866, English essayist and poet
Good without evil is not given to man.
[Gryll Grange 1861]

Plato, c. 428–348BC, Greek philosopher
No evil can happen to a good man, either in life or after death.

[*Apology*]

To prefer evil to good is not in human nature; and when a man is compelled to choose one of the two evils, no one will choose the greater when he might have the less.

[*Protagoras*]

It will never be possible to get rid of evil altogether, for there must always be something opposite to good.

[*Theaeteus c.* 360BC]

Alexander Pope, 1688–1744, English poet
Religion blushing veils her sacred fires,
And unawares Morality expires.

[*The Dunciad* 1728]

François, Duc de La Rochefoucauld, 1613–80, French writer
There is scarcely a single man clever enough to know all the evil he does.

[*Reflections, or Sentences and Moral Maxims* 1665]

Theodore Roosevelt, 1858–1919, 26th president of the United States
No man is justified in doing evil on the ground of expediency.

[*The Strenuous Life* 1900]

Jean Jacques Rousseau, 1712–78, Swiss-born French philosopher
Lacking all sense of right and wrong, a child can do nothing that is morally evil, or that merits either punishment or reproof.

[*Emile* 1762]

Bertrand [Arthur William] Russell, 3rd Earl Russell, 1872–1970, English philosopher
Those who forget good and evil and seek only to know the facts are more likely to achieve good than those who view the world through the distorting medium of their own desires.

[*A Free Man's Worship and Other Essays*]

We have, in fact, two kinds of morality side by side: one which we preach but do not practise, and another which we practise but seldom preach.

[*Sceptical Essays* 1928]

Jean-Paul Sartre, 1905–80, French philosopher and writer
Now I am weary and I can no longer tell Good from Evil, and I need someone to show me the way.

[*Electra and the Flies* 2 1947]

William Shakespeare 1564–1616, English dramatist
The evil that men do lives after them,
The good is oft interred with their bones.

[*Julius Caesar* 1 1598–1600]

George Bernard Shaw, 1856–1950, Irish playwright
An Englishman thinks he is moral when he is only uncomfortable.

[*Plays Unpleasant* preface 1898]

Adlai E[wing] Stevenson, 1900–65, American statesman
There is no evil in the atom; only in men's souls.

[Speech 1952]

Count Leo [Nikolayevich] Tolstoy, 1828–1910, Russian writer
There is only one way to put an end to evil, and that is to do good for evil.

[*What I Believe* 1884]

Garcilaso de la Vega ("El Inca"), c.1540–c.1616, Spanish poet
This is man's role:
to try evil, and if the outcome be evil,
to ask humbly for forgiveness for the act of depravity.

[*Second Eclogue*]

Voltaire [François Marie Arouet], 1694–1778, French philosopher and writer
We use ideas merely to justify our evil, and speech merely to conceal our ideas.

[*Dialogue XIV*]

John Wesley, 1703–91, English preacher
Do all the good you can,
By all the means you can,
In all the ways you can,
In all the places you can,
At all the times you can,
To all the people you can,
As long as ever you can.

[Letter 1915]

Oscar [Fingall O'Flahertie Wills] Wilde, 1854–1900, Irish writer
You can't make people good by Act of Parliament.

[*A Woman of No Importance* 1 1893]

William Butler Yeats, 1865–1939, Irish poet
The good are always the merry.

[*The Fiddler of Dooney* 1892]

Fame and Greatness

John Quincy Adams, 1767–1848, 6th president of the United States
He is too illiterate, unread, unlearned for his station and reputation.
[Referring to George Washington, 1st president of the United States]

Muhammad Ali, [Cassius Marcellus Clay], 1942– , American boxer
At home I am a nice guy: but I don't want the world to know. Humble people, I've found, don't get very far.
[In the *Sunday Express* 1963]

Fred Allen, [John Florence Sullivan], 1894–1956, American comedian
A celebrity is a person who works hard all his life to become known, then wears dark glasses to avoid being recognized.
[*Treadmill to Oblivion*]

Henri Frédéric Amiel, 1821–81, Swiss writer
Great men are the real men: in them nature has succeeded.
[*Journal* 13 August 1865]

Anne [Elizabeth Alice Louise], The Princess Royal, 1950– , British princess
When I appear in public people expect me to neigh, grind my teeth, paw the ground and swish my tail.
[In Noël St George's *Royal Quotes*]

Anonymous
Great persons seldom see their faces in a true glass.
[Proverb]
Great hopes make great men.
[Proverb]

Neil [Alden] Armstrong, 1930– , American astronaut
That's one small step for a man, one giant leap for mankind.
[On stepping on to the moon's surface, 21 July 1969]

Matthew Arnold, 1822–88, English poet and critic
Greatness is a spiritual condition worthy to excite love, interest, and admiration; and the outward proof of possessing greatness is that we excite love, interest, and admiration.
[*Culture and Anarchy* 1869]

John Barrymore, 1882–1942, American actor
I like to be introduced as America's foremost actor. It saves the necessity of further effort.
[Remark to journalists]

The Bible
Howbeit I believed not their words, until I came, and mine eyes had seen it: and, behold, the one half of the greatness of thy wisdom was not told me: for thou exceedest the fame that I heard.
[*2 Chronicles* 9:6]

Let us now praise famous men, and our fathers that begat us.
[*Ecclesiasticus* 44:1]

Humphrey Bogart, 1899–1957, American film actor
You're not a star until they can spell your name in Karachi.
[In David Brown's *Star Billing* 1985]

Emily Jane Brontë, 1818–48, English novelist and poet
Riches I hold in light esteem
And love I laugh to scorn;
And lust of fame was but a dream,
That vanished with the morn.

[*The Old Stoic*]

Elizabeth Barrett Browning, 1806–61, English poet
A great man,
Leaves clean work behind him, and requires
No sweeper up of the chips.

[*Aurora Leigh* 1857]

Robert Browning, 1812–89, English poet
That low man seeks a little thing to do,
Sees it and does it:
This high man, with a great thing to pursue,
Dies ere he knows it.
That low man goes on adding one to one,
His hundred's soon hit;
This high man, aiming at a million,
Misses an unit.

[*A Grammarian's Funeral*]

Jean de La Bruyère, 1645–96, French moralist
The nearer we come to great men the more clearly we see they are only men. They rarely seem great to their valets.
[*Caractères* 1688]

Bill [William] Bryson, 1951– , American travel writer
Now Stonewall Jackson is a man worth taking an interest in. Few people in history have achieved greater fame in a shorter period with less useful activity in the brainbox than General Thomas J. Jackson.
[*A Walk in the Woods* 1997]

377

Edward [George Earle Lytton] Bulwer-Lytton, 1st Baron, 1803–73, English statesman and writer

Beneath the rule of men entirely great,
The pen is mightier than the sword.

[*Richelieu* 1839]

Edmund Burke, 1729–97, Irish-born English political writer

It is the nature of all greatness not to be exact.

[Speech 1774]

Passion for fame; a passion which is the instinct of all great souls.

[Ibid]

Robert Burns, 1759–96, Scottish poet

Critics! – appall'd I venture on the name,
Those cut-throat bandits in the paths of fame.

[*Second Epistle to Robert Graham of Fintry*]

Byron, Lord George Gordon [Noel], 6th Baron Byron of Rochdale, 1788–1824, English poet

The only pleasure of fame is that it paves the way to pleasure, and the more intellectual our pleasure, the better for the pleasure and for us too. It was, however, agreeable to have heard our fame before dinner, and girl's harp after.

[*Journal* 1821]

I awoke one morning and found myself famous.

[Memorandum entry on the success of *Childe Harold*]

Pedro Calderón de la Barca, 1600–1681, Spanish dramatist

Fame, like water, bears up the lighter things, and lets the weighty sink.

[*Adventures of Five Hours*]

Sir Winston [Leonard Spencer] Churchill, 1874–1965, British statesman

[On Lord Charles Beresford] He is one of those orators of whom it was well said, "Before they get up they do not know what they are going to say; when they are speaking, they do not know what they are saying; and when they sit down, they do not know what they have said."

[Speech in the House of Commons 1912]

Stephen Grover Cleveland, 1837–1908, 22nd and 24th president of the United States

They love him most for the enemies he has made.

[Remark by Edward Stuyvesant Bragg, 1827–1912, seconding Cleveland's presidential nomination 1884]

Sir Noel [Pierce] Coward, 1899–1973, English actor and playwright

Don't put your daughter on the stage, Mrs Worthington.

[Song: *Mrs Worthington*]

Dante [Alighieri], 1265–1321, Italian poet

Chè, seggendo in piuma,
In fama non si vien, nè sotto coltre.
(For fame is not won by lying on a feather bed nor under a canopy.)

[*Inferno*]

John Dryden, 1631–1700, English dramatist

His grandeur he derived from Heaven alone,
For he was great, ere fortune made him so.

[*Heroic Stanzas after Cromwell's Funeral*]

How can the less the greater comprehend?
Or finite reason reach Infinity?

[*Religio Laic*]

[On Shakespeare] He is many times flat, insipid; his comic wit degenerating into clenches, his serious swelling into bombast. But he is always great when some occasion is presented to him.

[*Essay of Dramatic Poesy*]

Ralph Waldo Emerson, 1803–82, American writer

It is easy in the world to live after the world's opinion; it is easy in solitude after our own; but the great man is he who in the midst of the crowd keeps with perfect sweetness the independence of solitude.

[*Essays, First Series: Self-Reliance* 1841]

To be great is to be misunderstood.

[*Ibid*]

Nothing great was ever achieved without enthusiasm.

[*Essays: Circles*]

Henry Fielding, 1707–54, English novelist

Greatness consists in bringing all manner of mischief on mankind, and goodness in removing it from them.

[*Jonathan Wild the Great* 1743]

Gustave Flaubert, 1821–80, French novelist

We shouldn't touch our idols: the gilt comes off on our hands.

[*Madame Bovary* 1857]

Benjamin Franklin, 1706–90, American scientist and philosopher

It is a grand mistake of think of being great without goodness; and I pronounce it as certain that there was never yet a truly great man that was not at the same time truly virtuous.

[*The Busy-Body* 1729]

Thomas Fuller, 1608–61, English churchman and writer

The great and the little have need of one another.

[*Gnomologia: Adagies and Proverbs* 1732]

William Ewart Gladstone, 1809–98, British Prime Minister

He is the purest figure in history.

[Referring to George Washington, 1st president of the United States]

James Graham, 1st Marquis of Montrose, 1612–50, Scottish nobleman and general

I'll make thee glorious by my pen,
And famous by my sword.

[*My Dear and Only Love* 1642]

Kenneth Grahame, 1859–1932, English writer
The world has held great Heroes
As history-books have showed;
But never a name to go down to fame
Compared with that of Toad!

[*The Wind in the Willows* 1908]

[Henry] Grahame Greene, 1904–91, English novelist
Fame is a powerful aphrodisiac.

[In the *Radio Times* September 10 1964]

Lillian Hellman, 1905–84, American playwright
It is a mark of many famous people that they cannot part with their brightest hour: what
worked once must always work.

[*Pentimento* 1973]

George Herbert, 1593–1633, English poet
The great would have none great, and the little all little.

[*Jacula Prudentum* 1651]

There are many ways to fame.

[*Ibid*]

There would be no great ones if there were no little ones.

[*Ibid*]

John Keats, 1795–1821, English poet
Fame, like a wayward girl, will still be coy
To those who woo her with too slavish knees.

[*Sonnet: On Fame*]

Rudyard Kipling, 1865–1936, English writer
Four things greater than all things are, –
Women and Horses and Power and War.

[*Ballad of the King's Jest*]

Abraham Lincoln, 1809–65, 16th president of the United States
Let us have faith that right makes might, and in that faith let us to the end dare to do our duty
as we understand it.

[Address 1860]

Henry Wadsworth Longfellow, 1807–82, American poet
Lives of great men all remind us
We can make our lives sublime,
And, departing, leave behind us
Footprints on the sands of time.

[*A Psalm of Life* 1839]

The heights by great men reached and kept
Were not attained by sudden flight,
But they, while their companions slept,
Were toiling upward in the night.

[*The Ladder of Saint Augustine*]

Sophia Loren [Sofia Scicolone], 1934– , Italian film actress
They do not make stars like they used to. Every girl looks so thin, no personality, as if they have come off the production line.

[In the *Times* September 2002]

Clare Boothe Luce, 1903–87, American editor, writer and politician
You will feel that you are no longer clothing yourself; you are dressing a public monument.

No woman has ever so comforted, the distressed – or so distressed the comfortable.

[Referring to Eleanor Roosevelt, wife of Theodore Roosevelt and American First Lady]

Ralph McGill, 1898–1969, American editor, publisher and civil rights campaigner
One of the shameful chapters of this country was how many of the comfortable – especially those who profited from the misery of others – abused her . . . But she got even in a way that was almost cruel. She forgave them.

[Referring to Eleanor Roosevelt, wife of Theodore Roosevelt and American First Lady]

Dame Nellie Melba [Helen Porter Mitchell], 1861–1931, Australian soprano
One of the drawbacks of fame is that one can never escape from it.

[*Melodies and Memories* 1925]

John Milton, 1608–74, English poet
What needs my Shakespeare for his honour'd bones,
The labour of an age in piled stones,
Or that his hallow'd relics should be hid
Under a starry-pointing pyramid?
Dear son of memory, great heir of fame,
What need'st thou such weak witness of thy name?

[*On Shakespeare*]

Fame is the spur that the clear spirit doth raise
(That last infirmity of noble mind)
To scorn delights, and live laborious days.

[*Lycidas* 1637]

Fame is no plant that grows on mortal soil,
Nor in the glistering foil
Set off to th' world, nor in broad rumour lies.

[Ibid]

At last he rose, and twitch'd his Mantle blue:
Tomorrow to fresh Woods, and Pastures new.

[*Ibid*]

Michel [Eyquem] de Montaigne, 1533–1592, French essayist
Fame and tranquility can never be bedfellows.

[*Essays* 1580–88]

Thomas Moore, 1779–1852, Irish poet
Go where glory waits thee,
But, while fame elates thee,
Oh! still remember me.

[*Irish Melodies: Go where Glory waits thee* 1801–34]

381

Blaise Pascal, 1623–62, French mathematician and writer

Great and small have the same accidents, and the same vexations, and the same passions; but one is at the circumference of the wheel, and the other near the centre, and thus less agitated by the same movements.

[*Pensées* 1670]

Alexander Pope, 1688–1744, English poet

All crowd, who foremost shall be damned to fame.

[*The Dunciad* 1728]

If parts allure thee, think how Bacon shined,
The wisest, brightest, meanest of mankind:
Or, ravish'd with the whistling of a name,
See Cromwell, damn'd to everlasting fame!

[*An Essay on Man* 1732]

As yet a child, nor yet a fool to fame,
I lisp'd in numbers, for the numbers came.

[*Epistle to Dr Arbuthnot* 1735]

Fame is at best an unperforming cheat;
But 'tis substantial happiness, *to eat*.

[*Prologue for Mr D'Urfey's Last Play*]

Then teach me Heav'n! to scorn the guilty bays;
Drive from my breast that wretched lust of praise;
Unblemish'd let me live, or die unknown:
Oh, grant an honest Fame, or grant me none.

[*The Temple of Fame*]

Nor fame I slight, nor for her favours call;
She comes unlook'd for, if she comes at all.

[*Ibid*]

Theodore Roosevelt, 1858–1919, 26th president of the United States

It is better to be faithful than famous.

[In Riis's *Theodore Roosevelt, the Citizen*]

Arthur Meier Schlesinger Jr, 1917– , American historian

Above all [Kennedy] gave the world for an imperishable moment the vision of a leader who greatly understood the terror and the hope, the diversity and the possibility, of life on this planet and who made people look beyond nation and race to the future of humanity.

[*A Thousand Days: John F. Kennedy in the White House* 1965]

William Shakespeare 1564–1616, English dramatist

Let fame, that all hunt after in their lives,
Live register'd upon our brazen tombs,
And then grace us in the disgrace of death;
When, spite of cormorant devouring Time,
The endeavour of this present breath may buy
That honour which shall bate his scythe's keen edge
And make us heirs of all eternity.

[*Love's Labour's Lost* 1 1594–5]

Be not afraid of greatness: some are born great, some achieve greatness, and some have greatness thrust upon them.

[*Twelfth Night* 2:5:156 1598–1600]

Rightly to be great
Is not to stir without great argument,
But greatly to find quarrel in a straw
When honour's at the stake.

[*Hamlet* 4:4:53 1600–1601]

The soul and body rive not more in parting
Than greatness going off.

[*Antony and Cleopatra* 4 1606–7]

Farewell! a long farewell to all my greatness!
This is the state of man: today he puts forth
The tender leaves of hopes; tomorrow blossoms,
And bears his blushing honours thick upon him;
The third day comes a frost, a killing frost,
And, when he thinks, good easy man, full surely
His greatness is a-ripening, nips his root,
And then he falls, as I do.

[*King Henry VIII* 3:2:351 1613]

George Bernard Shaw, 1856–1950, Irish playwright
If a great man could make us understand him we should hang him.
[*Man and Superman: Maxims for Revolutionists* 1903]

Stephen Spender, 1909– , English poet
I think continually of those who were truly great –
The names of those who in their lives fought for life,
Who wore at their hearts the fire's centre.
[*I Think Continually of Those*]

Edmund Spenser, c.1552–1599, English poet
Dan Chaucer, well of English undefiled,
On Fame's eternal beadroll worthy to be filed.
[*The Faerie Queene* 1590–96]

Philip Dormer Stanhope, 4th Earl of Chesterfield, 1694–1773, English statesman
The fame of a conqueror; a cruel fame, that arises from the destruction of the human species.
[Letter 1757]

Adlai Stevenson, 1900–65, American politician
Falsity withered in her presence. Hypocrisy left the room . . . She would rather light candles
than curse the darkness.
[Referring to Eleanor Roosevelt, wife of Theodore Roosevelt and American First Lady]

Harriet Elizabeth Beecher Stowe, 1811–96, American writer
So this is the little lady who made this big war.
[Remark by Abraham Lincoln on the American Civil War over the abolition of slavery]

Tacitus [Publius Gaius Cornelius Tacitus], c. AD55–120, Roman historian
Love of fame is the last thing even learned men can bear to be parted from.
[*Histories*]

Alfred, Lord Tennyson, 1809–92, English poet
In me there dwells
No greatness, save it be some far-off touch
Of greatness to know well I am not great.

[*Idylls of the King: Lancelot and Elaine* 1859–85]

Horace Walpole, 4th Earl of Orford, 1717–97, English writer
They who cannot perform great things themselves may yet have a satisfaction in doing justice
to those who can.

[Attributed]

Andy Warhol [Andrew Warhola], 1926–87, American artist and filmmaker
In the future everybody will be world famous for fifteen minutes.

[Exhibition catalogue: *Andy Warhol* 1968]

John Wolcot ("Peter Pindar"), 1738–1819, English poet and physician
What rage for fame attends both great and small!
Better be d – – d than mentioned not at all!

[*More Lyric Odes to the Royal Academicians* 1782–5]

William Wordsworth, 1770–1850, English poet
Men are we, and must grieve when even the shade
Of that which once was great is pass'd away.

[*Sonnets Dedicated to Liberty*]

Edward Young, 1683–1765, English churchman and poet
One to destroy, is murder by the law;
And gibbets keep the lifted hand in awe;
To murder thousands, takes a specious name,
War's glorious art, and gives immortal fame.

[*Love of Fame* 1725–8]

Fate, Fortune and Luck

Anonymous

Fate leads the willing, but drives the stubborn.

[Proverb]

Fortune often lends her smiles as churls do money, to undo the debtor.

[Proverb]

Fortune wearies with carrying one and the same man always.

[Proverb]

Lucky men need no counsel.

[Proverb]

Francis Bacon, Baron Verulam of Verulam and Viscount of St Albans, 1561–1626, English philosopher

If a man look sharply, and attentively, he shall see Fortune: for though she may be blind, yet she is not invisible.

[*Essays: Of Fortune* 1625]

Samuel [Barclay] Beckett, 1906–89, Irish writer and playwright

What do I know of man's destiny? I could tell you more about radishes.

[*Six Residua* 1978]

Ambrose [Gwinnet] Bierce, 1842–1914, American writer

Calamities are of two kinds: misfortune to ourselves and good fortune to others.

[*The Devil's Dictionary* 1911]

Elizabeth Dorothea Cole Bowen, 1899–1973, Irish author

Fate is not an eagle, it creeps like a rat.

[*The House in Paris* 1935]

Anita Brookner, 1928– , English novelist and art historian

All good fortune is a gift of the gods, and . . . you don't win the favour of the ancient gods by being good, but by being bold.

[In George Plimpton's *Writers at Work* 1988]

Edward [George Earle Lytton] Bulwer-Lytton, 1st Baron, 1803–73, English statesman and writer

Fate laughs at probabilities.

[*Eugene Aram*]

Samuel Butler, 1612–80, English poet

I am not now in fortune's power:
He that is down can fall no lower.

[*Hudibras* 1663]

Raymond [Clevie] Carver, 1938–88, American writer and poet

So far, he had kept away from any real harm, from those forces he knew existed and that could cripple or bring down a man if the luck went bad, if things suddenly turned.

[*Cathedral* 1983]

Miguel de Cervantes [Saavedra], 1547–1616, Spanish dramatist and poet

Fortune leaves always some door open to come at a remedy.

[*Don Quixote* 1615]

Geoffrey Chaucer, c.1340–1400, English poet

For of fortunes sharpe adversitie,
The worste kind of infortune is this,
A man that hath been in prosperitie,
And it remember, when it passed is.

[*The Canterbury Tales: Troilus and Creseide* c.1387]

Fortune hath in her honey galle.

[*Ibid: The Monk's Tale*]

Anton [Pavlovoch] Chekhov, 1860–1904, Russian author and playwright

Tell mother that however dogs and samovars might behave themselves, winter comes after summer, old age after youth, and misfortune follows happiness (or the other way around). A person can not be healthy and cheerful throughout life. Losses lie waiting and man can not safeguard against death, even if he be Alexander of Macedonia. One must be prepared for anything and consider everything to be inevitably essential, as sad as that may be.

[Letter 1898]

Lydia Maria Child, 1802–80, American abolitionist and writer

Misfortune is never mournful to the soul that accepts it; for such do always see that every cloud is an angel's face. Every man deems that he has precisely the trials and temptations which are the hardest of all others for him to bear; but they are so, simply because they are the very ones he most needs.

[*Letters from New York* 1843]

Sir Winston [Leonard] Churchill, 1874–1965, British statesman

Which brings me to my conclusion upon Free Will and Predestination, namely let the reader mark it that they are identical.

[*My Early Life* 1930]

[William] Robertson Davies, Canadian novelist and journalist

What we call luck is the inner man externalized. We make things happen to us.

[*What's Bred in the Bone* 1985]

John Dryden, 1631–1700, English dramatist

Ill fortune seldom comes alone.

[*Cymon and Iphigenia* 1700]

Fate seemed to wind him up for fourscore years;
Yet freshly ran he on ten winters more.

[*Oedipus* 4]

Ralph Waldo Emerson, 1803–82, American writer
The vulgar call good fortune that which really is produced by the calculation of genius.

[*Speech* 1838]

Edward FitzGerald, 1809–83, English writer and translator
The moving Finger writes; and having writ, moves on.

[*The Rubaiyat of Omar Khayam* 1859]

[Paul] Joseph Goebbels, 1897–1945, German Nazi politician
(On the death of Roosevelt) This was the Angel of History! We felt its wings flutter through the room. Was that not the fortune we awaited so anxiously?

[*Diary*]

Johann Wolfgang von Goethe, 1749–1832, German poet and playwright
Fortunately, we can take in only so much misfortune; what exceeds that limit either destroys us or leaves us indifferent.

[*Elective Affinities* 1809]

James Graham, 1st Marquis of Montrose, 1612–50, Scottish nobleman and general
He either fears his fate too much,
Or his deserts are small,
That puts it not unto the touch
To win or lose it all.

[*My Dear and Only Love* 1642]

Richard Graves, 1715–1804, English poet
Each curs'd his fate, that thus their project cross'd:
How hard their lot who neither won nor lost.

[*An Incident in High Life*]

John Milton Hay, 1838–1905, American statesman and writer
Good luck is the gayest of all gay girls;
Long in one place she will not stay.

[*Good Luck and Bad Luck*]

Thomas Hardy, 1840–1928, English novelist and poet
Some folk want their luck buttered.

[*The Mayor of Casterbridge* 1886]

[Francis] Brett Harte, 1836–1902, American writer
The only sure thing about luck is that it will change.

[*The Outcasts of Poker Flat* 1869]

Nathaniel Hawthorne, 1804–64, American novelist
My fortune somewhat resembled that of a person who should entertain an idea of committing suicide, and, altogeher beyond his hopes, meet with the good hap to be murdered.

[*The Scarlet Letter* 1850]

W[illiam] E[rnest] Henley, 1849–1903, English writer
Under the bludgeonings of chance,
My head is bloody, but unbowed.

[*Echoes*]

I am the master of my fate:
I am the captain of my soul.

[*Echoes: In Memoriam*]

A[lfred E[dward] Housman, 1859–1936, English poet and scholar
Therefore, since the world has still
Much good, but much less good than ill,
And while the sun and moon endure
Luck's a chance, but trouble's sure,
I'd face it as a wise man would,
And train for ill and not for good.

[*A Shropshire Lad: The Welsh Marches* 1896]

Douglas William Jerrold, 1803–57, English writer
Some people are so fond of ill-luck that they run half-way to meet it.

[*Wit and Opinions of Douglas Jerrold* 1859]

Franz Kafka, 1883–1924, Austrian writer
Don Quixote's misfortune is not in his imagination but Sancho Panza.

[*Blue Octavo Notebooks*]

Stephen Butler Leacock, 1869–1944, Canadian economist and humorist
I am a great believer in luck, and I find that the harder I work, the luckier I get.

[*Literary Lapses* 1910]

Livy [Titus Livius], 59BC–AD17, Roman historian
Good fortune and a good disposition are rarely given to the same man.

[*Histories XXX*]

Frank Loesser, 1910–69, American songwriter
Luck be a lady tonight.

[Song: *Luck be a Lady*. In *Guys and Dolls* 1950]

Anita Loos, 1893–1981, American writer
Fate keeps on happening.

[*Gentlemen Prefer Blondes* 1925]

William Julius Mickle, 1735–88, Scottish poet
For there's nae luck about the house,
There's nae luck as a':
There's little pleasure in the house
When our gudeman's awa'.

[*The Mariner's Wife*]

Henry [Valentine] Miller, 1891–1980, American novelist
In this life I am god, and like God
I am indifferent to my own fate.

[*The Cosmological Eye*]

Napoleon I [Napoleon Bonaparte], 1769–1821, emperor of France
Has he luck?

[Question asked about potential officers. Attributed]

FATE, FORTUNE AND LUCK

Joyce Carol Oates, 1938– , American writer
The worst cynicism; a belief in luck.

[*Do What You Will*]

Alexander Pope, 1688–1744, English poet
Heaven from all creatures hides the book of Fate.

[*Essay on Man*]

Sir Karl Raimund Popper, 1902–94, Austrian-born English philosopher
We may become the makers of our fate when we have ceased to pose as its prophets.

[*The Open Society and Its Enemies* 1945]

E. Annie [Edna Ann] Proulx, 1935– , American journalist, novelist and short story writer
He got into the habit of walking around the trailer and asking aloud, "Who knows?" He said "Who knows?" For no one knew. He meant, anything could happen.
A spinning coin, still balanced on its rim, may fall in either direction.

[*The Shipping News* 1993]

François, Duc de La Rochefoucauld, 1613– 80, French writer
We are all strong enough to bear the misfortunes of others.

[*Reflections, or Sentences and Moral Maxims* 1665]

We are sensitive to good or ill fortune only in proportion to our self-love.

[*Ibid*]

Seneca, c.4BC–AD65, Roman philosopher
Everything may happen.

[*Epistolae Morales*]

William Shakespeare, 1564–1616, English dramatist
Ill blows the wind that profits nobody.

[*King Henry VI, Part III* 2 1591].

One writ with me in sour misfortune's book!

[*Romeo and Juliet* 5 1594–5]

Not the ill wind which blows man no good.

[*King Henry IV, Part II* 5 1597–8]

Let us sit and mock the good housewife Fortune from her wheel, that her gifts may hence-forth be bestowed equally.

[*As You Like It* 1 1598–1600]

Fortune is merry,
And in this mood will give us anything.

[*Julius Caesar* 3 1598–1600]

Sophocles, c.496–c.406BC, Greek poet
Fortune is not on the side of the faint-hearted.

[*Phaedra* 5th century BC]

Fortune raises up and fortune brings low both the man who fares well and the man who fares badly; and there is no prophet of the future for mortal men.

[*Antigone* 5th century BC]

Sir Richard Steele, 1672–1729, Anglo-Irish essayist

Every man is the maker of his own fortune.

[In the *Tatler*]

It was very prettily said, that we may learn the little value of fortune by the persons on whom heaven is pleased to bestow it.

[*Ibid*]

Terence [Publius Terentius Afer], c.195–159BC, Roman poet

Fortune aids the brave.

[*Phormio*]

James Thomson, 1700–48, Scottish poet

A lucky chance, that oft decides the fate
Of mighty monarchs.

[*The Seasons: Summer*]

I care not, Fortune, what you me deny:
You cannot rob me of free Nature's grace;
You cannot shut the windows of the sky,
Through which Aurora shows her brightening face;
You cannot bar my constant feet to trace
The woods and lawns, by living stream, at eve:
Let health my nerves and finer fibres brace,
And I their toys to the great children leave:
Of fancy, reason, virtue, naught can me bereave.

[*The Castle of Indolence*]

James Thomson, 1834–82, Scottish poet

The sense that every struggle brings defeat
Because Fate holds no prize to crown success;
That all oracles are dumb or cheat
Because they have no secret to express;
That none can pierce the vast black veil uncertain
Because there is no light beyond the curtain;
That all is vanity and nothingness.

[*The City of Dreadful Night*]

John Webster, c.1578–c.1632, English dramatist

Fortune's a right whore:
If she give aught, she deals it in small parcels,
That she may take away all at one swoop.

[*The White Devil* 1 1612]

And of all the axioms this shall win the prize, –
'Tis better to be fortunate than wise.

[*Ibid*]

Simone Weil, 1909–43, French essayist and philosopher

If we are suffering illness, poverty, or misfortune, we think we shall be satisfied on the day it ceases. But there too, we know it is false; so soon as one has got used to not suffering one wants something else.

[*Some Thoughts on the Love of God* 1942]

390

[Adeline] Virginia Woolf, 1882–1941, English novelist and critic
One likes people much better when they're battered down by a prodigious siege of misfortune than when they triumph.

[*Writer's Diary* 1921]

Sir Thomas Wyatt, 1503–42, English poet
Fortune's friend is mishap's woe.

[*The Lover Complaineth Himself Forsaken*]

Life

Douglas Adams, 1952– , English writer
Life . . . don't talk to me about life.

[*The Hitch Hiker's Guide to the Galaxy* 1979]

The Answer to the Great Question . . . Of Life, the Universe and Everything . . . Is . . . Forty-two.

[*Ibid*]

Woody Allen [Allen Stewart Konisberg], 1935– , American writer, actor and film director
Life is divided up into the horrible and the miserable.

[*Annie Hall* film 1977]

Life doesn't imitate art, it imitates bad television.

[*Husbands and Wives* film 1992]

Maya Angelou, 1928– , American author and poet
My life has been one great big joke,
A dance that's walked
A song that's spoke,
I laugh so hard I almost choke
When I think about myself.

[*Just Give Me a Cool Drink of Water 'fore I Die: When I Think About Myself* 1971]

Anonymous
Death is a port whereby we pass to joy,
Life is a lake that drowneth all in payn.

[*Comparison of Life and Death*]

Alan Bennett, 1934– , English playwright
Life, you know, is rather like opening a tin of sardines. We're all of us looking for the key.

[*Beyond the Fringe* 1960]

Bertolt Brecht, 1898–1956, German dramatist and poet
Life is short and so is money.

[*The Threepenny Opera* 1929]

Edward [George Earle Lytton] Bulwer-Lytton, 1st Baron, 1803–73, English statesman and writer
Life differs from the play only in this . . . it has no plot – all is vague, desultory, unconnected – till the curtain drops with the mystery unsolved.

[*Godolphin*]

Charlie Chaplin [Sir Charles Spencer Chaplin], 1889–1977, English-born film actor
Life is a tragedy when seen in close-up, but a comedy in long-shot.

[Quoted in his obituary in the *Guardian* December 28, 1977]

Jean Cocteau, 1891–1963, French poet and artist
Living is a horizontal fall.

[*Opium* 1930]

Shirley Conran 1932– , English designer and author
Life is too short to stuff a mushroom.

[*Superwoman* 1975]

William Cowper, 1731–1800, English poet
Ask what is human life – the sage replies,
With disappointment lowering in his eyes,
A painful passage o'er a restless flood,
A vain pursuit of fugitive false good,
A sense of fancied bliss and heartfelt care,
Closing at last in darkness and despair.

[*Hope*]

Variety's the very spice of life,
That gives it all its flavour.

[*The Task*]

Quentin Crisp, 1908–99, English eccentric and writer
Life was a funny thing that happened to me on the way to the grave.

[*The Naked Civil Servant* 1968]

Alexandre Dumas [fils], 1824–95, French writer
If God were suddenly condemned to live the life which he has inflicted upon men, he would kill himself.

[*Pensées d'Album*]

Ralph Waldo Emerson, 1803–82, American writer
Life is good only when it is magical and musical, a perfect timing and consent, and when we do not anatomize it . . . You must hear the bird's song without attempting to render it into nouns and verbs.

[*Society and Solitude: Works and Days*]

José Ortega y Gasset, 1883–1955, Spanish philosopher
Life is a petty thing unless there is pounding within it an enormous desire to extend its boundaries. We live in proportion to the extent to which we yearn to live more.

[*The Dehumanization of Art* 1925]

John Gay, 1685–1732, English poet and playwright
Life is a jest, and all things show it;
I thought so once, but now I know it.

[*My Own Epitaph*]

Johann Wolfgang von Goethe, 1749–1832, German poet and playwright
A useless life is an early death.

[*Iphiginie auf Taurus* 1 1787]

Thomas Gray, 1716–71, English poet
To each his sufferings: all are men,
Condemned alike to groan.

[*Ode on a Distant Prospect of Eton College* 1747]

Tom [Thomas J] Hanks, 1956– , American actor
My mama always said, life is like a box of chocolates. You never know what you're gonna get.

[*Forrest Gump* film 1994. Screenplay by Eric Roth, directed
by Robert Zemeckis, based on Winston Groom's novel]

Hippocrates, c.460–c.377BC, Greek physician
Life is short, art long, opportunity fleeting, experience treacherous, judgment difficult.
(Also known in the short form, *Ars longa, vita brevis* – Art is long, life short)

[*Aphorisms c*.400BC]

Oliver Wendell Holmes, 1809–94, American physician and writer
Life is a great bundle of little things.

[*The Professor at the Breakfast Table* 1860]

Life is a running shade, with fettered hands,
That chases phantoms over shifting sands.

[*The Old Player*]

Elbert Hubbard, 1856–1915, American writer and editor
Life is just one damned thing after another.

[*The Philistine* 1909]

Eugene Ionesco, 1912–94, Romanian-born French playwright
Life is an abnormal business.

[*Rhinoceros* 1 1959]

Henry James, 1843–1916, American-born English writer
Live all you can; it's a mistake not to. It doesn't so much matter what you do in particular, so
long as you have your life. If you haven't had that what have you had?

[*The Ambassadors* 1903]

Dr Samuel Johnson, 1709–84, English lexicographer
Human life is everywhere a state in which much is to be endured and little to be enjoyed.

[*Rasselas* 1759]

John Fitzgerald Kennedy, 1917–63, 35th president of the United States
There is always inequity in life. Some men are killed in a war and some men are wounded,
and some men never leave the country . . . Life is unfair.

[Press conference 1962]

Charles Kingsley, 1819–75, English churchman and writer
Life is too short for mean anxieties.

[*The Saint's Tragedy*]

Fran Lebowitz, 1951– , American journalist and writer
Life is something to do when you can't get to sleep.

[*Metropolitan Life* 1978]

Tom [Thomas Andrew] Lehrer, 1928– , American humorist and songwriter
Life is a sewer. What you take out depends on what you put into it.

[*We Will All Go Together When We Go* record album 1953]

LIFE

Henry Wadsworth Longfellow, 1807–82, American poet

Into each life some rain must fall.

[*Ballads and Other Poems: The Rainy Day* 1842]

Life is real! Life is earnest!
And the grave is not its goal;
Dust thou art, to dust returnest,
Was not spoken of the soul.

[*Voices of the Night: A Psalm of Life* 1839]

Our ingress into the world
Was naked and bare;
Our progress through the world
Is trouble and care.

[*The Student's Tale* 1874]

George Louis Palmella Busson Du Maurier, 1834–96, English artist and novelist

Life ain't all beer and skittles, and more's the pity; but what's the odds, so long as you're happy?

[*Trilby* 1894]

Henry [Valentine] Miller, 1891–1980, American novelist

The aim of life is to live, and to live means to be aware, joyously, drunkenly, serenely, divinely aware.

[*The Wisdom of the Heart* 1941]

Joni Mitchell, 1943– , Canadian-born American singer and songwriter

I've looked at life from both sides now
From up and down, and still somehow
It's life's illusions I recall
I really don't know life at all.

[Song: *Both Sides Now* 1969]

Michel [Eyquem] de Montaigne, 1533–92, French essayist

The unceasing labour of your life is to build the house of death.

[*Essais* 1580]

Thomas Moore, 1779–1852, Irish poet

Life is a waste of wearisome hours
Which seldom the rose of enjoyment adorns;
And the heart that is soonest awake to the flowers
Is always the first to be touch'd by the thorns.

[*Irish melodies: Oh! think not my spirits are always so light*]

Christopher [Darlington] Morley, 1890–1957, American writer

There are three ingredients in the good life: learning, earning and yearning.

[*Parnassus on Wheels* 1917]

Life is a foreign language: all men mispronounce it.

[*Thunder on the Left* 1925]

John Morley, 1st Viscount Morley of Blackburn, 1838–1923, English politician

The great business of life is to be, to do, to do without, and to depart.

[*Address on Aphorisms* November 1887]

[Thomas] Malcolm Muggeridge, 1903–90, English journalist

Human life . . . is only theatre, and mostly cheap melodrama at that.

[*Tread Softly for You Tread on My Jokes* 1966]

Ogden Nash, 1902–71, American humorous writer

When I consider how my life is spent,
I hardly ever repent.

[*Reminiscent Reflection*]

Friedrich Wilhelm Nietzsche, 1844–1900, German philosopher and poet

Believe me! The secret of reaping the greatest fruitfulness and the greatest enjoyment from life is to live dangerously!

[*The Gay Science* 1882]

Eugene O'Neill, 1888–1953, American playwright

Life is for each man a solitary cell whose walls are mirrors.

[*Lazarus Laughed* 1 1927]

Our lives are merely strange dark interludes in the electric display of God the Father.

[*Strange Interlude* 1928]

George Orwell [Eric Arthur Blair], 1903–50, English novelist and critic

Most people get a fair amount of fun out of their lives, but on balance life is suffering and only the very young or the very foolish imagine otherwise.

[*Shooting an Elephant* 1950]

Luigi Pirandello, 1867–1936, Italian dramatist and novelist

Life is little more than a loan shark: it exacts a very high rate of interest for the few pleasures it concedes.

[*The Pleasure of Honesty* 1917]

Francis Quarles, 1592–1644, English poet

He husbands best his life, that freely gives
It for the publick good; he rightly lives,
That nobly dies: 'tis greatest mastery,
Not to be fond to live, nor feare to die
On just occasion; he that (in case) despises
Life, earns it best; but he that overprizes
His dearest blood, when honour bids him die,
Steals but a life, and lives by robbery.

[*History of Esther : Meditation 15* 1621]

Antoine de Saint-Exupéry, 1900–1944, French aviator and writer

To live is to be slowly born.

[*Flight to Arras* 1942]

Each man must look to himself to teach him the meaning of life. It is not something discovered: it is something moulded.

[*Wind, Sand and Stars* 1939]

George Santayana, 1863–1952, Spanish-American philosopher

There is no cure for birth and death save to enjoy the interval.

[*Soliloquies in England* 1922]

396

Jean-Paul Sartre, 1905–80, French philosopher and writer
Human life begins on the far side of despair.

[*Les Mouches* 1943]

William Shakespeare, 1564–1616, English dramatist
The web of our life is of a mingled yarn, good and ill together: our virtues would be proud, if our faults whip'd them not; and our crimes would despair, if they were not cherished by our virtues.

[*All's Well that Ends Well* 4 1601–3]

George Bernard Shaw, 1856–1950, Irish playwright
Life is a disease; and the only difference between one man and another is the stage of the disease at which he lives.

[*Back to Methuselah* 1921]

There are two tragedies in life. One is not to get your heart's desire. The other is to get it.

[*Man and Superman* 1903]

[Lloyd] Logan Pearsall Smith, 1865–1946, American-born English writer
There are two things to aim at in life: first, to get what you want, and after that to enjoy it. Only the wisest of mankind achieve the second.

[*Afterthoughts* 1931]

Sir Tom Stoppard [Thomas Strassler], 1937– , Czech-born British dramatist
Life is a gamble at terrible odds – if it was a bet, you wouldn't take it.

[*Rosencrantz and Guildenstern are Dead* 1 1966]

Sir William Temple, 1628–99, English statesman and writer
When all is done, human life is, at the greatest and the best, but like a forward child, that must be played with and humoured a little to keep it quiet till it falls asleep, and then the care is over.

[*Esssay on Poetry*]

Paul Theroux, 1941– , American writer
We have become used to life being a series of arrivals or departures, of triumphs or failures, with nothing noteworthy in between.

[*The Old Patagonian Express: By Train Through the Americas* 1979]

Dylan Thomas, 1914–53, Welsh poet
Oh, isn't life a terrible thing, thank God?

[*Under Milk Wood* 1954]

Henry David Thoreau, 1817–62, American naturalist and writer
The mass of men lead lives of quiet desperation. What is called resignation is confirmed desperation.

[*Walden, or Life in the Woods* 1854]

Alice [Malsenior] Walker, 1944– , American novelist and poet
Not everyone's life is what they make it. Some poeple's life is what other people make it.

[*You Can't Keep a Good Woman Down: Source* 1981]

Walt[er] Whitman, 1819–92, American poet
And as to you Life I reckon you are the leavings of many deaths,
(No doubt I have died myself ten thousand times before).

[*Leaves of Grass* 1855]

George John Whyte-Melville, 1721–78, Scottish writer
What is life with all it grants us
But a hunting-run?

[*A Lay of the Ranston Bloodhounds*]

Tennessee Williams [Thomas Lanier Williams], 1911–83, American playwright
We're all of us sentenced to solitary confinement inside our own skins, for life.

[*Orpheus Descending* 1957]

Sir P[elham] G[reville] Wodehouse, 1881–1975, English-born writer
What a queer thing life is! So unlike anything else, don't you know, if you see what I mean.

[*My Man Jeeves* 1919]

[Adeline] Virginia Woolf, 1882–1941, English novelist and critic
The interest in life does not lie in what people do, nor even in their relations to each other, but largely in the power to communicate with a third party, antagonistic, enigmatic, yet perhaps persuadable, which one may call life in general.

[*The Common Reader*]

William Butler Yeats, 1865–1939, Irish poet
We begin to live when we have conceived life as a tragedy.

[*Autobiographies* 1926]

Edward Young, 1683–1765, English churchman and poet
Life is war –
Eternal war with woe: who bears it best,
Deserves it least.

[*Night Thoughts* 1742–45]

Men and Women

Anonymous
Men have many faults;
Poor women have but two:
There's nothing good they say,
And nothing right they do.
If ignorance is bliss then men have reached Nirvana.

[Graffiti]

Edward Franklin Albee, 1928– , American playwright
You asked me if I knew women. Well, one of the things I do not know about them is what they talk about while the men are talking. I must find out some time.

[*Who's Afraid of Virginaia Woolf?*, 1962]

Sir Kingsley Amis, 1922–95, English novelist and poet
Women are really much nicer than men:
No wonder we like them.

[*A Bookshop Idyll*]

Simone de Beauvoir, 1908–86, French writer
A man would never get the notion of writing a book on the peculiar situation of the human male.

[*The Second Sex* 1949]

Sir [Henry] Max[imilian] Beerbohm, 1872–1956, English writer
"After all," as a pretty girl once said to me, "women are a sex by themselves, so to speak."

[*The Pervasion of Rouge*]

You will find that the woman who is really kind to dogs is always the one who has failed to inspire sympathy in men.

[*Zuleika Dobson* 1912]

Most women are not so young as they are painted.

[*A Defence of Cosmetics*]

Alan Bennett, 1934– , English playwright
One of the few lessons I have learned in life is that there is invariably something odd about women who wear ankle socks.

[*The Old Country*]

399

Ambrose [Gwinnet] Bierce, 1842–1914, American writer
Women would be the most enchanting creatures on earth if, in falling into their arms one didn't fall into their hands.

[*The Devil's Dictionary* 1911]

James Brown, 1928– , American singer
It's a man's world
But it wouldn't be nothing without a woman or a girl.

[Song: *It's a Man's Man's Man's World* 1966]

Samuel Butler, 1835–1902, English writer
If God considered woman a fit helpmeet for man, he must have had a very poor opinion of man.

[*Notebooks* 1912]

Byron, Lord George Gordon [Noel], 6th Baron Byron of Rochdale, 1788–1824, English poet
Oh! too convincing – dangerously dear
In woman's eye the unanswerable tear!

[*The Corsair* 1814]

I hate a dumpy woman.

[*Don Juan* 1819–24]

Anton [Pavlovoch] Chekhov, 1860–1904, Russian author and playwright
Women can't forgive failure.

[*The Seagull* 2 1896]

Wendy Cope, 1945– , English poet
They say that men suffer,
As badly, as long.
I worry, I worry,
In case they are wrong.

[*Serious Concerns: I Worry* 1992]

Alan Coren, 1938– , English journalist and broadcaster
There is nothing less feminine than a woman drinking out of a jug.

[*Bin Ends*]

Sir Noel [Pierce] Coward, 1899–1973, English actor and playwright
Certain women should be struck regularly, like gongs.

[*Private Lives* 3 1930]

Walt[er Elias] Disney, 1901–66, American film producer
Girls bored me – they still do. I love Mickey Mouse more than any woman I've ever known.

[In *You Must Remember This*, W. Wagner 1975]

Michael Drayton, 1563–1631, English poet
Women be weak, and subject most to change,
Nor long to any can they steadfast be,
And as their eyes, their minds do ever range,
With every object varying that they see.

[*Eclogue*]

Marguerite Duras, 1914–96, French author
You have to be very fond of men. Very, very fond. You have to be fond of them to love them. Otherwise they're simply unbearable.

[Practicalities 1987]

George Eliot [Mary Ann Evans] 1819–80, English writer
To manage men one ought to have a sharp mind in a velvet sheath.

[Romola]

W.C. Fields [William Claude Dunkinfield], 1879–1946, American actor
Women are like elephants to me: I like to look at them, but I wouldn't want to own one.

[In *The Cynic's Lexicon* 1984]

F[rancis] Scott [Key] Fitzgerald, 1896–1940, American novelist
One girl can be pretty – but a dozen are only a chorus.

[The Last Tycoon 1941]

Marilyn French, 1929– , American feminist writer
Whatever they may be in public life, whatever their relations with men, in their relations with women all men are rapists, and that's all they are. They rape us with their eyes, their laws and their codes.

[The Women's Room 1977]

John Gay, 1685–1732, English poet and playwright
'Tis woman that seduces all mankind;
By her we first were taught the wheedling arts.

[The Beggar's Opera 1 1728]

Where is the woman that would scruple to be a wife if she had it in her power to be a widow whenever she pleased.

[Ibid]

If the heart of a man is depress'd with cares,
The mist dispels when a woman appears.

[Ibid 2]

[Hyppolyte] Jean Giraudoux, 1882–1944, French playwright and writer
To win a woman in the first place one must please her, then undress her, and then somehow get her clothes back on her. Finally, so she will allow you to leave her, you've got to annoy her.

[Amphitryon 38 1929]

Oliver Goldsmith, 1728–74, Irish-born English writer
Women and music should never be dated.

[She Stoops to Conquer 1773]

Germaine Greer, 1939– , Australian feminist writer
Probably the only place where a man can feel really secure is in a maximum security prison, except for the imminent threat of release.

[The Female Eunuch 1970]

James Howell, c.1593–1666, English writer
Women were created for the comfort of men.

[Familiar Letters, Bk II 1645–55]

Washington Irving, 1783–1808, American diplomat and writer
A woman's whole life is a history of the affections.

[*The Sketch Book* 1820]

Rudyard Kipling, 1865–1936, English writer
And a woman is only a woman, but a good cigar is a smoke.

[*The Betrothed*]

John Knox, c.1513–72, Scottish Protestant Reformer
The First Blast of the Trumpet against the Monstrous Regiment of Women.

[Title of Treatise 1558]

Alan Jay Lerner, 1918–86, American songwriter
Why can't a woman be more like a man?

[Song: *A Hymn to Him*]

I'd be equally as willing
For a dentist to be drilling
Than to ever let a woman in my life.

[*My Fair Lady* 1956]

Sir [Edward Montgue] Compton Mackenzie, 1883–1972, English novelist
Women do not find it difficult nowadays to behave like men; but they often find it extremely difficult to behave like gentlemen.

[*On Moral Courage*]

W[illiam] Somerset Maugham, 1874–1965, English novelist
A woman will always sacrifice herself if you give her the opportunity. It is her favourite form of self-indulgence.

[*The Circle* 3 1921]

H[enry] L[ouis] Mencken, 1880–1956, American critic and writer
A man's women folk, whatever their outward show of respect for his merit and authority, always regard him secretly as an ass, and with something akin to pity . . . In this fact, perhaps, lies one of the best proofs of feminine intelligence or, as the common phrase makes it, feminine intuition.

[*In Defense of Women* 1923]

Kate [Katherine] Murray Millett, 1934– , American feminist writer
Many women do not recognize themselves as discriminated against; no better proof could be found of the totality of their conditioning.

[*The Second Sex*]

Thomas Moore, 1779–1852, Irish poet
Disguise our bondage as we will,
'Tis woman, woman rules us still.

[*Miscellaneous poems: Sovereign Summer*1840]

Ogden Nash, 1902–71, American humorous writer
Some ladies smoke too much and some ladies drink too much and some ladies pray too much,
But all ladies think that they weigh too much.

[*Curl Up And Diet*]

Women would rather be right than reasonable.

[*Frailty, Thy Name is a Misnomer* 1942]

Aristotle Socrates Onassis, 1906–75, Turkish-born Greek shipping magnate
If women didn't exist, all the money in the world would have no meaning.

[Attributed]

P[atrick] J[ake] O'Rourke, 1947– , American satirist
There are a number of mechanical devices which increase sexual arousal, particularly in women. Chief among these is the Mercedes-Benz 380SL convertible.

[*Modern Manners* 1984]

Prince Philip, Duke of Edinburgh, 1921– , consort of Queen Elizabeth II
When a man opens the car door for his wife, it's either a new car or a new wife.

[Attributed]

Alexander Pope, 1688–1744, English poet
Men, some to bus'ness, some to pleasure take;
But ev'ry woman is at heart a rake:
Men, some to quiet, some to public strife;
But ev'ry lady would be Queen for life.

[*Epistles to Several Persons* 1735]

Alexander Sergeyevich Pushkin, 1799–1837, Russian poet and writer
With womankind, the less we love them, the easier they become to charm.

[*Eugene Onegin* 1831]

Helen Rowland, 1875–1950, American writer
Every man wants a woman to appeal to his better side, his nobler instincts and his higher nature – and another woman to help him forget them.

[*A Guide to Men* 1922]

Arthur Schopenhauer, 1788–1860, German philosopher
One needs only to see the way she is built to realise that woman is not intended for great mental labour.

[Attributed]

William Shakespeare, 1564–1616, English dramatist
A woman mov'd is like a fountain troubled,
Muddy, ill-seeming, thick, bereft of beauty.

[*The Taming of the Shrew* 5 1593–4]

Frailty, thy name is woman!

[*Hamlet* 1 1600–1]

Robert Southey, 1774–1843, English poet
What will not woman, gentle woman, dare,
When strong affection stirs her spirit up?

[*Madoc* 1805]

Muriel Spark, 1918– , Scottish novelist
From my experience of life I believe my personal motto should be "Beware of men bearing flowers."

[*Curriculum Vitae*]

Gloria Steinem, 1934– , American feminist writer
A woman without a man is like a fish without a bicycle.

[Attributed]

Alfred, Lord Tennyson, 1809–92, English poet
Men at most differ as Heaven and Earth,
But women, worst and best, as Heaven and Hell.

[*Merlin and Vivien*]

Margaret Hilda Thatcher, Baroness Thatcher of Kesteven, 1925– , British politician
One of the things being in politics has taught me is that men are not a reasoned or reasonable sex.

[Television interview 1972]

Anthony Trollope, 1815–82, English novelist
With many women I doubt whether there be any more effectual way of touching their hearts than ill-using them and then confessing it. If you wish to get the sweetest fragrance from the herb at your feet, tread on it and bruise it.

[*Miss Mackenzie* 1865]

Kenneth Peacock Tynan, 1927–80, English theatre critic
What, when drunk, one sees in other women, one sees in Garbo sober.

[In *Sunday Times* August 1963]

Evelyn [Arthur St John] Waugh, 1903–66, English writer
"I will not stand for being called a woman in my own house," she said.

[*Scoop*]

John Webster, c. 1580–c. 1625, English dramatist
There's nothing sooner dry than women's tears.

[*The White Devil* 1612]

Mae West, 1893–1980, American entertainer
A hard man is good to find.

[Attributed]

Give a man a free hand and he'll run it all over you.

[*Klondike Annie* film 1936]

A man in the house is worth two in the street.

[*She Done Him Wrong* film 1933]

John Greenleaf Whittier, 1807–92 American Quaker, poet and writer
Woman wronged, can cherish hate
More deep than manhood may.

[*Mogg Megone*]

Oscar [Fingall O'Flahertie Wills] Wilde, 1854–1900, Irish writer
A man who moralises is usually a hypocrite and a woman who moralises is invariably plain.
[*Lady Windermere's Fan* 1892]
One should never trust a woman who tells one her real age. A woman who would tell one that would tell one anything.

[*A Woman of No Importance* 1893]

Tennessee Williams [Thomas Lanier Williams], 1911–83, American playwright
Hysteria is a natural phenomenon, the common denominator of the female nature. It's the big female weapon, and the test of a man is his ability to cope with it.

[*The Night of the Iguana*]

[Adeline] Virginia Woolf, 1882–1941, English novelist and critic
The history of men's opposition to women's emancipation is more interesting perhaps than the story of that emancipation itself.

[*A Room of One's Own* 1929]

Edward Young, 1683–1765, English churchman and poet
Women were made to give our eyes delight.
A female sloven is an odious sight.

[*Love of Fame* 1725–8]

Countries and Their Peoples

Anonymous

In settling an island, the first building erected by a Spaniard would be a church; by a Frenchman, a fort; by a Dutchman, a warehouse; and by an Englishman, an alehouse.

[Proverb]

The Italian is wise before he undertakes a thing, the German while he is doing it, and the Frenchman when it is over.

[Proverb]

A Scotsman is aye wise a-hent the hand.

[Scots proverb]

Sir J[ames] M[atthew] Barrie, 1860–1937, Scottish playwright

There are few more impressive sights in the world than a Scotsman on the make.

[*What Every Woman Knows* 1908]

Brendan Behan, 1923–64, Irish writer and playwright

Other people have a nationality. The Irish and the Jews have a psychosis.

[*Richard's Cork Leg* 1 1973]

Louis de Bernières, 1954– , English author

Italians always act without thinking, it's the glory and downfall of your civilization. A German plans a month in advance what his bowel movements will be at Easter, and the British plan everything in retrospect, so it always looks as though everything occurred as they intended. The French plan everything whilst appearing to be having a party, and the Spanish . . . well, God knows.

[*Captain Corelli's Mandolin* 1994]

Maximilien de Béthune, Duc de Sully, 1560–1641, French financier

Ils s'amusent tristement.
The English take their pleasures sadly.

[*Memoires* 1630]

Sir John Betjeman, 1906–84, English poet

Think of what our Nation stands for,
Books from Boots' and country lanes,
Free speech, free passes, class distinction,
Democracy and proper drains.

[*John Betjeman's Collected Poems: In Westminster Abbey* 1958]

[Prince] Otto [Edward Leopold] von Bismarck, Duke of Lauenburg, 1815–98, Prussian statesman

The Russians do not possess the kind of self-restraint that would make it possible for us to live alone with them and France on the continent.

[Letter to his son 1886]

Gerald Brenan [Edward Fitz-Gerald Brenan], 1894–1987, English travel writer

Spain, since the loss of its Catholic faith, has been above all else a country in search of an ideology.

[*The Spanish Labyrinth* 1943]

Bill [William] Bryson, 1951– , American travel writer

There are certain idiosyncratic notions that you quietly come to accept when you live for a long time in Britain. One is that British summers used to be longer and sunnier. Another is that the England football team shouldn't have any trouble with Norway. A third is the idea that Britain is a big place. This last is easily the most intractable.

[*Notes From A small Island* 1995]

John Buchan, 1st Baron Tweedsmuir, 1875–1940, Scottish statesman and writer

You have to know a man awfully well in Canada to know his surname.

[In the *Observer* May 1950]

Byron, Lord George Gordon [Noel], 6th Baron Byron of Rochdale, 1788-1824, English poet

Italia! oh Italia! thou who hast
The fatal gift of beauty.

[*Childe Harold's Pilgrimage* 1812

Marquis Domenico Caracciolo, 1715–89, Neapolitan diplomat

In England there are sixty different religions and only one sauce.

[Attributed]

Thomas Carlyle, 1795–1881, Scottish historian and writer

France was a long despotism tempered by epigrams.

[*History of the French Revolution* 1837]

G[ilbert] K[eith] Chesterton, 1874–1936, English writer

There is nothing the matter with Americans except their ideals. The real American is all right; it is the ideal American who is all wrong.

[In the *New York Times* November 21, 1930]

[Sidonie-Gabrielle Claudine] Colette, 1873–1954, French novelist

In our part of the world, as you well know, they say raw meat is for cats and the English.

[*The Photographer's Missus*]

Quentin Crisp, 1908–99, English eccentric and writer

I don't hold with abroad and think that foreigners speak English when our backs are turned.

[*The Naked Civil Servant* 1968]

407

Countee Cullen, 1903–46, African-American poet

What is Africa to me: Copper sun or scarlet sea
Jungle star or jungle track
Strong bronzed men, or regal black
Women from whose loins I sprang
When the birds of Eden sang?

[*Color: Heritage* 1925]

Rhys Davies, 1903–78, Welsh writer

Sewn on, so to speak, like a patch of different material to England's robe of state, Wales nevertheless has succeeeded in retaining its own texture and colour.

[*The Story of Wales* 1943]

J[ames] P[atrick] Donleavy, 1926– , Irish author

To more than a few, Ireland remains a glowing sweet emerald vision having the fifteenth beer over some bereft bar counter at three a.m., in some outskirt corner of San Francisco, Hawaii, Boston, or the Bronx.

[*J.P. Donleavy's Ireland* 1986]

Roddy Doyle, 1958– , Irish novelist

The Irish are the niggers of Europe, lads. An' Dubliners are the niggers of Ireland . . . An' the northside Dubliners are the niggers o' Dublin. – Say it loud, I'm black an' I'm proud.

[*The Commitments* 1987]

Margaret Drabble, 1939– , English novelist

England's not a bad country. It's just a mean, cold, ugly, divided, tired, clapped-out, post-imperial, post-industrial slag-heap covered in polystyrene hamburger cartons.

[*A Natural Curiosity* 1989]

Ralph Waldo Emerson, 1803–82, American writer

An Englishman shows no mercy to those below him in the social scale, as he looks for none from those above him; any forbearance from his superiors surprises him, and they suffer in his good opinion.

[*English Traits* 1856]

William Faulkner, 1897–1962, American novelist

The Swiss . . . are not a people so much as a neat clean solvent business.

[*Intruder in the Dust* 1948]

John Kenneth Galbraith, 1908– , Canadian-born American economist

All races have produced notable economists, with the exception of the Irish, who doubtless can protest their devotion to higher arts.

[*The Age of Uncertainty* 1977]

Paul Gallico, 1897–1976, American novelist

No one can be as calculatedly rude as the British, which amazes Americans, who do not understand studied insult and can only offer abuse as a substitute.

[*The New York Times* January 14 1962]

Sir William Schwenck Gilbert, 1836–1911, English librettist
For he himself has said it;
And it's greatly to his credit
That he is an Englishman!
For he might have been a Rooshan,
A French, or Turk or Prooshan,
Or perhaps I-tal-i-an!
But in spite of all temptations
To belong to other nations,
He remains an Englishman!

[*H.M.S. Pinafore* 1]

Alasdair [James] Gray, 1934– , Scottish writer
I realised that Scotland was shaped like a fat messy woman with a surprisingly slender waist.
A threestranded belt of road, canal and railway crossed that waist joining Edinburgh, and the
ports facing Europe, to Glasgow and the ports facing Ireland and America.

[*Janine* 1982]

Germaine Greer, 1939– , Australian feminist writer
Australia is a huge rest home, where no unwelcome news is ever wafted on to the pages of the
worst newspapers in the world.

[In the *Observer* August 1982]

Margaret Halsey, 1910– , American writer
Listening to Britons dining out is like watching people play first-class tennis with imaginary
balls.

[*With Malice Towards Some* 1939]

The English never smash in a face. They merely refrain from asking it to dinner.

[*Ibid*]

[Christian Johann] Heinrich Heine, 1797–1856, German poet
The French and the Russians have shared out the land,
Britannia rules the oceans;
We reign unchallenged in the realm
Of dreamy abstract notions.

[*Deutschland: A Winter's Tale* 1844]

Katharine [Houghton] Hepburn, 1907–2003, American actress
First God made England, Ireland and Scotland. That's when he corrected his mistakes and
made Wales.

[In *Time* August 7 1978]

Thomas Hood, 1799–1845, English poet
Holland . . . lies so low they're only saved by being damned.

[*Up The Rhine* 1840]

Horace [Quintus Horatius Flaccus], 65–8 BC, Roman poet
Greece, once overcome, overcame her wild conquerer and brought the arts into rustic
Latium.

[*Epistles*]

[James] Langston Hughes, 1902–67, American poet, playwright and novelist
I, too, sing America.
I am the darker brother.

[*Selected Poems : I, Too* 1954]

Dr Samuel Johnson, 1709–84, English lexicographer
When two Englishmen meet, their first talk is of the weather.

[*The Idler* 1760]

Erica Jong, 1942– , American writer and poet
Every country gets the circus it deserves. Spain gets bull-fights. Italy gets the Catholic Church. America gets Hollywood.

[*How to Save Your Own Life* 1977]

James [Augustine Aloysius] Joyce, 1882–1941, Irish writer and poet
Ireland is the old sow that eats her farrow.

[*A Portrait of the Artist as a Young Man* 1916]

Thomas Keneally, 1935– , Australian novelist
In a way Australia is like Catholicism. The company is sometimes questionable and the landscape is grotesque. But you always come back.

[In *Woman's Day* July 4 1983]

John Fitzgerald Kennedy, 1917–63, 35th president of the United States
Ich bin ein Berliner.
I am a Berliner.

[Speech, West Berlin 1963]

Charles Kingsley, 1819–75, English churchman and writer
Oh, England is a pleasant place for them that's rich and high,
But England is a cruel place for such poor folks as I.

[*The Last Buccaneer* 1857]

Fran Lebowitz, 1951– , American journalist and writer
[Of Paris] If you're going there you would do well to remember this: no matter how politely or distinctly you ask a Parisian a question he will persist in answering you in French.

[*Metropolitan Life* 1979]

Alan Jay Lerner, 1918–86, American songwriter
The rain in Spain stays mainly in the plain.

[Song: *The Rain in Spain*]

Dame [Emilie] Rose Macauley, 1881–1958, English novelist and essayist
Owing to the weather, English social life must always have largely occurred either indoors, or, when out of doors, in active motion.

[*Life Among the English* 1942]

Hugh MacDiarmid [Christopher Murray Grieve], 1892–1978, Scottish poet
Whatever Scotland is to me,
Be it aye part o' a' men see
O' Earth and o' Eternity

[*A Drunk Man Looks at the Thistle* 1926]

Thomas Mann, 1875–1955, German novelist
The German is the eternal student, the eternal searcher, among the peoples of the earth.
[*Doctor Faustus* 1947]

Arthur Marshall, 1910–89, English humorous writer and broadcaster
The French are tremendous snobs, despite that rather showy and ostentatious Revolution.
[*I'll Let You Know*]

George Mikes, 1912– , Hungarian-born English humorous writer
Whatever else an Italian may lack, he has an Ego. Sometimes two. It is nice to think that even the poorest Italian may possess two Egos while even the richest Englishman, as a rule, has none.
[*How to be an Alien* 1946]
Continental people have sex lives. The English have hot water bottles.
[*Ibid*]
Switzerland, though lovely, is very full of the Swiss.
[*How to be Poor*]

Alice Duer Miller, 1874–1942, American writer and poet
I am American bred,
I have seen much to hate here – much to forgive,
But in a world where England is finished and dead,
I do not wish to live.
[*The White Cliffs* 1940]

Henry [Valentine] Miller, 1891–1980, American novelist
I have never been able to look upon America as young and vital but rather as prematurely old, as a fruit which rotted before it had a chance to ripen.
[*The Air-Conditioned Nightmare* 1945]

Jessica Mitford, 1917–96, English writer
Things on the whole are much faster in America; people don't *stand for election*, they *run for office*. If a person says he's *sick*, it doesn't mean regurgitating; it means *ill*. *Mad* means *angry*, not insane. Don't ask for the *left-luggage*; it's called a *check-room*. A *nice joint* means a *good pub*, not roast meat.
[*Hons and Rebels* 1960]

Robert Morley, 1908–92, English actor and humorist
The French are a logical people, which is one reason the English dislike them so intensely. The other is that they own France, a country which we have always judged to be much too good for them.
[*A Musing Morley* 1974]

Edna O'Brien, 1932– , Irish novelist and playwright
Irish? In truth I would not want to be anything else. It is a state of mind as well as an actual country. It is being at odds with other nationalities, having a quite different philosophy about pleasure, about punishment, about life, and about death. At least it does not leave one pusillanimous.
[*Mother Ireland* 1976]

P[atrick] J[ake] O'Rourke, 1947– , American satirist

Once you've been on a plane full of drunken Austrailians doing wallaby imitations up and down the aisles, you'll never make fun of Americans again.

[*Holidays in Hell* 1988]

George Orwell [Eric Arthur Blair], 1903–50, English novelist and critic

I have the most evil memories of Spain, but I have very few bad memories of Spaniards.

[*Homage to Catalonia* 1938]

Kerry [Francis Bullmore] Packer, 1937– , Australian media proprietor

If a British guy saw someone at the wheel of a Rolls-Royce, he'd say "come the revolution and we'll take that away from you, mate", where the American would say "one day I'll have one of those, when I have worked hard enough". It's unfortunate we Australians inherited the British mentality.

[In the *Guardian* September 1 1977]

Madame de Pompadour [Jeanne Antoinette Poisson, Marquise de Pompadour], 1721–64, French courtier and mistress of Louis XV

Canada is useful only to provide me with furs.

[Attributed]

Will[iam Penn Adair] Rogers, 1879–1935, American actor and humorist

The United Sates never lost a war or won a conference.

[*Saturday Review:A Roger's Thesaurus* 1962]

Saki [Hector Hugh Munro], 1870–1916, Scottish-born writer

The people of Crete unfortunately make more history than they can consume locally.

[*The Jesting of Arlington Stringham*]

Arthur Schopenhauer, 1788–1860, German philosopher

It is a curious failing in the German people that they search in the clouds for what lies at their feet.

[*Parerga und Paralipomena* 1851]

Sir Walter Scott, 1771–1832, Scottish novelist

O Caledonia! stern and wild,
Meet nurse for a poetic child!
Land of brown heath and shaggy wood,
Land of the mountain and the flood,
Land of my sires! what mortal hand
Can e'er untie the filial band,
That knits me to thy rugged strand!

[*The Lay of the Last Minstrel* 1805]

Charles Louis de Secondat, Baron de Montesquieu, 1689–1755, French philosopher

The English are a busy people. They haven't time to become polished.

[*Pensées c.*1750]

Walter Carruthers Sellar, 1898–1951 and Robert Julian Yeatman, 1897–1968, English writers

Holland is a low-lying country full of low, lying people whose main object in life is to deceive the English by holding *Dutch auctions*, displaying *Dutch courage*, and talking *Double-Dutch*.

[*And Now All This*]

George Bernard Shaw, 1856–1950, Irish playwright
England and America are two countries divided by a common language.
[Attributed]
There is nothing so bad or so good that you will not find Englishmen doing it; but you will never find an Englishman in the wrong. He does everything on principle. He fights you on patriotic principles; he robs you on business principles; he enslaves you on imperial principles.

[*The Man of Destiny* 1897]

Percy Bysse Shelley, 1792–1822, English poet
Thou Paradise of Exiles, Italy!

[*Julian and Maddalo*, 1818]

Sydney Smith, 1771–1845, English churchman
It requires a surgical operation to get a joke well into a Scotch understanding.

[In Lady Holland's *Memoir of the Reverend Sydney Smith* 1855]

[Of Scotland] That knuckle-end of England – that land of Calvin, oat-cakes and sulphur.

[In *Ibid*]

Gertrude Stein, 1874–1946, American writer
In the United States there is more space where nobody is than where anybody is. That is what makes America what it is.

[*The Geographical History of America*]

Laurence Sterne, 1713–68, English churchman and writer
[Of the French] They are a loyal, a gallant, a generous, an ingenious and good tempered people as is under heaven – if they have a fault, they are too serious.

A Sentimental Journey 1768]

Robert Louis [Balfour] Stevenson, 1850–94, Scottish novelist and poet
For that is the mark of the Scot of all classes: that he stands in an attitude towards the past unthinkable to Englishmen, and remembers and cherishes the memory of his forebears, good or bad; and there burns alive in him a sense of identity with the dead even to the twentieth generation.

[*Weir of Hermiston* 1896]

Paul Theroux, 1941– , American writer
The Japanese have perfected good manners and made them indistinguishable from rudeness.

[*The Great Railway Bazaar* 1975]

Hunter S[tockton] Thompson, 1939– , American journalist
America . . . just a nation of two hundred used car salesmen with all the money we need to buy guns and no qualms about killing anybody else in the world who tries to make us uncomfortable.

[*Fear and Loathing on the Campaign Trail* 1973]

Arnold Toynbee, 1889–1975, British historian
America is a large, friendly dog in a small room. Every time it wags its tail it knocks over a chair.

[Attributed]

Leon Trotsky [Lev Davidovich Bronstein], 1879–1940, Russian revolutionary
England is nothing but the last ward of the European madhouse, and quite possibly it will prove to be the ward for particularly violent cases.

[Diary in Exile 1959]

Mark Twain [Samuel Langhorne Clemens], 1835–1910, American writer
France has neither winter nor summer nor morals – apart from these drawbacks it is a fine country.

[Notebooks 1935]

Virgil or Vergil [Publius Vergilius Maro], 70–19BC, Roman poet
I fear the Greeks, even though they bring gifts.

[Aeneid BookII *c*29–19BC]

Evelyn [Arthur St John] Waugh, 1903-66, English writer
You never find an Englishman among the under-dogs – except in England, of course.

[The Loved One 1948]

Irvine Welsh, 1958– , Scottish author
Ah don't hate the English. They're just wankers. We are colonized by wankers. We can't even pick a decent, healthy culture to be colonized by. No. We're ruled by effete arseholes. What does that make us?

[Trainspotting 1993]

Walt[er] Whitman, 1819–92, American poet
The United Sates themselves are essentially the greatest poem.

[Leaves of Grass preface 1855]

Sir P[elham] G[reville] Wodehouse, 1881–1975, English-born writer
It is never difficult to distinguish between a Scotsman with a grievance and a ray of sunshine.

[In Usborne's*Wodehouse at Work*]

Israel Zangwill, 1864–1926, English writer
America is God's Crucible, the great Melting Pot where all the races of Europe are melting and re-forming!

[The Melting Pot 1908]

Sports and Games

Muhammad Ali [Cassius Marcellus Clay], 1942– , American boxer

Float like a butterfly, sting like a bee.

[Catchphrase]

It's just a job. Grass grows, birds fly, waves pound the sand. I beat people up.

[In the *New York Times* April 6 1977]

[Joe] Frazier is so ugly that he should donate his face to the US Bureau of Wild Life.

[In the *Guardian* December 1972]

Anonymous.

He plays well that wins.

[Proverb]

Fair play is good play.

[Proverb]

Jane Austen 1775–1817, English novelist

And it was not very wonderful that Catherine, who by nature had nothing very heroic about her, should prefer cricket, baseball, riding on horseback and running about the country, at the age of fouteen, to books.

[*Northanger Abbey* 1818]

Jacques Barzun, 1907– , American writer

Whoever wants to know the heart and mind of America had better learn baseball, the rules and realities of the game.

[*God's Country and Mine* 1954]

Alan Bennett, 1934– , English playwright

If you think squash is a competitive activity, try flower arrangement.

[*Talking Heads* 1988]

Arthur Asa Berger, 1933– , American writer and educator

Baseball represents America before the frontier ended, when there was plenty of space and plenty of time, and philosophic anarchists roamed about on verdant fields "doing their thing" with a free and reckless abandon. The game is relaxing and not particularly taxing on the players, who play many times each week. Football is tremendously difficult on the players and is so tiring that sixty minutes of clock time – which amounts to several hours of real time – exhausts them.

[*The TV-Guided American: Football and Television* 1976]

415

Sir John Betjeman, 1906–84, English poet
Miss J. Hunter Dunn, Miss J. Hunter Dunn,
Furnish'd and burnish'd by Aldershot sun,
What strenuous singles we played after tea
We in the tournament – you against me!

[*John Betjeman's Collected Poems: A Subaltern's Love-Song* 1958]

Pam, I adore you, you great big mountainous sports girl,
Whizzing them over the net, full of the strength of five.

[*Ibid: Pot Pourri from a Surrey Garden*]

The Bible
Know ye not that they which run in a race run all, but one receiveth the prize?

[*1 Corinthians* 9:24]

Wilfred Scawen Blunt, 1840–1922, English poet

I like the hunting of the hare
Better than that of the fox.

[*The Old Squire*]

Frank Bruno, 1961– , English boxer
Boxing is just show-business with blood.

[In the *Guardian* 1991]

Jimmy Cannon, 1890–1974, American sportswriter
Fishing, with me, has always been an excuse to drink in the daytime

[In J. Holtzman's *No Cheering in the Pressbox* 1973]

Linford Christie, 1960– , English athlete
I run with a controlled fear of losing. When you are frightened in that way it's amazing what you can achieve.

[Comment, 1992 Olympics. In *The Daily Telegraph Century of Sport* 1998]

[John] Calvin Coolidge, 1872–1933, 30th president of the United States
Baseball is our national game.

[Attributed]

William Cowper, 1731–1800, English poet
[On hunting] Detested sport, that owes its pleasure to another's pain.

[*The Task* 1785]

Joe DiMaggio [Joseph Paul Dimaggio], 1914–99, American baseball player
A ball player's got to be kept hungry to become a big-leaguer. That's why no boy from a rich family ever made the big leagues.

[In the *New York Times* 1961]

Chris[tine Marie] Evert, 1954– , American tennis player
In tennis, at the end of the day you're a winner or a loser. You know exactly where you stand . . . I don't need that any more. I don't need my happiness, my well-being, to be based on winning and losing.

[In *Sports Illustrated* May 25 1992]

F[rancis] Scott [Key] Fitzgerald, 1896–1940, American novelist
Baseball is a game played by idiots for morons.

[Attributed]

Sir William Schwenck Gilbert, 1836–1911, English librettist
The billiard sharp whom any one catches,
His doom's extremely hard –
He's made to dwell –
In a dungeon cell
On a spot that's always barred.
And there he plays extravagant matches
In fitless finger-stalls
On a cloth untrue
With a twisted cue
And elliptical billiard balls.

[*The Mikado* 1885]

Kenneth Grahame, 1859–1932, English writer
There is nothing – absolutely nothing – half so much worth doing as simply messing about in boats.

[*The Wind in the Willows* 1908]

John Woodcock Graves, 1795–1886, English poet and songwriter
D'ye ken John Peel with his coat so gay?
D'ye ken John Peel at the break of day?
D'ye ken John Peel when he's far, far away
With his hounds and his horn in the morning?

[Song: *John Peel* 1820]

Michael Frederick Green, 1927– , English humorous writer
Coarse Rugby is played by those who are too old, too young, too light, too heavy, too weak, too slow, too lazy, too cowardly, or too unfit for ordinary rugger.

[*The Art of Coarse Rugby* 1960]

Ernest [Miller] Hemingway, 1899–1961, American novelist
Bullfighting is the only art in which the artist is in danger of death and in which the degree of brilliance in the performance is left to the fighter's honour.

[*Death in the Afternoon*]

The formal bullfight is a tragedy, not a sport, and the bull is certain to be killed.

[*Ibid*]

James Hogg ("The Ettrick Shepherd"), 1770–1835, Scottish poet and novelist
Oh! for the channel-stane!
The fell good name the channel-stane!
There's no a game that e'er I saw
Can match auld Scotland's channel-stane!

[*The Channel-Stane*]

Nick Hornby, 1957– , English writer
The natural state of the football fan is bitter disappointment, no matter what the score.

[*Fever Pitch* 1992]

A[lfred E[dward] Housman, 1859–1936, English poet and scholar
Twice a week the winter through
Here stood I to keep the goal:
Football then was fighting sorrow
For the young man's soul.

Now in Maytime to the wicket
Out I march with bat and pad:
See the son of grief at cricket
Trying to be glad.

[*A Shropshire Lad* 1896]

Thomas Hughes, 1822–1896, English writer
[On cricket] It's more than a game. It's an institution.

[*Tom Brown's Schooldays* 1857]

John Irving, 1942– , American writer
[On baseball] It is a game with a lot of waiting in it; it is a game with increasingly heightened anticipation of increasingly limited results.

[*A Prayer for Owen Meany* 1989]

Bo [Vincent Edward] Jackson, 1962– , American football and baseball player
Baseball was fun when I was in college. It's my job now. But I like my 3–11 shift.

[In Paul Dickson's *Baseball's Greatest Quotations* 1991]

C[yril] L[ionel] R[obert] James, 1901–89, Trinidadian political activist and writer
Cricket is first and foremost a dramatic spectacle. It belongs with the theatre, ballet, opera and the dance.

[*Beyond a Boundary* 1963]

What do they know of cricket who only cricket know? West Indians crowding to Tests bring with them the whole past history and future hopes of the islands.

[*Ibid*]

Jerome K[lapka] Jerome, 1859–1927, English humorous writer
All that is required to make a good fisherman (some people say) is the ability to tell lies easily and without blushing.

[*Three Men in a Boat* 1889]

John Paul II [Karol Wojtyla], 1920– , Polish pope
It is unbecoming for a cardinal to ski badly.

[Attributed]

Dr Samuel Johnson, 1709–84, English lexicographer
Fly fishing may be a very pleasant amusement; but angling or float fishing I can only compare to a stick and a string, with a worm at one end and a fool at the other.

[Attributed]

I am sorry I have not learned to play cards. It is very useful in life: it generates kindness and consolidates society.

[In Boswell's *Journal of a Tour to the Hebrides* 1785]

Brian [Alexander] Johnston, 1912–94, English sports commentator and broadcaster
I evidently greeted listeners with the words: "You join us at an interesting time. Ray
Illingworth has just relieved himself at the pavilion end."

[*It's a Funny Game*]

The bowler's Holding, the batsman's Willey.

[Commentary remark, quoted in his obituary in the *Sunday Times* 1994]

Billie Jean King, 1943– , American tennis player
In the complete overall history of tennis, I figure I'll be worth a sentence or two . . . That's
why my place in the all-time rankings means so very little to me, because I know I won't be
anybody's number one, and it's that same old thing; if you're not number one, then what does
it really matter?

[*Billie Jean* 1982]

Andrew Lang, 1844–1912, Scottish writer
Golf is a thoroughly national game; it is as Scotch as haggis, cockie-leekie, high cheek-bones,
or rowanberry jam.

[*Lost Leaders* 1889]

Stephen Butler Leacock, 1869–1944, Canadian economist and humorist
Golf may be played on a Sunday, not being a game within the view of the law, but being a
form of moral effort.

[*Over the Footlights* 1923]

John Patrick McEnroe, 1959– , American tennis player
You cannot be serious!

[Complaint to Wimbledon umpire, which became a catchphrase.]

Diego Maradona, 1960– , Argentinian footballer.
[On a controversial goal against England in the World Cup] The goal was scored a little bit by
the hand of God, another bit by the head of Maradona.

[In the *Observer* 1986.]

A[lan] A[lexander] Milne, 1882–1956, English writer
Golf is the best game in the world at which to be bad . . . It is the bad player who gets the most
strokes.

[*Not That It Matters*]

Lewis Mumford, 1895–1990, American writer and critic
Sport in the sense of the mass-spectacle, with death to add to the underlying excitement,
comes into existence when a population has been drilled and regimented and depressed to
such an extent that it needs at least a vicarious participation in difficult feats of strength or
skill or heroism in order to sustain its waning life-sense.

[*Technics and Civilization* 1934]

Martina Navratilova, 1956– , Czech-born American tennis player
The moment of victory is much too short to live for that and nothing else.

[In the *Guardian* June 21 1989]

Denis Norden, 1922– , British humorist
It's a funny kind of month, October. For the really keen cricket fan it's when you discover that
your wife left you in May.

[In *She* October 1977]

Joyce Carol Oates, 1938– , American writer

Boxing is about being hit rather more than it is about the hitting, just as it is about feeling pain, if not devastating psychological paralysis, more than it is about winning.

[*One Boxing* 1987]

P[atrick] J[ake] O'Rourke, 1947– , American satirist

The sport of ski-ing consists of wearing three thousand dollars' worth of clothes and equipment and driving two hundred miles in the snow in order to stand around at a bar and get drunk.

[*Modern Manners* 1984]

George Orwell [Eric Arthur Blair], 1903–50, English novelist and critic

Serious sport has nothing to do with fair play. It is bound up with hatred, jealousy, boastfulness, disregard of all rules and sadistic pleasure in witnessing violence; in other words, it is war minus the shooting.

[*The Sporting Spirit*]

Camille Paglia, 1947– , American writer

Modern bodybuilding is ritual, religion, sport, art and science, awash in Western chemistry and mathematics. Defying nature, it surpasses it.

[*Sex, Art and American Culture* 1992]

Arnold Palmer 1929– , American golfer

The more I practise the luckier I get.

[Attributed]

Michael Parkinson, 1933– , English journalist and broadcaster

The most significant change in sport in my lifetime has been the transition of the game into a product.

[*The Daily Telegraph Century of Sport* 1998]

Nothing yet devised by man is worse for a sick hangover than a day's cricket in the summer sun.

[*Bats in the Pavilion* 1977]

Sidney Joseph Perelman, 1904–79, American humorist

Far from being a member of any gymnastic team, I could not jump over a sawhorse without sustaining multiple fractures.

[*The Last Laugh*]

Grantland Rice [Henry Grantland Rice], 1880–1954, American sports writer

For when the One Great Scorer comes to write against your name,
He marks – not that you won or lost – but how you played the Game.

[*Alumnus Football* 1941]

Philip [Milton] Roth, 1933– , American novelist

Baseball – with its lore and legends, its cultural power, its seasonal associations . . . its mythic transformation of the immediate – was the literature of my childhood.

[In the *New York Times: My Baseball Years* 1973]

Charles Monroe Schulz, 1922–2000, American cartoonist

No matter how hard you try, you just can't bounce a croquet ball.

[*For the Love of Peanuts* 1963]

Ayrton Senna [Ayrton Senna da Silva], 1960–94, Brazilian racing driver
[On the San Marino racing circuit] There are no small accidents on this circuit.
[Said before his fatal crash in the 1994 Grand Prix. In the *Independent* December 22 1994]

Bill [William] Shankly, 1913–81, Scottish footballer and manager
Some people think football is a matter of life and death . . . I can assure them it is much more serious than that.
[In the *Guardian* December 1973]

William Shakespeare, 1564–1616, English dramatist
What sport shall we devise here in this garden
To drive away the heavy thought of care?
[*King Richard II* 3 1592–3]

There be some sports are painful, and their labour
Delight in them sets off.
[*The Tempest* 3 1611–12]

Sir Philip Sidney, 1554–1586, English poet
Philip of Macedon reckoned a horse-race won at Olympus among his three fearful felicities.
[*Defence of Poesie* 1595]

Charles Hamilton Sorley, 1895–1915, Scottish poet
We swing ungirded hips,
And lightened are our eyes,
The rain is on our lips,
We do not run for prize.
[*The Song of the Upright Runners*]

Jock [John] Stein, 1922–85, Scottish footballer and manager
We do have the greatest fans in the world, but I've never seen a fan score a goal.
[In discussion of the World Cup in Spain 1982]

Philip Stubbes, c.1555–c.1593, English Puritan pamphleteer
Football . . .causeth fighting, brawling, contention, quarrel picking, murder, homicide and great effusion of bloode, as daily experience teacheth.
[*Anatomy of Abuses* 1583]

William Temple, 1881–1944, English prelate and Archbishop of Canterbury.
Personally, I have always looked on cricket as organised loafing.
[Attributed]

Henry David Thoreau, 1817–62, American naturalist and writer
The sport of digging the bait is nearly equal to that of catching the fish, when one's appetite is not too keen.
[*The Writings of Henry David Thoreau* 1906]

Mark Twain [Samuel Langhorne Clemens], 1835–1910, American writer and journalist
Golf is a good walk spoiled.
[Attributed]

Sir Herbert [Draper] Beerbohm Tree, 1853–1917, English actor

The national sport of England is obstacle-racing. People fill their rooms with useless and cumbersome furniture and spend the rest of their lives trying to dodge it.

[In Hesketh Pearson's *Beerbohm Tree*]

Sir Peter [Alexander] Ustinov, 1921– , British playwright and actor

Rowing seemed to me a monotonous pursuit, and somehow wasteful to be making all that effort to be going in the wrong direction.

[*Dear Me* 1977]

Izaak Walton, 1593–1683, English writer on fishing

With a fine needle and silk sew the upper part of [the frog's] leg, with only one stitch, to the arming-wire of your hook; or tie the frog's leg, above the upper joint, to the armed-wire; and, in so doing, use him as though you loved him, that is, harm him as little as you may possible, that he may live the longer.

[*The Compleat Angler* 1653]

Angling is somewhat like poetry: men are to be born so.

[*Ibid*]

We may say of angling as Dr Boteler said of strawberries: "Doubtless God could have made a better berry, but doubtless God never did": and so, if I might be judge, God never did make a more calm, quiet, innocent recreation than angling.

[*Ibid*]

Evelyn [Arthur St John] Waugh, 1903–66, English writer

Boys do get into such indelicate positions during the obstacle race.

[*Scoop* 1938]

H[erbert] G[eorge Wells, 1866–1946, English writer

The uglier a man's legs are the better he plays golf.

[*Bealby*]

Tennessee Williams [Thomas Lanier Williams], 1911–83, American playwright

Poker shouldn't be played in a house with women.

[*A Streetcar Named Desire* 1947]

Kenneth Wolstenholme, 1920– , British sports commentator

They think it's all over – it is now.

[Television commentary on last moments of World Cup final, July 30 1966]

Victoria Wood 1953– , English comedienne

Jogging is for people who aren't intelligent enough to watch television.

[*Mens Sana in Thingummy Doodah* 1990]

In Russia, show the least athletic aptitude and they've got you dangling off the parallel bars with a leotard full of hormones.

[*Up To You, Porky*]

Truth

Herbert [Sebastian] Agar, 1897–1980, American writer

The truth which makes men free is for the most part the truth which men prefer not to hear.

[*A Time for Greatness* 1942]

Anonymous

There's many a true word spoken in jest.

[Proverb]

Truth fears no trial.

[Proverb]

Truth is stranger than fiction

[Proverb]

Jean Anouilh, 1910–87, French dramatist

Nothing is true except what is not said.

[*Antigone* 1942]

Aristotle, 384–322BC, Greek philosopher

Plato is dear to me, but dearer still is truth.

[Attributed]

Matthew Arnold, 1822–88, English poet and critic

Truth sits upon the lips of dying men.

[*Sohrab and Rustum* 1853]

Francis Bacon, Baron Verulam of Verulam and Viscount of St Albans, 1561–1626, English philosopher

What is truth? said jesting Pilate; and would not stay for an answer.

[*Essays: Of Truth*]

Walter Bagehot, 1826–87, English economist and journalist

He believes, with all his heart and soul and strength, that there is such a thing as truth; he has the soul of a martyr and the intellect of an advocate.

[*Mr Gladstone*]

Stanley Baldwin, 1st Earl Baldwin of Bewdley, 1867–1947, British statesman

A platitude is simply a truth repeated until people get tired of hearing it.

[Attributed]

[Joseph] Hilaire [Pierre] Belloc, 1870–1953, English writer
Matilda told such Dreadful Lies,
It made one Gasp and Stretch one's Eyes;
Her Aunt, who, from her Earliest Youth,
Had kept a Strict Regard for Truth,
Attempted to Believe Matilda:
The effort very nearly killed her.

[*Matilda* 1907]

Simone de Beauvoir, 1908–86, French writer
I tore myself away from the safe comfort of certainties through my love for truth; and truth rewarded me.

[*All Said and Done* 1974]

Saul Bellow, 1915– , American writer
A man may say, "From now on I'm going to speak the truth." But the truth hears him and runs away and hides before he's even done speaking.

[*Herzog* 1964]

There were two varieties of truth, one symbolized by the Tree of Knowledge, the other by the Tree of Life, one the truth of striving and the other the truth of receptivity.

[*More die of Heartbreak* 1987]

George Berkeley, 1685–1753, Irish Anglican bishop and philosopher
Truth is the cry of all, but the game of the few.

[*Siris*]

The Bible
Ye are of your father the devil, and the lusts of your father ye will do. He was a murderer in the beginning, and abode not in the truth, because there is no truth in him. When he speaketh a lie, he speaketh of his own: for he is a liar, and the father of it.

[*John* 8:44]

I am the way, the truth, and the life: no man cometh unto the father, but by me.

[*John* 14:1]

Pilate therefore said unto him, Art thou a king then? Jesus answered, Thou sayest that I am a king. To this end was I born, and for this cause came I into the world, that I should bear witness unto the truth. Every one that is of the truth heareth my voice.
Pilate said unto him, What is truth?

[*John* 18:38–9]

William Blake, 1757–1827, English poet and artist
When I tell any Truth it is not for the sake of convincing those that do not know it, but for the sake of defending those who do.

[Speech]

Elizabeth Dorothea Cole Bowen, 1899–1973, Irish author
Nobody speaks the truth when there's something they must have.

[*The Heat of the Day*]

Georges Braque, 1882–1963, French artist
Truth exists; only lies are invented.

[*Notebooks: Day and Night* 1952]

Robert Browning, 1812–89, English poet
All's over, then; does truth sound bitter
as one at first believes?

[*The Lost Mistress*]

Charles Bukowski, 1920–94, German-born American writer
There is nothing as boring as the truth.

[*Notes of a Dirty Old Man* 1969]

Samuel Butler, 1835–1902, English writer
Some men love Truth so much that they seem to be in continual fear lest she should catch
cold through over-exposure.

[*Note-Books c.* 1890]

Richard Clarke Cabot, 1868–1939, American physician
Before you tell the "truth" to the patient, be sure you know the "truth", and that the patient
wants to hear it.

[*Journal of Chronic Diseases*]

James Callaghan, 1912– , British politician
A lie can be halfway round the world before the truth has got its boots on.

[Speech 1976]

Thomas Campbell, 1777–1844, Scottish poet
Truth, ever lovely, since the world began
The foe of tyrants, and the friend of man.

[*Pleasures of Hope* 1799]

Louis-Ferdinand Céline [Louis-Ferdinand Destouches], 1894–1961, French novelist
Truth is a never-ending agony. The truth of this world is death. One must choose – die or lie.
I've never been able to kill myself.

[*Voyage au bout de la nuit* 1932]

Geoffrey Chaucer, c.1340–1400, English poet
Trouthe is the hyeste thyng that man may kepe.

[*The Canterbury Tales: The Franklin's Tale c.*1387]

Marcus Tullius Cicero, 106–43 BC, Roman statesman
If the truth were self-evident, eloquence would be unnecessary.

[*De Oratore* 55 BC]

Jean Cocteau, 1891–1963, French poet and artist
I am a lie who always speaks the truth.

[*Opéra* 1925]

Sir Arthur Conan Doyle, 1859–1930, English novelist
How often have I said to you that when you have eliminated the impossible, whatever
remains, however improbable, must be the truth.

[*The Sign of Four* 1890]

William Congreve, 1670–1729, English dramatist
No mask like open truth to cover lies,
As to go naked is the best disguise.

[*The Double Dealer* 5 1694]

William Cowper, 1731–1800, English poet
He is the freeman whom the truth makes free.

[*The Winter Morning Walk*]

George Crabbe, 1754–1832, English poet and churchman
I paint the Cot
As Truth will paint it, and as Bards will not.

[*The Village* 1783]

John Dewey, 1859–1952, American philosopher
Truth, in short, from a psychological standpoint, is agreement of relations; falsity, disagreement of relations.

[*Psychology* 1887]

Emily Dickinson, 1830–86, American poet
Tell all the Truth but tell it slant –
Success in Circuit lies
too bright for our infirm Delight
The Truth's superb surprise.

[*Tell all the Truth but Tell It Slant*]

Benjamin Disraeli, 1st Earl of Beaconsfield, 1804–81, British statesman and novelist
Something unpleasant is coming when men are anxious to tell the truth.

[Speech]

John Donne, c.1571–1631, English poet
On a huge hill,
Cragged, and steep, Truth stands, and he that will
reach her, about must, and about must go;
And what the hill's suddenness resists, win so.

[*Satyre III*]

Umberto Eco, 1932– , Italian novelist and semiotician
Perhaps the mission of those who love mankind is to make people laugh at the truth, *to make truth laugh*, because the only truth lies in learning to free ourselves from insane passion for truth.

[*The Name of the Rose* 1980]

Albert Einstein, 1879-1955, German-born mathematical physicist
Ethical axioms are found and tested not very differently from the axioms of science. Truth is what stands the test of exoperience.

[*Out of My Later Years* 1950]

Gerald R[udolf] Ford, 1913– , 38th president of the United States
Truth is the glue that holds the government together.

[Speech August 1974]

Mohandas Karamchand ("Mahatma") Gandhi, 1869–1948, Indian political leader
I have nothing new to teach the world. Truth and Non-violence are as old as the hills. All I have done is to try experiments in both on as vast a scale as I could.

[*Harijan* 1936]

[Henry] Grahame Greene, 1904–91, English novelist
The truth has never been of any real value to any human being – it is a symbol for mathematicians and philosophers to pursue. In human relations kindness and lies are worth a thousand truths.

[*The Heart of the Matter* 1948]

Sir William Hamilton, 1788–1856, Scottish philosopher
Truth, like a torch, the more it's shook it shines.

[*Discussions on Philosophy* 1852]

Lillian Hellman, 1905–84, American playwright
Truth made you a traitor as it often does in a time of scoundrels.

[*Scoundrel Time* 1976]

Thomas Hobbes, 1588–1679, English political philosopher
True and false are attributes of speech, not of things. And where speech is not, there is neither truth nor falsehood.

[*Leviathan* 1651]

Thomas Henry Huxley, 1825–95, English biologist
Irrationally held truths may be more harmful than reasoned errors.

[*Science and Culture, and Other Essays* 1881]

William James, 1842–1910, American philosopher
There is no worse lie than a truth misunderstood by those who hear it.

[*The Varieties of Religious Experience* 1902]

Jerome K[lapka] Jerome, 1859–1927, English humorous writer
It is always the best policy to speak the truth, unless of course you are an exceptionally good liar.

[*The Idler*]

Karl Kraus, 1874–1936, Austrian writer
Truth is a clumsy servant that breaks the dishes while cleaning them.

[In Harry Zohn's *Karl Kraus* 1971]

Baron Gottfried Wilhelm von Leibniz, 1646–1716, German philosopher
There are two kinds of truths: truths of *reasoning* and truths of *fact*. Truths of *reasoning* are necessary and their opposite is impossible; those of *fact* are contingent and their opposite is possible.

[*Monadology* 1714]

Gotthold Ephraim Lessing, 1729–61, German writer
If God were to hold out enclosed in His right hand all Truth, and in His left hand just the active search for Truth, though with the condition that I should ever err therein, and should say to me: Choose! I should humbly take His left hand and say: Father! Give me this one: absolute Truth belongs to Thee alone.

[*Wolfenbüttler Fragmente*]

James Russell Lowell, 1819–91, American editor and poet
Once to every man and nation
Comes the moment to decide,
In the strife of Truth and Falsehood,
For the good or evil side.

[*The Present Crisis*]

Edward Verrall Lucas, 1868–1938, English writer
By always telling the truth one saves oneself from a multitude of fatiguing cares.

[*Rose and Rose*]

Mary McCarthy, 1912–89, American writer
There are no new truths, but only truths that have not been recognized by those who have perceived them without noticing. A truth is something that everybody can be shown to know and to have known, as people say, all along.

[*On the Contrary: The Vita Activa*]

Thomas Mann, 1875–1955, German novelist
A great truth is a truth whose opposite is also a great truth.

[*Essay on Freud* 1937]

Henry [Valentine] Miller, 1891–1980, American novelist
What does it matter how one comes by the truth so long as one pounces on it and lives by it?

[*Tropic of Capricorn* 1939]

John Milton, 1608–74, English poet
Though all the winds of doctrine were let loose to play upon the earth, so Truth be in the field, we do injuriously by licensing and prohibiting to misdoubt her strength. Let her and Falsehood grapple; who ever knew Truth put to the worse, in a free and open encounter?

[*Areopagitica* 1644]

Dame Iris Murdoch, 1919–99, English novelist and philosopher
As for truth – well, it's like brown – it's not in the spectrum . . . Truth is *sui generis*.

[*The Philosopher's Pupil* 1983]

Friedrich Wilhelm Nietzsche, 1844–1900, German philosopher and poet
Truths are illusions about which one has forgotten that this is what they are; metaphors which are worn out and without sensuous power; coins which have lost their pictures and now matter only as metal, no longer as coins.

[*On Truth and Lie in an Extra-Moral Sense*]

Richard Milhous Nixon, 1913–94, 37th president of the United States
Let us begin by committing ourselves to the truth, to see it like it is and to tell it like it is, to find the truth, to speak the truth and live with the truth. That's what we'll do.

[Nomination acceptance speech 1968]

Peter Ouspensky, 1878–1947, Russian philosopher
Truths that become old become decrepit and unreliable; sometimes they may be kept going artificially for a certain time, but there is no life in them . . . Ideas can be too old.

[A New Model of the Universe]

TRUTH

William Penn, 1644–1718, English founder of Pennsylvania
Truth often suffers more by the heat of its defenders than from the arguments of its opposers.
[*Some Fruits of Solitude* 1693]

Plato, c.428–348BC, Greek philosopher
But, my dearest Agathon, it is truth which you cannot contradict; you can without any difficulty contradict Socrates.
[*Symposium*]

J[oseph] B[oynton] Priestley, 1894–1984, English novelist and playwright
Telling the truth is about as healthy as skidding round a corner at sixty.
[*Dangerous Corner* 1 1932]

François Rabelais, c.1494–1553, French physician and satirist
Speak the truth and shame the Devil.
[*Gargantua and Pantagruel* 1546]

Jean Jacques Rousseau, 1712–78, Swiss-born French philosopher
Truth is no road to fortune.
[*The Social Contract* 1762]

George Santayana, 1863–1952, Spanish-American philosopher
The truth is cruel, but it can be loved, and it makes free those who have loved it.
[Introduction to Spinoza's *Ethics*]

William Shakespeare, 1564–1616, English dramatist
When my love swears that she is made of truth,
I do believe her, though I know she lies.
[Sonnet]

O, while ye live, tell truth, and shame the devil!
[*King Henry IV, Part I* 1 1597–8]

Alexander Solzhenitsyn, 1918– , Russian novelist
When truth is discovered by someone else, it loses something of its attractiveness.
[*Candle in the Wind*]

Susan Sontag, 1933– , American critic and writer
The truth is always something that is told, not something that is known. If there were no speaking or writing there would be no truth about anything. There would only be what is.
[*The Benefactor* 1963]

Henry David Thoreau, 1817–62, American naturalist and writer
It takes two to speak the truth – one to speak, and another to hear.
[*A Week on the Concord and Merrimack Rivers* 1849]

Mark Twain [Samuel Langhorne Clemens], 1835–1910, American writer and journalist
Truth is the most valuable thing we have. Let us economize it.
[*Following the Equator* 1897]

When in doubt, tell the truth.
[*Pudd'nhead Wilson: Pudd'nhead Wilson's Calendar* 1894]

John [Hoyer] Updike, 1932– , American writer
Truth should not be forced; it should simply manifest itself, like a woman who has in her privacy reflected and coolly decided to bestow herself upon a certain man.
[*Self-Consciousness: Memoirs* 1989]

Voltaire [François Marie Arouet], 1694–1778, French philosopher and writer
We owe respect to the living; to the dead we owe only truth.
[*Oevres* I 1785]

George Washington, 1732–99, 1st president of the United States
Father, I cannot tell a lie. I did it with my little hatchet.
[In M.L. Weems' *Life of George Washington* 1810]

Oscar [Fingall O'Flahertie Wills] Wilde, 1854–1900, Irish writer
The truth is rarely pure, and seldom simple.
[*The Importance of Being Earnest* 1 1895]

Tennessee Williams [Thomas Lanier Williams], 1911–83, American playwright
I am the opposite of the stage magician. He gives you illusion that has the appearance of truth. I give you truth in the pleasant disguise of illusion.
[*The Glass Menagerie* 1945]

Ludwig Joseph Johann Wittgenstein, 1889–1951, Austrian-born British philosopher
When one is frightened of the truth . . . then it is never the *whole* truth that one has an inking of.
[*Notebooks 1914–1916*]

[Adeline] Virginia Woolf, 1882–1941, English novelist and critic
Let a man get up and say, "Behold, this is the truth," and instantly I perceive a sandy cat filching a piece of fish in the background. Look, you have forgotten the cat, I say.
[*The Waves* 1931]

Virtues and Vices

Joseph Addison, 1672–1719, English essayist
Unbounded courage and compassion joined,
Tempering each other in the victor's mind,
Alternately proclaim him good and great,
And make the hero and the man complete.

[*Cato* 1713]

Content thyself to be obscurely good.
When vice prevails, and impious men bear sway,
The post of honour is a private station.

[*Ibid*]

Anonymous
What you do when you are drunk, you must pay for when you are sober.

[Scottish proverb]

Bacchus hath drowned more men than Neptune.

[Proverb]

Charity begins at home.

[Proverb]

Forbidden fruit is sweet.

[Proverb]

Virtue and happiness are mother and daughter.

[Proverb]

Hannah Arendt, 1906–75, German-born American philosopher
What makes it plausible to assume that hypocrisy is the vice of vices is that integrity can indeed exist under the cover of all other vices except this one. Only crime and the criminal, it is true, confront us with the perplexity of radical evil; but only the hypocrite is really rotten to the core.

[*On Revolution* 1963]

Tallulah Bankhead, 1903–68, American actress
Here's a rule I recommend. Never practise two vices at once.

[*Tallulah* 1952]

The Bible
Pride goeth before destruction, and an haughty spirit before a fall.

[*Proverbs* 16:18]

A bishop then must be blameless, the husband of one wife, vigilant, sober, of good behaviour, given to hospitality, apt to teach.

Not given to wine, no striker, not greedy of filthy lucre; but patient, not a brawler, not covetous.

[*1 Timothy* 3:2]

Ambrose [Gwinnet] Bierce, 1842–1914, American writer
Patience: a minor form of despair, disguised as a virtue.

[*The Devil's Dictionary* 1911]

Samuel Butler, 1835–1902, English writer
Half the vices which the world condemns most loudly have seeds of good in them and require moderate use rather than total abstinence.

[*The Way of All Flesh* 1903]

Byron, Lord George Gordon [Noel], 6th Baron Byron of Rochdale, 1788–1824, English poet
So for a good old-gentlemanly vice,
I think I must take up with avarice.

[*Don Juan* 1819–24]

Lewis Carroll [Charles Lutwidge Dodgson], 1832–92, English mathematician and writer
"I'm very brave generally," he went on in a low voice: "only today I happen to have a headache."

[*Through the Looking-Glass and What Alice Found There* 1872]

Albert Camus, 1913–60, Algerian-born French philosopher and novelist
Too many people have decided to do without generosity in order to practise charity.

[*The Fall* 1956]

Jimmy [James Earl] Carter, 1924– , 39th president of the United States
I've looked on a lot of women with lust. I've committed adultery in my heart many times. God recognises I will do this and forgives me.

[Interview in *Playboy* November 1976]

[Arthur] Joyce Lunel Cary, 1888–1957, English novelist
Sara could commit adultery at one end and weep for her sins at the other, and enjoy both operations at once.

[*The Horse's Mouth* 1944]

Miguel de Cervantes [Saavedra], 1547–1616, Spanish dramatist and poet
Diligence is the mother of good fortune; and the goal of a good intention was never reached through its opposite, laziness.

[*Don Quixote* 1615]

G[ilbert] K[eith] Chesterton, 1874–1936, English writer
Charity is the power of defending that which we know to be indefensible.

[*Heretics*]

Bill [WilliamJefferson] Clinton, 1946– , 42nd president of the United States

When I was in England, I experimented with marijuana a time or two and I didn't like it. I didn't inhale.

[In the *Washington Post* March 30 1992]

[On his alleged adulterous affair with Monica Lewinsky] I did not have sexual relations with that woman.

[1998]

Indeed I did have a relationship with Ms Lewinsky that was not appropriate. In fact, it was wrong. It constituted a critical lapse in judgement and a personal failure on my part for which I am solely and completely responsible.

[Televised speech to the American nation August 17 1998]

Samuel Taylor Coleridge, 1771–1834, English poet

And the Devil did grin, for his darling sin
Is pride that apes humility.

[*The Devil's Thoughts* 1799]

[Sidonie Gabrielle Claudine] Colette, 1873–1954, French novelist

Smokers, male and female, inject and excuse idleness in their lives every time they light a cigarette.

[*Earthly Paradise: An Autobiography* 1966]

My virtue's still far too small, I don't trot it out and about yet.

[*Claudine at School* 1900]

Confucius [K'ung fu-tzu], 551–479BC, Chinese philosopher

To be able to practise five things everywhere under heaven constitutes perfect virtue . . . Gravity, generosity of soul, sincerity, earnestness and kindness.

[*Analects*]

Cyril [Vernon] Connolly, 1903–74, English writer

If one is too lazy to think, too vain to do a thing, too cowardly to admit it, one will never attain wisdom.

[*The Unquiet Grave* 1944]

Quentin Crisp, 1908–99, English eccentric and writer

Vice is its own reward. It is virtue which, if it is to be marketed with consumer appeal, must carry Green Shield stamps.

[*The Naked Civil Servant* 1968]

Dalai Lama, [Tenzin Gyatso], 1935– , Tibetan spiritual leader

It is the enemy who can truly teach us to practise the virtues of compassion and tolerance.

[*Ocean of Wisdom: Guidelines for Living* 1989]

Thomas Dekker, c. 1570–1632, English dramatist

The best of men
That e'ere wore earth about him was a sufferer;
A soft, meek, patient, humble, tranquil spirit.
The first true gentleman that ever breathed.

[*The Honest Whore, Part I* 1604]

René Descartes, 1596–1650, French philosopher

The greatest minds are capable of the greatest vices as well as of the greatest virtues.

[*Le Discours de la Méthode* 1637]

Charles [John Huffam] Dickens, 1812–70, English novelist

I am well aware that I am the 'umblest person going . . . My mother is likewise a very 'umble person. We live in a numble abode.

[*David Copperfield* 1850]

John Dryden, 1631–1700, English dramatist

And virtue, though in rags, will keep me warm.

[*Imitation of Horace* 1685]

Finlay Peter Dunne ("Mr Dooley"), 1867–1936, American humorist

Vice is a creature of such hideous mien that the more you see it the better you like it.

[*Mr Dooley's Opinions* 1901]

George Eliot [Mary Ann Evans] 1819–80, English writer

I've never any pity for conceited people, because I think they carry their comfort about with them.

[*The Mill on the Floss* 1860]

Ralph Waldo Emerson, 1803–82, American writer

Every hero becomes a bore at last.

[*Representative Men* 1850]

William Faulkner, 1897–1962, American novelist

A man shouldn't fool with booze until he's fifty; then he's a damn fool if he doesn't.

[In J.M. Webb and A. Wigfall Green's *William Faulkner of Oxford* 1965]

No man can cause more grief than that one clinging blindly to the vices of his ancestors.

[*Intruder in the Dust* 1948]

W.C. Fields [William Claude Dunkinfield], 1879–1946, American actor

I exercise extreme self-control. I never drink anything stronger than gin before breakfast.

[In R.L. Taylor's *W. C. Fields, His Follies and Fortunes* 1949]

F[rancis] Scott [Key] Fitzgerald, 1896–1940, American novelist

Everyone suspects himself of at least one of the cardinal virtues, and this is mine: I am one of the few honest people that I have ever known.

[*The Great Gatsby* 1925]

Sir Clement [Raphael] Freud, 1924– , British broadcaster and writer

If you resolve to give up smoking, drinking and loving, you don't actually live longer; it just seems longer.

[In the *Observer* December 27 1964]

Christopher [Harris] Fry, 1907– , English poet and playwright

I apologize
For boasting, but once you know my qualities
I can drop back into a quite brilliant
Humility.

[*The Lady's Not For Burning* 1949]

André [Paul Guillaume] Gide, 1869–1951, French novelist

True kindness presupposes the faculty of imagining as one's own the suffering and joy of others.

[*Portraits and Aphorisms* 1903]

Adam Lindsay Gordon, 1833–70, Australian poet
Life is mostly froth and bubble,
Two things stand like stone,
Kindness in another's trouble,
Courage in your own.

[*Ye Wearie Wayfarer*]

Kenneth Grahame, 1859–1932, English writer
It is the restrictions placed upon vice by our social code which makes its pursuit so peculiarly
agreeable.

[*Pagan Papers* 1893]

Joseph Hall, 1574–1656, English prelate and writer
Moderation is the silken string running through the pearl chain of virtues.

[*Christian Meditations*]

William Hazlitt, 1778–1830, English essayist
The greatest offence against virtue is to speak ill of it.

[*Sketches and Essays: On Disagreeable People* 1839]

[William] Stanley Houghton, 1881–1913, English playwright
When things are helpless patience must be used.

[*Englishmen for my Money*]

E[dgar] W[atson] Howe, 1853–1937, American writer
A modest man is often admired – if people ever hear of him.

[*Ventures in Common Sense* 1919]

Elbert Hubbard, 1856–1915, American writer and editor
An ounce of loyalty is worth a pound of cleverness.

[*The Note Book* 1927]

James VI of Scotland and I of England, 1566–1625, British monarch
[On tobacco smoking] A branch of the sin of drunkenness, which is the root of all sins.

[*A Counterblast to Tobacco* 1604]

Carl Gustav Jung, 1875–1961, Swiss psychiatrist
Every form of addiction is bad, no matter whether the narcotic be alcohol or morphine or idealism.

[*Memories, Dreams, Reflections* 1962]

Franz Kafka, 1883–1924, Austrian writer
There are two cardinal sins from which others spring: impatience and laziness.

[Letters, in Max Brod's *Franz Kafka*]

Charles Lamb, 1775–1834, English essayist
For thy sake, Tobacco, I
Would do anything but die.

[*The Poetical Works of Charles Lamb: A Farewell to Tobacco* 1836]

Walter Savage Landor, 1775–1864, English writer
Around the child bent all the three
Sweet Graces: Faith, Hope, Charity.
Around the man bend other faces:
Pride, Envy, Malice, are his Graces.

[Around the Child]

Philip Arthur Larkin, 1922–85, English poet
Selflessness is like waiting in a hospital
In a badly-fitting suit on a cold wet morning.
Selfishness is like listening to good jazz
With drinks for further orders and a huge fire.

[None of the Books Have Time 1960]

Don[ald Robert Perry] Marquis, 1878–1937, American novelist, playwright and poet
honesty is a good
thing but
it is not profitable to
its possessor
unless it is
kept under control.

[archys life of mehitabel: archygrams 1927]

Groucho [Julius Henry] Marx, 1895–1977, American comedian
There is one way to find out if a man is honest – ask him. If he says "Yes", you know he is
crooked.

[In The Cynic's Lexicon 1984]

W[illiam] Somerset Maugham, 1874–1965, English novelist
Hypocrisy is the most difficult and nerve-wracking vice that any man can pursue; it needs an
unceasing vigilance and a rare detachment of spirit. It cannot, like adultery or gluttony, be
practised at spare moments; it is a whole-time job.

[Cakes and Ale 1930]

George Meredith, 1828–1909, English poet and novelist
Want of courage is want of sense.

[The Tragic Comedian]

Thomas Middleton, 1580–1627, English dramatist
Lands mortgag'd may return, and more esteem'd,
But honesty once pawned, is ne'er redeemed.

[A Trick to Catch the Old One]

Michel [Eyquem] de Montaigne, 1533–92, French essayist
One may be humble out of pride.

[Essays 1580–88]

Dame Iris Murdoch, 1919–99, English novelist and philosopher
Humility is not a peculiar habit of self-effacement, rather like having an inaudible voice, it is a
selfless respect for reality and one of the most difficult and central of all the virtues.

[The Sovereignty of Good 1970]

Virtues and Vices

Ogden Nash, 1902–71, American humorous writer
I am a conscientious man, when I throw rocks at seabirds I leave no tern unstoned.
[Everybody's Mind to Me a Kingdom Is]

Denis Norden, 1922– , British humorist
If I were asked to enumerate the Seven Deadly Virtues, the one I'd put right at the top of my list is Female Tidiness.
[Oh, My Word]

Matthew Prior, 1664–1721, English diplomat and poet
Be to her virtues very kind;
Be to her faults a little blind.
[An English Padlock]

Publilius Syrus, *fl.* 1st century BC, Roman writer
If you would live innocently, seek solitude.
[Sententiae c.50 BC]

François, Duc de La Rochefoucauld, 1613–80, French writer
Hypocrisy is the homage that vice pays to virtue.
[Reflections, or Sentences and Moral Maxims 1665]
What makes other people's vanity intolerable is that it wounds our own
[Ibid]
Our virtues are most frequently but vices in disguise.
[Ibid]

John Ruskin, 1819–1900, English art critic and writer
Your honesty is *not* to be based either on religion or policy. Both your religion and policy must be based on *it*. Your honesty must be based, as the sun is, in vacant heaven; poised, as the lights in the firmament, which have rule over the day and over the night.
[Time and Tide 1867]

John Selden, 1584–1654, English scholar
Humility is a virtue all preach, none practice; and yet everybody is content to hear.
[Table Talk: Humility 1689]

Seneca, c.4BC–AD65, Roman philosopher
Drunkenness doesn't create vices, but it brings them to the fore.
[Letters to Lucilius]

William Shakespeare, 1564–1616, English dramatist
In law, what plea so tainted and corrupt
but, being season'd with a gracious voice,
Obscures the show of evil? In religion,
What damned error, but some sober brow
Will bless it and approve it with a text,
Hiding the grossness with fair ornament?
There is no vice so simple but assumes
Some mark of virtue in its outward parts.
[The Merchant of Venice 2 1596–7]
There's neither honesty, manhood, nor good fellowship in thee.
[King Henry IV, Part I 1 1597–8]

O, beware, my lord, of jealousy;
It is the green-eyed monster which doth mock
The meat it feeds on.

[*Othello* 2 1604–5]

True hope is swift, and flies with swallow's wings;
Kings it makes gods, and meaner creatures kings. [*King Richard III* 5 1592–3]

George Bernard Shaw, 1856–1950, Irish playwright
Gambling promises to the poor what Property performs for the rich; that is why the bishops dare not denounce it fundamentally.

[*Man and Superman: Maxims for Revolutionists* 1903]

Self-denial is not a virtue: it is only the effect of prudence on rascality.

[*Ibid*]

Thomas Southerne, 1660–1746, Anglo-Irish dramatist
There is no courage but in innocence;
No constancy but in an honest cause.

[*The Fate of Capua*]

Edmund Spenser, c. 1552–99, English poet
Who will not mercie unto others show,
How can he mercie ever hope to have?

[*The Fairie Queen*]

Jonathan Swift, 1667–1745, Irish-born English writer
'Tis eminence makes envy rise,
As fairest fruits attract the flies.

[*To Dr Delaney*]

Dylan Thomas, 1914–53, Welsh poet
An alcoholic is someone you don't like who drinks as much as you do.

[Attributed]

Anthony Trollope, 1815–82, English novelist
As for conceit, what man will do any good who is not conceited? Nobody holds a good opinion of a man who has a low opinion oF himself.

[*Orley Farm* 1862]

Anne Tyler, 1941– , American novelist and short story writer
Oh, what is it that makes some people more virtuous than others? Is it something they know from birth? Don't they ever feel that zingy, thrilling urge to smash the world to bits? Isn't it possible, maybe, that good people are just *luckier* people?

[*A Patchwork Planet* 1998]

H[erbert] G[eorge] Wells, 1866–1946, English writer
Moral indignation is jealousy with a halo.

[*The Wife of Sir Isaac Harman*]

Patrick White, 1912–90, Australian writer
Virtue is . . . frequently in the nature of an iceberg, the other parts of it submerged.

[*The Tree of Man* 1955]

Language, Words and Speech

Anonymous
Sticks and stones
May break my bones
But words will never hurt me.

[Children's rhyme]

Carelss talk costs lives.

[British wartime slogan 1940s]

Words are but wind, but seeing is believing.

[Proverb]

Words may pass, but blows fall heavy.

[Proverb]

Speech is silver, but silence is gold.

[German proverb]

Paddy [Jermey John Durham] Ashdown, 1941– , English politician
Lord, make my words sweet and reasonable. For some day I may have to eat them.
[Speech at Liberal Party Conference, September19 1992]

Samuel [Barclay] Beckett, 1906–89, Irish writer and playwright
They had no conversation properly speaking. They made use of the spoken word in much the
same way as the guard of a train makes use of his flags or of his lantern.

[*Malone Dies* 1951]

The Bible
Who is this that darkeneth counsel by words without knowledge?

[*Job* 38:2]

The preacher sought to find out acceptable words: and that which was written was upright,
even words of truth.
The words of the wise are as goads, and as nails fastened by the masters of assemblies, which
are given from one shepherd.

[*Ecclesiastes* 12:10–11]

More smooth than butter were his words,
while in his speech was war;
His speeches were more soft than oil,
and yet drawn swords they are.

[*Psalms* 56:21]

Nicholas Boileau-Despréaux, 1636–1711, French poet
Of every four words I write, I strike out three.

[*Satires* 1666]

Bertolt Brecht, 1898–1956, German dramatist and poet
And I always thought: the very simplest words
Must be enough. When I say what things are like
Everyone's heart must be torn to shreds.

[*And I Always Thought*]

Byron, Lord George Gordon [Noel], 6th Baron Byron of Rochdale, 1788–1824, English poet
But words are things, and a small drop of ink,
Falling, like dew, upon a thought, produces
That which makes thousands, perhaps millions, think.

[*Don Juan* 1819–24]

No words suffice the secret soul to show,
For truth denies all eloquence to woe.

[*The Corsair*]

Thomas Carlyle, 1795–1881, Scottish historian and writer
Be not the slave of Words.

[*Sartor Resartus* 1834]

Sir Winston [Leonard] Churchill, 1874–1965, British statesman
This is the sort of English up with which I will not put.

[In Gowers' *Plain Words* 1948]

Personally I like short words and vulgar fractions.

[*Closing the Ring*]

Confucius [K'ung fu-tzu], 551–479BC, Chinese philosopher
Without knowing the force of words, it is impossible to know men.

[*Analects*]

Joseph Conrad [Josef Teodor Konrad Korzeniowski], 1857–1924, Polish-born English novelist
Words, as is well known, are great foes of reality.

[*Under Western Eyes* 1911]

Dame Ivy Compton-Burnett, 1884–1969, English novelist
We must use words as they are used or stand aside from life.

[*Mother and Son* 1955]

John Dewey, 1859–1952, American philosopher
There is all the difference in the world between having something to say, and saying something.

[In M. Dworkin's *Dewey on Education* 1959]

Philip K[indred] Dick, 1928–82, American science-fiction author
The basic tool for the manipulation of reality is the manipulation of words. If you can control the meaning of words, you can control the people who must use the words.

[*I Hope I Shall Arrive Soon* 1986]

T[homas] S[tearns] Eliot, 1888–1965, American-born English poet
For last year's words belong to last year's language
And next year's words await another voice.

[*Four Quartets: Little Gidding* 1943]

Ralph Waldo Emerson, 1803–82, American writer
Language is fossil poetry.

[*The Poet* 1844]

Johann Wolfgang von Goethe, 1749–1832, German poet and playwright
Whoever is not acquainted with foreign languages knows nothing of his own.

[*On Art and Antiquity* 1827]

Václav Havel 1936– , Czech playwright and statesman
I really do inhabit a system in which words are capable of shaking the entire structure of government, where words can prove mightier than ten military divisions.

[Speech 1989]

Ernest [Miller] Hemingway, 1899–1961, American novelist
All my life I've looked at words as though I were seeing them for the first time.

[Letter 1945]

George Herbert, 1593–1633, English poet
Words are women, deeds are men.

[*Jacula Prudentum* 1651]

Adolf Hitler, 1889–1945, German dictator
The broad masses of the people can be moved only by the power of speech. All great movements are popular movements, volcanic eruptions of human passions and emotional sentiments, stirred either by the cruel Goddess of Distress or by the firebrand of the word hurled among the masses.

[*Mein Kampf* 1925]

Thomas Hobbes, 1588–1679, English political philosopher
For words are wise men's counters, they do but reckon by them; but they are the money of fools.

[*The Leviathan*]

Henry James, 1843–1916, American-born English writer
Most English talk is a quadrille in a sentry-box.

[*The Awkward Age*]

Dr Samuel Johnson, 1709–84, English lexicographer
I am not yet so lost in lexicography, as to forget that words are the daughters of earth, and that things are the sons of heaven. Language is only the instrument of science, and words are but the signs of ideas.

[*A Dictionary of the English Language* 1755]

Ben[jamin] Jonson, 1572–1637, English poet
Talking and eloquence are not the same: to speak, and to speak well, are two things.

[*Timber, or Discoveries Made upon Men and Matter* 1641]

Walter Savage Landor, 1775–1864, English writer
How many verses have I thrown
Into the fire because the one
Peculiar word, they wanted most,
Was irrevocably lost.

[*Verses Why Burnt*]

D[avid] H[erbert] Lawrence, 1885–1930, English novelist and poet
Be still when you have nothing to say; when genuine passion moves you, say what you've got to say, and say it hot.

[*Studies in Classic American Literature* 1923]

Fran Lebowitz, 1951– , American journalist and writer
The opposite of talking isn't listening. The opposite of talking is waiting.

[*Social Studies: People* 1981]

David Lehman, 1948– , American poet and writer
Words can have no single fixed meaning. Like wayward electrons, they can spin away from their initial orbit and enter a wider magnetic field. No one owns them or has a proprietary right to dictate how they will be used.

[*Signs of the Times* 1991]

David Lloyd-George, 1st Earl Lloyd-George of Dwyfor, 1863–1945, Welsh-born British politician
The finest eloquence is that which gets things done and the worst is that which delays them.

[In the *Times* January 20 1919]

Thomas Mann, 1875–1955, German novelist
An art whose medium is language will always show a high degree of critical creativeness, for speech is itself a critique of life: it names, it characterises, it passes judgement, in that it creates.

[*Essays on Three Decades* 1942]

Norman Alexander McCaig, 1910–96, Scottish poet
Hear my words carefully,
Some are spoken
not by me, but
by a man in my position.

[*A Man in My Position* 1969]

I learned words, I learned words: but half of them
died for lack of exercise. And the ones I use
often look at me
with a look that whispers, *Liar*.

[*Ineducable Me* 1980]

Eugenio Montale, 1896–1981, Italian poet
Words
are everyone's property and in vain
do they hide in dictionaries,
for there's always a rogue
who digs up the rarest
and most stinking truffles.

[*New Poems: Words* 1976]

Robert Morley, 1908–92, English actor and humorist
Beware of the conversationalist who adds "in other words". He is merely starting afresh.
[In the *Observer* December 6 1964]

[Philip] Michael Ondaatje, 1943– , Sri Lankan-born Canadian poet and novelist
She had always wanted words, she loved them, grew up on them. Words gave her clarity, brought reason, shape. Whereas I thought words bent emotions like sticks in water.
[*The English Patient* 1992]

George Orwell [Eric Arthur Blair], 1903–50, English novelist and critic
The great enemy of clear language is insincerity.
[*Politics and the English Language*]

Thomas Love Peacock, 1785–1866, English essayist and poet
He remembered too late on his thorny green bed,
Much that well may be thought cannot wisely be said.
[*Crochet Castle: The Priest and the Mulberry Tree* 1831]

Pliny the Younger, AD62–c.114, Roman statesman
The living voice is that which sways the soul.
[In Melmoth's *The Letters of Pliny the Consul* 1747]

Plutarch, c.AD46–c.12, Greek historian and philosopher
It is a point of wisdom to be silent when occasion requires, and better than to speak, though never so well.
[*Of the Training of Children*]

Alexander Pope, 1688–1744, English poet
Words are like leaves; and where they most abound,
Much fruit of the sense beneath is rarely found.
[*An Essay on Criticism* 1711]

Sir Ralph David Richardson, 1902–83, English actor
The most precious things in speech are pauses.
[Attributed]

Cardinal Richelieu [Armand Jean Duplessis, Duc de Richelieu], 1585–1642, French prelate and statesman
Wounds inflicted by the sword heal more easily than those inflicted by the tongue.
[*Testament Politique* 1688]

Philip [Milton] Roth, 1933– , American novelist
Conversation isn't just crossfire where you shoot and get shot at! Where you've got to duck for your life and aim to kill! Words aren't only bombs and bullets – no, they're little gifts, containing *meanings*!
[*Portnoy's Complaint* 1969]

George Santayana, 1863–1952, Spanish-American philosopher
Trust the man who hesitates in his speech and is quick and steady in action, but beware of long arguments and long beards.
[*Soliloquies in England: The British Character*]

Jean-Paul Sartre, 1905–80, French philosopher and writer

You get the impression that their normal condition is silence and that speech is a slight fever which attacks them now and then.

[*Nausea* 1949]

Siegfried Sassoon, 1886–1967, English poet

He spoke with homicidal eloquence, keeping the game alive with genial and well-judged jokes.

[*Memoirs of an Infantry Officer*]

[Johann Christoph] Friedrich von Schiller, 1759–1805, German poet

What's the short meaning of this long harangue?

[*Piccolomini* 1 1800]

Sir Walter Scott, 1771–1832, Scottish novelist

There is a southern proverb – fine words butter no parsnips.

[*A Legend of Montrose* 1819]

William Shakespeare, 1564–1616, English dramatist

But words are words; I never yet did hear
That the bruis'd heart was pierced through the ear.

[*Othello* 1 1604–5]

Speak to me as to thy thinkings,
As thou dost ruminate; and give thy worst of thoughts
The worst of words.

[*Ibid* 3]

George Bernard Shaw, 1856–1950, Irish playwright

Make me a beautiful word for doing things tomorrow, for that surely is a great and blessed invention.

[*Methuselah Pt I*, 1]

Remember that you are a human being with a soul and the divine gift of articulate speech: that your native language is the language of Shakespeare and Milton and the Bible; and don't sit there crooning like a bilious pigeon.

[*Pygmalion* 1914]

The English have no respect for their language, and will not teach their children to speak it. It is impossible for an Englishman to open his mouth without making some other Englishman hate or despise him.

[*Pygmalion* 1912]

With the single exception of Homer, there is no eminent writer, not even Sir Walter Scott, whom I can despise so entirely as I despise Shakespeare when I measure my mind against his.

[*Dramatic Opinions and Essays*]

Paul Simon, 1941– , American singer and songwriter

And the sign said, "The words of the prophets
Are written on the subway walls
And tenement halls"
And whispered in the sounds of silence.

[Song: *The Sounds Of Silence* 1964]

444

Gertrude Stein, 1874–1946, American writer
Ida never spoke, she just said what she pleased. Dear Ida.

[*Ida*]

Claude Lévi-Strauss, 1908– , French philosopher and social anthropologist
Language is a kind of human reason, which has its own internal logic of which man knows nothing.

[*The Savage Mind* 1962]

Jonathan Swift, 1667–1745, Irish-born English writer
Nor do they trust their tongue alone,
But speak a language of their own;
Can read a nod, a shrug, a look,
Far better than a printed book;
Convey a libel in a frown,
And wink a reputation down.

[*The Journal of a Modern Lady*]

Alfred, Lord Tennyson, 1809–92, English poet
For words, like Nature, half reveal
And half conceal the soul within.

[*In Memoriam A.H.H.* 1850]

Peter De Vries, 1910–93, American novelist and journalist
This person has a deluge of words and a drizzle of thought.

[*Comfort Me with Apples* 1956]

John Webster, c.1580–c.1625, English dramatist
A mere tale of a tub, my words are idle.

[*The White Devil* 1612]

E[lwyn] B[rooks] White, 1899–1985, American humorist
The dream of the American male is for a female who has an essential languor which is not laziness, who is unaccompanied except by himself, and who does not let him down. He desires a beautiful, but comprehensible creature who does not destroy a perfect situation by forming a complete sentence.

[*The Second Tree from the Corner*]

Alfred North Whitehead, 1861–1947, English mathematician and philosopher
Language is incomplete and fragmentary, and merely registers a stage in the average advance beyond ape-mentality. But all men enjoy flashes of insight beyond meanings already stabilized in etymology and grammar.

[*Adventures of Ideas Part I*]

John Greenleaf Whittier, 1807–92 American Quaker, poet and writer
For of all the sad words of tongue or pen,
The saddest are these: "It might have been!"

[*Maud Müller*]

George Wither, 1588–1667 English poet and pamphleteer
And I oft have heard defended
Little said is soonest mended.

[*The Shepherd's Hunting*]

Ludwig Joseph Johann Wittgenstein, 1889–1951, Austrian-born British philosopher

Everyday language is a part of the human organism and is no less complicated than it.

[Tractatus Logico-Philosophicus 1921]

All philosophy is "Critique of language".

[Ibid]

Royalty

Alexander the Great, 356–323BC, king of Macedonia
If I were not Alexander, I would be Diogenes.

[In Plutarch's *Life of Alexander*]

Anonymous
| The word of a king ought to be as binding as the oath of a subject.

[Italian proverb]

A king promises, but observes only what he pleases.

[Proverb]

Hark! The herald angels sing
Mrs Simpson pinched our king.

[1936]

Walter Bagehot, 1826–87, English economist and journalist
Throughout the greater part of his life George III was a kind of "consecrated obstruction".

[*The Monarchy*]

Queen Anne was one of the smallest people ever set in a great palace.

[*Checks and Balances*]

Sir Cecil [Walter Hardy] Beaton, 1904–80, English photographer
On coronation day the Queen looked extremely minute under her robes and crown, her nose and hands chilled, her eyes tired. "Yes," in reply to my question, "the Crown does get rather heavy."

[*The Strenuous Years* 1973]

Edmund Clerihew Bentley, 1875–1956, English writer
George the Third
Ought never to have occurred.
One can only wonder
At so grotesque a blunder.

[*More Biography* 1929]

Ambrose [Gwinnet] Bierce, 1842–1914, American writer
King: a male person commonly known in America as a "crowned head", although he never wears a crown and has usually no head to speak of.

[*The Devil's Dictionary* 1911]

447

Tony [Anthony Charles Linton] Blair, 1953– , British politician
[Of Princess Diana] She was the people's princess, and that is how she will stay, how she will remain in our hearts and our memories forever.

[Speech following the death of Princess Diana August 31 1997]

Catherine II, the Great, 1729–96, Empress of Russia
I shall be the autocrat: that's my trade. And the good Lord will forgive me: that's his.

[Attributed]

Sir Noel [Pierce] Coward, 1899–1973, English actor and playwright
Ma'am or Sir,
Sir or Ma'am
Makes every royal personage as happy as a clam.

[*Sir or Ma'am* 1962]

Charles I, 1600–49, King of England, Scotland and Ireland
I die a Christian, according to the Profession of the Church of England, as I found it left me by my father.

[Speech before his execution]

Charles [Philip Arthur George], Prince of Wales, 1948– , British prince
The one advantage of marrying a princess – or someone from a royal family – is that they know what happens.

[Attributed]

She was quite simply the most magical grandmother you could possibly have, and I was utterly devoted to her.

[Television tribute to Elizabeth the Queen Mother April 1 2002]

Sir Winston [Leonard] Churchill, 1874–1965, British statesman
Here at the summit of our worldwide community is a lady whom we respect because she is our queen and whom we love because she is herself.

[Broadcast 1953]

Diana, Princess of Wales, 1961–97, British princess
I'd like to be a queen of people's hearts, in people's hearts, but I don't see myself being Queen of this country. I don't think many people will want me to be Queen.

[Television interview November 24 1995]

Edward VIII, 1894–1972, king of Great Britain and Northern Ireland
I have found it impossible to carry the heavy burden of responsibility and to discharge my duties as King as I would wish to do without the help and support of the woman I love.

[Abdication broadcast 1936]

Elizabeth the Queen Mother [née Elizabeth Bowes-Lyon], 1900–2002
I'm glad we've been bombed. It makes me feel I can look the East End in the face.

[Attributed remark after bombing of Buckingham Palace 1940]

Elizabeth I, 1533–1603, Queen of England and Ireland
The queen of Scots is this day leichter of a fair son, and I am but a barren stock.

[*Memoirs of Sir James Melville*]

Elizabeth II, 1926– , Queen of Great Britain and Northern Ireland
Nineteen ninety-two is not a year I shall look back on with undiluted pleasure. In the words of one of my more sympathetic correspondents, it has turned out to be an "Annus Horribilis".
[Speech to mark her fortieth anniversary, London November 1992.]
I think everybody really will concede that on this, of all days, I should begin my speech with the words, "My husband and I".
[25th wedding anniversary speech, London November 20 1972]

Farouk I, 1920–65, King of Egypt
Soon there will be only five kings left – the King of England, the King of Spades, the King of Clubs, the King of Hearts and the King of Diamonds.
[In *Life* April 10 1950]

Frederick the Great [Frederick II], 1712–86, King of Prussia
I am tired of ruling over slaves. We are over the mountain, we shall go better now.
[Dying words, attributed]
My people and I have come to an agreement which satisfies us both. They are to say what they please, and I am to do what I please.
[Attributed]
[Of George III] The King of England changes his ministers as often as he changes his shirts.
[Attributed]

Pierre Marc Gaston, Duc de Lévis, 1764–1830, French writer
Nobless oblige.
Nobility has its obligations.
[*Maximes et Réflexions* 1812]

George III, 1738–1820, king of Great Britain and Ireland and King of Hanover
Born and educated in this country I glory in the name of Briton.
[Speech 1660]

George V, 1865–1936, king of Great Britain and Northern Ireland
I'm really quite an ordinary sort of chap.
[Attributed 1935]

Sir William Schwenck Gilbert, 1836–1911, English librettist
Oh, 'tis a glorious thing, I ween,
To be a regular Royal Queen!
No half-and-half affair, I mean,
But a right-down regular Royal Queen!
[*The Gondoliers* 1899]

Spurn not the nobly born
With love affected,
Nor treat with virtuous scorn
The well-connected.
[*Iolanthe* 1882]

Henry VIII, 1491–1547, king of England
[On meeting Anne of Cleves] You have sent me a Flanders mare.
[In Tobias Smollet's *A Complete History of England* 1759]

Robert Herrick, 1591–1674, English churchman and poet
'Twixt kings and tyrants there's this difference known;
Kings seek their subjects' good: tyrants their own.

[Kings and Tyrants]

Catherine Howard, 1521–42, queen of England, wife of Henry VIII
I die a Queen, but I would rather die the wife of Culpepper. God have mercy on my soul.
Good people, I beg you pray for me.

[Last words before her execution. Attributed]

James V, 1512–42, king of Scotland
The Devil do with it! It will end as it began; it cam' wi' a lass, it will gang wi' a lass.

[Dying words, referring to his newly-born daughter Mary, the future Queen of Scots]

David Lloyd-George, 1st Earl Lloyd-George of Dwyfor, 1863–1945, Welsh-born British politician
A fully equipped Duke costs as much to keep as two Dreadnoughts, and Dukes are just as great a terror, and they last longer.

[Speech 1909]

Louis XIV, 1638–1715, king of France
Why are you weeping? Did you imagine that I was immortal?

[Attributed, on his deathbed 1715]

Niccolo Machiavelli, 1469–1527, Italian political philosopher
Titles do not reflect honour on men, but rather men on their titles.

[Dei Discorsi]

As a prince must be able to act just like a beast, he should learn from the fox and the lion; because the lion does not defend himself against traps, and the fox does not defend himself against wolves. So one has to be a fox in order to recognize traps, and a lion to frighten off wolves.

[The Prince 1513]

Princess Margaret Rose, 1930–2002, British princess
My children are not royal, they just happen to have the Queen as their aunt.

[In *The Oxford Book of Royal Anecdotes*]

Arthur Marshall, 1910–89, English humorous writer and broadcaster
Queen Victoria economised on lavatory paper and substituted back numbers of the *Times*.

[Sunny Side Up]

Dame Nellie Melba [Helen Porter Mitchell], 1861–1931, Australian soprano
Never fall in love with royalty, they'll break your heart.

[Attributed]

A[lan] A[lexander] Milne, 1882–1926, English writer
King John was not a good man –
He had his little ways.
And sometimes no one spoke to him
For days and days and days.

[*Now We Are Six: King John's Christmas* 1927]

I often wish I were a King,
And then I could do anything.

[*When We Were Very Young: If I Were King* 1924]

Nancy Freeman Mitford, 1904–73, English writer

An aristocracy in a republic is like a chicken whose head has been cut off: it may run about in a lively way, but in fact it is dead.

[*Nobless Oblige* 1956]

Louis [Francis Albert Victor Nicholas] Mountbatten, 1st Earl Mountbatten of Burma, 1900–79, English naval commander and statesman

During the first part of my life I was an ordinary conventional naval officer, trying not to be different in the sense of being royal, trying not to show myself off as being rich and ostentatious – like always using a small car to drive to the dockyard instead of my Rolls-Royce.

[In Richard Hough's *Mountbatten, Hero of Our Time* 1980]

Sir, I suffer from the congenital weakness of believing I can do anything.

[Remark to Winston Churchill In Collins and Lapierre's *Freedom at Midnight*,]

Lady Carolina Nairne [née Oliphant], 1766–1845, Scottish songwriter

Charlie is my darling, the young Chevalier.

[Song: *Charlie Is My Darling*]

Prince Philip, Duke of Edinburgh, 1921– , consort of Queen Elizabeth II

Dendopedology is the science of opening your mouth and putting your foot in it. I've been practising it for years.

[Quoted in *Time* magazine November 21 1960]

Matthew Prior, 1664–1721, English diplomat and poet

What is a king? A man condem'd to bear
The public burden of the nation's care.

[*Solomon* 1718]

Theodore Roosevelt, 1858–1919, 26th president of the United States

Kings and such like are just as funny as politicians.

[Attributed]

Antoine de Saint-Exupéry, 1900–1944, French aviator and writer

It took me a long time to learn where he came from. The little prince, who asked me so many questions, never seemed to hear the ones I asked him. It was from words dropped by chance that, little by little, everything was revealed to me.

[*The Little Prince* 1943]

Sarah, Duchess of York [née Sarah Margaret Ferguson]

I want to thank the American people, because some time ago I came to these shores having made a bit of nonsense in the UK.

[In the *Times* September 28 2002]

[Johann Christoph] Friedrich von Schiller, 1759–1805, German poet

Kings are only slaves of their own position who may not follow their own heart.

[*Maria Stuart* 1800]

Walter Carruthers Sellar, 1898–1951 and Robert Julian Yeatman, 1897–1968, English writers

James I slobbered at the mouth and had favourites; he was thus a bad king.

[*1066 and All That*]

George Bernard Shaw, 1856–1950, Irish playwright

Titles distinguish the mediocre, embarrass the superior, and are disgraced by the inferior.

[*Man and Superman: Maxims for Revolutionists* 1903]

He who slays a king and he who dies for him are alike idolaters.

[*Ibid*]

William Shakespeare, 1564–1616, English dramatist

Gives not the hawthorn bush a sweeter shade
To shepherds looking on their silly sheep,
Than doth a rich embroider'd canopy
To kings that fear their subjects' treachery?

[*King Henry VI, Part III* 2 1591]

A king of shreds and patches.

[*Hamlet* 3 1600–1601]

Ay, every inch a king.

[*King Lear* 4 1605–6]

It is well done, and fitting for a princess
Descended of so many royal kings.

[*Antony and Cleopatra* 5 1606–7]

A horse! a horse! my kingdom for a horse!

[*King Richard III* 5 1592–3]

Not all the water in the rude rough sea
Can wash the balm from an anointed king.

[*King Richard II* 3 1595–6]

For God's sake let us sit upon the ground
And tell sad stories of the death of kings:
How some have been deposed; some slain in war;
Some haunted by the ghosts they have deposed;
Some poison'd by their wives; some sleeping kill'd;
All murder'd: for within the hollow crown
That rounds the mortal temples of a king
Keeps Death his court

[*Ibid*]

Here I and sorrows sit;
Here is my throne, bid kings come bow to it.

[*King John* 3 1596–7]

Uneasy lies the head that wears a crown.

[*King Henry IV, Part II* 3 1597–8]

Wallis Simpson, Duchess of Windsor [née Bessie Wallis Warfield], 1896–1986, American socialite, wife of Edward, Duke of Windsor

I married the Duke for better or worse, but not for lunch.

[In J. Bryan and J.V. Murphy's *The Windsor Story* 1979]

Charles Spencer, Earl Spencer, Viscount Althorp, 1964– , British businessman
It is a point to remember that of all the ironies about Diana, perhaps the greatest was this – a girl given the name of the ancient goddess of hunting was, in the end, the most hunted person of the modern age.

[Tribute at the funeral of his sister, Diana, Princess of Wales September 6 1997]

Victoria, 1819–1901, queen of Great Britain and Ireland
[On her forthcoming coronation] I look forward to the event which it seems is likely to occur soon, with calmness and quietness. I am not alarmed at it, and yet I do not suppose myself quite equal to all; I trust, however, that with good-will, honesty, and courage I shall not, at all events, fail.

[Journal June 1837]

They wished to treat me like a little girl, but I will show them that I am Queen of England.

[Letter 1839]

We are not amused.

[Attributed]

Arthur Wellesley, 1st Duke of Wellington, 1769–1852 English soldier and statesman
I believe I forgot to tell you I was made a duke.

[Letter to Henry Wellesley, 1814]

Sir P[elham] G[reville] Wodehouse, 1881–1975, English-born writer
Unlike the male codfish which, suddenly finding itself the parent of three-and-a-half million little codfish, cheerfully resolves to love them all, the British aristocracy is apt to look with a somewhat jaundiced eye on its younger sons.

[In Usborne's*Wodehouse at Work to the End*]

Thomas Wolsey, c.1475–1530, English churchman and politician
[Of Henry VIII] He is a prince of royal courage and hath a princely heart; and rather than he will miss or want part of his appetite, he will hazard the loss of one half of his kingdom.

[Attributed]

Wit and Humour

Joseph Addison, 1672–1719, English essayist
In all thy humours, whether grave or mellow,
Thou'rt such a touchy, testy, pleasant fellow,
Hast so much wit, and mirth, and spleen about thee,
There is no living with thee, nor without thee.

[*The Spectator: Translation of Martial*]

Edward Franklin Albee 1928– , American playwright
I have a fine sense of the ridiculous, but no sense of humour.

[*Who's Afraid of Virginia Woolf?* 1 1962]

Aristotle, 384–322BC, Greek philosopher
Wit is educated insolence.

[*The Art of Rhetoric*]

Ronnie Barker [Ronald William George Barker], 1929– , English comedian
The marvellous thing about a joke with a double meaning is that it can only mean one thing.

[*Sauce* 1977]

Sir [Henry] Max[imilian] Beerbohm, 1872–1956, English writer
Humour undiluted is the most depressing of all phenomena. Humour must have its
background of seriousness. Without this contrast there comes none of that incongruity which
is the mainspring of laughter.

[*Around Theatres*]

Ambrose [Gwinnet] Bierce, 1842–1914, American writer
Wit: the salt with which the American humorist spoils his intellectual cookery by leaving it
out.

[*The Devil's Dictionary* 1911]

Lenny Bruce [Leonard Alfred Schneider] 1925–66, American comedian
The only honest art form is comedy. You can't fake it.

[In *The Essential Lenny Bruce* Cohen 1967]

**Edward [George Earle Lytton] Bulwer-Lytton, 1st Baron, 1803–73, English statesman
and writer**
Wit is but truth made amusing.

[*The Parisians*]

Samuel Butler, 1835–1902, English writer
We grant, although he had much wit,
He was very shy of using it.

[*Hudibras* 1663]

Byron, Lord George Gordon [Noel], 6th Baron Byron of Rochdale, 1788–1824, English poet
And if I laugh at any mortal thing,
'Tis that I may not weep.

[*Don Juan* 1819–24]

Thomas Carlyle, 1795–1881, Scottish historian and writer
No man who has once heartily and wholly laughed can be altogether irreclaimably bad.

[*Sartor Resartus* 1834]

Miguel de Cervantes [Saavedra], 1547–1616, Spanish dramatist and poet
Don't put too fine a point to your wit, for fear it should get blunted.

[*The Little Gypsy*]

Charlie Chaplin [Sir Charles Spencer Chaplin], 1889–1977, English-born film actor
All I need to make a comedy is a park, a policeman and a pretty girl.

[*My Autobiography* 1964]

G[ilbert] K[eith] Chesterton, 1874–1936, English writer
I have never in my life said anything merely because I thought it was funny; though, of course, I have an ordinary human vainglory, and may have thought it funny because I said it.

[*Orthodoxy*]

Charles Churchill, 1731–64, English poet
A joke's a very serious thing.

[*The Ghost* 1763]

[Sidonie-Gabrielle Claudine] Colette, 1873–1954, French novelist
A total absence of humour makes life impossible.

[*Chance Acquaintances*]

Peter [Edward] Cook, 1937–95, English actor and comedian
there's terrific merit in having no sense of humour, no sense of irony, practically no sense of anything at all. If you're born with these so-called defects you have a very good chance of getting to the top.

[In Ronald Bergan's *Beyond the Fringe . . . and Beyond* 1989]

Umberto Eco, 1932– , Italian novelist and semiotician
But laughter is weakness, corruption, the foolishness of our flesh.

[*The Name of the Rose* 1980]

George Eliot [Mary Ann Evans] 1819–80, English writer
A difference of taste in jokes is a great strain on the affections.

[*Daniel Deronda* 1876]

Marty Feldman, 1933–82, English comedian
Comedy, like sodomy, is an unnatural act.

[In the *Times* 1969]

Robert [Lee] Frost, 1874–1963, American poet
Forgive, O Lord, my little jokes on Thee
And I'll forgive Thy great big one on me.

[*In the Clearing: Cluster of Faith* 1962]

John Gay, 1685–1732, English poet and playwright
He makes a foe who makes a jest.

[*Fables*]

Ian Hay [John Hay Beith], 1876–1952, Scottish dramatist
What do you mean, funny? Funny peculiar, or funny ha-ha?

[*Housemaster* 3 1936]

William Hazlitt, 1778–1830, English essayist
Wit is the salt of the conversation, not the food.

[*On Wit and Humour* 1819]

[James] Langston Hughes, 1902–67, American poet, playwright and novelist
Humour is laughing at what you haven't got when you ought to have it.

[*The Book of Negro Humour* 1966]

Brian Keenan, 1950– , Irish teacher and writer
A man emerges back into life, not because of anything I have said, but the lunacy and the laughter that is at the heart of our life beckon him back and he cannot resist it. There are many things a man can resist – pain, torture, loss of loved ones – but laughter ultimately he cannot resist.

[*An Evil Cradling* 1992]

Garrison [Gary] Keillor, 1942– , American broadcaster and writer
Humour, a good sense of it, is to Americans what manhood is to Spaniards and we will go to great lengths to prove it.

[*We Are Still Married* 1989]

Milan Kundera, 1929– , Czech-born French novelist
The sound of laughter is like the vaulted dome of a temple of happiness.

[*The Book of Laughter and Forgetting* 1980]

Charles Lamb, 1775–1834, English essayist
Jokes come in with candles.

[*Popular Fallacies* 1833

Walter Savage Landor, 1775–1864, English writer
The better wit is, the more dangerous it is.

[*Imaginary Conversations*]

Stephen Butler Leacock, 1869–1944, Canadian economist and humorist
I can see nothing funny in the Cockney humour. The Cockney accent seems to me one of the most debased forms of utterance. I like nearly all the forms of broken-down English – Yorkshire and Somerset accents and so on – bit no outside nation can admire the Cockney. Cockney humour invariably depends upon bad taste, cruelty, or callousness.

[In the *Evening Standard* September 27 1921]

WIT AND HUMOUR

C[live] S[taples] Lewis, 1898–1963, English writer
The coarse joke proclaims that we have here an animal which finds its own animality either objectionable or funny.

[*Miracles*]

W[illiam] Somerset Maugham, 1874–1965, English novelist
Impropriety is the soul of wit.

[*The Moon and Sixpence* 1919]

John Milton, 1608–74, English poet
Enjoy your dear wit, and gay rhetoric,
That hath so well been taught her dazzling fence.

[*Paradise Regained* 1671]

Haste thee, Nymph, and bring with thee
Jest, and youthful jollity,
Quips, and cranks, and wanton wiles,
Nods, and becks, and wreathèd smiles.

[*L'Allegro*]

Molière [Jean-Baptiste Poquelin], 1622–73, French playwright
C'est une étrange entreprise, que celle de faire rire les honnêtes gens.
It's a strange business, making honest people laugh.

[*L'École des Femmes* 1662]

Frank Muir, 1920–98, English writer and broadcaster
Wit is a weapon. Jokes are a masculine way of inflicting superiority. But humour is the pursuit of a gentle grin, usually in solitude.

[In the *Daily Mail* April 26 1990]

Sean O'Casey, 1880–1964, Irish playwright
Laughter is the wine of the soul – laughter soft, or loud and deep, tinged through with seriousness . . . the hilarious declaration made by man that life is worth living.

[*Green Crows* 1956]

Dorothy [Rothschild] Parker, 1893–1967, American writer
Wit has truth in it . . . wisecracking is simply calisthenics with words.

[In Leslie Frewin's *The Late Mrs Dorothy Parker* 1986]

Thomas Parnell, 1679–1718, Irish-born English poet
Wit is the Muse's horse, and bears on high
The daring rider to the Muse's sky.

[*On Different Styles of Poetry*]

Alexander Pope, 1688–1744, English poet
Wit and judgement often are at strife,
Though meant each other's aid, like man and wife.

[*An Essay on Criticism* 1711]

True wit is Nature to advantage dressed,
What oft was thought, but ne'er so well expressed;
Something whose truth convinced at sight we find,
That gives us back the image of our mind.

[*Ibid*]

J[oseph] B[oynton] Priestley, 1894–1984, English novelist and playwright

Comedy, we may say, is society protecting itself – with a smile.

[*George Meredith* 1926]

Jean [Baptiste] Racine, 1639–99, French dramatist

He who laughs on Friday will cry on Sunday.

[*Les Plaideurs* 1668]

François, Duc de La Rochefoucauld, 1613– 1680, French writer

The greatest fault of a penetrating wit is to go beyond the mark.

[*Reflections, or Sentences and Moral Maxims* 1665]

Will[iam Penn Adair] Rogers, 1879–1935, American actor and humorist

Everything is funny as long as it is happening to somebody else.

[*The Illiterate Digest* 1924]

I don't make jokes – I just watch the government and report the facts.

[*Saturday Review: A Roger's Thesaurus* 1962]

Rafael Sabatini, 1875–1950, Italian-born British novelist

He was born with a gift of laughter and a sense that the world was mad.

[*Scaramouche* 1921]

Françoise Sagan [Françoise Quoirez] 1935– , French novelist

To jealousy, nothing is more frightful than laughter.

[*La Chamade* 1966]

William Shakespeare, 1564–1616, English dramatist

A jest's prosperity lies in the ear
Of him that hears it, never in the tongue
Of him that makes it.

[*Love's Labours Lost* 4 1594–5]

A good wit will make use of anything: I will turn diseases to commodity.

[*King Henry IV, Part II* 1 1597–8]

Better a witty fool than a foolish wit.

[*Twelfth Night* 1 1598–1600]

Brevity is the soul of wit.

[*Hamlet* 2 1600–1]

George Bernard Shaw, 1856–1950, Irish playwright

My way of joking is to tell the truth. It's the funniest joke in the world.

[*John Bull's Other Island* 2 1904]

Philip Dormer Stanhope, 4th Earl of Chesterfield, 1694–1773

If you have wit, use it to please, and not to hurt; you may shine, like the sun in the temperate zones, without scorching. Here it is wished for; under the Line, it is dreaded.
[Letter to his son September1748]

Wit is so shining a quality that everybody admires it; most people aim at it, all people fear it, and few love it unless in themselves. A man must have a good share of wit himself to endure a great share of it in another.

[Letter to his Godson December 1765]

WIT AND HUMOUR

Paul Theroux, 1941– , American writer
In the best comedy, there is clearly something wrong, but it is secret and understated – not even implied – comedy is the public version of a private darkness.

[*My Secret History* 1996]

Henry David Thoreau, 1817–62, American naturalist and writer
With respect to wit, I learned that there was not much difference between the half and the whole.

[*Walden, or, Life in the Woods* 1854]

James Grover Thurber, 1894–1961, American humorist and cartoonist
The laughter of man is more terrible than his tears, and takes more forms – hollow, heartless, mirthless, maniacal.

[In the *New York Times* December 7 1958]

Humour is emotional chaos remembered in tranquility.

[In the *New York Post* February 29 1960]

Mark Twain [Samuel Langhorne Clemens], 1835–1910, American writer
Wit and humour – if any difference, it is in duration – lightning and electric light. Same material, apparently; but one is vivid, and can do damage – the other fools along and enjoys elaboration.

[Notebook 1885]

Sir Peter [Alexander] Ustinov, 1921– , British playwright and actor
Laughter would be bereaved if snobbery died.

[In the *Observer* March 13 1955]

H[erbert] G[eorge] Wells, 1866–1946, English writer
Cynicism is humour in ill-health.

[*Short Stories: The Last Trump*]

Mae West, 1892–1980, American entertainer
It's hard to be funny when you have to be clean.

[In J. Weintraub's *The Wit and Wisdom of Mae West* 1967]

Nathanael West [Nathan Wallenstein Weinstein] 1903–40, American novelist
He could go on finding the same joke funny thirty times a day for months on end.

[*Miss Lonelyhearts* 1933]

Ella Wheeler Wilcox, 1850–1919, American poet
Laugh, and the world laughs with you;
Weep, and you weep alone;
For the sad old earth must borrow its mirth,
But has trouble enough of its own.

[*Solitude*]

George Wither, 1588–1667 English poet and pamphleteer
Though I am young, I scorn to flit
On the wings of borrowed wit.

[*The Shepherd's Hunting*]

Sir P[elham] G[reville] Wodehouse, 1881–1975, English-born writer
She had a penetrating sort of laugh. Rather like a train going into a tunnel.

[*The Inimitable Jeeves*]

[Adeline] Virginia Woolf, 1882–1941, English novelist and critic
Humour is the first of the gifts to perish in a foreign tongue.

[*The Common Reader* 1925]

Edward Young, 1683–1765, English churchman and poet
Dull is the jester when the joke's unkind.

[*The Love of Fame*]

Israel Zangwill, 1864–1926, English writer
She was a pale, bent woman, with spectacles, who believed in the mission of Israel, and wrote domestic novels to prove that she had no sense of humour.

[*Children of the Ghetto* 1892]

Index

Ace, Jane, 1905–74, American actress 137

Acheson, Dean, 1893–1971, American statesman 76

Adams, Douglas, 1952–2001, English writer 362, 392

Adams, Henry [Brooks], 1838–1918, American historian 7, 126, 192, 342

Adams, John Quincy, 1767–1848, 6th president of the United States 47, 126, 137, 319, 376

Adams, Sarah Flower, 1805–48, English poet 205

Addison, Joseph, 1672–1719, English essayist 22, 47, 101, 126, 137, 153, 205, 257, 264, 431, 454

Ade, George, 1866–1944, American humorist, writer and dramatist 342, 362

Aeschylus, 525–456BC, Greek poet 7, 247, 257

Agar, Herbert [Sebastian], 1897–1980, American writer 423

Akers, Elizabeth Chase, 1832–1911, American writer 7

Akins, Zoë, 1886–1958, American playwright 7

Albee, Edward Franklin, 1928–, American playwright 399, 454

Alcott, [Amos] Bronson, 1799–1888, American philosopher 58, 126, 153,

Aldrich, Henry, 1647–1710, English churchman 171

Alexander the Great, 356–323BC, king of Macedonia 257, 447

Alexander, Cecil Frances, 1818–95, English poet 205

Alexander, Samuel, 1859–1938, Australian philosopher 369

Alexander, Sir William, Earl of Stirling, c. 1567–1640, Scottish poet 183

Alfonso the Wise [Alfonso X], 1221–84, king of Castile and Leon 331

Algren, Nelson, 1909–81, American novelist 362

Ali, Muhammad [Cassius Marcellus Clay], 1942–, American boxer 351, 376, 415

Allainval, Abbé Leonor Jean d', c. 1700–53, French writer 319

Allen, Fred [John Florence Sullivan], 1894–1956, American comedian 376

Allen, Woody [Allen Stewart Konigsberg], 1935–, American writer, actor and film director 88, 101, 137, 205, 319, 392

Allingham, William, 1824–89, Irish poet and diarist 58

al-Sadat, Anwar 1918–81, president of Egypt 242, 339

Ames, Fisher, 1758–1808, American politician 229

Amiel, Henri Frederic, 1821–81, Swiss writer 7, 205, 257, 376

Amis, Martin, 1949–, English writer 319

Amis, Sir Kingsley, 1922–95, English novelist and poet 101, 206, 399

Anacreon, 563–478BC, Greek poet 36

Anaxandrides, fl. 376BC, Greek writer 101

Andrewes, Lancelot, 1555–1626, English theologian and bishop 206

Angelou, Maya, 1928–, American author and poet 392

Anne [Elizabeth Alice Louise], The Princess Royal, 1950–, British princess 376

Anonymous 7, 22, 36, 47, 58, 76, 88, 101, 126, 137, 153, 171, 183, 192, 206, 229, 247, 257, 264, 275, 311, 319, 331, 342, 362, 369, 376, 385, 392, 399, 415, 423, 431, 439

Anouilh, Jean, 1910–87, French dramatist 247, 275, 311, 423

Anthony, Susan B[rownell], 1820–1906, American reformer 47, 76, 153

Antiphanes of Macedonia, fl. 360BC 58

Apollonius of Tyana, 3BC–c. 97AD, Greek philosopher 331

Arendt, Hannah, 1906–75, German-born American philosopher 88, 369, 431

Aristophanes, c. 448–c. 388BC, Greek playwright 7, 153, 229

Aristotle, 384–322BC, Greek philosopher 22, 137, 192, 229, 247, 264, 423, 454

Armistead, Lewis Addison, 1817–63, American general 351

Armstrong, Neil [Alden], 1930–, American astronaut 342, 376

Arnold, Matthew, 1822–88, English poet and critic 58, 206, 275, 376, 423

Arnold, Thomas, 1795–1842, English schoolmaster 206

Asaf, George, 1880–1951, English songwriter 362

Ashdown, Paddy [Jeremy John Durham], 1941–, English politician 439

Astley, Sir Jacob, 1579–1652, English soldier 206

Atkinson, [Justin] Brooks, 1894–1984, American essayist 76

Attlee, Clement Richard 1st Earl Attlee, 1883–1967, British statesman 229

INDEX

Pliny the Elder, 23–79AD, Roman naturalist 270
Pliny the Younger, 62–c. 114AD, Roman statesman 147, 443
Plotinus, c. 205–c. 270AD, Greek philosopher 41
Plutarch, c. 46–c. 120AD, Greek historian and philosopher 443
Poe, Edgar Allan, 1809–49, American writer 30, 41, 188, 199, 253, 295
Pollock, Edward, 1823–58, English poet 115
Polybius, c. 203–120BC, Greek historian 359
Pompadour, Madame de [Jeanne Antoinette Poisson, Marquise de Pompadour], 1721–64, French courtier and mistress of Louis XV 412
Pope, Alexander, 1688–1744, English poet 15, 31, 41, 69, 96, 115, 133, 148, 164, 200, 221, 241, 253, 270, 296, 338, 366, 374, 382, 389, 443, 457
Popper, Sir Karl Raimund, 1902–94, Austrian-born English philosopher 53, 389
Porter,Cole [Albert], 1891–1964, American composer 31
Portillo, Michael, 1953–, British Conservative politician 241
Posidippus, fl. c. 275BC, Greek writer 115
Post, Sir Laurens [Jan] Van der, 1906–96, South African-born writer 272, 307, 350
Pound, Ezra [Loomis], 1855–1972, American poet 70, 133, 148, 165, 296
Pratt, Sir Charles, 1st Earl Camden, 1714–94, English lawyer and statesman 241
Previn, André, 1929–, American conductor 31
Priestley, J[oseph] B[oynton], 1894–1984, English novelist and playwright 429, 458
Prince Philip, Duke of Edinburgh, 1921–, consort of Queen Elizabeth II 403, 451
Princess Margaret Rose, 1930–2002, British princess 450
Prior, Matthew, 1664–1721, English diplomat and poet 262, 437, 451
Proudhon, Pierre Joseph, 1809–65, French social philosopher and writer 96
Proulx, E. Annie [Edna Ann], 1935–, American journalist, novelist and short story writer 148, 389
Proust, Marcel, 1871–1922, French novelist 115, 148
Publilius Syrus, fl. 1st century BC, Roman writer 148, 165, 253, 262, 271, 347, 437
Pushkin, Alexander Sergeyevich, 1799–1837, Russian poet and writer 403
Quarles, Francis, 1592–1644, English poet 31, 253, 262, 396
Quincey, Thomas De, 1785–1859, English writer 96
Quintilian [Marcus Fabius Quintilianus], c. 35–c. 96ad, Roman rhetorician 31
Raban, Jonathan, 1942–, English travel writer 347
Rabelais, François, c. 1494–c. 1553, French physician and satirist 179, 262, 429
Racine, Jean [Baptiste], 1639–99, French dramatist 296, 458
Raleigh, Sir Walter Alexander, 1861–1922, English academic 133, 297
Raleigh, Sir Walter, c. 1552–1618, English explorer and poet 115, 148, 296

Ralph Waldo Emerson, 1803–82, American writer and philosopher 27, 38, 63, 92, 107, 142, 196, 214, 234, 249, 259, 286, 322, 335, 344, 371, 379, 387, 434, 441
Reagan, Ronald Wilson, 1911–, 40th president of the United States 241
Red Cloud, 1822–1909, American Oglala Sioux Indian chief 54
Redgrave, Vanessa, 1937–, English actress 31
Reed, Thomas Brackett, 1839–1902, American legislator 271
Renan, Ernest, 1823–92, French historian 221
Reynolds, Sir Joshua, 1723–92, English painter 83
Rhodes, Cecil John, 1853–1902, South African politician 115, 133
Rhys, Ernest Percival, 1859–1946, Welsh writer 297
Ricardo, David, 1772–1823, English economist 83
Rice, [Henry] Grantland, 1880–1954, American sports writer 420
Rice, Robert, 1916–, American criminologist 96
Richards, Keith, 1943–, British rock musician 364
Richardson, Sir Ralph David, 1902–83, English actor 443
Richelieu, Cardinal [Armand Jean Duplessis, Duc de Richelieu], 1585–1642, French prelate and statesman 443
Richter, Jean Paul, 1763–1825, German novelist 42, 221, 253, 297
Robert Southwell, 1561–95, English poet 151
Robinson, Joan [Violet], 1903–83, English economist 327
Rochefoucauld, François, Duc de La, 1613–80, French writer 200, 253, 262, 271, 297, 374, 389, 437, 458
Roddenberry, Gene, 1921–91 American television writer and producer 347
Rogers, Samuel, 1763–1855, English poet 297
Rogers, Will[iam Penn Adair], 1879–1935, American actor and humorist 70, 148, 241, 412, 458
Roosevelt, Franklin Delano, 1882–1945, 32nd president of the United States 83, 241
Roosevelt, Theodore, 1858–1919, 26th president of the United States 84, 115, 241, 316, 327, 338, 366, 374, 382, 451
Rosen, Michael Wayne, 1946–, English writer and poet 179
Rossetti, Christina Georgina, 1830–94, English poet 115
Rossetti, Dante Gabriel, 1828–82, English poet 116, 200
Rossini, Gioacchino Antonio, 1792–1868, Italian composer 31
Roth, Philip [Milton], 1933–, American novelist 420, 443
Rousseau, Jean Jacques, 1712–78, Swiss-born French philosopher 54, 96, 241, 327, 429
Routh, Martin Joseph, 1755–1854, English academic 70
Rowe, Nicholas, 1674–1718, English playwright 116
Rowland, Helen, 1875–1950, American writer 189, 403

475

Rowling, J[oanne] K[athleen], 1965–, English author 366

Roy, Arundhati, 1961–, Indian novelist 116

Rushdie, [Ahmed] Salman, 1947–, British novelist 54

Rushton, Willie [William George], 1937–96, English actor, writer and broadcaster 366

Ruskin, John, 1819–1900, English art critic and writer 15, 31, 42, 70, 241, 297, 327, 347, 359, 437

Russell, Bertrand [Arthur William] 3rd Earl Russell, 1872–1970, English philosopher 70, 84, 165, 189, 254, 271, 297 327 374

Sabatini, Rafael, 1875–1950, Italian-born British novelist 458

Sackville-West, Vita [Victoria Mary], 1892–1962, English writer, poet and gardener 148

Sagan, Françoise [Françoise Quoirez] 1935–, French novelist 458

Saikaku, Ihara [Hirayama Togo], 1642–93, Japanese novelist 165

Saint-Exupéry, Antoine de, 1900–44, French aviator and writer 16, 297, 396, 451

Saki [Hector Hugh Munro], 1870–1916, Scottish-born writer 42, 116, 165, 179, 412

Salignac de la Mothe Fénélon, François de, 1651–1715, French churchman 175

Salinger, J[erome] D[avid], 1919–, American novelist 116

Sallust [Caius Sallustius Crispus] 86–c. 34BC, Roman historian 359

Salluste, Guillaume de, Seigneur du Bartas, 1544–90, French poet 16

Sampson, Anthony, 1926–, English writer 84

Sandburg, Carl, 1878–1967, American poet 70

Santayana, George, 1863–1952, Spanish-American philosopher 16, 32, 148, 200, 254, 396, 429, 443

Sappho, c. 650BC–?, Greek poet 32, 42

Sarah, Duchess of York [née Sarah Margaret Ferguson] 451

Sartre, Jean-Paul, 1905–80, French philosopher and writer 54, 70, 148, 374, 397, 444

Sassoon, Siegfried, 1886–1967, English poet 179, 359, 444

Savile, George, 1st Marquis of Halifax, 1633–95, English statesman 297

Schiller, [Johann Christoph] Friedrich von, 1759–1805, German poet 32, 149, 189, 221, 444, 451

Schlesinger, Arthur Meier Jr, 1917–, American historian 382

Schopenhauer, Arthur, 1788–1860, German philosopher 116, 222, 403, 412

Schubert, Franz [Peter], 1797–1828, Austrian composer 271

Schulz, Charles Monroe, 1922–2000, American cartoonist 165, 179, 254, 271, 420

Scott, Alexander, c. 1525–c. 84, Scottish poet 298

Scott, C[harles] P[restwich], 1846–1932, English newspaper editor 316

Scott, Robert Falcon, 1868–1912, English explorer 347

Scott, Sir Walter, 1771–1832, Scottish novelist and poet 16, 116, 133, 149, 222, 242, 298, 327, 412, 444

Scott, William, Baron Stowell, 1745–1836, English lawyer 84

Secondat, Charles Louis de, Baron de Montesquieu, 1689–1755, French philosopher 96, 222 242 339

Seeger, Alan, 1888–1916, English poet 116

Seeger, Peter ("Pete"), 1919–, American folksinger 117, 133

Seeley, Sir John Robert, 1834–95, English historian 242

Segal, Erich, 1937–, American author and filmwriter 298

Selden, John, 1584–1654, English antiquary and politician 32, 96, 179, 200, 242

Sellar, Walter Carruthers, 1898–1951 English writer 412, 452

Seneca, c. 4bc–65ad, Roman philosopher 16, 97, 149, 179, 200, 262, 271, 339, 347, 389, 437

Senna, Ayrton [Ayrton Senna da Silva], 1960–94, Brazilian racing driver 421

Sewall, Samuel, 1652–1730, American judge 117

Sextus Propertius, c. 50BC–c. 16AD, Roman poet 296

Shadwell, Thomas, c. 1642–92, English dramatist 254, 298

Shakespeare, William, 1564–1616, English dramatist 16, 32, 42, 54, 70, 84, 97, 117, 133, 149, 165, 180, 189, 200, 222, 242, 254, 262, 271, 299, 317, 328, 339, 347, 359, 366, 382, 389, 397, 403, 421, 429, 437, 444, 458

Shankly, Bill [William], 1913–81, Scottish footballer and manager 421

Shaw, George Bernard, 1856–1950, Irish playwright 17, 33, 43, 54, 85, 120, 167, 180, 223, 243, 254, 303, 348, 383, 397, 413, 438, 444, 452, 458

Sheed, Wilfred [John Joseph], 1930–, English-born American novelist 120

Sheen, Fulton John, 1895–1979, American bishop 223

Sheffield, John, 1st Duke of Buckingham and Normandy, 1648–1721, English politician and poet 72, 134

Shenstone, William, 1714–63, English gardener and poet 190, 263

Sheridan, Philip Henry, 1831–88, American general 224

Sheridan, Richard Brinsley, 1751–1816, English dramatist 34, 72, 134, 167, 243, 254, 271, 304, 317

Sherman, William [Tecumseh], 1820–91, American Unionist general 360

Shirley, James, 1596–1666, English dramatist 243

Sica, Vittorio De, 1902–74, Italian film director 271

Sidney, Sir Philip, 1554–86, English soldier, statesman and poet 72, 304, 421

Simon, Paul, 1941–, American singer and songwriter 444

Simonides of Ceos, c. 556–c. 468BC, Greek poet 121

Simpson, O[renthal] J[ames], 1947–, American football player 99

Simpson, Wallis, Duchess of Windsor [née Bessie Wallis Warfield], 1896–1986, American socialite, wife of Edward, Duke of Windsor 452